Mathematics
applied to business
problems

M. D. MacPherson
Professor of Business
Dutchess Community College, Poughkeepsie, New York

Mathematics applied to business problems

1982

BUSINESS PUBLICATIONS, INC.   Plano, Texas   75075
Irwin-Dorsey Limited   Georgetown, Ontario   L7G 4B3

©BUSINESS PUBLICATIONS, INC., 1982

All rights reserved. No part of this publication may be reproduced, stored in a retrieval system, or transmitted, in any form or by any means, electronic, mechanical, photocopying, recording, or otherwise, without the prior written permission of the publisher.

ISBN 0-256-02565-7
Library of Congress Catalog Card No. 80-69964
Printed in the United States of America

1 2 3 4 5 6 7 8 9 0 ML 8 7 6 5 4 3 2

Preface

The subjects in the book were selected to meet the requirements of a one-semester business math course. The contents of the text are appropriate for community college students as well as for adult students who may or may not have a knowledge of algebra or who have not studied business math for some time. The text will also serve business education students preparing to teach at the secondary school level.

The text is divided into 12 study units, each representing an application of the arithmetic process to a business procedure or subject. The emphasis in each study unit is on the mathematical procedures required to solve business problems, rather than on an in-depth study of concepts; thus, descriptive material has been kept to a minimum. The mathematical procedures are summarized in a set of Rules of Procedures, followed by step-by-step solution(s) to example problems. To develop your skill and accuracy in the solution of problems, a series of practice exercises follows each rule or set of rules. Review problems at the end of each study unit provide meaningful practice in solving problems that are similar to those included in the unit.

Unit 1 is designed to refresh your computation skill in the basic function of numbers and to introduce the application of arithmetic to applied business problems. If you need further practice to achieve a satisfactory level of competency, additional drill is included in the Appendix. Although this material was written to give general instructions in the use of electric or hand calculators, it can also be used for further practice in basic arithmetic functions.

Unit 2, Percents—Percentage, is perhaps the most important study unit in the development of your skill in solving applied problems. The rules of procedure and example problems of finding base, rate, and percentage are outlined in detail. In many businesses, percents are used as a measurement in controlling costs and in indicating changes in profits and prices. An understanding of and skill in computing percents will greatly enhance your value to an employer. The principles outlined in this study unit will be applied to problems in subsequent study units.

Unit 3, Solving Word Problems, suggests a method of solving problems that will be applicable to the solution of problems in the remaining study units in the text.

Units 4 through 12 represent the applied problems of business. The sequence of study units has no significance about the level of difficulty or preference but rather were selected at the recommendation of former students and business people. The emphasis in all study units is on the arithmetic involved in solving the types of problems you may encounter in other business courses. Each study unit includes the rules of procedure and step-by-step solutions to example problems. Review problems at the end of each study unit are designed to prepare you for the study unit tests. I recommend that you complete all review problems before taking the study unit test.

If your course is being taught by the module method, your instructor will review the requirements of this method of instruction and supply additional material relevant to the procedures.

A genuine thank you to the faculty of Dutchess Community College, who have taught business math, for their suggestions and patience in completing the classroom testing of the text material. A special thank you to Ms. Joan Artz, Ms. Janet Junge, and Mr. William Harwood of Dutchess Community College for their assistance in preparing the manuscript and their suggestions for the presentation of the text subject matter. Special acknowledgment to Ms. Helen Etherington of Onondaga Community College, Mr. Robert Ek of Seminole Community College, and Mr. Robert Hammond of Utah State University for their complete and thoughtful critiques. Recognition is also given to Mr. Gregg Voght of I.B.M. Corporation for his contributions.

M. D. MacPherson

Contents

STUDY UNIT 1
REVIEW OF FUNDAMENTAL ARITHMETIC OPERATIONS

Addition, 3
Whole numbers, 3
Decimal numbers, 6

Subtraction, 8
Whole numbers, 8
Decimal numbers, 9

Multiplication, 10
Whole numbers, 10
Decimal numbers, 12

Division, 13
Whole numbers, 13
Decimal numbers, 15

Fractions and mixed numbers, 16
Conversion of fractions to decimals, 16

Common or proper fractions, 18
Addition, 18
Subtraction, 20
Multiplication, 20
Division, 22

Mixed numbers, 22
Addition, 22
Subtraction, 24
Multiplication, 24
Division, 26

Applied math problems, 27
Checking account records, 27
Bank statement reconciliation, 29
Word problems, 33

Review problems, 35

STUDY UNIT 2
PERCENTS—PERCENTAGE

Rules of procedure, 40
Rate or percent of (%) to a decimal number, 40
Percent (%) to a common fraction, 41
Decimal number to a percent, 43

Rules of percents/percentage, 44
Definitions, 44
To find a percentage, 44
To find a rate, 47
To find a rate of increase/decrease, 49
To find a base, 52

Review problems, 55

STUDY UNIT 3
SOLVING WORD PROBLEMS

Rules for word problem solving, 59

Formulas, 59
To find a base, 60
To find a total, 63

Equations, 67
Arithmetic of an equation, 68
Distribution of a total, 71

Metric system, 73

Review problems, 77

STUDY UNIT 4
TRADE AND CASH DISCOUNT

Trade discount
Definitions, 84

Rules for applying trade discounts, 84
Calculation of net price, 84
Net price equivalent or percent, 89
Single discount equivalent, 89

Cash discount, 92
Definitions, 92
Calculation of net price, 94

Trade and cash discounts, 102

Review problems, 107

STUDY UNIT 5
SIMPLE INTEREST—BANK DISCOUNT

Definitions, 115

Calculation of interest, 116
Interest days, 116
Interest year, 117
Due date, 118
Maturity value, 119
Interest tables, 123

Bank discount procedures, 127
Definitions, 127
Rules of discount, 127

Proceeds of a bank loan, 128
Proceeds of a noninterest-bearing note, 128
Proceeds of interest notes, 130

Compound interest, 134
Compound interest table, 136

Review problems, 139

STUDY UNIT 6
RETAIL MERCHANDISING

Definitions, 145

Rules of markup, 146
Selling price when markup is based on cost, 147
Cost when markup is based on selling price, 148
Markup percent, 151
Rate of markup based on cost, 151
Rate of markup based on selling price, 152

Markdown, 153

Net markup and net markdown, 157

Profits and losses, 159

Review Problems, 163

STUDY UNIT 7
CONSUMER CREDIT

Introduction, 169

Rules of procedure, 170
Installment charges, 170
Amount financed, 170
Add-on interest, 173
Monthly interest rates, 176
Annual interest rate, 176
Annual percentage rate, 176
  APR from a table, 176
  APR by formula, 178
Installment payments, 181
  Simple add-on interest, 182
  Amortized installment payments, 183

Open-end credit plans, 187
Total amount due, 189

Review problems, 193

STUDY UNIT 8
PAYROLL COMPUTATIONS

Hourly wages, 199
Gross pay, 200

Ovetime pay, 200
Straight overtime pay, 201
Excess overtime payments, 202

Incentive pay plans, 205

Salaries, 211

Commission payment plans, 214

Commission merchant payment plans, 217

Review problems, 223

STUDY UNIT 9
TAXES

Federal taxes, 229
Federal Insurance Contribution Act (FICA), 229
Federal income withholding tax, 231
Net income, 233

Local taxes, 236
Sales tax, 236
Property taxes, 240
  Tax rate, 241
  Property taxes, 242
  Assessed value, 242

Review problems, 245

STUDY UNIT 10
ACCOUNTING PROCEDURES

Methods of depreciation, 251
Straight-line depreciation, 252
Book value, 257
Declining-balance depreciation, 261
Sum-of-the-year's-digits method, 262

Distribution of overhead, 265

Inventory evaluation, 266
Fifo inventory evaluation, 266
Lifo inventory evaluation, 267
Average unit cost, 268

Review problems, 273

STUDY UNIT 11
STOCKS AND BONDS

Stocks, 279
Price of a share, 279
Stock quotations, 279
Value of stock owned, 281
Commissions, 283
Sale and purchase of stock, 286
Stock dividends, 290

Bonds, 294
Quotations, 294
Interest, 295
Purchase and sale, 299

Review problems, 303

STUDY UNIT 12
INTRODUCTION TO STATISTICS

Measurements of central tendencies, 309
Means, 309

To calculate the mean, 309
Median, 310
Median value of a quantity of a series, 310
Mode, 311
To determine the mode of a series, 311
Weighted average, 312
To calculate the weighted average mean, 312

Frequency distribution, 314
The range of the items in a series of data, 314
Class intervals, 314
To prepare a frequency distribution table, 314
Weighted average mean, 315

Standard deviation, 315

Graphs, 318
Line graphs, 318
Bar graphs, 319
Circle graphs, 320
The distribution of a circle to component parts of a whole, 320

**APPENDIX
USE OF THE ELECTRIC CALCULATOR, 325**

INDEX, 339

STUDY UNIT **1**

Review of fundamental arithmetic operations

ADDITION: WHOLE NUMBERS, DECIMALS

SUBTRACTION: WHOLE NUMBERS, DECIMALS

MULTIPLICATION: WHOLE NUMBERS, DECIMALS

DIVISON: WHOLE NUMBERS, DECIMALS

FRACTIONS/MIXED NUMBERS
    Conversion of fractions
    Common or proper fractions:
        Addition, subtraction,
        multiplication, division
    Mixed numbers:
        Addition, subtraction,
        multiplication, division

APPLIED MATH PROBLEMS:
    Checking account records
    Bank statement reconciliation

INTRODUCTION

If you have a hand or desk electric calculator available, refer to the Appendix for the rules and exercises in the use of the calculator.

This unit concentrates on the review of basic arithmetic functions used in the solutions of applied business problems that are presented in subsequent chapters.

The extensive use of both the hand and desk electric calculators, where the arithmetic functions are completed by depressing a key or button, does not mean that a skill in fundamental arithmetic operations is not necessary for success on employment or civil service tests, on problem solving, or on understanding the relationship of numbers in applied business problems.

You have learned the basic arithmetic functions in your elementary or high school education. Thus, emphasis in this study unit is simply to review the functions of addition, subtraction, multiplication, and division of whole numbers, decimal numbers, and fractions, and the rules of numbers. If you have an acceptable computation skill, a review of the rules of numbers and the applied business problems will serve to increase your speed and accuracy in these basic arithmetic functions. If you have some computational weakness, review the rules of numbers and complete the exercises and the applied problems before completing the unit review problems.

ADDITION

WHOLE NUMBERS The number system used in our monetary system, as well as in business problems, is based on the decimal system, where the value of a number depends upon its position from the decimal point. Note the proper "names" of the decimal positions both to the right and left of the decimal point indicated on the following table.

```
                                              decimal place
     millions   thousands    hundreds      1   2   3   4
                                           ↓   ↓   ↓   ↓
            9 , 8   1   2 , 3   4   5 . 6   7   8   9
            ·   ·   ·   ·   ·   ·   ·   ·   ·   ·   ·
            ·   ·   ·   ·   ·   ·   ·   ·   ·   ·   ·
            m   1   1   t   h   t   o   "   h   t   1
            i   0   0   h   u   e   n   a   u   h   0
            l   0       o   n   n   e   n   n   o
            l       t   u   d   s   s   d   d   u   t
            i   t   h   s   r       /   "   r   s   h
            o   h   o   a   e       u       e   a   o
            n   o   u   n   d       n       d   n   u
                u   s   d   s       i       t   d   s
                s   a               t       h   t   a
                a   n               s       s   h   n
                n   d                               s   d
                d   s                                   s
                    s                                   
```

Rule 1: ADDITION OF WHOLE NUMBERS.

Whole numbers are the numbers or integers to the left of the decimal point. To find the sum or total of a series of whole numbers, add each column of digits, starting with the right-hand column and continue to each column to the left. If the total of a column is more than 9, carry the digit to the next column.

Example 1
Vertical addition

Add each column of digits and carryover digit from prior column:

```
  1 11 ← (carryover)
   893
    32
 1,234
     6
 2,165
```

Example 2
Vertical addition

Add each column separately and indent the answers. Total the column answers.

```
   893
    32
 1,234
     6
    15   total of column 1
    15   total of column 2
   1 0   total of column 3
   1     total of column 4
 2,165   (Ans.)
```

Example 3
Horizontal addition

Add the first digit in each number and note the total. Add each remaining set of digits, indent the totals, and add the total of the digits.

Digits (3) (2) (1)   (2) (1)   (4) (3) (2) (1)   (1)
         8   9   3 + 3   2 + 1, 2   3   4   + 6

```
       Add 1st digits    3 + 2 + 4 + 6 =    15
       Add 2d digits     9 + 3 + 3     =    15
       Add 3d digits     8 + 2         =   10
       Add 4th digit     1             =  1
       Total                              2,165
```

Rule 2: TO INCREASE SPEED AND ACCURACY IN ADDING A SERIES OF WHOLE NUMBERS, GROUP TWO OR MORE NUMBERS IN THE COLUMN THAT TOTAL 10 OR A MULTIPLE OF 10.

Example 1

```
              2 (carry)
          ┌─ 73 ┐
   10 = ──┤      │ = 5
          └─ 82 ┘
          ┌─ 52
          │
   10 = ──┤─ 46 ┐
   10 = ──┤─ 34 │ = 10
          │      
          └─ 18 ──┘ = 10
            ───         ──
            305         25  (carry the 2)
```

Rule 3: PROOF OF THE ACCURACY OF ADDITION.

a. Re-add the column in the opposite direction. If you added the column down, re-add it upward.

b. Use a different method of adding. If you added by carrying over to the next column, re-add by using separate totals for each column and indent the separate totals and add.

Practice exercises

Add the following problems and prove your answers:

1.	2.	3.	4.
18	23	86	219
92	56	73	426
24	31	51	508
86	38	37	172
43	77	22	386
81	89	51	514
39	26	6	317
383 (Ans.)	___ (Ans.)	326 (Ans.)	___ (Ans.)

5.	6.	7.
123	728	2,467
456	261	1,926
531	121	8,409
890	345	6,147
757	643	5,208
113	127	24,157 (Ans.)
843	106	
3,713 (Ans.)	___ (Ans.)	

8.	9.	10.
4,269	9,642	7,936
5,086	8,071	5,678
3,867	3,937	3,034
2,208	4,981	4,827
7,573	1,267	1,649
___ (Ans.)	27,898 (Ans.)	___ (Ans.)

1 REVIEW OF FUNDAMENTAL ARITHMETIC OPERATIONS / 5

Add the following problems horizontally:　　　　　　　　　　　Answer
11. 32 + 28 + 59 + 40 + 43 + 21 = 　　　　　　　　　　　　　223
12. 43 + 65 + 32 + 29 + 26 + 13 = 　　　　　　　　　　　　　_____
13. 206 + 94 + 817 + 943 + 631 + 643 = 　　　　　　　　　　3,334
14. 112 + 882 + 626 + 793 + 461 + 27 = 　　　　　　　　　　_____
15. 123 + 47 + 684 + 721 + 505 + 692 = 　　　　　　　　　　2,772
16. 7,936 + 5,678 + 3,034 + 4,827 + 1,649 = 　　　　　　　　_____
17. 7,780 + 2,721 + 8,909 + 3,654 + 6,981 = 　　　　　　　　30,045
18. 62 + 7 + 568 + 340 + 3,122 + 10,358 = 　　　　　　　　　_____
19. 1,236 + 3 + 549 + 3,410 + 12,345 = 　　　　　　　　　　17,543
20. 15 + 456 + 19 + 8 + 32,549 + 587 = 　　　　　　　　　　_____

Add the following problems by any method and prove your answer:

	21.		22.		23.	
	65		6,026		58	
	4,021		4		3	
	4		764		781	
	137		92		9,189	
	826		11,126		146	
	11,101		236		6,264	
	16,154 (Ans.)		_____ (Ans.)		16,441 (Ans.)	

	24.		25.		26.	
	4,099		863		732	
	384		2,973		4,987	
	12		31,419		2,319	
	19,640		26		58	
	96		272		25,323	
	846		2		216	
	_____ (Ans.)		35,555 (Ans.)		_____ (Ans.)	

	27.		28.		29.	
	35,234		5,508		4,228	
	129,555		251		27,412	
	9,234		91		61	
	1,183		199		69	
	5		6,648		420	
	17		36,016		916	
	175,228 (Ans.)		_____ (Ans.)		33,106 (Ans.)	

DECIMAL NUMBERS　　All digits to the right of the decimal point represent a fractional part of any power of the whole number 10.

Rules for rounding decimals

Step 1. Decide the number of decimal places desired or required by the problem.

Note: If the problem requires an answer in dollars and cents, the decimal is always rounded to the 2d decimal place.

Step 2. Refer to the digit to the right of the required digit. If this digit is 5 or more, add 1 to the last retained digit. If this digit is 4 or less, retain the last digit in the required decimal place.

Example 1 Round .168476 to the 4th decimal place.
Step 1. The 4th decimal digit is 4.
Step 2. The first digit to the right of 4 is 7. Since 7 is greater than 5, the 4 will be raised to 5.

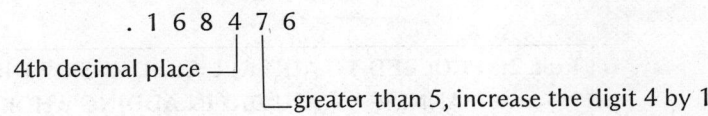

(Ans.) .1685

Example 2 Round $16.26124 to the 2d decimal place.
Step 1. The 2d decimal digit is 6.
Step 2. The first digit to the right of 6 is 1. Since 1 is less than 5, do not change the 6.

$16.26124
2d decimal place ⌐ ⌐ less than 5, do not change the 6

(Ans.) $16.26

Practice exercises

		Answer
1. Round the following to the 1st decimal place (tenths):		
a. 12.4627		12.5
b. .9634		1.0
c. .39645		.4
d. .8423		.8
2. Round the following to the 2d decimal place (hundredths):		
a. .1208		___
b. .7809		___
c. 16.476		___
d. $23.382		___
3. Round the following to the 3d decimal place (thousandths):		
a. .953125		.953
b. .45694		.457
c. 45.8125		45.813
d. 112.9826		112.983
4. Round the following to the 4th decimal place (ten thousandths):		
a. .765625		___
b. 16.489629		___
c. 89.008923		___
d. .76539		___

Addition of decimal numbers

> **Rule 1: PLACEMENT OF THE DECIMAL POINT:**
> Place the decimal points in a vertical column regardless of the number of digits in the decimal number.

1 REVIEW OF FUNDAMENTAL ARITHMETIC OPERATIONS / 7

Example   Add: 1.098 + .34692 + .067 + 11.3

Rewrite as: 1.098
.34692
.067
11.3

> Rule 2:   PROCEED TO ADD ALL COLUMNS OF DIGITS IN THE SAME MANNER AS YOU DID IN ADDING WHOLE NUMBERS.
> It may be more convenient to add zeros to each number to equal the largest decimal.

Example

1.09800
.34692
.06700
11.30000
12.81192 (Ans.)

Practice exercises

Add the following numbers: Answer
1.   .003 + 41.1 + 7.8002 + .6 + 8.04 =   57.5432
2.   .125 + 16.68 + 2.0041 + 3.6097 + .00056 =   _____
3.   .097 + 175.096 + .46 + .0048 + 4.0905 =   179.7483
4.   .35 + 11.23 + 6.00897 + .0002 + .0672 =   _____
5.   117.26 + 2.00468 + .874 + .9 + .4286 =   121.46728
6.   12.1 + 16.28 + 2.09 + .0875 + .375 + .9642 =   _____
7.   626.84 + 5.095 + .8775 + .012 + .9 =   633.7245
8.   .01 + .9604 + .12896 + 1.375 + .6667 =   _____
9.   .14106 + .7245 + 17.63 + 9.834 + 3.6 + .10054 =   32.0301
10. .031 + 6.04 + 112.9 + 3.9084 + .3075 =   _____

SUBTRACTION

WHOLE NUMBERS   Subtraction is the process of reducing one number by another. The function of subtraction is indicated by the "−" sign, the word *minus*, or the word *from*.

> Rule 1:   TO FIND THE DIFFERENCE BETWEEN TWO NUMBERS, REDUCE THE LARGER NUMBER BY THE SMALLER NUMBER.

Example   Subtract 60 from 872:

    872
 −   60
    812 (Ans.)

> Rule 2:   IF A DIGIT IN THE LARGER NUMBER IS SMALLER THAN THE DIGIT TO BE SUBTRACTED IN THE SMALLER NUMBER, BORROW A VALUE OF 10 FROM THE DIGIT IN THE LARGER NUMBER THAT IS IMMEDIATELY TO THE LEFT.

Example   Subtract 60 from 812:

```
 812
-  60    0 subtracted from 2 = 2.
 752     Borrow 1 from the 8.
         Add 10 to the 1.
         Subtract 6 from 11 = 5.
         Subtract 0 from 7 = 7.
```

> **Rule 3:** PROOF: ADD THE DIFFERENCE TO THE SMALLER NUMBER. THE SUM MUST EQUAL THE LARGER NUMBER.

Example   Subtract 60 from 812:   Proof:

```
  812                          752
-  60                        + 60
  752                          812
```

Practice exercises

		Answer
1.	Find the difference in the following problems:	
	a. 623 − 402 =	221
	b. 835 − 323 =	512
	c. 741 − 520 =	221
	d. 538 − 217 =	321
	e. 457 − 389 =	68
2.	Subtract 2,896 from 4,582	
3.	16,058 minus 8,639 equals	7,419
4.	999 less 788 equals	
5.	2,360 − 926 equals	1,434
6.	Subtract 7,399 from 96,427.	
7.	14,712 − 9,865 equals	4,847
8.	8,353 less 1,963 equals	
9.	Subtract 11,976 from 32,402.	20,426
10.	9,860 less 3,897 equals	

DECIMAL NUMBERS   The subtraction function is completed in the same manner as it is in whole numbers. The rule of borrowing applies, as does proving the accuracy of the difference or answer.

> **Rule 1:** THE DECIMAL POINTS MUST BE ALIGNED IN A VERTICAL COLUMN FOR ALL DECIMAL NUMBERS TO BE SUBTRACTED.

Example   Subtract 42.716 from 115.39:

```
 115.390
 -42.716
  72.674
```

1 REVIEW OF FUNDAMENTAL ARITHMETIC OPERATIONS / 9

Practice exercises

		Answer
1.	2,193.57 less 95.907 =	2,097.663
2.	5.3778 minus 3.0674 =	
3.	Subtract .0959 from .1348 =	.0389
4.	.005 − .0005 =	
5.	1.6382 less .9768 =	.6614
6.	1.432 less .568 =	
7.	Subtract 3.843 from 13.609	9.766
8.	117.65 less 7.962 =	
9.	1.0476 minus .9387 =	.1089
10.	Subtract .08381 from .96432 =	
11.	.0625 − .0275 =	.035
12.	.875 minus .006 =	
13.	42.86 less 4.29 =	38.57
14.	Subtract 19.8347 from 106.0256 =	

MULTIPLICATION

WHOLE NUMBERS

The multiplication function is a short method of repeated additions. It involves 2 or more factors that when multiplied results in an increase in value or quantity. For example, if an item cost $16 and a merchant buys 4 of the items, the total cost would be 16 + 16 + 16 + 16 = $64 or $16 × 4 = $64.

The function of multiplication is indicated by the "×" sign, a dot above the line •, the word *times*, or the words *multiplied by*.

Example   Multiply 123 by 32:

```
    123   (multiplicand)
×    32   (multiplier)
    246   (partial product)
  3 69    (partial product)
  3,936   (sum of partial products) Product
```

> **Rule 1:** USE THE SMALLER NUMBER IN THE PROBLEM AS THE MULTIPLIER.

> **Rule 2:** IF MORE THAN 1 MULTIPLIER IS INVOLVED IN THE PROBLEM, COMPLETE THE MULTIPLICATION BY ONE MULTIPLIER BEFORE APPLYING SUBSEQUENT MULTIPLIERS.

Example   Multiply 308 × 18 × 8 × 4 =

```
   308              5,544                44,352
×   18            ×     8              ×      4
  2 464            44,352 (product)     177,408 (product)
  3 08
  5,544 (product)
```

> **Rule 3:** TO MULTIPLY BY 10 OR ANY MULTIPLE OF 10, ADD THE NUMBER OF ZEROS TO THE MULTIPLICAND (the other number involved in the multiplication).

Examples   812 × 10 = 812 plus one zero for the zero in 10 = 8,120
812 × 100 = 812 plus 2 zeros for the 2 zeros in 100 = 81,200
812 × 1,000 = 812 plus 3 zeros for the 3 zeros in 1,000 = 812,000
812 × 50 = 812 plus one zero × 5 or 8120 × 5 = 40,600
812 × 400 = 812 plus two zeros × 4 or 81,200 × 4 = 324,800

> **Rule 4:** TO PROVE THE ACCURACY OF THE PRODUCT, DIVIDE THE PRODUCT BY EITHER THE MULTIPLIER OR THE MULTIPLICAND.

Example   Multiply 845 by 125:

```
      845
    × 125
    4 225
   16 90
   84 5
  105,625  (product)
```

Proof:

```
          845                      125
125 ⟌ 105,625     or     845 ⟌ 105,625
      100 0                    84 5
        5 62                   21 12
        5 00                   16 90
          625                   4 225
          625                   4 225
```

Practice exercises

		Answer
1.	1,426 × 75 =	106,950
2.	11,135 × 30 =	————
3.	137 × 12 =	1,644
4.	107 × 63 =	————
5.	182 × 57 =	10,374
6.	2,796 × 517 =	————
7.	9,047 × 624 =	5,645,328
8.	6,258 × 300 =	————
9.	11,426 × 1,105 =	12,625,730
10.	26,439 × 40 =	————
11.	96 × 8 × 4 =	3,072
12.	167 × 4 × 2 =	————
13.	906 × 12 × 3 =	32,616
14.	1,046 × 7 × 5 =	————
15.	469 × 16 × 9 =	67,536
16.	2,681 × 73 =	————
17.	7,029 × 52 =	365,508
18.	8,426 × 167 =	————
19.	1,327 × 824 =	1,093,448
20.	6,427 × 393 =	————

DECIMAL NUMBERS

The multiplication function of decimal numbers is completed in the same manner as it is in the multiplication of whole numbers. The decimal place in the product of multiplied decimal numbers is the sum of the decimal places in all factors involved in the multiplication or it may be rounded to a desired decimal place.

> **Rule 1:** MULTIPLY THE MULTIPLICAND BY EACH DIGIT IN THE MULTIPLIER IN THE SAME MANNER THAT IS USED IN MULTIPLYING WHOLE NUMBERS.

> **Rule 2:** POINT OFF AS MANY DECIMAL PLACES IN THE PRODUCT AS THERE ARE IN THE MULTIPLICAND, PLUS ALL MULTIPLIERS. IF THERE ARE MORE DECIMAL PLACES THAN NUMBERS IN THE PRODUCT, ADD SUFFICIENT ZEROS TO COMPLY WITH THE REQUIRED NUMBER OF DECIMAL PLACES.

Example 1 Multiply 92.45 by 2.2:

```
  92.45  (2 decimal places)
×  2.2   (1 decimal place)
 18490
 18490
203390  = 203.390  (3 decimal places)
```

Example 2 Multiply 1.806 by .008:

```
  1.806  (3 decimal places)
×  .008  (3 decimal places)
  14448  = .014448  (6 decimal places)
```

Example 3 Multiply $192.55 by .0675:

```
$  192.55  (2 decimal places)
×   .0675  (4 decimal places)
    96275
   134785
   115530
 12997125  = $13.00  Rounded to 2 decimal places because the answer is in
                     dollars and cents.
```

Practice exercises

		Answer
1.	Multiply 185.9 by .46 =	85.514
2.	452.57 × .008 =	
3.	.0608 × .234 =	.0142272
4.	Multiply 148.50 by 56.13 =	
5.	What is the product of 4.67 times .003?	.01401
6.	486.95 × .085 =	
7.	Multiply 573 by .68 =	389.64
8.	How much is $5,575 times .125?	
9.	358.23 × .89 =	318.8247
10.	$158.60 × .35 =	

11. Multiply 98.421 by .347 and round answer to the 4th decimal place.   34.1521
12. .075 times .009 =   _____
13. $6,500 multiplied by .1125 equals $731.25
14. .125 × .004 =   _____
15. Round your answer to the third decimal place. Multiply 82.645 by 14.652.   1,210.915
16. 3.0755 × .034 =   _____
17. Round answer to the first decimal place when you multiply 1,235 by .0675.   83.4
18. $275.50 times .206 =   _____
19. 3,245 × .1072 =   347.864
20. 4.0725 × .6667 =   _____

DIVISION

WHOLE NUMBERS   Division is a procedure that determines how many times one number is contained in another number. For example, 812 is divided by 4:

(divisor) 4 $\overline{)812}$ 203 (quotient)
(dividend)

Thus 4 is contained 203 times in 812. The division function is indicated by the division sign "÷", the words *divided by*, or *divide into*.

Terms   *Dividend.* The number to be divided.
Divisor. The number that is divided into the dividend.
Quotient. The answer, and it indicates the number of times the divisor is contained in the dividend.
Remainder. The portion of the dividend into which the divisor will not divide evenly.

> Rule 1: REMAINDERS: If a divisor is not contained in a dividend an even number of times, there will be a remainder.

A remainder may be expressed as a fraction.

Fraction

The remainder is the numerator of the fraction and the divisor is the denominator.

Example   Divide 40,000 by 813:

$$813 \overline{)40000} \quad 49$$
$$\underline{3252}$$
$$7480$$
$$\underline{7317}$$
$$163 \text{ (remainder)} = \frac{163}{813}$$

Ans. = $49\frac{163}{813}$

Decimal

Place a decimal point to the right of the last digit in the dividend and directly above it in the quotient. Continue the division process to the desired decimal place. Round the final decimal digit in the quotient by the same rounding rules outlined under Decimal Numbers.

Example   Divide 40,065 by 814 and round answer to the nearest hundredths (2 decimal places):

```
           49.219 = 49.22  Ans.
    814 |40065.000
         3256
         ────
          7505
          7326
          ────
           179 0
           162 8
           ────
            16 20
             8 14
            ─────
             8 060
             7 326
             ─────
               734
```

> **Rule 2:** TO DIVIDE BY 10 OR ANY MULTIPLE OF 10, MOVE THE DECIMAL POINT AS MANY PLACES TO THE LEFT IN THE DIVIDEND AS THERE ARE ZEROS IN THE DIVISOR.

Examples   Divide 812 by 10 = 81.2

Note: There is an unwritten decimal point to the right of the last digit in a whole number.

Divide 812 by 100 = 8.12
Divide 812 by 1,000 = .812

Practice exercises

		Answer
1.	Express the remainders in the following problems as fractions.	
a.	$34 \div 6 =$	$5^2/_3$
b.	$110 \div 8 =$	$13^3/_4$
c.	Divide 334 by 16	$20^7/_8$
d.	$1{,}422 \div 171 =$	$8^6/_{19}$
e.	$32{,}604 \div 144 =$	$226^5/_{12}$
f.	Divide 136 into 1,687	$12^{55}/_{136}$
g.	What is 135,783 divided by 1,200?	$113^{61}/_{400}$
h.	$59 \div 13 =$	$4^7/_{13}$
i.	Divide 683 by 133	$5^{18}/_{133}$
j.	$1{,}916 \div 121 =$	$15^{101}/_{121}$
2.	Express the remainders in the following problems as a decimal rounded to the 2d decimal place.	
a.	$1{,}467 \div 27 =$	_____
b.	$18{,}693 \div 164 =$	_____
c.	Divide 34 into 7,297	_____

14 /

  d. Divide 72,846 by 426   _____
  e. 1,112 ÷ 86 =   _____

3. Express the remainders in the following problems as a decimal rounded to the 3d decimal place:
 a. 1,217 ÷ 20 =   60.850
 b. Divide 16 into 686   42.875
 c. Divide 27,687 by 337   82.157
 d. 18,645 ÷ 152 =   122.664
 e. 11,346 ÷ 114 =   99.526

4. Express the remainders in the following problems as decimals rounded to the 4th decimal place:
 a. Divide 1,429 by 18   _____
 b. 19,348 ÷ 126 =   _____
 c. 196,413 ÷ 612 =   _____
 d. Divide 156,421 by 37   _____
 e. 376,933 ÷ 1,704   _____

5. Divide 119,456 by 1,000   119.456
6. Divide 5,600 by 10   _____
7. 113,689 ÷ 100 =   1,136.89
8. 95 ÷ 100 =   _____
9. 450,123 ÷ 1,000 =   450.123
10. 37 ÷ 1,000 =   _____

DECIMAL NUMBERS The division process for decimal numbers is completed in the same manner that is used in dividing whole numbers.

> **Rule 1:** WHEN THE DIVISOR INCLUDES A DECIMAL NUMBER, MOVE THE DECIMAL POINT IN THE DIVIDEND TO THE RIGHT AS MANY DECIMAL PLACES AS THERE ARE IN THE DIVISOR. IF NECESSARY, ADD ZEROS TO THE DIVIDEND.

Example Divide 12.6 by .003:

    .003 ⟌12.6 *or* 003 ⟌12600.

> **Rule 2:** PLACE THE DECIMAL POINT IN THE QUOTIENT DIRECTLY ABOVE THE DECIMAL POINT IN THE NEW DIVIDEND.

Example 003 ⟌12600.

> **Rule 3:** REMAINDERS MAY BE EXPRESSED AS A FRACTION OR AS A DECIMAL IN THE SAME MANNER AS WHEN DIVIDING WHOLE NUMBERS.

Practice exercises

1. Express any remainder as a decimal number rounded to the 2d decimal place.   Answer
 a. 76.1 ÷ 50 =   1.52
 b. 669.2 ÷ 139.3 =   4.80
 c. Divide 1,382.4 by 3.476   397.70

  d. Divide .0098 into .073   7.45
  e. 62.8 ÷ 2.5 =   25.12
2. Express any remainder as a decimal number rounded to the 3d decimal place.
  a. 6.31 ÷ .061 =   _____
  b. 7.3 ÷ .243 =   _____
  c. Divide 74.8 by .088   _____
  d. Divide 36.8 into 1,582.43   _____
  e. .073 ÷ .0098 =   _____

Proof of division

The accuracy of the answer or quotient of any division problem may be proven by multiplying the quotient by the divisor.

Example 1   Divide 694.40 by 124:

```
          5.6
124 ) 694.4
      620
       74 4
       74 4
        0 0
```

Proof: 124 × 5.6 = 694.40

FRACTIONS AND MIXED NUMBERS

Fractions provide a method of computing the value, quantity, or number that is part of a whole value, quantity, or number. For example, if ⅙ of a shipment of goods is damaged, the shipment of goods is the whole quantity; ⅙ is the part of the whole quantity that can be computed.

A fraction consists of a numerator (the top number) and a denominator (the bottom number), which are separated by a line (– or /) that means "divide by." Thus:

$\frac{1}{6}$ 1 . . . . . . is the numerator
    6 . . . . . . is the denominator

The denominator (6) indicates that the whole shipment was divided into 6 equal parts. The numerator (1) indicates the number of these parts that are required by the problem.

A *common or proper fraction* is one where the numerator is less than the denominator.

An *improper fraction* is one where the numerator is larger than the denominator. For example, ⅜ is an improper fraction.

CONVERSION OF FRACTIONS TO DECIMALS

The increased use of electric calculators in solving problems that include proper fractions or mixed numbers requires that fractions be converted to their decimal equivalents. Skill in the use of either a fraction or its decimal equivalent will increase not only your accuracy but your speed in completing all types of calculations.

The decimal equivalent of a fraction can be computed by dividing the numerator of the fraction by the denominator. For example, the fraction ¼ can be converted to the decimal of .25 (4 ⟌1.00) without changing the value of the fraction.

The more frequently used fractions and their decimal equivalents rounded to the 4th decimal place are listed on the following table. If you are not familiar with the decimal equivalents, take the time to memorize the table.

½ = .5	⅗ = .6	⅛ = .125
⅓ = .3333	⅘ = .8	⅜ = .375
⅔ = .6667	⅙ = .1667	⅝ = .625
¼ = .25	⅚ = .8333	⅞ = .875
¾ = .75	1/7 = .1429	1/9 = .1111
⅕ = .2	4/7 = .5714	4/9 = .4444
⅖ = .4	1/16 = .0625	3/16 = .1875

Example 1   Convert the fraction 9/11 to its decimal equivalent rounded to the 4th decimal place.

Step 1. Write the fraction as a division problem:

$$\frac{9}{11} = 11\overline{)9}$$

Step 2. Add the decimal point and sufficient zeros to calculate the answer to the required decimal place. In this example, 4 zeros are added:

11 ⟌9.0000

Step 3. Complete the division rounding the quotient to the 4th decimal place:

```
        .8181
  11 ⟌9.0000
       8 8
       ---
         20
         11
         --
         90
         88
         --
         20
         11
         --
          9
```
Note: Since the remainder of 9 is greater than ½ of the divisor, increase the 4th digit of 1 to 2.

.8182 = **Ans.**

Example 2   Write 125⅜ as a mixed decimal rounded to the 4th decimal place.

Step 1. The whole number 125 is not involved in the conversion. Write the fraction ⅜ as a division problem:

$$\frac{3}{8} = 8\overline{)3}$$

Step 2. Add the decimal point and 4 zeros:

8 ⟌3.0000

Step 3. Complete the division. Round answer to 4th decimal place:

```
       .3750
    8 )3.0000
       2 4
       ———
         60
         56
         ——
          40
          40
          ——
          00
```

125.3750 = Mixed decimal to the 4th decimal place

Practice exercises

1.	3/11	=	.2727	11.	116 1/6	=	116.1667
2.	2/5	=	_____	12.	42 11/25	=	_____
3.	5/16	=	.3125	13.	9 7/8	=	9.875
4.	5/8	=	_____	14.	64 3/8	=	_____
5.	4/23	=	.1739	15.	308 1/16	=	308.0625
6.	9/13	=	_____	16.	916 5/6	=	_____
7.	1/11	=	.0909	17.	33 1/3	=	33.3333
8.	1/12	=	_____	18.	816 2/3	=	_____
9.	8/15	=	.5333	19.	1,426 3/16	=	1,426.1875
10.	4/17	=	_____	20.	444 3/4	=	_____

COMMON OR PROPER FRACTIONS

ADDITION

Example 1   Add:

3/8 + 4/5 + 2/3 + 4/9 + 5/6

Step 1. Determine the denominator that all fractions in the series have in common. One method to do this is:

a. Set down all the denominators in a line.
b. Divide at least 2 denominators by any prime number. A prime number is one that is divisible only by 1 or itself. For example, 2, 3, 5, 7, 11, 13 are all prime numbers.
c. Continue to divide each line of denominators until no further divisions can be made. If a denominator is not divisible, drop it to the next line. (See "8" and "5" in example.)
d. Multiply all the divisors on the left and continue multiplying by the remainders of the divisions.

```
3 |8 5 3 9 6
   ↓ ↓
2 |8 5 1 3 2
   ↓ ↓ ↓ ↓   no prime number will divide into 2 of the remainders.
   4 5 1 3 1
```

3 × 2 × 4 × 5 × 1 × 3 × 1 = 360

Step 2. Convert all fractions to their common denominator.

$3/8 = 135/360$ (360 ÷ 8 = 45 × 3)
$4/5 = 288/360$ (360 ÷ 5 = 72 × 4)
$2/3 = 240/360$ (360 ÷ 3 = 120 × 2)
$4/9 = 160/360$ (360 ÷ 9 = 40 × 4)
$5/6 = 300/360$ (360 ÷ 6 = 60 × 5)

Step 3. Add the numerators:

135 + 288 + 240 + 160 + 300 = 1,123

Step 4. Place the total of the numerators over the common denominator:

$$\frac{1123}{360}$$

Step 5. Express the answer in its lowest term (mixed number):

$$\frac{1123}{360} = 3\frac{43}{360}$$

Example 2 Add:

$$\frac{3}{4} + \frac{3}{5} + \frac{7}{8} + \frac{3}{10} + \frac{1}{6}$$

Step 1.

```
2 | 4  5  8  10  6
2 | 2  5  4   5  3
5 | 1  5  2   5  3
    1  1  2   1  3
```

2 × 2 × 5 × 1 × 1 × 2 × 1 × 3 = 120

Step 2.

$\frac{3}{4} = \frac{90}{120}$ (120 ÷ 4 = 30 × 3)

$\frac{3}{5} = \frac{72}{120}$ (120 ÷ 5 = 24 × 3)

$\frac{7}{8} = \frac{105}{120}$ (120 ÷ 8 = 15 × 7)

$\frac{3}{10} = \frac{36}{120}$ (120 ÷ 10 = 12 × 3)

$\frac{1}{6} = \frac{20}{120}$ (120 ÷ 6 = 20 × 1)

Step 3. Add the numerators:

90 + 72 + 105 + 36 + 20 = 323

Step 4. Place the total of the numerators over the common denominator:

$$\frac{323}{120}$$

Step 5. Express the answer in its lowest terms:

$$\frac{323}{120} = 2\frac{83}{120}$$

SUBTRACTION

Example 1 Subtract $1/12$ from $7/8$.

Step 1. Determine the denominator that the fractions have in common:

```
2 | 12  8
2 |  6  4
     3  2
```

$2 \times 2 \times 3 \times 2 = 24$

Step 2. Convert the fractions to the common denominator:

$$\frac{7}{8} = \frac{21}{24} \quad (24 \div 8 = 3 \times 7)$$

$$\frac{1}{12} = \frac{2}{24} \quad (24 \div 12 = 2 \times 1)$$

Step 3. Subtract the numerators:

$21 - 2 = 19$

Step 4. Place the new numerator over the common denominator:

$$\frac{19}{24}$$

Step 5. Express answer in lowest terms. (Since the fraction $19/24$ cannot be reduced, it is in its lowest terms.)

Example 2 $15/16$ less $7/12$.

Step 1. Determine the denominator that both fractions have in common:

```
2 | 16  12
2 |  8   6
     4   3
```

$2 \times 2 \times 4 \times 3 = 48$

Step 2. Convert all fractions to the common denominator:

$15/16 = 45/48 \quad (48 \div 16 = 3 \times 15)$
$7/12 = 28/48 \quad (48 \div 12 = 4 \times 7)$

Step 3. Subtract the numerators:

$45 - 28 = 17$

Step 4. Place the new numerator over the common denominator:

$17/48$

Step 5. Express the answer in its lowest terms. The fraction $17/48$ cannot be reduced and is the lowest term.

MULTIPLICATION

Example 1 Multiply $3/8$ by $2/3$.

Step 1. Cancel any numerators and denominators that have a common divisor.

a. Cancel by common divisor of 3:

$$\frac{\cancel{3}^{1}}{8} \times \frac{2}{\cancel{3}_{1}} = \frac{1}{8} \times \frac{2}{1}$$

b. Cancel by common divisor of 2:

$$\frac{1}{\cancel{8}_{4}} \times \frac{\cancel{2}^{1}}{1} = \frac{1}{4} \times \frac{1}{1}$$

Step 2. Multiply the numerators and the denominators:

$$\frac{1}{4} \times \frac{1}{1} = \frac{1 \times 1}{4 \times 1} = \frac{1}{4}$$

Step 3. Reduce the answer to its lowest terms. Answer cannot be reduced. Answer is ¼.

Example 2   Multiply $\frac{8}{21} \times \frac{7}{20} \times \frac{15}{32}$.

Step 1. Cancel any numerators and denominators that have a common divisor.

a. Cancel by common divisor of 8:

$$\frac{\cancel{8}^{1}}{21} \times \frac{7}{20} \times \frac{15}{\cancel{32}_{4}} = \frac{1}{21} \times \frac{7}{20} \times \frac{15}{4}$$

b. Cancel by common divisor of 7:

$$\frac{1}{\cancel{21}_{3}} \times \frac{\cancel{7}^{1}}{20} \times \frac{15}{4} = \frac{1}{3} \times \frac{1}{20} \times \frac{15}{4}$$

c. Cancel by common divisor of 5:

$$\frac{1}{3} \times \frac{1}{\cancel{20}_{4}} \times \frac{\cancel{15}^{3}}{4} = \frac{1}{3} \times \frac{1}{4} \times \frac{3}{4}$$

d. Cancel by common divisor of 3:

$$\frac{1}{\cancel{3}_{1}} \times \frac{1}{4} \times \frac{\cancel{3}^{1}}{4} = \frac{1}{1} \times \frac{1}{4} \times \frac{1}{4}$$

Step 2. Multiply the numerators and the denominators:

$$\frac{1 \times 1 \times 1}{1 \times 4 \times 4} = \frac{1}{16}$$

Step 3. Reduce answer to lowest terms:

$\frac{1}{16}$. Answer cannot be reduced: $\frac{1}{16}$ = **Ans.**

1 REVIEW OF FUNDAMENTAL ARITHMETIC OPERATIONS / 21

DIVISION

Example 1 Divide $1/3$ by $4/9$.

Step 1. Write the problem stating the divisor as the second factor:

$$\frac{1}{3} \div \frac{4}{9}$$

Step 2. Invert the divisor and change the arithmetic sign to multiplication:

$$\frac{1}{3} \div \frac{4}{9} = \frac{1}{3} \times \frac{9}{4}$$

Step 3. Complete the multiplication, including any cancellation where possible:

$$\frac{1}{\cancel{3}_1} \times \frac{\cancel{9}^3}{4} = \frac{3}{4}$$

Step 4. Express the answer in its lowest terms. $3/4$ cannot be reduced further; thus it is the lowest terms.

Example 2 Divide $8/11$ by $16/33$.

Step 1. Write the problem stating the divisor as the second factor:

$$\frac{8}{11} \div \frac{16}{33} =$$

Step 2. Invert the divisor and change the arithmetic sign to multiplication:

$$\frac{8}{11} \div \frac{16}{33} = \frac{8}{11} \times \frac{33}{16}$$

Step 3. Complete the multiplication, including any cancellation:

$$\frac{\cancel{8}^1}{\cancel{11}_1} \times \frac{\cancel{33}^3}{\cancel{16}_2} \begin{array}{l}(33 \div 11)\\(16 \div 8)\end{array} = \frac{3}{2}$$

Step 4. Express the answer in its lowest terms:

$$\frac{3}{2} = 3 \overline{)2}\,^{1\frac{1}{2}} = 1\frac{1}{2} \quad \text{Ans.}$$

MIXED NUMBERS

ADDITION The addition of MIXED NUMBERS is a combination of the procedures that is used to add whole number and to add fractions.

Example 1 Add:

$$11\frac{1}{4} + 8\frac{1}{8} + 15\frac{1}{5} + 22\frac{3}{4} + 16\frac{2}{15}$$

Step 1. Add the fractions. Follow the procedure that is used to add fractions.

$11\frac{1}{4}$ $\frac{1}{4}$ = $\frac{30}{120}$ Common denominator = 120

$8\frac{1}{8}$ $\frac{1}{8}$ = $\frac{15}{120}$

$15\frac{1}{5}$ $\frac{1}{5}$ = $\frac{24}{120}$

$22\frac{3}{4}$ $\frac{3}{4}$ = $\frac{90}{120}$

$16\frac{2}{15}$ $\frac{2}{15}$ = $\frac{16}{120}$

Step 2. Add the numerators:

30 + 15 + 24 + 90 + 16 = 175

Step 3. Place the total of the numerators over the common denominator:

$$\frac{175}{120}$$

Step 4. Express the fraction in its lowest terms:

$\frac{175}{120}$ = $120\overline{)175}^{1}$
$\phantom{\frac{175}{120} = 120}\underline{120}$
$\phantom{\frac{175}{120} = 120\ }\frac{55}{120} = \frac{11}{24}$

$1\frac{11}{24}$ Ans.

Step 5. Add the whole numbers, including the sum of the fractions:

11
 8
15
22
$\underline{16}$
72
+ $\underline{1^{11}/_{24}}$
$73^{11}/_{24}$ Ans.

Example 2   Add:

$3^3/_4 + 2^5/_6 + 4^1/_2 + 2^4/_9$

Step 1. Add the fractions:

$3^3/_4$ $^3/_4$ = $^{27}/_{36}$ Common denominator = 36
$2^5/_6$ $^5/_6$ = $^{30}/_{36}$
$4^1/_2$ $^1/_2$ = $^{18}/_{36}$
$2^4/_9$ $^4/_9$ = $^{16}/_{36}$

Step 2. Add the numerators:

27 + 30 + 18 + 16 = 91

Step 3. Place the total of the numerators over the common denominator:

$$\frac{91}{36}$$

1 REVIEW OF FUNDAMENTAL ARITHMETIC OPERATIONS / 23

Step 4. Express the fraction in its lowest terms:

$$\frac{91}{36} = 36\overline{)91} \quad \frac{72}{19} = \frac{19}{36}$$

$2\frac{19}{36}$ Ans.

Step 5. Add the whole numbers including the sum of the fractions:

$$\begin{array}{r} 3 \\ 2 \\ 4 \\ 2 \\ 11 \\ + \ 2^{19}/_{36} \\ \hline 13^{19}/_{36} \text{ Ans.} \end{array}$$

SUBTRACTION
Example 1

Subtract $22\frac{4}{5}$ from $61\frac{2}{3}$.

Step 1. Subtract the fractions. Follow the same procedures outlined previously.

$$61\frac{2}{3} \quad \frac{2}{3} = \frac{10}{15}$$
$$22\frac{4}{5} \quad \frac{4}{5} = \frac{12}{15}$$

Step 2. If, after converting the fraction to the common denominator fraction, the numerator of the subtrahend (the bottom fraction) is larger than the numerator in the minuend (the top fraction), borrow 1 or $^{15}/_{15}$ from the whole number 61.

$$61\frac{10}{15} = 60\frac{25}{15}$$

Step 3. Subtract the whole numbers and the numerators of the fractions:

$$\begin{array}{r} 60^{25}/_{15} \\ -\ 22^{12}/_{15} \\ \hline 38^{13}/_{15} \text{ Ans.} \end{array}$$

Example 2

$934\frac{7}{12}$ less $546\frac{3}{7}$.

Step 1. Subtract the fractions:

$$934\frac{7}{12} \quad \frac{7}{12} = \frac{49}{84} \quad \text{Common denominator} = 84$$
$$546\frac{3}{7} \quad \frac{3}{7} = \frac{36}{84}$$
$$\overline{388} \qquad\qquad \frac{13}{84} \quad \text{Borrowing is not necessary}$$

$388\frac{13}{84}$ Ans.

MULTIPLICATION
Example 1

Multiply $46\frac{3}{8}$ by $6\frac{2}{5}$.

Step 1. Convert the mixed numbers to improper fractions:

$$46\frac{3}{8} = 46 \times 8 + 3 = \frac{371}{8}$$

$$6\frac{2}{5} = 6 \times 5 + 2 = \frac{32}{5}$$

Step 2. Cancel any numerator and denominator that have a common divisor:

$$\frac{371}{\cancel{8}_{1}} \times \frac{\cancel{32}^{4}}{5} =$$

Step 3. Multiply both numerators and denominators:

$$371 \times \frac{4}{5} = \frac{1484}{5}$$

Step 4. Express the improper fraction as a mixed number:

$$\frac{1484}{5} = 5 \overline{)1484}$$

$$\begin{array}{r} 296 \\ \underline{10} \\ 48 \\ \underline{45} \\ 34 \\ \underline{30} \\ 4 \end{array} = \frac{4}{5}$$

$$296\frac{4}{5} \text{ Ans.}$$

Example 2 Multiply $4\frac{1}{4} \times 3\frac{3}{7} \times 6\frac{3}{14}$.

Step 1. Convert the mixed numbers to improper fractions:

$$4\frac{1}{4} = 4 \times 4 + 1 = \frac{17}{4}$$

$$3\frac{3}{7} = 3 \times 7 + 3 = \frac{24}{7}$$

$$6\frac{3}{14} = 6 \times 14 + 3 = \frac{87}{14}$$

Step 2. Cancel any numerator and denominator that have a common divisor:

$$\frac{17}{\cancel{4}_{1}} \times \frac{\cancel{24}^{3}}{7} \times \frac{87}{\cancel{14}_{7}} \qquad \begin{array}{l}(24 \div 2, 14 \div 2)\\ (12 \div 4, 4 \div 4)\end{array}$$

Step 3. Multiply both the numerators and the denominators:

$$\frac{17}{1} \times \frac{3}{7} \times \frac{87}{7} = \frac{4437}{49}$$

Step 4. Express the improper fraction as a mixed number:

$$\frac{4437}{49} = 49 \overline{)4437}$$

$$\begin{array}{r} 90 \\ \underline{441} \\ 27 \end{array} = \frac{27}{49}$$

$$90\frac{27}{49} \text{ Ans.}$$

1 REVIEW OF FUNDAMENTAL ARITHMETIC OPERATIONS / 25

DIVISION
Example 1

Divide $16\frac{2}{9}$ by $7\frac{1}{3}$.

Step 1. Convert each mixed number to an improper fraction.

$$16\frac{2}{9} = 16 \times 9 + 2 = \frac{146}{9}$$

$$7\frac{1}{3} = 7 \times 3 + 1 = \frac{22}{3}$$

Step 2. Write problem stating the divisor as the second factor:

$$\frac{146}{9} \div \frac{22}{3}$$

Step 3. Invert the divisor and change the arithmetic sign to multiplication:

$$\frac{146}{9} \div \frac{22}{3} = \frac{146}{9} \times \frac{3}{22}$$

Step 4. Complete the multiplication after making any cancellation by a common divisor in the numerators and denominators:

$$\frac{\overset{73}{\cancel{146}}}{\underset{3}{\cancel{9}}} \times \frac{\overset{1}{\cancel{3}}}{\underset{11}{\cancel{22}}} = \frac{73}{3} \times \frac{1}{11} = \frac{73}{33}$$

Step 5. Express the improper fraction as a mixed number:

$$\frac{73}{33} = 33 \overline{)\begin{array}{c} 2 \\ 73 \\ \underline{66} \\ 7 \end{array}} = \frac{7}{33}$$

$2\frac{7}{33}$ Ans.

Practice exercises

		Answer
1.	Add: 5,429 + 8,694 + 7,283 + 1,998 + 6,289	29,693
2.	Add: .097 + 175.096 + .46 + .0048 + 4.0905	_____
3.	Subtract $356\frac{5}{6}$ from $770\frac{7}{8}$	$414\frac{1}{24}$
4.	What is $\frac{15}{16}$ less $\frac{7}{12}$?	_____
5.	Multiply 1,936 by 427.	826,672
6.	Multiply: $\frac{14}{15} \times \frac{9}{28} \times \frac{5}{6}$	_____
7.	Add: $\frac{13}{14} + \frac{3}{35} + \frac{3}{4} + \frac{24}{25}$	$2\frac{507}{700}$
8.	Divide: $1,382.40 by 3.476; round to the 2d decimal place.	_____
9.	Divide: $116\frac{7}{8}$ by $3\frac{7}{16}$.	34
10.	Subtract: 8,353 less 1,963	_____
11.	Multiply: $17\frac{2}{7} \times 3\frac{5}{8} \times \frac{9}{11}$	$51\frac{15}{56}$
12.	Divide: $\frac{8}{11}$ by $\frac{16}{33}$	_____
13.	Add: $15 + 103\frac{5}{8} + 21\frac{2}{3} + 6\frac{2}{5}$	$146\frac{83}{120}$
14.	Multiply: 14.7 by 3.04 by 12.67. Round answer to the 4th decimal place.	_____

15. Multiply: 358.23 by .89   318.8247
16. Divide: 18,693 by 164. Round answer to the 4th decimal place.   _____
17. Subtract: 95.907 from 2,193.57   2,097.663
18. Divide: 35,425 by 96. Express remainder as a fraction.   _____
19. Divide: $12/33$ by $6/11$ $2/3$
20. Multiply: $32\frac{5}{8}$ by $6\frac{1}{3}$ _____

APPLIED MATH PROBLEMS

CHECKING ACCOUNT RECORDS
The checkbook

To maintain an accurate record of the cash balance in the bank, all deposits made and checks written are recorded in the checkbook. Deposits, which increase the bank balance, are added to the previous balance, and checks, which decrease the bank balance, are subtracted from the previous balance. (See Figure 1–1.)

Figure 1–1

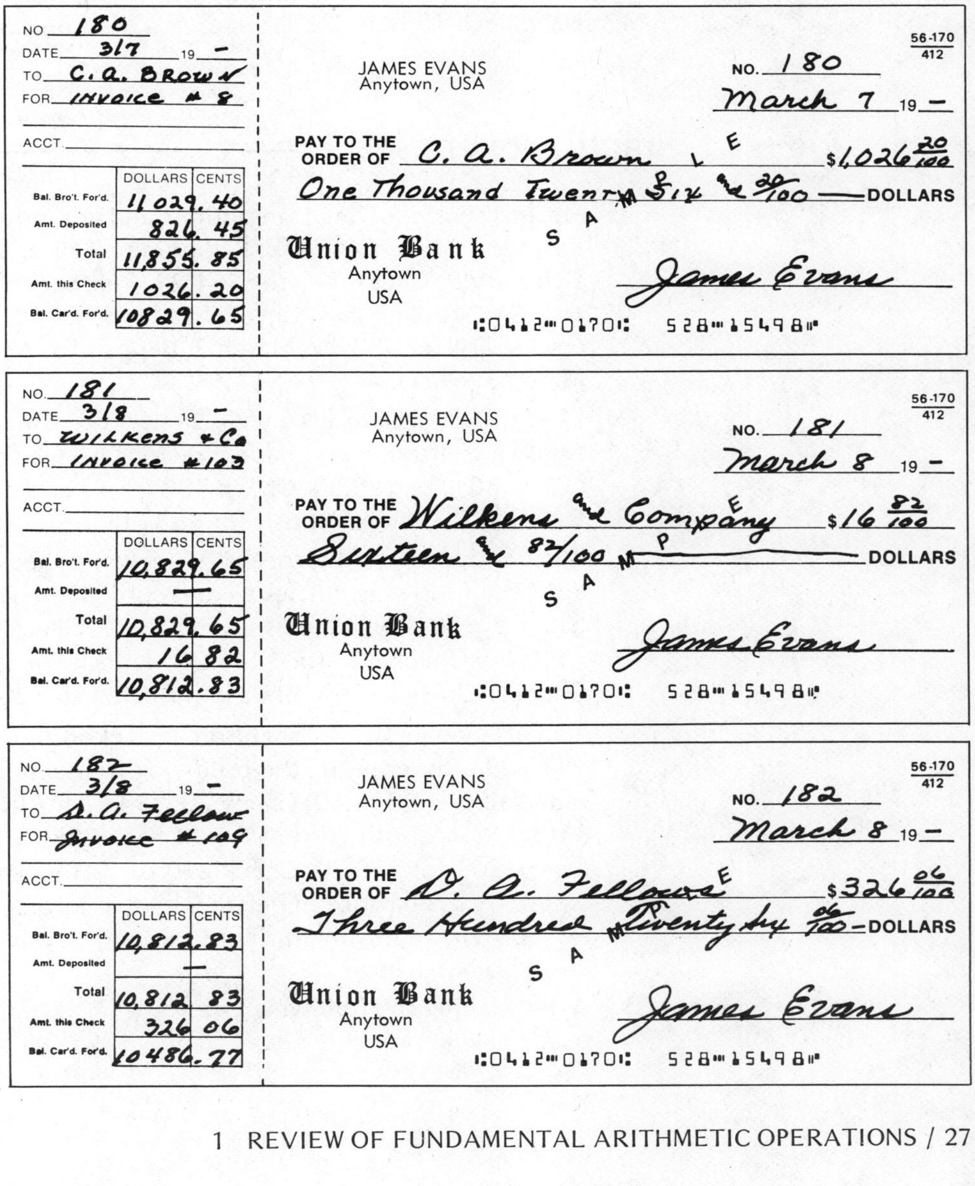

Example   The checkbook also provides a record of the date of the check, the check number, and the name of the party to whom the check was payable. The date when deposits are made is also recorded in the checkbook.

Find the balance of a checkbook at the close of business on March 9. Beginning balance, $11,029.40; a deposit dated March 7 for $826.45 was made; Check 180 dated March 7 for $1,026.20; Check 181 dated March 8 for $16.82; Check 182 dated March 8 for $326.06; deposit dated March 9 for $286.10 and Check 183 dated March 9 for $756.34 were also entered.

Solution

Beginning balance	$11,029.40
March 7 deposit	+ 826.45
Balance	$11,855.85
March 7 Check 180	−1,026.20
Balance	$10,829.65
March 8 Check 181	− 16.82
Balance	$10,812.83
March 8 Check 182	− 326.06
Balance	$10,486.77
March 9 deposit	+ 286.10
Balance	$10,772.87
March 9 Check 183	− 756.34
	$10,016.53

Practice exercises

                                                                                                        Answer

1. Record the following transactions and compute the balance in the checkbook. Beginning balance, $316.47; February 2, Check 412 for $64.25; February 2, deposit for $913.40; March 3, Check 413 for $124.10; March 3, Check 414 for $34.12; March 3, deposit for $337.82; March 3, Check 415 for $54.63. $1,290.59

2. Find the balance in J. L. Wells's checkbook after the following entries were made. Previous balance, $214.16; Check 301 for $89.20; Check 302 for $11.51; Check 303 for $303.20; and a deposit for $387.00.   ————

3. What is the correct balance in Ms. Ryan's checkbook after the following entries were recorded? Beginning balance, $801.20; a deposit of $216.20; Check 421 for $119.62; Check 422 for $436.20; deposit for $11.87; Check 423 for $27.91 and a deposit for $46.20. $491.74

4. The balance in Mary Donaldson's checkbook was $416.29 after entering the following transactions. Beginning balance, $216.40; Check 206, $43.21; Check 207, $106.18; a deposit for $350.00; Check 208 for $4.37; Check 209 for $56.72; Check 210 for $109.00.
    a. Is the balance in her checkbook correct?   ————
    b. What adjustment, if any, should be made in the checkbook balance?   ————

5. After making the following entries, what is the balance in the checkbook? Previous balance, $89.20; Check 42,

$11.46, Check 43, $25.00, deposit, $165.50; Check 44,
$51.45; Check 45, $62.83; Check 46, $37.27. $66.69

BANK STATEMENT RECONCILIATION

Periodically a bank will send its checking account depositors a statement listing all deposits made and all checks written that have been processed through the bank records during a stated time.

The account balance shown on the bank statement will seldom agree with the balance shown in the checkbook. The purpose of the bank reconciliation is to make certain that the checkbook balance agrees with the bank statement balance.

To complete this agreement, it will be necessary to make adjustments in both the bank statement balance and the checkbook balance. The following types of adjustments and their effect on balances are quite common in completing a bank statement reconciliation. (See Figure 1-2 for one type of statement.)

Figure 1-2
Bank Statement

UNION CITY BANK
Some Place
U S A

Statement: Period for:
Mr. James T. Wilson   March 1 through
420 Midland Ave.   March 31, 19-
Mapleview, U.S.A.

DATE	CHECKS	DEPOSITS	BALANCE
3/1/19-	Balance		$8,941.40
3/4	$129.40 42.60	$865.50	9,634.90
3/12	$406.20 101.45		
	92.34	612.50	
3/17	$312.40 86.19	101.85	
	36.20	335.65	
			9,650.12
3/24	$11.09 218.16		
	361.20 816.80	907.00	
	298.00		8,851.87
3/29	$206.42 15.40		
	23.85	500.00	
	Service Charge 3.00		
	Collect. fee 3.00		9,100.20

Adjustments usually made to the bank statement balance:

1. *Add to statement balance all deposits not recorded on the statement* but included in the checkbook balance.
2. *Add any errors* made in recording deposits and checks that increases the balance of the statement.
3. *Subtract outstanding checks.* These are checks that are not included on the bank statement but have been deducted in the checkbook.

1 REVIEW OF FUNDAMENTAL ARITHMETIC OPERATIONS / 29

4. *Subtract any errors* in recording deposits and checks that decrease the statement balance.

Adjustments usually made to the checkbook:

1. *Add items* such as a note or draft collected by the bank but not recorded in the checkbook.
2. *Add any error* in recording deposits or checks that increases the balance in the checkbook.
3. *Subtract any fees*, collection charges, or service fees that the bank charges but have not been recorded in the checkbook.
4. *Subtract any error* in recording deposits and checks that decreases the checkbook balance.

Example 1   Complete a bank statement reconciliation of the following checkbook and bank statement:

Balance on bank statement	$9,104.20
Balance in checkbook	8,537.50
Deposit not included on the bank statement	420.00

Outstanding checks:
   #801 $119.10
   #807   36.80
   #811   92.80

Service charge	3.00
Note collected by the bank but not recorded in checkbook	500.00
Collection fee charged by bank	3.00

Error made by bank on deposit for $709 that was recorded as $907
A check for $316.20 was listed as $361.20 by the bank
Errors found in checkbook included a check for $69.20 that was entered as $60.20; a deposit for $186.00 was entered as $86.

Step 1.   Adjustments to bank statement:

Balance	$9,104.20
Deposit not recorded	+ 420.00
Outstanding checks:	
$119.10 + 36.80 + 92.80	− 248.70
Errors:	
Deposit for $709 that was recorded as $907	
(error reduces balance)	− 198.00
Check for $316.20 that was recorded as $361.20	
(error increases balance)	+ 45.00
Adjusted statement balance	$9,122.50

Step 2.   Adjustments to checkbook:

Balance	$8,537.50
Note collected by bank	+ 500.00
Service charge by bank	− 3.00
Collection fee due bank	− 3.00

Errors found in checkbook:
 Check for $69.20; check recorded as $60.20
  (error decreases balance) .... − 9.00
 Deposit for $186.00, deposit recorded as $86.00
  (error increases balance) .... + 100.00
Adjusted checkbook balance $9,122.50

Step 3. Complete reconciliation:

Adjusted bank statement balance $9,122.50
Adjusted checkbook balance 9,122.50
Adjusted balances agree.

Practice exercises

1. Complete a bank statement reconciliation for the following accounts: Answer

    Balance on bank statement $1,096.00
    Balance in checkbook 414.00
    Outstanding checks: $ 96.20
                           113.80
                           316.00
                            40.00
    Deposits not recorded by bank:
                          $216.75
                           101.25
    Errors made by bank:
      Check for $87.75 recorded as $97.75
      Check for $135.00 recorded as $105.00
      Deposit for $416.00 recorded as $641.00
    Errors made in checkbook:
      Deposit for $281 recorded as $180
      Check for $149.50 recorded as $194.50
      Check for $306.20 recorded as $360.20
    Service charge $8.00
    Collection fee $3.00 $603.00

2. Complete a reconciliation from the following information:

    Checkbook balance $1,064.50
    Bank statement balance 1,314.60
    Outstanding checks
      not recorded by bank:
        $27.15, $216.20, $189.40
    Deposits omitted from checkbook:
      $216.00
    Deposits not recorded by bank:
      $146.20, $316.00
    Note collected by the bank 238.50
    Service charge 4.00
    Check omitted from checkbook 19.00

1 REVIEW OF FUNDAMENTAL ARITHMETIC OPERATIONS / 31

Errors made by bank:
  Deposit for $775.00
    recorded as $575.00
  Check for $525
    recorded as $575
Errors found in checkbook:
  Check for $234.45
    recorded as $332.50

3. Prepare a bank statement reconciliation from the following data:

Balance in checkbook	$ 812.80
Balance on bank statement	1,064.20
Deposit omitted from statement	600.00
Outstanding checks:	
$16.45, $143.20, $311.60, $71.25	
Errors on bank statement:	
Check for $320	
recorded as $302	
Check for $102.00	
recorded as $322.00	
Deposit for $428.30	
recorded as $482.30	
Note collected by the bank	585.00
Service charge	7.00
Errors found in checkbook:	
Deposit for $178.90 omitted	
Check for $116.20	
recorded as $16.20	
Check for $255	
recorded as $55	$1,269.70

4. Complete the reconciliation of the checkbook and the bank statement from the following information:

Balance on bank statement	$16,750.00
Balance in checkbook	15,250.00
Outstanding checks:	
$912.80, $132.20, $314.50	
Service charge	6.00
Stop payment charge	5.00
New check charge	12.00
Deposit not on statement	274.50
Errors made by bank:	
Check for $1,392	
recorded as $1,300	
Deposit for $750	
recorded as $700	
Errors found in checkbook:	
Deposit for $196 was omitted	
Check for $240	
recorded as $440	

WORD PROBLEMS

		Answer
1.	The Eatum Produce Company had 4,218 barrels of apples in its inventory. Each barrel contained 323 pounds. Find the total pounds of apples.	1,362,414
2.	The following items were purchased by a hardware supply company:	

    82 feet of lumber at 13 cents per foot.
   783 quarts of white paint at $3.85 per quart.
   320 cans of linseed oil at 69 cents per can.
    84 paint brushes at $2.94 each.

    Find the total of the invoice. _____

3. Find the total amount on an invoice for the following merchandise:

   $15\frac{3}{5}$ yards of linen at $4.89 per yard.
    $8\frac{3}{10}$ yards of cotton at $2.45 per yard. $96.62

4. A produce dealer sold 9 crates of apples containing 21, 19, 23, 24, 20, 25, 18, 22, and 21 dozen apples at $22.60 per crate. The merchant who purchased the apples found 14 dozen apples were spoiled. If the merchant sold the apples for $1.35 a dozen, what was the profit? (Selling price − Cost = Profit.) _____

5. A large estate was divided into 72 farms of $27\frac{7}{8}$ acres each. Find the total number of acres in the estate.   2,007 acres

6. Find the total gross payroll of the Fisk Manufacturing Company, which employs the following people:

   a. Mr. J. C. Holmes, who worked 40 hours at $4.15 per hour.
   b. Ms. I. T. Parker, who worked 36 hours at $4.35 per hour.
   c. Mr. E. O. Keefer, who worked 32 hours at $4.00 per hour.
   c. Ms. R. T. Keith, who worked 38 hours at $5.85 per hour. _____

7. At an egg auction, a "lot" of eggs was sold for $52.54. How many dozen eggs were in the lot if the price was $.74 per dozen?   71 dozen

8. A 27-story building is 258 feet high. How high is it up to and including the 12th floor? _____

9. A real estate broker owned $215\frac{3}{8}$ acres of land. An additional $87\frac{5}{8}$ acres were purchased and later $103\frac{3}{4}$ acres were sold. How many acres of land were still owned? $199\frac{1}{4}$

10. If 1,567 yards of plastic cloth was purchased at $1.23½ per yard and 638 yards of cording were purchased for $81\frac{3}{8}$ cents per yard, what was the total amount of the purchase? _____

11. If .625 of an estate was left to the widow, .0625 each to the son and daughter, and the remainder to charity, what amount was left to charity from an estate valued at $130,000? (Note: the total estate is equal to 1.000.) $32,500

1 REVIEW OF FUNDAMENTAL ARITHMETIC OPERATIONS / 33

12. May Bailey earned a gross salary of $10,686 per year. If $18 was deducted from her weekly salary, what was her take-home weekly salary? _____

13. A stockbroker sold stock for the XYZ Corp. for a total of $136,500. If the price of the stock was $9⅜ per share, how many shares were sold?   14,560

14. The C & A Auction purchased 480 cut-glass bowls for $8,600. They sold ⅛ of the bowls for $18.75 each, ⅙ at $19.95, and ¼ at $21.30. The remainder of the bowls were sold for $22.15 each.
    a. How many bowls were sold for $22.15? _____
    b. What profit did the C & A Auction make? _____
    (Selling price − Cost = Profit.)

15. James, Schooly, Ford, and Keats are equal partners in a hardware business. James sells ⅓ of his interest in the business to Schooly, ¼ to Keats, and the balance to Ford. If the business was worth $145,000, what is the value of the share sold to Ford? $15,104.17 or $15,105.38

16. If the cost of an item is ⅕ less than the selling price, find the cost if the selling price is $450. (S.P. − ⅕ S.P. = C.) _____

17. If the total cost of producing a product was $3,212.53 and the cost for each product was $.755, how many products were produced?   4,255

18. An employer is required to contribute .088 of the total payroll to the union welfare fund. How much was contributed in a week in which the total payroll was $4,656.84? _____

19. If a case of merchandise contains 12 cartons and each carton contains 2 dozen articles, what is the value of 12 cases if the articles are priced to sell for $1.875 each? $6,480.00

20. An employee is paid at the rate of $4.875 per hour. Find the gross pay for a week in which the following hours were worked: 8½ hours on Monday, 12¼ hours on Tuesday, 6⅖ hours on Wednesday, 11¾ hours on Thursday, and 4¼ hours on Friday. _____

Review problems

		Answer
1.	Multiply 1,936 by 427.	826,672
2.	$1,422 divided by 171 equals what amount?	_____
3.	Add: 4/5 + 1/6 + 5/12 + 13/24.	1 37/40
4.	Divide 4 5/6 by 4/9.	_____
5.	321 × 1/12 ÷ 6.8 =	3.9338
6.	Convert the following fractions to their decimal equivalents: a. 1/8 c. 6/11 b. 4/9 d. 3/16	_____ _____ _____ _____
7.	Subtract 11.0375 from 131.8.	120.7625
8.	Multiply 22 3/5 by 110.9 by $26.	_____
9.	Divide 81.03 by 3.02. (Round answer to the 4th decimal.)	26.8311
10.	Divide 32,604 by 144. (State remainder as a fraction.)	_____
11.	If it takes 1 5/6 pounds of plastic to produce a toy truck, how many complete trucks can be produced from 846 pounds of plastic?	461

12. Find the checkbook balance after the following transactions were entered:

    Beginning balance $1,420.90
    Checks written and entered
       in the checkbook:
          $13.20, $315.80, $1,106.95 and $4.38
    A deposit of $227.85 was also made.

13. Prepare a reconciliation of the checkbook and the bank statement from the following data:

Bank statement balance	$	876.25
Checkbook balance		660.50
Deposit omitted on the statement		245.25
Service charge		4.50
Stop Payment charge by bank		6.50

    Errors in checkbook:
       Deposit for $296.20
          entered as $96.20
       Check for $416.50
          entered as $306.50
       Check for $62.50
          entered as $6.50
    Errors made by bank:
       Deposit for $526.00
          recorded as $626.00
       Check for $526.00
          recorded as $625.00
    Note collected by bank 437.00 $1,120.50

1 REVIEW OF FUNDAMENTAL ARITHMETIC OPERATIONS

14. Bryant Department Store purchased the following merchandise:

    72 yards of cotton cloth at $2.065 per yard
    84 yards of woolen cloth at $5.15 per yard
    16 yards of linen cloth at $4.875

    Find the amount due on the invoice. _____

15. The production of a milling machine averaged 6 units per hour. What is the expected production if the machine is operated for 6.6 hours per day and 6½ days per week at the end of 4 weeks?   1,029.6

16. Profits for the year were divided among 3 partners according to their interest in the company. If J. C. Lippman owned .365 of the company, N. O. Nyman owned .418 of the company and M. B. Thomas owned the balance, what amount did Thomas receive as her share of the profits of $86,420?   _____

17. Find the total value of 200 shares of stock purchased for $34⅛ per share and 38 shares purchased for $16⅝ per share. $7,456.75

18. Prepare a reconciliation of the checkbook and the bank statement from the following data:

Balance on bank statement	$ 380.20
Balance on checkbook	226.60
Outstanding checks: $42.90, $18.25, and $25.95	
Deposit omitted from bank statement	216.00
Deposit not included in the checkbook	162.00
Service charge	6.50
Error found in checkbook: Check for $226.40 entered as $353.40	

    _____

19. If the cost of an item is .265 less than its selling price, find the profit if the selling price is $145.50 (Selling price − Cost = Profit.) $38.56

20. Sales District 10 sold ²⁄₉ of the total sales for the month of October. Sales District 11 sold ⅗ of the October sales. Find the sales made in Sales District 12 if total sales for October were $76,855 in the three districts.   _____

36 /

STUDY UNIT **2**

Percents—percentage

RULES OF PROCEDURE
   Convert a percent (%) to a decimal
   Convert a percent (%) to a fraction
   Convert a decimal to a percent (%)

RULES OF PERCENT/PERCENTAGE
   To find a percentage
   To find a rate
   To find a rate of increase/decrease
   To find a base

To express a relationship or to make a meaningful comparison between two or more numbers or values, a businessperson frequently relies on a percent (%) to indicate such a relationship or comparison. Tax rates, interest rates, and markups or markdowns may be expressed as a percent. The comparison of production, income, sales, expenses, prices and many other business indicators in one time period are often compared to another time period and expressed as a percent of increase or decrease.

In this study unit, we will review the definitions and procedures as well as the mathematics involved in percent-percentage calculations by use of the following formulas:

(1) Base × Rate = Percentage
$$B \times R = P$$

(2) $$\frac{Percentage}{Base} = Rate$$
$$\frac{P}{B} = R$$

(3) $$\frac{Percentage}{Rate} = Base$$
$$\frac{P}{R} = B$$

Percent-Percentage problems involve three components:

Percentage, Rate (Percent), and Base

Two of these components are generally stated in the problem and you are required to compute the third component.

Figure 2-1

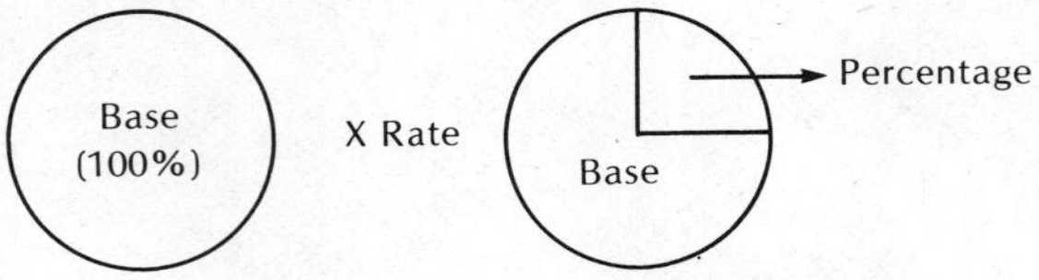

Figure 2-1 indicates the relationship between these components.

The following Rules of Procedure, definitions, formulas, and problems are designed to increase your skill in solving business problems that involve the calculation of a percentage, rate or base.

RULES OF PROCEDURE

The computation involved in a percent/percentage problem may require a change in one or more of the components in order to complete the calculations.

> **Rule 1: TO CONVERT A RATE OR PERCENT (%) TO A DECIMAL NUMBER:**
> a. Change any fraction in the percent to its decimal equivalent.
> b. Remove the % sign and move the decimal point 2 places to the left. If necessary, add zeros to complete the required 2 places.
> Note: the percent (%) sign equals the hundredths (two) decimal places.

Example 1   Write 16% as a decimal number.

Step 1. Remove the % sign and move decimal point 2 decimal places to the left:

16% is written as 16.
16. is written as .16

Step 2.

16 % = .16

Example 2   Write 6% as a decimal number.

Step 1. Remove the % sign:

Write 6% as 6.

Step 2. Move the decimal point 2 places to the left and, if necessary, add zeros to complete 2 decimal places:

Write 6. as .06
6% = .06

Example 3   Write ¼% as a decimal number.

Step 1. Change any fraction in the percent to its decimal equivalent:

¼% = .25%

Step 2. Remove the % sign:

Write .25% as .25

Step 3. Move the decimal point 2 places to the left, and if necessary, add zeros to complete 2 decimal places:

Write .25 as .0025
¼% = .0025

40 /

Example 4 Write 8½% as a decimal number.
  Step 1. Change any fraction in the percent to its decimal equivalent:

$$8\tfrac{1}{2}\% = 8.5\%$$

  Step 2. Remove the % sign:

  Write 8.5% as 8.5

  Step 3. Move the decimal point 2 places to the left and, if necessary, add zeros to complete 2 decimal places:

  Write 8.5 as .085
  8.5% = .085

Practice exercises

Round answers to the 4th decimal place.

#	Question	Answer
1.	Write 27% as a decimal number.	.27
2.	Write 72% as a decimal number.	_____
3.	What decimal is equal to 31⅛%?	.3113
4.	12½% is equal to what decimal number?	_____
5.	Write 16¼% as a decimal number.	.1625
6.	Write 9⅓% as a decimal number.	_____
7.	How is 56.8% written as a decimal number?	.568
8.	Write 7.284% as a decimal number.	_____
9.	What decimal number is equal to 112½%?	1.125
10.	Write 237½% as a decimal number.	_____
11.	66⅔% is written as what decimal number?	.6667
12.	8⅓% is written as what decimal number?	_____
13.	⅙% is written as what decimal number?	.0017
14.	3/16% is written as what decimal number?	_____
15.	106¼% is equal to what decimal number?	1.0625
16.	19% is equal to what decimal number?	_____
17.	Write ⅞% as a decimal number.	.0088
18.	What decimal number is equal to 11⅑%?	_____
19.	14¾% is written as what decimal number?	.1475
20.	⅘% is written as what decimal number?	_____

> **Rule 2: TO CONVERT A PERCENT (%) TO A COMMON FRACTION:**
>   *a.* Remove the percent (%) sign and move decimal point 2 places to the left.
>   *b.* Place the decimal number over 1 plus as many zeros as there are decimal places in the decimal number.
>   *c.* Reduce the fraction to its lowest term.

Example 1 Write 6% as a common fraction.
  Step 1. Remove the percent sign and move the decimal point 2 places to the left:

  Write 6% as 6.
  Write 6. as .06

2 PERCENTS—PERCENTAGE / 41

Step 2. Place decimal number over 1, plus as many zeros as there are decimal places in the decimal number:

$$.06 = \frac{6}{100} \quad \text{(2 places)} \quad \begin{array}{l} \longrightarrow \text{decimal number} \\ \longrightarrow \text{1 plus 2 zeros} \end{array}$$

Step 3. Reduce the fraction to its lowest term:

$$\frac{6}{100} = \frac{3}{50}$$

Thus $6\% = \frac{3}{50}$

Example 2   Write $\frac{1}{8}\%$ as a common fraction.
Step 1. Change fraction in percent to a decimal:

$$\frac{1}{8}\% = .125\%$$

Step 2. Remove the percent sign and move decimal point 2 places to the left:

Write .125% as .00125

Step 3. Place decimal number over 1, plus as many zeros as there are decimal places in the decimal number:

$$.00125 \text{ (5 places)} = \frac{125}{100,000} \quad \begin{array}{l} \longrightarrow \text{decimal number} \\ \longrightarrow 1 + 5 \text{ zeros} \end{array}$$

Step 4. Reduce fraction to its lowest term:

$$\frac{125}{100,000} = \frac{1}{800}$$

Thus $\frac{1}{8}\% = \frac{1}{800}$

Example 3   Write $14\frac{1}{4}\%$ as a common fraction.
Step 1. Change fraction in percent to a decimal:

Write $14\frac{1}{4}\%$ as 14.25%

Step 2. Remove the percent sign and move decimal point 2 places to the left:

Write 14.25% as .1425

Step 3. Place decimal number over 1, plus as many zeros as there are decimal places in the decimal number:

$$\frac{.1425}{(4 \text{ places})} = \frac{1425}{10,000} \quad \begin{array}{l} \longrightarrow \text{decimal number} \\ \longrightarrow (1 + 4 \text{ zeros}) \end{array}$$

Step 4. Reduce fraction to its lowest term:

$$\frac{1425}{10,000} = \frac{57}{400}$$

Thus $14\frac{1}{4}\% = \frac{57}{400}$

Practice exercises

Round decimals to the 5th decimal place when necessary.

		Answer
1.	Write 16% as a fraction.	$\frac{4}{25}$
2.	How is ⅙% written as a fraction?	_____
3.	87½% is written as what fraction?	$\frac{7}{8}$
4.	Write .5% as a fraction.	_____
5.	What fraction is equal to 6.125%?	$\frac{49}{800}$
6.	.072% is written as what fraction?	_____
7.	Write 66⅔% as a fraction.	$\frac{2}{3}$
8.	How would you write 11⅛% as a fraction?	_____
9.	What fraction is equal to 4.25%?	$\frac{17}{40}$
10.	Write 92% as a fraction.	_____
11.	What fraction is equal to .75%?	$\frac{3}{400}$
12.	Write .8% as a fraction.	_____
13.	42% written as a fraction is equal to what?	$\frac{21}{50}$
14.	Write 12% as a fraction.	_____
15.	What fraction is equal to 4⅗%?	$\frac{23}{500}$
16.	9⅛% is equal to what fraction?	_____

Rule 3: TO CONVERT A DECIMAL NUMBER TO A PERCENT:
    a. Move the decimal point 2 places to the right.
    b. Add the % sign.

Example 1   Write .06 as a percent.
    Step 1. Move decimal 2 places to the right:

$$.06 = 06.$$

    Step 2. Add the % sign:

$$06. = 6\%$$

Example 2   Write .00125 as a percent.
    Step 1. Move the decimal 2 places to the right:

$$.00125 = .125$$

    Step 2. Add the % sign:

$$.125 = .125\%$$

Example 3	Write .0825 as a percent.
Step 1. Move the decimal 2 places to the right:

$$.0825 = 8.25$$

Step 2. Add the % sign:

$$8.25 = 8.25\%$$

Practice exercises

		Answer
1.	Write .1275 as a percent.	12.75%
2.	How is .0067 written as a percent?	_____
3.	What percent is equal to .0375?	3.75%
4.	Write .875 as a percent.	_____
5.	.055 is what percent?	5.5%
6.	What percent is equal to .5467?	_____
7.	How is .11125 written as a percent?	11.125%
8.	Write .1667 as a percent.	_____
9.	How is 1.255 written as a percent?	125.5%
10.	Write .6667 as a percent.	_____
11.	What percent is equal to .0025?	.25%
12.	.8725 is written as what percent?	_____
13.	How is 1.6475 written as a percent?	164.75%
14.	What percent is equal to .0094?	_____
15.	Write .375 as a percent.	37.5%
16.	How is 1.06375 written as a percent?	_____

RULES OF PERCENTS/PERCENTAGE

DEFINITIONS   *Percentage.* A percentage is always a part of a base (see Figure 2-1) and is expressed in the same term as the base.

Example   If the base is pounds, the percentage will be expressed in pounds.
If the base is dollars, the percentage will be expressed in dollars.
Rate. A rate is a decimal part of the base. The words *rate* and *percent* refer to the same thing and are used interchangeably.

Example   An interest rate is expressed as 11% and means the rate is 11 parts of 100. The rate may be written as .11 or $^{11}/_{100}$.
Base. The base is generally the amount, value, or quantity that is the basis of the problem. In many problems the base will follow the "rate" and the words *of, more than,* or *less than.* The base is always equal to 100% (see Figure 2-1).

Rule 4: TO FIND A PERCENTAGE:
   A percentage is calculated by substituting the facts stated in the problem in this formula:

$$\text{Base} \times \text{Rate} = \text{Percentage}$$
$$B \times R = P$$

Step 1. Identify the facts stated in the problem.
Note: The *rate* will include the % sign.
The *base* will be the whole quantity amount or the value stated in the problem.
Step 2. Substitute the facts stated in the problem in the percentage formula.
Step 3. Complete the arithmetic required by the formula.

Example 1 What amount is 8% of $240?
Step 1. Identify the facts stated in the problem.

$$\text{Base } \$240 \times \text{Rate } .08 = \text{Percentage} \rightarrow \text{the Amount}$$

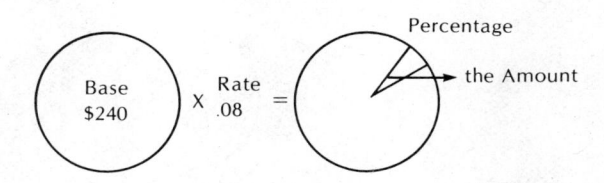

Step 2. Substitute facts in the percentage formula:

$$B \times R = P$$
$$\$240 \times .08 = P$$

Step 3. Complete the required arithmetic:

$$\$240 \times .08 = \$19.20 \textbf{ Ans.}$$

Example 2 What is ¼% of 420 pounds?
Step 1. Identify the facts stated in the problem.

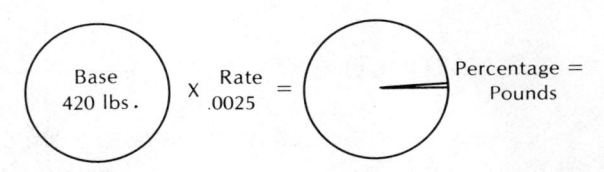

$$\text{Base } 420 \text{ lbs.} \times \text{Rate } .0025 = \text{Percentage} = \text{Pounds}$$

Step 2. Substitute the facts stated in the problem in the percentage formula:

$$B \times R = P$$
$$420 \times .0025 = P$$

Step 3. Complete the required arithmetic:

$$420 \times .0025 = 1.05 \text{ pounds}$$

Example 3 A salesman's commission is 9½% of his total sales. Find the commission if total sales were $11,828.
Step 1. Identify the facts stated in the problem.

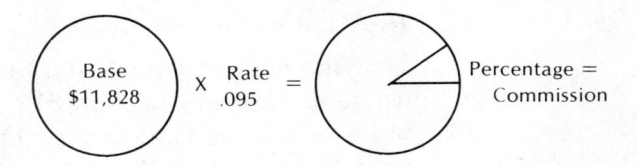

$$\text{Base } \$11,828 \times \text{Rate } .095 = \text{Percentage} = \text{Commission}$$

Step 2. Substitute the facts stated in the problem in the percentage formula:

2 PERCENTS—PERCENTAGE / 45

$$B \times R = P$$
$$\$11,828 \times .095 = P$$

Step 3. Complete the required arithmetic:

$$\$11,828 \times .095 = \$1,123.66$$

Example 4 The Durant Manufacturing Company planned to increase production by 7% during the next year. If production in the current year was 140,000 units, by how many units would production be increased?

Step 1. Identify the facts stated in the problem:

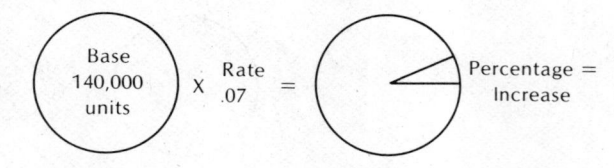

Base 140,000 units X Rate .07 = Percentage = Increase

Step 2. Substitute the facts stated in the problem in the percentage formula:

$$B \times R = P$$
$$140,000 \times .07 = P$$

Step 3. Complete the required arithmetic:

$$140,000 \times .07 = 9,800 \text{ units.}$$

Practice exercises

Round all decimals to the 4th decimal place. If answer is dollars and cents, round to the nearest cent.

		Answer
1.	How much is 62.5% of $35?	$21.88
2.	3½% of $466 is what percentage?	_____
3.	¼% of $501.20 is what amount?	$1.25
4.	How much is 15.6% of $5,400?	_____
5.	How much is 5½% of $27.40?	$1.51
6.	What is 12½% of 14,600?	_____
7.	⅔% of $6,600 is what amount?	$44.22 or $44.00
8.	How much is 22% of 11,846 pounds?	_____
9.	115% of 8,063 tons is how many tons?	9,272.45
10.	16⅔% of 916 people equals how many people?	_____
11.	The sales tax in a certain city was 5½%. How much tax would be paid on a sale of $812.65?	$44.70
12.	Ms. Brown earns a commission of 11.125% on total sales. If her sales on Monday are $642.50, $706.12 on Tuesday, $319.40 on Wednesday, $509.04 on Thursday, and $814.28 on Friday, how much commission did she earn for the week?	_____

13. Jim Kercher received an 8⅓% raise in his salary. If his salary was $9,325 a year, what was the amount of his raise? $776.77

14. The will of R. W. Smythe left 35% of his estate to his wife, 12% to his business partner, and 18½% to each of his two sons. The balance of the estate was left to charity. How much was given to charity if the total estate was $118,750? _____

15. 27.6% of the production of T. C. Reynolds Company was sold in the New England area. If total production was valued at $837,550, what is the expected New England area sales? $231,163.80

16. Ms. R. Walters borrowed $3,250 to buy a new car. She was to pay 9½% interest per year. How much interest would she pay? _____

17. C. R. Brown sold to Olt Garage tools that cost $1,018.20. How much commission did he earn if his commission was 16⅔% of total sales? $169.73

18. A 15% cash discount was allowed on an invoice of $4,719.85. How much discount was allowed? _____

19. The Smythe Company expected a profit of 9% over the cost of manufacturing wooden stepladders. If the cost of one ladder was $27.15, how much profit would be made on each ladder they manufactured? $2.44

20. Ms. R. Keith, sales manager for the Kelley Company, planned to increase sales by 11% over last year's sales. How much would sales increase if last year's sales were $112,890? _____

Rule 5: TO FIND A RATE:
The rate indicates what portion the percentage is of a base. It is computed by substituting the facts stated in a problem in this formula:

$$\frac{\text{Percentage}}{\text{Base}} = \text{Rate}$$

Step 1. Identify the facts stated in the problem. The smaller number, quantity, or value is generally the percentage.
Step 2. Substitute the facts stated in the problem in the rate formula.
Step 3. Complete the arithmetic required by the formula.
Step 4. Write the decimal answer as a percent.

Note: Answers to the examples and practice exercises have been rounded to the 4th decimal place.

Example 1   Find the rate if the percentage is $26.50 and the base is $212.00
   Step 1. Identify the facts stated in the problem:

   $26.50 is the Percentage
   $212.00 is the Base

   Step 2. Substitute facts stated in the problem in the rate formula:

   $$\frac{P}{B} = R \quad \frac{\$26.50}{\$212.00} = R$$

2 PERCENTS–PERCENTAGE / 47

Step 3. Complete the arithmetic required:

$$212 \overline{)26.50} = .125$$

Step 4. Write decimal answer as a percent:

$$.125 = 12.5\%$$

Example 2 The sales tax on an invoice was $14.08. The amount of the sale was $256.00. Find the sales tax rate.

Step 1. Identify the facts stated in the problem:

$14.08 is the Percentage
$256.00 is the Base

Step 2. Substitute the facts stated in the problem in the rate formula:

$$\frac{P}{B} = R \quad \frac{14.08}{256.00} = R$$

Step 3. Complete the required arithmetic:

$$256 \overline{)14.08} = .055$$

Step 4. Write decimal answer as a percent:

$$.055 = 5.5\%$$

Example 3 A clothing manufacturer produces 1,208 women's coats, 1,612 men's overcoats, and 1,420 children's snowsuits. What percent of the total production is the children's snowsuits?

Step 1. Identify the facts stated in the problem:

1,420 is the Percentage
1,208 + 1,612 + 1,420 = 4,240 is the Base

Step 2. Substitute the facts stated in the problem in the rate formula:

$$\frac{P}{B} = R \quad \frac{1,420}{4,240} = R$$

Step 3. Complete the required arithmetic:

$$4,240 \overline{)1,420} = .3349$$

Step 4. Write the decimal answer as a percent:

$$.3349 = 33.49\%$$

Practice exercises

Round all answers to 4 decimal places.

		Answer
1. Percentage is 51, base is 621, what is the rate?		8.21%
2. If the base is 392 and the percentage is 206, what is the rate?		

3. Find the rate if the base is 586 and the percentage is 106.8. **18.23%**
4. What percent is 97 of 387.50? _____
5. If a base is $88.00, the percentage is $9.12, what is the rate? **10.36%**
6. What percent of $1,129 is $627? _____
7. If the base is 11,420 pounds and the percentage is 3,026 pounds, what is the rate? **26.50%**
8. $512 is what percent of $2,330? _____
9. Find the percent 92 is of 816.375. **11.27%**
10. What percent is 10.80 of 42? _____
11. If 264 crates of oranges are spoiled, what was the percent of loss from spoilage in a shipment of 3,624 crates? **7.28%**
12. The population of a village included 1,420 women, 1,392 men, and 1,406 children. What percent of the total population were children? _____
13. A baseball team won 65 games and lost 14 games. What percent of the total games played did the team win? **82.28%**
14. In the manufacturing of 1,160 women's coats, 96 did not pass inspection. What percent of the total coats did not pass inspection? _____
15. A commission paid to a salesperson amounted to $1,687.50 on total sales of $11,250. What was the rate of commission paid? **15%**
16. The gross income of Baker Manufacturing Company was $198,420. Selling expenses amounted to $3,626. What percent of the gross income was the selling expense? _____
17. Children's jackets cost $21.85 to manufacture. They were priced to sell for $26.95. What percent of the selling price was the cost? **81.08%**
18. In a class of 126 students, 14 students failed to pass the course. Find the percent of failures. _____
19. The value of the total production of electric irons was $7,896,000. If $896,420 of the total production was shipped to foreign buyers, what percent of the production was sold to foreign buyers? **11.35%**
20. Find the rate if the base is 708 and the percentage is 117. _____

The rate or percent of increase or decrease indicates a change in value, amount, or units that occur in one period of time when compared to another period of time.

Rule 6: TO FIND A RATE OF INCREASE/DECREASE:
  a. **Subtract the data of one time period from data in another time period.**
  b. **Substitute the facts in the rate formula.**

Step 1. Calculate the amount of increase or decrease by subtracting the data of one time period from data in another time period.

Step 2. Identify the percentage and the base.
Note: The increase or decrease calculated in Step 1 will be the *percentage*. The *base* will be the amount that changed or the amount from the earlier time period.
Step 3. Substitute the facts in the rate formula:

$$\frac{P}{B} = R$$

Step 4. Complete the required arithmetic.

Example 1   Sales during year 1 were $867,570 and in year 2 were $976,884. Find the rate of increase.
Step 1. Subtract data of one time period from data of another period:

Year 2 .... $976.884
Year 1 .... −867,570
Increase $109,314

Step 2. Identify the percentage and the base:

Increase of $109,314 = Percentage
Year that changed, $867,570 = Base

Step 3. Substitute facts in the rate formula:

$$\frac{P}{B} = R \quad \frac{\$109,314}{\$867,570} = \text{Rate}$$

Step 4. Complete the required arithmetic:

$$867{,}570 \overline{)109{,}314.} \quad .126 = 12.6\% \text{ of increase}$$

Example 2   Profits for the first 6 months of a year were $69,855. For the second 6 months, profits were $52,964. What was the rate of decrease?
Step 1. Subtract data of one time period from data of another period:

1st 6 months $69,855
2d 6 months   52,964
Decrease $16,891

Step 2. Identify the percentage and the base:

Decrease $16,891 = Percentage
$69,855, the amount that decreased = Base

Step 3. Substitute data in Rate formula:

$$\frac{P}{B} = R \quad \frac{\$16,891}{\$69,855} = \text{Rate}$$

Step 4. Complete the required arithmetic:

$$69{,}855 \overline{)16{,}891.} \quad .2418 = 24.18\% \text{ of decrease}$$

Example 3   (It may be necessary to first calculate a base.)
In the canning process, 204 pounds of tomatoes were lost in the cooking operation. If 820 pounds remained after cooking, what was the percent of decrease in the original pounds started in the canning process?

Step 1. Calculate the original pounds:

$$\begin{array}{ll} \text{Pounds lost} & 204 \\ \text{Pounds remaining} & +\ 820 \\ \text{Original pounds} & \overline{1,024} \end{array}$$

Step 2. Identify the fact stated in the problem:

Pounds lost, 204 = Percentage
Original pounds, 1,024 = Base

Step 3. Substitute facts in the rate formula:

$$\frac{P}{B} = R \quad \frac{204}{1,024} = \text{Rate}$$

Step 4. Complete the required arithmetic:

$$1,024 \overline{)204.} \quad .1992 = 19.92\% \text{ of decrease}$$

Practice exercises

Round all answers to the 4th decimal place.

		Answer
1.	The E. F. Phelps Company employed 1,209 women in year 1 and 1,082 in year 2. What was the rate of decrease?	**10.5%**
2.	Jane Keller's salary was $963 per month. After a raise, she earned $1,043. Find the percent of increase in her salary.	_____
3.	Production costs increased from $8.15 per unit to $9.50. What was the rate of increase?	**16.56%**
4.	T. B. Hagan Company increased their house paint orders for outside white from 189 gallons to 222 gallons. What was the percent of increase?	_____
5.	The property tax rate in year 1 was $32.45 per $1,000 of assessed property value. In year 2, the rate was $30.67. What was the percent of decrease in the tax rate?	**5.49%**
6.	Enrollment in a business management course was 312 students; in an English composition course, enrollment was 906 students. The following semester enrollment in the business management course was 276 students and in the English composition course, 944 students. Find the rate of increase or decrease in the enrollments in both courses.	_____ _____
7.	In processing woolen goods, 105 pounds of wool were lost due to shrinkage. If 355 pounds remained after the processing, what was the percent of decrease due to shrinkage?	**22.83%**
8.	The Brown family traveled 3,036 miles on their vacation to Yellowstone National Park. The following year they traveled 4,047 miles. What was the percent of increase in the miles they traveled?	_____

9. If the National Forest Service planted 11,086 new trees during the spring and 8,900 during the fall, what was the rate of decrease in trees planted? 19.72%

10. A compact car averaged 24.7 miles per gallon of gasoline. After being driven 40,000 miles, the average miles per gallon was 20.9. What percent of change was there in the average miles per gallon? _____

11. A toy manufacturer started 3,950 pounds of plastic to produce toy trucks. Each truck required 1 pound of plastic. If total production was 3,150 trucks, what was the percent of loss in the plastic used in the production process? 20.25%

12. A fast food chain served 9,025 cheeseburgers in March. During April 10,420 cheeseburgers were served. Find the rate of increase in cheeseburgers served. _____

13. The cost of manufacturing a product increased from $1.89 per pound to $2.16 per pound. Find the percent of increase in the cost of 150 pounds of the product. 14.29%

14. If 14,420 tons of apples were sold after a loss of 1,027 tons from spoilage, what was the percent of loss in the original tonnage from spoilage? _____

15. The sale of bathing suits in March averaged 285 and 467 in June. What percent of increase in the average number of suits sold could be expected? 63.86%

16. Ms. Zimmer's travel expenses during the 1st quarter of the year amounted to $846.50. During the 2d quarter her travel expenses increased to $1,049.66. What was the rate of increase in her expenses? _____

> **Rule 7: TO FIND A BASE:**
> The base is always regarded as equal to 100% (see Figure 2-1). It is the quantity, value, or number that, when multiplied by a rate, results in a percentage.

The base will often follow the word *of*. To calculate a base, substitute the facts stated in the problem in the base formula.

$$\frac{\text{Percentage}}{\text{Rate}} = \text{Base}$$

Step 1. Identify all the facts stated in the problem.
Step 2. Substitute the facts in the problem in the formula:

$$\frac{P}{R} = B$$

Step 3. Complete the required arithmetic:

96.36 is 12% of what number?

Example 1 Step 1. Identify all the facts stated in the problem:

96.36 = Percentage
12% = Rate
Number = Base

Step 2. Substitute the facts in the problem in the base formula:

$$\frac{P}{R} = B \quad \frac{96.36}{.12} = \text{Base}$$

Step 3. Complete the required arithmetic:

$$.12 \overline{)96.36} = 803 \qquad \text{Number} = 803$$

Example 2   Find total sales if the rate of commission paid was 9% of total sales and the commission received amounted to $1,156.50.

Step 1. Identify all the facts stated in the problem:

$$\$1,156.50 = \text{Percentage}$$
$$9\% = \text{Rate}$$
$$\text{Total sales} = \text{Base}$$

Step 2. Substitute the facts in the problem in the base formula:

$$\frac{P}{R} = B \quad \frac{\$1,156.50}{.09} = \text{Base}$$

Step 3. Complete the required arithmetic:

$$.09 \overline{)1,156.50} = \$12,850 \qquad \text{Total sales} = \$12,850$$

Practice exercises

		Answer
1.	85 is 5% of what number?	1,700
2.	140 is 140% of what number?	_____
3.	Janet Kaye earned a commission of $875. The rate of commission paid was 8¼% of the total sales. Find the total sales.	$10,606.06
4.	The drafting department of a large manufacturing company is charged with 11% of the total rent expense. What is the total rent expense if the amount charged to the drafting department is $1,908.80?	_____
5.	The owner of a clothing store planned a profit of 33⅓% of the cost of a suit. Find the cost if the profit amounted to $36.75.	$110.26 or $110.25
6.	8% of the total production of the assembly department did not pass inspection. If 456 units did not pass, find the total production of the department.	_____
7.	The cost of doing business is 35% of gross sales. If the cost of doing business is $18,500, what must be the gross sales?	$52,857.14
8.	The selling expenses of the Greene Company were equal to 23% of gross sales. If the selling expenses totaled $4,991, find the gross sales.	_____
9.	45% of how many dollars is $19.50?	$43.33

10. J. R. Mackey plans to purchase a new house. He has saved the required down payment of $7,600. Find the price of the house if the down payment is 14.5% of the total price. _____

11. Ms. Ball owns 46% of the common stock of the ABC Corporation. If Ms. Ball's stock is valued at $79,870, what is the total value of the common stock of the ABC Corporation? $173,630.43

12. 27.42 is 6% of what number? _____

13. The operating expenses of the Graymore Company were 12% of total sales. Find total sales if the operating expenses amounted to $69,420. $578,500

14. Faith Hays received a raise in salary of 8%. If the amount of her raise was $784, what was her salary before the raise? _____

15. If 354 units did not pass inspection and this number was 6% of the total units started in production, find:
    a. The total number of units started. 5,900
    b. The total units that did pass inspection. 5,546

16. Expenses of a company last year amounted to $19,895. If this amount was 23% of gross sales, what were the gross sales? _____

17. The selling expenses of a musical instrument company were equal to 23% of gross sales. Selling expenses amounted to $4,991. Find gross sales. $21,700

18. The cost of doing business was 35% of gross sales. If the cost of doing business was $18,500, what were the gross sales? _____

19. Sales returns for the week amounted to $450.72. This amount was equal to 6% of weekly sales. Find the amount of weekly sales. $7,512

20. Find the weekly salary of J. T. Keys if $31.59 withholding tax was deducted from his gross pay and this amount was 15.6% of his gross pay. _____

Review problems

1. Change the following percents to a decimal number. (Round all answers to the 4th decimal place.)
   a. 87½% = .875
   b. 125% = 1.25
   c. 33⅓% = .3333
   d. 11% = .11
   e. ⅙% = .0017
   f. 26⅖% = .2640
   g. 9²⁄₇% = .0929
   h. 7⅑% = .0711

2. Change the following percents to a common fraction.
   a. 19% = _____
   b. 1.3% = _____
   c. 37.5% = _____
   d. 127.5% = _____
   e. 25.3% = _____
   f. 87½% = _____
   g. 60% = _____
   h. 66⅔% = _____

3. Write the following decimals as percents.
   a. .125 = 12.5%
   b. 1.455 = 145.5%
   c. .102 = 10.2%
   d. .0025 = .25%
   e. .6 = 60%
   f. .625 = 62.5%
   g. .0083 = .83%
   h. 1.42⅝ = 142.625

	Answer
4. How much is 62.5% of $35.00?	_____
5. ⅙% of $501.20 is what amount?	$ .85
6. What is 12½% of 14,600?	_____
7. 16⅔% of 916 equals what number?	152.70
8. Ms. Ray, who had a net income of $1,100 per month, had a budget which included 40% of her net income for housing, 30% for food, 16% for operating expenses. How much did Ms. Ray have for all other expenses?	_____
9. Jane Allgood received a raise equal to 9⅛% of her weekly salary which was $212.50. What was the amount of her raise?	$ 19.39
10. In the month of June, the total production of Warren Manufacturing Company was 143,875 units. If 11⅖% of the total production was sold in the state of Delaware, how many units were sold in Delaware?	_____
11. R. W. Ramsey was paid a commission of 8⅓% of total sales he completed. Find his commission for a week in which he completed $820.18 sales on Monday, $716.15 on Tuesday, $218.14 on Wednesday, did not work on Thursday, and $1,146.50 on Friday.	$241.65
12. All items in a clothing store were sold at a 30% discount off the regular selling price. If the regular selling price of a suit Ms. Stone selected was $165.00, what did she pay for the suit if a 4% sales tax was added to the discount price?	_____
13. What percent is 102 of 416.8?	24.47%
14. $381 is what percent of $4,352?	_____

15. J. C. Morris produced a total of 912 units, but 103 units of his production did not pass inspection. What percent of his total production did pass inspection? 88.71%

16. If it cost $7,000 to manufacture goods that sold for a total of $9,702, find the percent the cost was of the selling price. _____

17. Corporate stock that was purchased for $8,950 was sold for $7,518. What was the percent of decrease in the value of the stock? 16%

18. The population in the town of Wells Grove was 14,826 in 1968. In 1978 the population increased to 18,948. Find the rate of increase in the population. _____

19. The price of a car was quoted as $5,629. Extras increased the total price to $6,480.39. What percent of increase in the price of the car was due to the extras? 15.125%

20. The selling price of an item was $90.75. What percent of profit (increase) was made on the sale of the item if its cost was $72.65? _____

21. Mary Adams drove her car 30,560 miles in one year. The following year she drove 19,940 miles. What was the percent of change in miles she drove? 34.75% decrease

22. The requirements of an order received by a dress manufacturer indicated that the present stock of 252 yards of material was only 45% of the job requirement. How many yards of material are required to fill the order? _____

23. $29.50 is 6% of what number? $491.67

24. Mr. Cramer was given an increase of $825 in his salary, which was a 20% raise. What was his salary after he received the increase? _____

25. A jobber sold a "lot" of goods for $32.39 which was 18% of the original price. What was the original price? $179.94

26. A salesperson earns a salary of $95 per week, plus a commission of 6% of sales. Find the amount of sales in a week in which a total of $135.95, including salary, was received. _____

27. A contractor estimated the cost of installing plumbing in a new house would be $8,425. This amount was 12½% of the total cost of the house. What is the expected cost of the house? $67,400

28. Property taxes were 23⅖% of the assessed value of Mr. White's property. What property tax did he pay if the assessed value of his property was $14,615.50? _____

29. Ms. T. Walls borrowed $5,750 from the First National Bank for one year. The interest rate was 11.5%. How much interest would Ms. Walls pay on the loan? $661.25

30. A publishing company sold 8,420 books in sales district 12. The total edition was 44,907 books. What percent of the total edition was sold in district 12? _____

STUDY UNIT 3

Solving word problems

RULES FOR SOLVING WORD PROBLEMS

FORMULAS

CALCULATING A BASE

CALCULATING TOTAL VALUE

EQUATIONS
   To find the whole value
   Distribution of a total

METRIC SYSTEM

Study Unit 3 concentrates on the solution of word problems by applying the fundamentals of arithmetic reviewed in Study Units 1 and 2 and by using formula substitution and simple equations. Although there is no one single rule or method that can be applied to all types of problems, the knowledge of the more frequently used formulas in business and the skill in writing simple equations will enhance your skill in analyzing and solving a variety of word problems.

RULES FOR WORD PROBLEM SOLVING
1. Read the problem carefully, several times if necessary.
2. Analyze the problem and identify all numbers, values, or quantities as well as the unknown term.
3. Write a formula or simple equation to solve for the unknown term.
4. Substitute all facts stated in the problem in the formula or equation.
5. Complete the arithmetic required by the formula or equation.

FORMULAS
A formula may be defined as a statement of a rule or method by which a *specific* type of problem may be solved by the substitution of facts stated in a problem.

Some of the more frequently used formulas in solving business problems include:

1 Cost + Markup (profit) = Selling Price

Example Find the selling price of a sweater that cost $14.50 if the merchant had a markup of 15% of the cost.

$$\text{Cost} + \text{Markup} = \text{Selling price}$$
$$\$14.50 + (.15 \times 14.50) = \text{Selling price}$$
$$\$14.50 + \$2.18 = \$16.68$$

2   List price − Discount = Net price

Example   The price of merchandise was $840. A discount of 5% was given for cash payment. Find the net price of the merchandise if cash payment was made.

$$\text{List price} - \text{Discount} = \text{Net price}$$
$$\$840 - (.05 \times 840) = \text{Net price}$$
$$\$840 - \$42.00 = \$798.00$$

3   Gross pay − Withholding tax = Net pay

Example   Harry Webber earned $265 per week. Total withholding tax deducted from his pay amounted to $53. What net pay did he receive?

$$\text{Gross pay} - \text{Withholding tax} = \text{Net pay}$$
$$\$265 - \$53 = \$212$$

You will use these formulas and many others in subsequent study units.

A modification of the formula, to Find a Base, used in Study Unit 2, can be applied to several types of problems.

Rule 1: TO FIND A BASE:

Divide the total stated in the problem by 100% plus the stated rate, if the total is more than the base. Substitute terms given in the problem in the formula:

$$\text{Base} = \frac{\text{Total}}{100\% + \text{Rate}}$$

Step 1. Identify the facts stated in the problem:
   a. The base will be the unknown fact and equal to 100%.
   b. The rate will include the % sign.
   c. The total will be the amount, value, or quantity stated in the problem.

Step 2. Substitute the facts stated in the problem in the formula.

Step 3. Complete the required arithmetic.

Example 1   How many dollars + 7% is equal to $820.50?

Step 1. Identify the facts stated in the problem:

$$\text{Dollars} = \text{the base of } 100\%$$
$$\text{Rate} = 7\%$$
$$\text{Total} = \$820.50$$

Step 2. Substitute the facts stated in the problem in the formula:

$$B = \frac{\text{Total}}{100\% + \text{Rate}}$$

$$B = \frac{\$820.50}{100\% + 7\%} = \frac{\$820.50}{1.07}$$

Step 3. Complete the required arithmetic:

$$1.07 \overline{)820.50} \quad \begin{array}{c} 766.82 \end{array} = \$766.82$$

Example 2 The selling price of an item is $28.75. Find the cost of the item if a profit of 15% of the cost is included in the selling price.

Step 1. Identify the facts stated in the problem:

$$\text{Cost} = \text{the base of } 100\%$$
$$\text{Rate} = 15\%$$
$$\text{Total} = \$28.75$$

Step 2. Substitute the facts stated in the problem in the formula:

$$B = \frac{\text{Total}}{100\% + 15\%}$$

$$B = \frac{\$28.75}{100\% + 15\%} = \frac{\$28.75}{1.15}$$

Step 3. Complete the required arithmetic:

$$1.15 \overline{)28.75}^{\,25.00} \quad \$25.00 = \text{cost}$$

Example 3 Inventory this year was 7% more than last year. If this year's inventory was 12,840 units, how many units were included in last year's inventory?

Step 1. Identify the facts stated in the problem:

Last year's inventory = base of 100%
Rate = 7%
Total = 12,840

Step 2. Substitute the facts stated in the problem in the formula:

$$B = \frac{\text{Total}}{100\% + 7\%} = \frac{12,840}{1.07}$$

Step 3. Complete the required arithmetic:

$$1.07 \overline{)12,840} = 12,000 \text{ units}$$

Practice exercises

		Answer
1.	How many dollars + 11% equals $1,248.75?	$1,125
2.	9,300 pounds equals how many pounds plus 16¼%?	_____
3.	A retailer priced an item to sell for $72.60, which was 10% more than its cost. Find the cost of the item.	$66.00
4.	How many bushels plus 8¼% equals 127.5?	_____
5.	If a product shrinks 12% of the finished production while being processed, how many pounds of finished products can be processed from 560 pounds?	500 lbs.
6.	A salesperson is paid a salary plus a bonus of 15.5% on the salary. If the salesperson received a total pay of $1,285 in July, what was the salary of the salesperson?	_____
7.	F. T. Thomas earns $235.44 per week after receiving a raise of 8% of his original salary. Find his original salary.	$218.00

8. Marie Jones earns $360 a week, which is 20% more than Henry Brown earns. What is Brown's weekly salary? _____

9. If the selling price of an item was $146.53 after an increase of 12½% in the original price, what was the original price? $130.25

10. The total production in Plant A was 11,554 units during March. If this production represents an increase of 9% over February production, what was the number of units produced during February? _____

> **Rule 2: TO FIND A BASE:**
> Divide the total stated in the problem by 100% *minus* the stated rate, if the total is less than the base.
>
> $$\text{Base} = \frac{\text{Total}}{100\% - \text{Rate}}$$

Step 1. Identify facts stated in the problem:
   a. The *base* = the unknown term and 100%.
   b. The *rate* will include the % sign.
   c. The *total* is the number, quantity, or value stated in the problem.

Step 2. Substitute all facts stated in the problem in the formula:

$$\text{Base} = \frac{\text{Total}}{100\% - \text{Rate}}$$

Step 3. Complete the required arithmetic.

Example 1 The selling price of an item was $285.00, which was 14% less than its cost. Find the cost of the item.

Step 1. Identify the facts stated in the problem:

$$\text{Total} = \$285.00$$
$$\text{Rate} = 14\%$$
$$\text{Base} = \text{The cost or } 100\%$$

Step 2. Substitute the facts in the formula:

$$\text{Base} = \frac{\text{Total}}{100\% - \text{Rate}}$$

$$\text{Cost} = \frac{\$285.00}{100\% - 14\%} = \frac{\$285.00}{86\%}$$

Step 3. Complete the required arithmetic:

$$.86\overline{)\$285.00} = \$331.40 = \text{Cost}$$

Example 2 If 25% of perishable vegetables spoiled while being transported to market, how many pounds were shipped if 7,650 pounds of unspoiled vegetables arrived at the market?

Step 1. Identify the facts stated in the problem:

$$\text{Total} = 7,650$$
$$\text{Rate} = 25\%$$
$$\text{Base} = \text{Pounds shipped or } 100\%$$

Step 2. Substitute the facts in the formula:

$$\text{Base} = \frac{\text{Total}}{100\% - \text{Rate}}$$

$$\text{Pounds shipped} = \frac{7{,}650}{100\% - 25\%} = \frac{7{,}650}{75\%}$$

Step 3. Complete the required arithmetic:

$$\text{Pounds shipped} = .75 \overline{)7{,}650} = 10{,}200 \text{ Pounds shipped}$$

Practice exercises

		Answer
1.	If 12.5% of the original quantity of steel is lost from shrinkage in processing, find the original tons if 1,890 tons were produced.	2,160
2.	How many dollars less 6% is $596.90?	_____
3.	An item sold for $279.50, which was 14% less than its cost. What was the cost of the item?	$325.00
4.	How many dollars less 8⅓% is equal to $435?	_____
5.	A tank contained 2,001 gallons of gasoline after a loss of 8% of the original contents from evaporation. Find the original contents of the tank.	2,175 gals.
6.	Mary Williams received a salary of $118.50 after tax deductions. Deductions were 14% of her total salary. What was her total salary?	_____
7.	450 yards of finished cloth remained after the dyeing process. If 10% of the original yards started were lost from shrinkage, how many yards of cloth were started?	500 yards
8.	R. A. Raymond's salary after taxes was $175. The tax rate was 9.5% of his gross salary. Find Raymond's gross salary.	_____
9.	Clerical salary expenses were $18,920, which also were 38.2% less than selling expenses. Find the selling expenses.	$30,614.89
10.	460 perfect dishes were produced by the day shift. The manager knows that 8% of the total dishes started in production are spoiled. How many dishes were started?	_____

Rule 3: TO FIND A TOTAL:
   If the total amount, number, or quantity is larger than the base, multiply the base by 100% *plus* the stated rate.

   Base × (100% + Rate) = Total

Step 1. Identify the facts stated in the problem:
   a. The base will be the amount, number, or quantity stated in the problem.
   b. The rate will include the % sign.
   c. The total will be the unknown term.

Step 2. Substitute the facts stated in the problem in the formula:

Base × (100% + Rate) = Total

Step 3. Complete the required arithmetic.

Example 1 James Bailey's salary was $175 a week. How much did he earn after he received a raise of 9.5% of his salary?

Step 1. Identify the facts stated in the problem:

Base = $175 and 100%
Rate = 9.5%
Total = Salary after the raise

Step 2. Substitute facts stated in the problem in the formula:

Base × (100% + Rate) = Total
$175 × (100% + 9.5%) = Total

Step 3. Complete the required arithmetic:

$175 × 1.095 = $191.63 Salary after the raise

Example 2 Inventory of raw material included 46,000 tons of high grade steel. After the inventory was increased by 11.4%, how many tons of steel were in the inventory?

Step 1. Identify the facts stated in the problem:

Base = 46,000 and 100%
Rate = 11.4%
Total = Tons of steel after the increase

Step 2. Substitute facts stated in the problem in the formula:

Base × (100% + Rate) = Total
46,000 × (100% + 11.4%) = Total

Step 3. Complete the required arithmetic:

46,000 × 1.114 = 51,244 Tons

Example 3 An item that cost $6.20 was sold for a profit of 12¼% of its cost.
a. Find the selling price of the item.
b. What profit would be made on a sale of 160 items?

a: **Step 1.** Identify the facts stated in the problem:

Base = $6.20 and 100%
Rate = 12¼%
Total = Selling price

Step 2. Substitute facts stated in the problem in the formula:

Base × (100% + Rate) = Total
$6.20 × (100% + 12¼%) = Total

Step 3: Complete the required arithmetic:

$6.20 × 1.1225 = $6.96 Selling price

b: **Step 1.** Substitute facts in the formula:

Units sold × Profit per unit = Total profit
160 × ($6.96 − $6.20) = Total profit

Step 2. Complete the required arithmetic:

$$160 \times .76 = \$121.60 \text{ Total profit}$$

Practice exercises

		Answer
1.	A base of 1,142 was increased by 15.5%. Find the total.	$1,319.01
2.	If the base is $165.50 and the rate of increase was 7¾%, what was the total?	_____
3.	The price of a living room set was $1,426. The sales tax was 6.5%. What was the total cost of the living room set?	$1,518.69
4.	The cost of an item was $49.50; profit was $11.25. What was the selling price?	_____
5.	The Ballard Company planned to increase the personnel in its sales department by 16%. If there were 50 people in the department, how many people would be employed after the increase?	58
6.	The hourly rate for the employees in the shipping department was increased by 10.8%. If the average hourly rate was $5.165, what was the increased average hourly rate?	_____
7.	Mileage drive by a vending machine serviceman was 380 miles per week. Additional machines added to his route and required an increase of 17.4% in miles driven per week. Find the total miles he will drive after the increase.	446.12
8.	Doris Hogan owned 216 shares of common stock. She increased her shares by 33⅓%. If the price of the stock was $112.60 per share, what was the value of her total shares after the increase?	_____
9.	The price of a car was quoted as $5,629. Additional equipment added 15⅛% cost to the quoted price. What was the total price of the car?	$6,480.39
10.	The weight of raw cotton increased by 28⅜% from absorption of moisture. If the original weight was 9,012, how much will it cost to ship the cotton after the additional pounds are added, if the shipping charges are 14.8 cents per pound?	_____

Rule 4: TO FIND A TOTAL:
  If the total amount, number, or quantity is less than the base, multiply the base by 100% *minus* the stated rate.

  Base × (100% − Rate) = Total

Step 1. Identify the facts stated in the problem:
a. The Base will be the amount, number or quantity stated in the problem.
b. The Rate will include the % sign.
c. The Total will be the unknown term.

Step 2. Substitute the facts stated in the problem in the formula:

$$\text{Base} \times (100\% - \text{Rate}) = \text{Total}$$

Step 3. Complete the required arithmetic.

Example 1 The selling price of an item was $98.20. Markup was 23½% of the selling price. Find the cost of the item.

Step 1. Identify the facts stated in the problem:

$$\text{Base} = \$98.20$$
$$\text{Rate} = 23\frac{1}{2}\%$$
$$\text{Total} = \text{Cost of the item}$$

Step 2. Substitute the facts stated in the problem in the formula:

$$\text{Base} \times (100\% - \text{Rate}) = \text{Total}$$
$$\$98.20 \times (100\% - 23\frac{1}{2}\%) = \text{Total}$$

Step 3. Complete the required arithmetic:

$$\$98.20 \times .765 = \$75.12$$

Example 2 Of the original pounds of wool started in the dyeing process, 9% was lost to shrinkage. If 940 pounds were started;
  a. How many pounds remained after dyeing?
  b. What was the dollar value of the loss, if the price of wool was $1.06 per pound?

Step 1. Identify the facts stated in the problem:

$$\text{Base} = 940 \text{ pounds}$$
$$\text{Rate} = 9\%$$
$$\text{Total} = \text{Pounds remaining}$$

Step 2. Substitute facts stated in the problem in the formula:

$$\text{Base} \times (100\% - \text{Rate}) = \text{Total}$$
$$940 \times (100\% - 9\%) = \text{Total}$$

Step 3. Complete the required arithmetic:

  a. $940 \times .91 = 855.4$ Pounds remaining
  b. $940 - 855.4 = 84.6$ Pounds lost
  $84.6 \times \$1.06 = \$89.68$ Loss

Practice exercises

		Answer
1.	Gross sales minus sales returns equals net sales. Find gross sales if net sales were $8,426.30 and sales returns were $294.92.	$8,721.22
2.	The Collins Manufacturing Company employs a total of 1,869 people. If 55% of the total employees were women, how many men were employed?	————
3.	W. J. Willey sold a car that had cost him $3,698 at a loss of 14.8%. What was the selling price of the car?	$3,150.70
4.	The Plumb Manufacturing Company offered a customer a discount of 12⅛% if he purchased the entire stock of children's shoes. If the entire stock cost $12,839, what did the customer pay for the shoes?	————

5. Tea loses 15⅖% of its weight in the drying process. How many pounds of dried tea resulted if 1,960 pounds of tea were started in the drying process?   1,658.16

6. 9% of the total work units produced by department 43 did not pass inspection. If total work unit production was 5,700 units, how many work units did pass inspection?   _____

7. Mrs. T. Young paid 20% of the balance of her charge account, which was $4,475. What was the amount still due on the account? $3,580

8. Loss from a fire in a warehouse was estimated to be 35% of the merchandise stored. Find the value of the loss if 7,040 items were stored at the time of the fire and each item was valued at $4.85.   _____

EQUATIONS

The use of simple equations is a useful tool in analyzing and solving problems for which there are no established formulas.

> **Rule 1: TO WRITE A SIMPLE EQUATION:**
> Arrange the facts stated in the problem in such a manner that facts stated on the *left* side of the = sign are of the same number, quantity, or value as the facts stated on the *right* side.

Step 1. Identify the facts stated in the problem that are of equal value.
Step 2. Arrange the equal facts in an equation.

Example 1 If ⅕ of an acre cost $200, what would 1 acre cost?
Step 1. Identify equal facts:

$\frac{1}{5}$ acre is one fact.

$200 is another fact.

Step 2. Arrange as an equation:

$\frac{1}{5}$ acre cost = $200

Example 2 If 14 bushels of wheat cost $399.50, what is the cost of 1 bushel?
Step 1. Identify equal facts:

14 bushels is one fact.
$399.50 is another fact.

Step 2. Arrange as an equation:

14 bushels cost = $399.50

Example 3 In District 1, 25% of total sales were made. If the sales in District 1 amounted to $16,436, what were the total sales?
Step 1. Identify equal facts:

25% of total sales is one fact
$16,436 is another fact

Step 2. Arrange as an equation:

.25 of total sales = $16,436

Example 4   Not passing inspection were 412 work units. Find total production if 8½% of work units produced did not pass inspection.

Step 1.   Identify equal facts:

.085 of total production is one fact
412 work units is another fact

Step 2.   Arrange as an equation:

.085 of total production = 412

Rule 2: TERMS OF AN EQUATION:
The terms on both sides of the = sign in an equation must always be equal in number, value, or quantity, and this equality will *not* change if 4 criteria, which follow, are met.

---

a. The same number is *added* to both the left and right sides of the = sign.

$$\begin{array}{rl} \text{Example:} & 2 + 4 = 6 \quad \text{(equation)} \\ \text{Add} & +2 = +2 \\ \hline & 4 + 4 = 8 \quad \text{(equation)} \end{array}$$

b. If the same number is *subtracted* from both the left and right sides of the = sign.

$$\begin{array}{rl} \text{Example:} & 2 + 4 = 6 \quad \text{(equation)} \\ \text{Subtract} & -2 = -2 \\ \hline & 0 + 4 = 4 \quad \text{(equation)} \end{array}$$

c. If both the *left* and *right* sides of the = sign are *multiplied* by the same number.

$$\begin{array}{rl} \text{Example:} & 2 \times 4 = 8 \quad \text{(equation)} \\ \text{Multiply} & \times 2 = \times 2 \\ \hline & 4 \times 4 = 16 \quad \text{(equation)} \end{array}$$

d. If both the *left* and *right* sides of the = sign are *divided* by the same number.

$$\begin{array}{rl} \text{Example:} & 4 \div 2 = 2 \quad \text{(equation)} \\ \text{Divide} & \div 2 = \div 2 \\ \hline & 2 \div 2 = 1 \quad \text{(equation)} \end{array}$$

Rule 3: TO COMPLETE THE ARITHMETIC OF AN EQUATION WHEN ONE MEMBER IS UNKNOWN:
a. Write the facts stated in the problem as an equation.
b. Transfer all stated numbers to the same side of the = sign by applying Rule 2 *a, b, c,* or *d.*
c. Complete the arithmetic function required by the final equation.

Example 1   If ⅕ of an acre of land cost $2,000, find the cost of 1 acre.

Step 1.   Write the facts stated in the problem as an equation:

$$\frac{1}{5} \text{ acre cost} = \$2,000$$

Step 2.
     × 5   = × 5   Rule 3 *b*

Step 3.   1 acre cost = $10,000 Rule 3 *c*

Example 2   The selling price of 14 bushels of wheat was $163.85. What is the selling price of 1 bushel?

  Step 1.   Write the facts stated in the problem as an equation:

$$14 \text{ bushels cost} = \$163.85$$

  Step 2.

      ÷ 14   = ÷ 14   Rule 3 *b*

  Step 3.   1 bushel cost = $\dfrac{\$163.85}{14}$

$$14 \overline{)\$163.85}^{\;11.70} = \$11.70 \text{ Cost of 1 bushel}$$

Example 3   The labor cost necessary to produce a product was 80% of the total product cost. Labor cost amounted to $22.80. Find the total cost of the product.

  Step 1.   Write the facts stated in the problem as an equation:

$$.80 \text{ of total cost} = \$22.80$$

  Step 2.

      ÷ .80   = ÷ .80

  Step 3.   1 total cost = $\dfrac{\$22.80}{.80}$

$$.80 \overline{)22.80.00}^{\;\$28.50} = \text{Total product cost} = \$28.50$$

Example 4   The cost of 1 pound of untreated wool was 52¢. What is the cost of 215 pounds?

  Step 1.

$$1 \text{ pound of wool cost} = \$.52$$

  Step 2.

      × 215   = × 215   Rule 3 *b*

  Step 3.   215   = 215 × .52 Rule 3 *c*

$$\begin{array}{r} \$\;\;215 \\ \times\;\;\;.52 \\ \hline 4\;30 \\ 107\;5\;\; \\ \hline \$111.80 \end{array} = \text{Cost of 215 pounds}$$

Practice exercises

		Answer
1.	Interest on a loan for one year amounted to $488.75. What was the amount of the loan if the interest was 8½% of the loan?	$5,750
2.	Ms. J. Willis made a down payment of $380 on a piece of office equipment. If the down payment was ⅕ of the total price, what was the price of the equipment?	_____
3.	The sales tax on an item was $136.15. If the sales tax was 5.5% of the selling price, find the selling price of the item.	$2,475.45
4.	If a tank contained 670 gallons of liquid and was ⅔ full, what was the full capacity of the tank?	_____
5.	A salesperson receives a commission of 1/12 of the total sales completed. Find the total sales for a week in which $175 was received in just commissions.	$2,100.84 or $2,100.00
6.	Find the selling price of an item that had a markup of 24% of the selling price if the markup amounted to $6.18.	_____
7.	Find the net income of the Acme Food Market if their annual expenses amounted to $192,690 and this amount was equal to 9/20 of net income.	$428,200
8.	The total cost of 4,025 pounds of wool was $13,101.38. The manufacturer planned a markup of $.165 per pound. Find the selling price per pound. (Cost + Markup = Selling price.)	_____
9.	A ladies apparel shop sold 25 ladies jackets for a total of $687.50. They made a profit of 30% of the selling price. Find the profit that was made on the sale of the 25 jackets.	$206.25
10.	Inventory records showed a total of 1,026 units in stock, which cost a total of $2,123.82. Find the cost of units used to complete job 412, which required 96 units.	_____
11.	G & T Sports Center sold 12 basketballs for a total profit of $69. The basketballs cost a total of $194.40. Find the selling price of 1 basketball. (Selling price − Profit = Cost.)	$21.95
12.	Ms. J. Greene's travel expenses amounted to $68.15 for a week in which she traveled a total of 3249.5 miles. Find the cost per mile.	_____
13.	The GRF Appliance Company sold 15 air conditioners, which cost a total of $7,650. If markup was ¼ of the cost, what was the selling price of each air conditioner? (Cost + Markup = Selling price.)	$637.50
14.	If the deductions from Jane White's weekly salary were 12.5% of her gross salary and the deductions amounted to $22.65, what was her net salary?	_____
15.	The markup on a pair of ladies shoes was ⅜ of the cost. If the markup was $9.15, find the selling price of one pair of shoes.	$33.55

16. If a bottling machine has a production capacity of 2,120 bottles in an 8-hour day, how many bottles will be produced in 32 hours? _____

17. The selling expenses of a musical instrument company were equal to 23% of gross sales. If the selling expenses totaled $4,991, find the gross sales. $21,700

18. Ms. Carson was given a raise of $825, which was an increase of 20% in her salary. What was her salary after she received the raise? _____

19. Sales returns amounted to $450.72 for the week. This amount was equal to 6% of total sales. Find the total weekly sales. $7,512

20. If the withholding tax is 15.6% of total salary, what is J. T. Keye's total salary if $31.59 was withheld? _____

Rule 4: DISTRIBUTION OF A TOTAL BETWEEN 2 TERMS OF DIFFERENT VALUE, QUANTITY, OR NUMBERS:
   a. Write an equation including the terms stated in the problem.
   b. Analyze the equation based on requirements of the problem.
   c. Write a 2d equation based on the analysis.
   d. Complete the arithmetic of the revised equation.

This type of problem may be identified by the words *more than, less than*, or *times*. In the example problems, note the difference in the equation used for problems that include "more than" and "less than" and the problems that include "times."

Example 1 The town of Valley Green had a total population of 18,000 people. There were 2 times *more* women *than* men. Find the number of women in the total population.

Note: This type of problem requires that the total population of 18,000 be so distributed between men and women that the number of women is 2 times *more than* the number of men.

Step 1. Write an equation including the terms of the problem:

Number of women + Number of men = 18,000

Step 2. Analyze the equation based on requirements of the problem:

Number of women = Number of men + 2 × Number of men
Number of men = Number of men
―――――――――――――――――――――――――――――――
Total   = 4 × Number of men

Step 3. Write a 2d equation based on the analysis:

4 Number of men = 18,000

Step 4. Complete the arithmetic of the revised equation:

4 Number of men = 18,000
÷ 4   = ÷ 4
―――――――――――――――――――――――――
Number of men = $\frac{18,000}{4}$ = 4,500

Total − Number of men =   Number of women
18,000 −   4,500   = 13,500 Number of women

3 SOLVING WORD PROBLEMS / 71

Example 2 The total of $22.50 represents the cost of a product and the package. Find the cost of the product if it cost 3 *times* that of the package.

Step 1. Write an equation including the terms of the problem:

$$\text{Cost of product} + \text{Cost of package} = \$22.50$$

Step 2. Analyze the equation based on the requirements of the problem:

Cost of product = 3 × Cost of package
Total   = 3 Cost of package + 1 Cost of package

Step 3. Write a 2d equation based on the analysis:

$$4 \text{ Cost of package} = \$22.50$$

Step 4. Complete the arithmetic of the revised equation:

4 Cost of package = $22.50
÷ 4   = ÷ 4

$$\text{Cost of package} = \frac{\$22.50}{4} = \$5.63$$

Total   − Cost of package =   Cost of product
$22.50 − $5.63   = $16.87 Cost of product

Example 3 If Joan Green earned 1.5 times more than Bob Kelly and together they earned $525 in one week, what is Joan's salary?

Step 1. Write an equation including the terms of the problem:

$$\text{Green's salary} + \text{Kelly's salary} = \$525$$

Step 2. Analyze the equation based on the requirements of the problem:

Green's salary = Kelly's salary + 1.5 × Kelly's salary
Kelly's salary = Kelly's salary
Total   =   3.5 of Kelly's salary

Step 3. Write a 2d equation based on the analysis:

$$3.5 \text{ of Kelly's salary} = \$525.00$$

Step 4. Complete the arithmetic of the revised equation:

3.5 Kelly's salary = $525.00
÷ 3.5   = ÷ 3.5

$$\text{Kelly's salary} = \frac{525}{3.5} = \$150.00$$

Total   − Kelly's salary =   Green's salary
$525.00 − $150.00   = $375.00 Green's salary

Practice exercises

Answer

1. A parcel of real estate was sold for $87,500. The buildings on the parcel of land were valued at 2 times more than the land. Find the value of the buildings. $65,625

2. The total monthly salary expenses of the Watkins Manufacturing Company amounted to $78,500. If the salaries of the executive personnel were 3 times more than the

salaries paid to production management, find the monthly salary paid to executive personnel. _____

3. The Jesse Company rented store space on the first floor and office space on the fifth floor of an office building. Rent for both locations amounted to $2,750 per month. If the rent for the store was 4 times the rent of the office space, how much was the monthly store rent? $2,200

4. Profits of the Bailey Furniture Store for the year amounted to $36,460. Joan Smythe's share of the profits was 3 times the amount received by Walter Dalton. How much did each receive? _____

5. The annual budget for advertising and selling expenses allowed a total of $182,000. If the advertising budget was 4.5 times more than the selling expenses, find the average monthly advertising expense budget. $12,833.33

6. The Baker Manufacturing Company employs a total of 680 employees. Find the number of women employed if 6.5 times more women than men are employed. _____

7. Sales of the Wilson Insurance Agency for the 3d quarter of the year were 4 times the sales of the 2d quarter. Find the sales for the 3d quarter if total sales for both quarters were $206,850. $165,480

8. The total production for October was 4,557 units. If the production of Plant A was 2.5 times the production of Plant B, find the production of Plant A. _____

9. The selling price of an item included cost + a markup. If the selling price was $29.80 and the cost was 2½ times the markup, what was the cost of the item? $21.29

10. A car dealer sold 2 used pickup trucks for a total of $12,690. Selling price of one truck was 1½ times selling price of the second truck. Find the price of each. _____

11. A time and motion study completed at the Allen Food Processing Plant showed that it took the second shift 1.8 times longer to process 4 tons of tomatoes as it did the first shift. If the total time of both shifts was 1,176 minutes, what was the average minutes it took the second shift to process 1 ton of tomatoes? 189

12. Ms. Allen invested a total of $16,800 in common stock of the Bailer Investment Company and of the Applebee Manufacturing Company. The value of stock in Applebee Manufacturing was 5.5 times more than the value of the Bailer Investment. What was the value of the Applebee Manufacturing Company stock? _____

THE METRIC SYSTEM OF WEIGHTS AND MEASURES

The *metric system* is an international decimal system of weights and measures. The basic unit to measure length is the *meter,* to measure weight the *gram* is used, and to indicate capacity, the *liter* is the basic unit. All other measurements are determined by dividing by 10 to find a smaller measurement or multiplying by 10 to find a larger measurement.

The United States has been using the old English system of weights and measures and is now one of the last industrialized countries of the world to adopt the *metric system*. The Metric Conversion Act of 1975 does not make the use of the metric system compulsory, but with the increase in the extent of international trade and the world-wide adoption of the metric system the American businessman has had to change the terms of weights and measures used in the manufacturing of machine parts, the packaging of products, and the measurement of distances. The old familiar terms of inches, feet, yards, miles, pints, quarts, and gallons have become millimeters, centimeters, meters, kilometers, grams, kilograms, and so on.

The dual measurements on packages of milk, processed food, automobile speedometers, and highway signs are a few of the examples of changes that the businessman has made to comply with the metric system.

The following conversion tables will assist you in converting from one metric measurement to another, as well as from the English system to the metric system of measurements.

Procedure

The math functions remain the same regardless of the system of weights and measures used.

To convert a measurement from the English system to the metric system, refer to the conversion tables on pages 74 and 75.

Table 3-1
Conversion table of weights and measures

When you know	You can find	By multiplying by*
inches	millimeters	25
feet	centimeters	30
yards	meters	.9
miles	kilometers	1.6
millimeters	inches	.04
centimeters	inches	.4
meters	yards	1.1
kilometers	miles	.6
square inches	square centimeters	6.5
square feet	square meters	.09
square yards	square meters	.8
square miles	square kilometers	2.6
acres	square hectometers (hectares)	.4
square centimeters	square inches	.16
square meters	square yards	1.2
square kilometers	square miles	.4
square hectometers (hectares)	acres	2.5
ounces	grams	28
pounds	kilograms	.45
short tons	metric ton	.9
grams	ounces	.035
kilograms	pounds	2.2
metric tons	short tons	1.1
Fahrenheit degrees	Celsius	Subtract 32 and multiply by $5/9$.
Celsius	Fahrenheit degrees	Celsius $\times$ $5/9$, add 32 degrees.
ounces	milliliters	30
pints	liters	.47
quarts	liters	.95
gallons	liters	3.8
milliliters	ounces	.034
liters	pints	2.1
liters	quarts	1.06
liters	gallons	.26

*Approximate equivalents.

Table 3-2
Metric equivalent measurements

1 milligram	(mg)	=	.001 gram	(g)
1 gram	(g)	=	1,000 milligrams	(mg)
1 gram	(g)	=	100 centigrams	(cg)
1 kilogram	(kg)	=	1,000 grams	(g)
1 metric ton	(m)	=	1,000 kilograms	(kg)
1 centimeter	(cm)	=	10 millimeters	(mm)
1 decimeter	(dm)	=	10 centimeters	(cm)
1 meter	(m)	=	100 centimeters	(cm)
1 meter	(m)	=	10 decimeters	(dm)
1 dekameter	(dkm)	=	10 meters	(m)
1 hektometer	(hm)	=	100 meters	(m)
1 hektometer	(hm)	=	10 dekameters	(dkm)
1 kilometer	(km)	=	1,000 meters	(m)
1 kilometer	(km)	=	10 hektometers	(hm)
1 liter	(l)	=	1,000 milliliters	(ml)
1 liter	(l)	=	100 centiliter	(cl)
1 hectare	(ha)	=	10,000 square meters	

Step 1. Locate the measurement given in the problem in the left column of the conversion table.

Step 2. Multiply by the conversion factor to find the required measure.

Step 3. Complete the arithmetic required by the problem.

Example 1 A salesperson is paid a commission of .125 of total sales. Find the commission on a sale of 4,128 kilograms of wheat, which was sold for $11.50 per 100 pounds.

Step 1. Locate the measurement given in the problem on the conversion table.

Note: Change *kilograms* to *pounds*.

Step 2. Multiply by the conversion factor:

Conversion factor from table is 2.2.
4,128 kilograms × 2.2 = 9,081.6 pounds

Step 3. Complete the arithmetic required:

$$\frac{9{,}081.6 \text{ lbs.}}{100} \times \$11.50 = \$1{,}044.38 \text{ Total sale}$$

Step 4. Calculate commission:

$$\$1{,}044.38 \times .125 = \$130.55 \text{ Commission}$$

To convert one metric measure to another metric measure

Step 1. Refer to the Metric Equivalent Table for the measurement stated in the problem.

Step 2. Complete the required arithmetic.

Example 1 How many centimeters are in 60 meters?

Step 1. Refer to Table 3-2:

100 centimeters = 1 meter

Step 2. Complete the required arithmetic:

100 centimeters × 60 = 6,000 centimeters

$$\frac{6{,}000}{100} \text{ centimeters} = 60 \text{ meters}$$

Practice exercises

		Answer
1.	After one day a bicyclist had ridden 25 kilometers, which was ⅖ of the distance to his destination.	
	a. What was the total distance of his trip?	62.5 km
	b. What was the total distance in miles?	37.5 mi.
2.	If the temperature was 95 degrees Fahrenheit, what was the temperature in Celsius degrees?	_____
3.	A lumber dealer kept his pine lumber inventory by feet at a selling price of $.27 per foot. He received an order for 6.6 meters of pine lumber. How much will he charge the buyer for the lumber?	$5.88 or $5.94
4.	A container of milk is marked 946 milliliters. How many ounces of milk are in the container?	_____
5.	A box of corn flakes weighs 280 grams. How many boxes can be filled from 428.4 kilograms?	1,530
6.	The Gray Taxi Company purchased 890 gallons of gasoline for its fleet of cabs. It received a bill that quoted the price of the gasoline as $.618 per liter. How much was the bill?	_____
7.	A real estate developer owned a plot of land that measured 208 square hectometers. He planned to construct homes of ½-acre lots. How many homes can he build?	1,040
8.	A drug company had an inventory of 390 kilograms of pills to be put into bottles holding 240 grams each. How many bottles will be needed?	_____
9.	A manufacturer of paper bags must change the weight printed on his bags to the equivalent metric measurement in kilograms. What kilogram weight will they print on 5- and 10-pound bags?	(5 lb) 2.25 kg (10 lb) 4.5 kg
10.	In converting dress sizes to the metric measure of centimeters, a dress manufacturer will change dress size 32 inches to how many centimeters?	_____
11.	A formula for a chemical compound requires that a mixture be brought to a 129.2 degrees Fahrenheit temperature. To comply with the metric temperature measurement, what Celsius degrees will be used?	54
12.	How many liters would it take to fill 6 containers if each container held 946 milliliters?	_____
13.	If the temperature in a florist hothouse is kept at 18 degrees Celsius, what Fahrenheit degrees must the florist use to maintain the equivalent temperature?	42 degrees
14.	A shipment of wheat weighed 3 metric tons. How many grams are in the shipment?	_____
15.	How many meters of lumber are required to build a fence around a lot that is 16 feet long and 12 feet wide?	16.8

Review problems

		Answer
1.	The selling price of an item was $119.75. Find the cost of the item if the markup was 18½% of the cost.	$101.05
2.	How many dollars plus 7% = $820.50?	$142.50 or $142.49
3.	Ms. Ashley's salary was reduced by ⅓. If she received $95 a week after the reduction, how much did she earn before the reduction?	
4.	The weight of raw cotton shrinks 40% in the washing process. How many kilograms of raw cotton must be used to produce 3,915 kilograms of clean cotton?	_____
5.	A store planned to sell an item for $26.80. They also planned a markup of ⅜ of the cost.	
	a. Find the cost of the item.	$19.49
	b. How much was the markup?	$7.31
6.	798 crates of lettuce arrived at its destination after a loss of 16% from spoilage.	
	a. How many crates were shipped?	_____
	b. What was the loss if the price of a crate was $16.86?	_____
7.	A number increased 4.6% times its own value was $567.00. What was the number?	$542.07
8.	Find the selling price of an item that cost $86.20 if a markup of 15.5% of the cost is charged?	_____
9.	The selling price of a used car was $3,685. A sales tax of 6.2% was charged on the selling price. What was the total price to the buyer?	$3,913.47
10.	Men's overcoats were on sale for 26½% less than the regular price. If the regular price of the coat Mr. Myles selected was $146, what did he pay for the coat on which a 4½% sales tax was charged?	_____
11.	Anne K. Fish earned a gross weekly salary of $206. What was her take-home pay if 13⅕% was deducted from gross earnings?	$178.81
12.	The profit on an item was 37.5% of its cost. If the profit amounted to $9.27, what was the cost of the item?	_____
13.	If 3/7 of the cost of producing ladies' handbags was $245, what is the total cost of producing the handbags?	$571.67 or $571.63
14.	A brand of cough medicine was sold at a markup of 40% of the selling price. If the markup was $.96, what was the selling price?	_____
15.	The Whitney Company agreed to pay 70.5% of the cost of establishing a retirement fund. The remaining cost was to be contributed by the employees. If the company's share	

was $103,480, what amount must the employees contribute? $43,300.14

16. The Thomas Furniture Store made a payment of $462 on an invoice for dining room furniture. Find the total invoice price if the down payment was ⅛ of the total price. _____

17. The profits of the R.S. & T. Investment brokers for the year amounted to $102,847.60. By prior agreement, Ms. Reynolds was guaranteed $64,000. The balance of the profits were so divided that Ms. Smith was to receive 2.3 times the profits received by Ms. Thomas. What share of the profits did Smith and Thomas receive?
Thomas: $11,772.00
Smith: $27,075.60

18. If profits of $16,142 are to be so divided that one partner would receive 4 times what the other 3 partners would receive, how much was the share of that one partner? _____

19. The total cost of marketing a new product amounted to $11,520. The research costs were 5 times the packaging costs. How much were the research costs? $9,600

20. The commission earned by a salesperson in November and December amounted to $4,265.50. Commissions earned in December were 1.65 times the November commissions. Find the commissions earned in December. _____

21. The total bonus paid to the sales managers of Districts 1 and 2 amounted to $16,848. The manager of District 2 received 3.4 times more than the manager of District 1. What bonus did each manager receive?
#1: $3,120
#2: 13,728

22. The production cost of the box department of the Frame Manufacturing Company for the 2d quarter of the fiscal year was 2.3 times more than the production cost for the 1st quarter. Total cost for the 1st and 2d quarters amounted to $94,785. What was the production cost for the 2d quarter? _____

23. Total production of Plant A and Plant B was 2,000 work units in an 8-hour day. If the production in Plant A was 50% more than the production in Plant B, what was the 8-hour production in Plant A. 1,200 units

24. Production costs in the press department were 2.8 times more than the production costs in the print shop. If total production costs were $27,940, find the production cost in the press department. _____

25. The sales tax on 3 tables was $216.90, which was ⅛ of the selling price of the tables before the sales tax. Find the price of one table, including the sales tax. $650.70

26. A merchant sold radios that cost him $547.80 per dozen

78 /

at a price that was 2.5 times the cost. Find the markup on one radio.

27. Profit on an item was ⅜ of the cost of an item. Find the selling price if the profit was $4.56.   **$16.72**

28. If ⁵⁄₁₂ of a yard of silk cost $6.55, find the cost of 3¼ yards.

29. An office equipment company purchased a calculator at a cost of $230. During a sale, they sold the calculator for 20% less than the original selling price. What was the sale price of the calculator?   **$191.67**

30. A chain grocery store spent $175,000 for advertising during the first 8 months of the budget year. This amount represents ⅔ of the total advertising budget for the year. How much of the remaining budget can be spent in each of the remaining 4 months?

STUDY UNIT **4**

Trade and cash discount

TRADE DISCOUNTS
   Net price
   Net price equivalent
   Single net price

CASH DISCOUNTS
   Discount dates
   Net price
   Additional charges
   Returned goods
   Partial payments

TRADE AND CASH DISCOUNTS

TRADE DISCOUNTS

Many manufacturers, wholesalers, or middlemen offer retail buyers discounts on merchandise they buy. To encourage retail buyers to purchase large quantities of merchandise or special items at certain times of the year, one or more discounts may be offered. To provide lower prices to certain classes of customers, such as schools, hospitals, or nonprofit organizations, the wholesaler or manufacturer will make special prices available to them by offering additional discounts.

Most manufacturers and wholesalers sell their products from catalogs that show pictures of their products, installation instructions, and recommended retail prices. Rather than reprint the catalog when there is a change in prices, the manufacturer or wholesaler will supply the retail buyer with discount sheets giving the latest discounts available to them. Such discounts are called *trade discounts*. Trade discounts are not available to consumers, but are necessary for the retail buyer to determine the cost of merchandise he purchases for resale.

Trade discounts are shown on the bill or invoice and on the discount sheets as either one discount, such as $33\frac{1}{3}\%$, or as two or more discounts, such as 20%, 10%, 5%. When two or more discounts are available, they are referred to as *a series of discounts*. Very often the percent sign (%) is indicated by a diagonal line (/) separating the discounts. For example, discounts of 25%, 20%, 5% may be written as 25/20/5.

Trade discounts apply only to the list or catalog price of the merchandise. Such items as transportation charges, shipping cost, insurance, or special handling charges may be included in the total invoice price, but such charges must be subtracted from the total invoice price before discounts are applied. These charges, however, must be paid by the buyer and are added to the net price of the merchandise. Read carefully the following Definitions,

Rules for Applying Trade Discounts, and the Example Solutions before completing the Practice Exercises and Unit Review Problems.

DEFINITIONS

List price or catalog price. This is the total price of merchandise purchased that is listed on the invoice. It is the amount to which discount rates are applied.

Trade discount. It is the amount the buyer is permitted to deduct from the list price of merchandise purchased. Discount is calculated by:

$$\text{List price} \times \text{Rate of discount} = \text{Discount}$$
$$\$ \qquad \% \qquad = \qquad \$$$

Trade discount rate. The percents stated in the terms of the sale.

Net price equivalent or percent. The net price equivalent is the percent a net price is of the original list price. For example, if the list price of an item was $1.00, subject to trade discounts of 25/20/10, the net price of the item would be $.54 (1.00 × .75 × .80 × .90 = .54). The .54 is also the net price equivalent that could be applied to the full list price of all invoices subject to trade discounts of 25/20/10. Thus, if the list price of an invoice was $325, the net price would be $175.50 ($325 × .54 = $175.50).

Single discount rate or equivalent. This is one discount rate that is equal to a series of discounts. If it is desirable to know the single discount rate or equivalent, subtract the net price percent from $1.00. For example:

$$\$1.00 - \text{Net price percent} = \text{Single discount rate}$$

Net price. This is the amount the buyer will pay for merchandise purchased. Net price is calculated by:

$$\text{List price} - \text{Discounts} = \text{Net price}$$

RULES FOR APPLYING TRADE DISCOUNTS

A number of methods are equally applicable in computing a net price. Review carefully the methods outlined under Rule 1 and note that all the methods produce the same net price. The method selected to solve a problem is optional. If you are using a calculator, Method 1 will be the most convenient. If you are not using a calculator, Method 4 may be the most convenient.

> **Rule 1: CALCULATION OF NET PRICE:**
> The net price that is payable by the buyer may be computed by any one of the following methods.

Method 1

Multiply *list price* by the *complements of the discount rates.*

Step 1. Determine the decimal complement for each of the discount rates allowed.

Note: The complement of a decimal is any number that when added to the discount decimal will equal "1."

Example: Trade discounts 25/20/05:

Decimal equivalents =	.25	.20	.05
Decimal complements =	.75	.80	.95
	1.00	1.00	1.00

Step 2. Multiply the list price by the decimal complement of the discount rates.

Example 1   The Allen Hardware Store received an invoice from the Allied Wholesale Supply Company in the amount of $890 with trade discount terms of 25%. Find the net price the Allen Hardware Store will pay.

Step 1. Determine the decimal complement:

$$\text{Decimal equivalent} = .25$$
$$\text{Decimal complement} = .75$$

Step 2. Multiply list price by decimal complement:

$$\$890.00 \times .75 = \$667.50 \text{ Net price}$$

Example 2   The Allen Hardware Store received an invoice for $1,256.50, with discount terms of 20/10/3. Find the net price they will pay.

Step 1. Determine the decimal complements:

$$\text{Decimal equivalents} = .20 \ .10 \ .03$$
$$\text{Decimal complements} = .80 \ .90 \ .97$$

Step 2. Multiply *list price by each decimal complement:*

$$\$1{,}256.50 \times .80 \times .90 \times .97 = \$877.54 \text{ Net price}$$

Example 3   Find the net price the buyer would pay on the following invoice.

INVOICE

ALLIED WHOLESALE SUPPLY CO.
8 MAIN STREET
OLDSVILLE, U.S.A.

NO. 11154
DATE March 7
YOUR ORDER NO. 238

SOLD TO: Allen Hardware Store
7 Market Street
Cedarville, U.S.A.

SHIPPED TO: Same

OUR ORDER NO.	SALESMAN	TERMS	F.O.B.	DATE SHIPPED	SHIPPED VIA
14	DFR	25/15/5	—	March 7	Truck

QUANTITY ORDERED	QUANTITY SHIPPED	STOCK NUMBER/DESCRIPTION	PRICE	UNIT	AMOUNT
30	30	#12 hammers	14.65	ea.	439.50
24	24	Hand saws	18.00	ea.	432.00
50	50	White housepaint	7.20	gal.	360.00
		Total due			1,231.50

ORIGINAL

Step 1. Determine the decimal complements:

$$\text{Decimal equivalents} = .25 \ .15 \ .05$$
$$\text{Decimal complements} = .75 \ .85 \ .95$$

Step 2. Multiply list price, by decimal complements:

$$\$1{,}231.50 \times .75 \times .85 \times .95 = \$745.83 \text{ Net price}$$

List price less discount (method 2)   Multiply the List Price by each trade discount rate and subtract the s-discount from each list price.
  Step 1. Multiply the list price by a discount rate:

  List price × Discount rate = Discount

  Step 2. Subtract the discount from each decreasing list price:

  List price − Discount = Net price

Example 1   The Allen Hardware Store received an invoice for $890, with trade discount terms of 25%. Find the net price it will pay.
  Step 1. Multiply list price by a discount rate:

  $890.00 × .25 = $222.50 Discount

  Step 2. Subtract the discount from each decreasing list price:

  List price − Discount = Net price
  $890.00 − $222.50 = $667.50

Example 2   The Allen Hardware Store received an invoice for $1,256.50, with trade discount terms of 20/10/3. Find the net price of the invoice.
  Step 1. Multiply list price by a discount rate:

  $1,256.50 × .20 = $251.30

  Step 2. Subtract the discount from each decreasing list price:

  $1,256.50 − $251.30 = $1,005.20

Step 1, 2d discount.

  List price × Discount rate = Discount
  $1,005.20 ×   .10   = $100.52

Step 2.

  List price − Discount = Decreased list price:
  $1,005.20 − $100.52 = $904.68

Step 1, 3d discount.

  List price × Discount rate = Discount
  $904.68 ×   .03   = $27.14

Step 2.

  List price − Discount = Net price
  $904.68 − $27.14   = $877.54

List price times fraction equivalent (method 3)   Multiply list price by the fraction equivalent of each trade discount; this equals discount. Then subtract the discount from list price.
  Step 1. Convert each discount rate to its fraction equivalent. For example:

  Trade discounts   = 25/10/5
  Fraction equivalent = $\frac{1}{4}$ $\frac{1}{10}$ $\frac{1}{20}$

  Step 2. Multiply the list price by each fraction equivalent:

  List price × Fraction equivalent = Discount

Step 3. Subtract discount from list price:

$$\text{List price} - \text{Discount} = \text{Net price}$$

Note: If a series of discounts apply, find the discount of each fraction equivalent based on the decreasing list price.

Example 1 The Allen Hardware Store received an invoice for $890, with trade discount terms of 25%. Find the net price of the invoice.

Step 1.

$$\text{Trade discount} = 25\%$$
$$\text{Fraction equivalent} = \frac{1}{4}$$

Step 2.

List price × Fraction equivalent = Discount:
$890.00 × $\frac{1}{4}$ = $222.50

Step 3.

List price − Discount = Net price:
$890.00 − $222.50 = $667.50

Example 2 The Allen Hardware Store received an invoice for $1,256.50, with trade discount terms of 20/10/3. Find the net price of the invoice.

Step 1.

$$\text{Trade discounts} = .20 \quad .10 \quad .03$$
$$\text{Fraction equivalents} = \frac{1}{5} \quad \frac{1}{10} \quad \frac{3}{100}$$

Step 2.

List price × Fraction equivalent = Discount
$1,256.50 × $\frac{1}{5}$ = $251.30

Step 3.

List price − Discount = Net price
$1,256.50 − $251.30 = $1,005.20

Step 2, 2d discount.

List price × Fraction equivalent = Discount
$1,005.20 × $\frac{1}{10}$ = $100.52

Step 3.

List price − Discount = Net price
$1,005.20 − $100.52 = $904.68

Step 2, 3d discount.

List price × Fraction equivalent = Discount
$904.68 × $\frac{3}{100}$ = $27.14

List price times fraction compliment (method 4)

Step 3.

List price − Discount = Net price
$904.68 − $27.14 = $877.54

To find *net price*, multiply the list price by the fraction complement of each trade discount rate.

Step 1. Determine the fraction complement of each trade discount rate.

Note: The fraction complement is any fraction that when added to the fraction equivalent will equal 1.

Example

Trade discount	=	$33\frac{1}{3}\%$
Fraction equivalent	=	$\frac{1}{3}$
Fraction complement	=	$\frac{2}{3}$
Trade discounts	=	20% 10% 3%
Fraction equivalents	=	$\frac{1}{5}$ $\frac{1}{10}$ $\frac{3}{100}$
Fraction complements	=	$\frac{4}{5}$ $\frac{9}{10}$ $\frac{97}{100}$

Step 2. Multiply the list price by the fraction complements of each trade discount rate.

Example 1 The Allen Hardware Store received an invoice for $890, with trade discount terms of 25%. Find the net price of the invoice.

Step 1.

Trade discount	=	.25
Fraction equivalents	=	$\frac{1}{4}$
Fraction complements	=	$\frac{3}{4}$

Step 2.

List price × Fraction complement = Net price:

$890.00 × $\frac{3}{4}$ = $667.50

Example 2 The Allen Hardware Store received an invoice for $1,256.50, with trade discount terms of 20/10/3. Find the net price of the invoice.

Step 1.

Trade discounts	=	.20 .10 .03
Fraction equivalents	=	$\frac{1}{5}$ $\frac{1}{10}$ $\frac{3}{100}$
Fraction complements	=	$\frac{4}{5}$ $\frac{9}{10}$ $\frac{97}{100}$

Step 2.

List price × Fraction complements = Net price:

$1,256.50 × $\frac{4}{5} \times \frac{9}{10} \times \frac{97}{100}$ = $877.54

If a number of invoices are subject to the same trade discount rates, it may be desirable to calculate a net price equivalent that can be applied to all the invoices rather than repeat the discounting of each individual invoice.

> **Rule 2: NET PRICE EQUIVALENT OR PERCENT:**
> To find the *net price equivalent,* multiply the decimal or fraction complements of all the discount rates.

Step 1. Determine the decimal or fraction complement of each trade discount.

Step 2. Multiply all the discount complements.

Example 1 Find the net price equivalent that could be applied to 5 invoices, all of which are subject to trade discounts of 20/10/5.

Step 1.

$$\begin{array}{lccc} \text{Trade discounts} & .20 & .10 & .05 \\ \text{Decimal complements} & .80 & .90 & .95 \end{array}$$

Step 2.

$$.80 \times .90 \times .95 = .684$$

Note: Net price of each of the invoices could be calculated by applying .684 to the list price of the invoice.

Example 2 The Hillman and Stores Company had 6 invoices, all subject to trade discounts of 15/10/2½.

a. Find the net price equivalent that would apply to all invoices.

b. Find the net price of one of the invoices with a list price of $416.80.

Step 1.

$$\begin{array}{lccc} \text{Trade discounts} & = .15 & .10 & .025 \\ \text{Decimal complements} & = .85 & .90 & .975 \end{array}$$

Step 2.

$$.85 \times .90 \times .975 = .7459 \text{ (4th decimal)}$$
Net price equivalent = .7459 (**Ans.** *a*)

Step 3.

List price × Net price equivalent = Net price
$416.80 × .7459 = $310.89
Net price = $310.89 (**Ans.** *b*)

It may be desirable to know what single discount rate equals the series of trade discounts, to compare the discounts available in several companies; this will assist the buyer in deciding which company offers the lower discounts. The trade discount rates in a series cannot be added to get a single discount, because each trade discount in the series applies to a different list price. To calculate a single discount equivalent, use the following procedure.

> **Rule 3: SINGLE DISCOUNT EQUIVALENT:**
> Subtract the net price equivalent from 1.00.

Step 1. Calculate the net price equivalent for the trade discount series.
Step 2. Subtract the net price equivalent from 1.00.

Example 1   Find the single discount equivalent for the following trade discount rates:
  a. 33⅓/20/5.
  b. 25/15/2½.

Step 1, a.

 Trade discounts   .3333 .20 .05
 Decimal complements .6667 .80 .95
 .6667 × .80 × .95 = Net price equivalent
      .5067 = Net price equivalent

Step 2.

 1.00 − Net price equivalent = Single discount equivalent
 1.00 − .5067 = .4933

Step 1, b.

 Trade discounts   .25 .15 .025
 Decimal complements .75 .85 .975
 .75 × .85 × .975 = Net price equivalent
      .6216 = Net price equivalent

Step 2.

 1.00 − Net price equivalent = Single discount equivalent
 1.00 − .6216 = Single discount equivalent
      .3784 = Single discount equivalent

Practice exercises

	Answer
1. A clothing store ordered 40 dozen wool caps at $92.50 per dozen, less trade discounts of 25/20/5. What net price will the store pay on this invoice?	$2,109
2. A furniture dealer ordered a dozen armchairs listed on the invoice at $45 each, less trade discounts of 20/10/5. What is the net price of the invoice?	_____
3. A line of cosmetics was sold to retailers at trade discounts of 33⅓%, 5%, and 2%. Find the net price that would be paid on an invoice that totaled $2,675.50	$1,660.60 or $1,660.68
4. If the list price of an invoice is $1,245, with trade discount terms of 33⅓%, 20%, and 10%, what is the net price the buyer will pay?	_____
5. Company A quotes a price of $150, less trade discounts of 30/25/6. Company B quotes a price of $160, less trade discounts of 40/15/12½. Which company offers the lower net price and by how much?	Company B $2.63
6. The Reynolds Manufacturing Company allowed trade discounts of 30/10/2. The Burk Company allowed trade discounts of 25/20. The Jones Company planned to order $1,687 worth of merchandise. Which company offers the lower net price?	_____

7. The list price on an invoice was $640. Find the amount of discount if trade discount terms of 20/10/5 were allowed the buyer. $202.24

8. What amount of discount would the buyer of 6 chairs priced at $52.50 each receive if trade discount terms were 20/5?   _____

9. An invoice listed merchandise worth $1,634.50. Terms of the sale included trade discounts of 33⅓/15/5. What net price would the buyer pay? $879.95

10. The cost of merchandise listed on the invoice totaled $865.20, with trade discount terms of 20/10/2½. What net price would the buyer pay?   _____

11. A manufacturer of women's slacks shipped 2,000 pairs of slacks to a wholesale merchant at a price of $8.25 per pair. Terms of the sale included trade discounts of 25/20/10. What net price will the wholesaler pay for the shipment? $8,910.00

12. The Dryden Dish Company sold 400 dozen dinner plates to a wholesale distributor for $2.80 per plate, with trade discount terms of 30%, 10%, 2½%. What amount will the wholesaler pay the Dryden Dish Company for the shipment?   _____

13. The manufacturer's suggested list price for a living room set was $1,450. How much would a wholesaler pay for the set if trade discount terms were 25/20/5? $826.50

14. A clothing store ordered 40 dozen pairs of wool socks at $1.90 per pair, less trade discounts of 20/10/5. What is the net price of the invoice?   _____

15. Ms. G. Walker had 4 invoices from several suppliers all subject to trade discounts of 30/10/5.
    a. Find the net price equivalent that could apply to all the invoices.   .5985
    b. What is the single discount equivalent?   .4015

16. The A & D Sporting Goods Store received an invoice from a supplier for $637.50. Terms included trade discounts of 20/10/5. Find the net price due on the invoice.   _____

17. The owner of a hardware store had received 5 invoices from several wholesale distributors, all of which were subject to trade discounts of 15/10/2½.
    a. Find the net price equivalent that could be used to find the net price of the invoices. (Round to the 4th decimal place)   .7459
    b. What is the single discount equivalent?   .2541

18. Renshaw Manufacturing Company received an invoice for $2,812.75 for merchandise it ordered from the Young & Young Company. Terms of the sale included trade discounts of 30/15/5. What net price will Renshaw pay on the invoice?   _____

4 TRADE AND CASH DISCOUNT / 91

19. The Cowan Manufacturing Company sells merchandise to wholesale distributors, with trade discount terms of 25/15/5. If a distributor has 5 invoices from the Cowan Manufacturing Company, what net price equivalent could the distributor use to calculate the net price of the 5 invoices? (Round answer to the 4th decimal place)   .6056

20. The Gilson Wholesale Grocery Company had the following invoices, all of which had trade discount terms of 20/10/2½.

    Find the net price equivalent that could be applied to each of the invoices. _____

    Find the net price of the invoices that were due for payment.

    Invoice 1: list price = $ 402.80   _____
    Invoice 2: list price =   2,611.25 _____
    Invoice 3: list price =   1,006.20 _____

CASH DISCOUNTS

To encourage customers to pay their bills or invoices promptly, many manufacturers, wholesalers, and distributors offer the buyer a cash discount if payment is made within a stated number of days.

DEFINITIONS   **Cash discount.** The amount the buyer may deduct from the invoice price if payment is made within the discount period.

Discount period. The exact number of days within which the buyer must pay the invoice in order to deduct the cash discount.

Terms of sale (or discount). A variety of terms are available to the buyer. The following are among those used more frequently.

Ordinary dating. The discount period starts at the date of the invoice and ends the exact number of days stated in the terms of the sale.

Example
    Date of invoice: April 4
    Terms of the sale: 3/10, 1/20, n/30.

These terms mean that:

a. 3% discount may be taken if payment is made within 10 days after date of the invoice.
b. 1% discount may be taken if payment is made within 20 days of the date of the invoice.
c. If payment is not made within the discount periods, the full amount of the invoice is due in 30 days.

    Note:

        3 / 10, 1 / 20, net / 30
        %   days, %   days, net / days

E.O.M. dating. This term of a sale means that the discount period begins at the end of the month in which the invoice is dated. If the invoice date is on or after the 26th day of the month, it is customary to extend the discount period an additional month.

Example

Invoice date: April 4
Terms of sale: 3/10, 1/20, n/30 EOM
E.O.M. April   April 30
Discount days for 3%   + 10 days
End of discount period   May 10

If payment is made on or before May 10, the 3% discount applies to the invoice price. If payment is made on or before May 20 but after May 10, the 1% discount would apply.

Example

Invoice date: April 28
Terms of sale: 3/10, 1/20, n/30 EOM
E.O.M. April   April 30
Additional month   May 31
  (Invoice date is after the
  26th of the month)
Discount days for 3%. . . . . . . + 10 days
End of discount period . . . . . . June 10

If payment is made on or before June 10, the 3% discount applies to the invoice price. If payment is made by June 20 after June 10, the 1% discount would apply.

R.O.G. dating. This means Receipt of Goods. The discount period starts on the date the goods are received.

Example

Invoice date: April 10
Terms of sale: 3/10, 1/20, n/30 ROG
Goods received   April 19
Discount days for 3%   + 10
End of discount period   April 29

If payment is made on or before April 29, 3% discount may be deducted from the invoice price. If payment is made on or before May 9 (April 19 + 20 days), the 1% discount may be deducted from the invoice price.

> **Rule 1: TO DETERMINE THE LAST DAY ON WHICH PAYMENT CAN BE MADE TO TAKE ADVANTAGE OF THE CASH DISCOUNTS:**

Step 1. Add the number of discount days to the beginning date of the discount period as indicated by the terms of the sale.

Example 1 Invoice dated May 6 with terms 3/10, 1/20, n/30 (ordinary dating).
Step 1.

Invoice date   May 6
Discount days   + 10 days
Last date for 3% discount May 16

Example 2 Invoice date May 6 with terms 3/10, 1/20, n/30 EOM.
Step 1.

Invoice date   May 6
E.O.M. May   May 31
Discount days   + 10
Last day for 3% discount   June 10
Last day for 1% discount   June 20

Example 3   Invoice dated May 6 with terms 3/10, 1/20, n/30 ROG. Goods received May 14.

Step 1.

Receipt of Goods	May 14
Discount days	+ 10 days
Last date for 3% discount	May 24
Last date for 1% discount	June 3

Rule 2: TO FIND THE NET PRICE TO BE PAID:
  a. Invoice price × Complement of the applicable discount rate = Net price
  or
  b. Invoice price × Applicable rate of discount = Discount
  c. Invoice price − Discount = Net price

Step 1. Determine the last day of which payment can be made to take advantage of each rate of discount.

Step 2. Calculate the net price if payment is made within the discount periods.

Example 1   What amount would be due on the following invoice on September 17?

```
                                                        INVOICE
        A & B SUPPLY CO.                    NO. 11156
          11 MAIN STREET                    DATE Sept. 8
          OURTOWN, U.S.A.                   YOUR ORDER NO. _____

SOLD TO  J.C. Campbell Co.                  SHIPPED TO
         9 Oak Street                       Same
         Fairview, U.S.A.
```

OUR ORDER NO.	SALESMAN	TERMS	F.O.B.	DATE SHIPPED	SHIPPED VIA
132	TRS	4/10, 2/20 n/30	—	Sept. 8	Truck

QUANTITY ORDERED	QUANTITY SHIPPED	STOCK NUMBER/DESCRIPTION	PRICE	UNIT	AMOUNT
30	30	#412 woolen cloth	7.06	yd.	211.80
25	25	White cotton cloth	4.75	yd.	118.75
25	25	Yellow cotton cloth	6.226	yd.	155.65
		Total invoice price			486.20

ORIGINAL

Step 1. Determine the last day on which discount can be taken:

Date of invoice	September 8
Discount days for 4%	+ 10
Last day for 4% discount	September 18
Date of payment	September 17
4% discount allowed	

Step 2. Calculate net price:

$$\$486.20 \times .96 = \$466.75 \text{ Net price}$$
or
$$\$486.20 \times .04 = \$19.45 \text{ Discount}$$
$$\$486.20 - \$19.45 = \$466.75 \text{ Net price}$$

Example 2 R. T. Mack received an invoice for merchandise that was dated August 4, with cash discount terms of 3/10, 1/20, n/30 EOM for $712.50.

   a. On what dates must payment be made to take the 3% discount and the 1% discount?

   b. What net price will R. T. Mack pay on September 9?

Step 1. Determine the latest date on which payment must be made to take advantage of the cash discounts:

Invoice date	August 4
EOM date	August 31
Discount days for 3%	+ 10 days
Payment date for 3% discount	September 10
Discount days for 1%	August 31
	+ 20 days
Payment date for 1%	September 20

Step 2. Calculate net price:

$$\$712.50 \times .97 = \$691.12 \text{ Net price}$$
or
$$\$712.50 \times .03 = \$21.38 \text{ Discount}$$
$$\$712.50 - \$21.38 = \$691.12$$

Rule 3: ADDITIONAL CHARGES:

When the *invoice price* includes additional charges, calculate *net price* by:

Total invoice price	XXXX.XX
− Additional charges	XXX.XX
Invoice price	XXXX.XX
× **Complement of discount rate**	
+ **Additional charges**	= Net price

Additional charges may include such charges as:

Prepaid freight.   Insurance costs.
Shipping charges.   Special handling charges.

If such charges are included in the total invoice price, they must be subtracted from the total price before applying any discount rates. If such charges are not included in the invoice price, discount rate is applied to the invoice price of the merchandise.

Additional charges are always added to the net price to find the *amount to be paid* by the buyer.

Step 1. Determine the latest date on which discount can be taken.

Step 2. Subtract additional charges that are included in the invoice price.

Step 3. Calculate net price:

> Total invoice price
> <u>- Additional charges</u>
> Invoice price × Complement of the discount rate = Net price

Step 4. Add additional charges to the net price to find the total amount due.

Example 1 Ms. M. R. Thomas received an invoice dated August 3, with terms of 2/10, 1/20, n/30 EOM for $432, which included $108.50 prepaid freight charges. What amount will Ms. Thomas pay on September 7?

Step 1. Determine the latest date on which discount can be taken:

Invoice date	August 3
EOM discount date	August 31
Discount days for 2%	+ 10 days
Last day for 2% discount	September 10
Date of payment	September 7
2% discount applies	

Step 2. Calculate net price:

Invoice price	$432.00
Less freight charges	-108.50
Basis of discount	$323.50

Step 3. Calculate net price:

$323.50 × .98 = $317.03 Net price

Step 4.

| Add freight charges | +108.50 |
| Amount to be paid | $425.53 |

Rule 4: TO FIND NET PRICE WHEN INVOICE INCLUDES CHARGES FOR GOODS THAT HAVE BEEN RETURNED FOR CREDIT:
Invoice price (total)
-Goods returned
Invoice price × Complement of discount rate = Net price

Step 1. Determine the latest date on which discount may be taken.
Step 2. Subtract credit for goods returned from total invoice price.
Step 3. Calculate the net price:

Total invoice price - Returned goods = Invoice price
Invoice price × Complement of discount rate = Net price

Example 1 Dr. R. Walters received an invoice dated October 3, with discount terms of 3/10, 1/20, n/30 ROG for $637.35. The merchandise was received on October 15 but Dr. Walters returned $72 worth of damaged merchandise to the seller.

   a. On what date must Dr. Walters make payment to take the 3% discount?
   b. What amount will be paid?

Step 1. Determine the latest date on which payment must be made to take the discounts:

Date goods received	October 15
Discount days for 3%	+ 10 days
Last date for 3% discount	October 25 (**Ans.** *a*)

Step 2. Subtract goods returned for credit from total invoice price

Total invoice price	$637.35
Less credit	− 72.00
Invoice price	$565.35

Step 3. Calculate net price:

$565.35 × .97 = $548.39 Net price (**Ans.** *b*)

Example 2 W. C. Digby received an invoice dated March 6 for $1,106.24. An additional charge for shipping of $123.12 was not included in the invoice price, but was due for payment. Mr. Digby had returned $216.40 worth of merchandise for credit. Terms of the sale were 5/10, 2/20, n/30.

  a. What is the last date on which the 2% discount may be taken?
  b. What amount is due on this date?

Step 1: Determine the latest date on which the discount may be taken:

Invoice date	March 6
Discount days for 2%	+ 20 days
Last date for 2% discount	March 26 (**Ans.** *a*)

Step 2. Subtract goods returned from total invoice price:

Invoice price	$1,106.24
Goods returned	− 216.40
Invoice price total	$ 889.84

Step 3. Calculate net price:

$889.84 × .98 = $872.04 Net price

Step 4. Add additional charges:

$872.04 + $123.12 = $995.16 Amount due (**Ans.** *b*)

If a buyer pays only part of the invoice price within the discount periods, discount is given on the payment by allowing the buyer credit for more than the amount of the payment. If several payments are made, each payment is subject to the discount rate applicable at the date of the payment. Balance due on the invoice is found by *invoice price − credit = balance due.*

Rule 5: PARTIAL PAYMENTS:
  To find the credit due on a partial payment made within the discount period:

$$\frac{\text{Payment}}{\text{Complement of the discount rate}} = \text{Credit}$$

Example 1 An invoice dated October 14, for $600, with cash discount terms of 3/10, 1/20, n/30. The buyer paid $200 on October 23. Find the amount of credit the buyer would receive for the payment.

4 TRADE AND CASH DISCOUNT / 97

Step 1. Determine the latest date on which discount would be given:

Invoice date	October 14
Discount days for 3%	+ 10 days
Latest date for discount	October 24
Payment date	October 23
3% discount applies	

Step 2. Calculate credit to be given for the payment made on October 23:

$$\frac{\$200}{.97} = \$206.19 \text{ Credit}$$

Example 2 Invoice dated November 2 for $850 had cash discount terms of 5/10, 2/20, n/30. On November 10 the buyer paid $200, and another payment of $150 on November 20.
   a. What credit would the buyer receive for the $200 payment?
   b. What credit would be given for the $150 payment?
   c. Find the balance due on the invoice.

Step 1. Determine the latest dates on which discount may be taken:

Invoice date	November 2
Discount days for 5%	+10
Latest date for 5% discount	November 12
Payment date of $200	November 10
5% discount applies	

Step 2. Calculate credit given for $200 payment:

$$\frac{\$200}{.95} = \$210.53 \ (a)$$

Step 1.

Invoice date	November 2
Discount days for 2%	+ 20
Latest date for 2% discount	November 22
Payment date for $150	November 20
2% discount applies	

Step 2.

$$\frac{\$150}{.98} = \$153.06 \ (b)$$

Step 3. Calculate *balance due* on the invoice:

Invoice price	$850.00
Credit for $200 payment	−210.53
Credit for $150 payment	−153.06
Balance due on invoice	$486.41 (c)

Example 3 Ms. H. Henry received an invoice dated March 28 for $1,106, with cash discount terms of 5/10, 3/20, n/30 EOM.
   a. Find the amount of credit the seller will give for a payment of $250 made on May 5.
   b. What credit will be given for a payment of $300 made on May 18?
   c. What balance is still due on the invoice on May 25?

Step 1. Determine the latest date on which the discount may be taken:

  Invoice date   March 28
  EOM date   March 31 + 30 days in April
      + 10 days in May   = May 10
  Latest date for 5% discount   = May 10
  Payment date for $250   May 5
    5% discount applies

Step 2. Calculate credit given for $250 payment:

$$\frac{\$250}{.95} = \$263.16 \text{ Credit} \quad (\textbf{Ans. } a)$$

Step 1.

  Invoice date   March 28
  EOM date = March 31 + 30 days in April
         + 20 days in May
  Latest date for 3% discount   = May 20
  Payment date of $300   = May 18
    3% discount applies

Step 2.

$$\frac{\$300}{.97} = \$309.28 \text{ Credit} \quad (\textbf{Ans. } b)$$

Step 3. Calculate *balance due* on the invoice on May 25:

Invoice price	$1,106.00
Less credit for $250 payment	− 263.16
Less credit for $300 payment	− 309.28
Balance due on invoice	$ 533.56

Practice exercises

                                 Answer

1. An invoice dated July 15 had cash discount terms of 3/10, 2/20, n/30. The amount of the invoice was $1,750 and was paid in full on July 24. What amount was paid? $1,697.50

2. James A. Walters sent an invoice to A. W. Myers for $3,820. The invoice was dated April 27, with cash discount terms of 3/10, n/60.
   - a. What is the latest date on which discount may be taken?   _____
   - b. What amount would be paid on this date?   _____

3. The total price on an invoice dated June 4 was $308.95 including transportation charges of $16.45. Cash discount terms were 4/10, 2/20, n/30 EOM.
   - a. On what date must the invoice be paid to take advantage of the 4% discount?   July 10
   - b. What amount will be paid on this date? $297.25

4. An invoice for $1,750, including shipping charges of $86.40, was dated January 5, with cash discount terms of 3/20, 1/30, n/60 EOM.
   a. What is the latest date on which 3% may be taken? _____
   b. Find the amount that would be paid on the above date. _____

5. The total invoice price including freight charges of $142.12 was $1,649.52. The buyer returned damaged merchandise worth $248.12. Find the total amount the buyer would pay on May 17 if the invoice was dated May 9, with cash discount terms of 4/10, n/30. $1,351.03

6. Ms. C. Williams received an invoice from one of her suppliers for $986.20, including $84 for shipping charges. Defective merchandise worth $126.50 was returned for credit. The invoice was dated July 20, with cash discount terms of 4/15, 2/20, n/30. Find the amount Williams will pay on August 3. _____

7. An invoice for $303.63 is dated October 29, with cash discount terms of 3/10, 1/20, n/30 ROG. The goods were received on December 5.
   a. Find the latest date on which 3% discount may be taken. December 15
   b. What amount will be due on the above date? $294.52

8. An invoice for $326.85, with cash discount terms of 5/5, 2/15, n/30 ROG, was dated April 12. The goods were received on May 5.
   a. On what date must the invoice be paid to take the 5% discount? _____
   b. What amount would be paid on May 20? _____

9. T. C. Wells received an invoice for merchandise he had ordered for $618.35, with cash discount terms of 3/10, 1/20, n/30 EOM. Prepaid shipping charges of $26.12 were due in addition to the invoice price of the merchandise. The invoice was dated July 16. What is the latest date on which Mr. Wells can take the 3% discount? August 10

10. An invoice for merchandise dated September 28, with cash discount terms of 4/15, 2/30, n/60 EOM, totaled $541.20. Additional shipping charges for $70.20 were also due.
    a. What is the latest date on which the 4% discount may be taken? _____
    b. What amount is due on or before this date? _____

11. Ms. W. Dillon received an invoice dated August 12 from one of her suppliers for $1,109.50, which included $164.50 shipping charges. Merchandise worth $231 was returned for credit. Cash discount terms were 3/10, 1/20, n/30 EOM.

  a. What is the latest date on which Dillon can pay the invoice and take 1% discount?   September 20
  b. What amount would she pay on September 7? $857.08

12. An invoice dated November 20 for $2,472.50 included shipping charges of $206.50 and had cash discount terms of 4/15, 2/30, n/30 EOM. The buyer returned $65 worth of damaged goods.
  a. Find the latest date on which 2% discount may be taken.   _____
  b. What amount would be paid on December 14?   _____

13. An invoice for $606.20 was dated October 12, with cash discount terms of 2/10, 1/20, n/30. The buyer paid $125 on October 20 and $300 on November 1. How much did the buyer still owe on the invoice? $175.62

14. A. W. Evans received an invoice dated July 10, with cash discount terms of 5/10, 3/20, n/30 for $826.50. Mr. Evans paid $225 on July 18 and made another payment of $150 on July 29. What balance is due on the invoice after credit is given for the payments?   _____

15. Ms. D. Thomas received an invoice dated July 28 for merchandise that totaled $314.85. Prepaid shipping charges of $71.30 was also due on the shipment. Cash discount terms were 5/10, 2/20, n/30 EOM. Ms. Thomas paid $150 on September 8.
  a. What credit would Ms. Thomas receive from the seller for the payment? $157.89
  b. What balance is still due on the invoice? $228.26

16. An invoice dated September 29 for $927.15 was subject to discounts of 3/10, 1/20, n/30 EOM. The buyer made a payment of $275 on November 9.
  a. What credit would the seller give for the payment?   _____
  b. What balance is still due on the invoice?   _____

17. The Wool Shop purchased 3 dozen woolen sweaters for $8.45 each. Terms of the sale on the invoice, which was dated February 14, were 4/10, 2/20, n/30 ROG. When the sweaters were received on March 19, Ms. Seaman found that 5 of the sweaters were defective and returned them to the seller for credit. Ms. Seaman paid $100 on account on March 24.
  a. What credit would the seller give Ms. Seaman for the payment? $104.17
  b. What balance is still due on the invoice? $157.78

18. An invoice listed 4 dozen pairs of children's shoes at $9.85 per pair. The invoice was dated January 14, with cash discount terms of 3/10, 1/20, n/30 ROG. When the shipment was received on February 17, the buyer returned 6 pairs of damaged shoes for credit. On February 26 the buyer paid $210 on account.

    a. What credit would the buyer receive for the payment? _____

    b. What balance is still due on the invoice? _____

19. An invoice dated July 16 listed merchandise for $320. Terms of the sale were 3/10, 1/20, n/30. Payment in full was made on August 4. What net amount will the buyer pay? $316.80

20. D. R. Paulsen purchased merchandise for his hardware store from the Dickson Supply Company. The invoice was dated May 12 and had a total of $906.25, subject to discounts of 5/10, 2/20, n/30. How much did Mr. Paulsen pay on June 1? _____

TRADE AND CASH DISCOUNTS

A manufacturer, wholesaler, or distributor may offer the buyer both trade and cash discounts. To calculate the amount due on an invoice subject to both trade and cash discounts, apply the rules stated previously under *trade discounts* and *cash discounts*. The following formulas will summarize the procedure to find the amount due on an invoice subject to both types of discounts.

To find List Price of merchandise:

    Invoice price − Additional charges − Returned goods = List price

To find Net Price of merchandise:

    List price × Complements of trade discounts = Net price

To find the Discount Date:

  Invoice date + Days in discount period = Discount date
  Receipt of goods date + Days in discount period = Discount date

To find Amount Due:

    Net price × Complement of applicable cash discount rate
        + Prepaid additional charges = Amount due

To find amount of Credit for a partial payment:

$$\frac{\text{Payment}}{\text{Complement of discount rate}} = \text{Credit}$$

To find Balance Due:

    Net price − Credit = Balance due

Example 1   Trade discounts allowed were 30/6/3. The list price of the merchandise on the invoice was $785. The invoice was dated February 15, with cash discount terms of 5/10, n/20. If payment in full was made on February 23, what amount would the buyer pay?

    Step 1. Find the net price of the merchandise:

        $785.00 × .70 × .94 × .97 = $501.03 Net price

    Step 2. Determine discount date:

Invoice date	February 15
Discount days	+ 10 days
Last date for 5% discount	February 25

Step 3. Find the amount due:

$501.03 × .95 = $475.98 Amount due

Example 2 The Reynolds Company sent an invoice dated May 8 to Ms. J. Curtis in the amount of $816.20, including $87.80 for prepaid shipping charges. Terms included trade discounts of 20/10/5 and cash discounts of 5/10, 3/20, n/60. Ms. Curtis decided to pay 45% of the invoice on May 17.
  a. What credit would Ms. Curtis receive for the payment?
  b. What balance is due on June 1?

Step 1. Find the list price of the merchandise:

$816.20 − $87.80 = $728.40 List price

Step 2. Find the next price of the merchandise:

$728.40 × .80 × .90 × .95 = $498.23 Net price

Step 3. Find the discount date:

Invoice date	May 8
Discount days at 5%	+ 10 days
Last date for 5% discount	May 18

Step 4. Calculation of credit:

$498.23 × .45 = $224.20 Payment

$$\frac{\$224.20}{.95} = \$236.00 \text{ Credit for payment}$$

Step 5. Balance due:

Net price for merchandise	$498.23
Less credit for payment	−236.00
Add: Shipping charges	+ 87.80
Balance due June 1	$350.03

Example 3 Mr. Nyman received the following invoice from the R & D Company. He returned $316 worth of damaged goods on this invoice and on July 2 paid 40% of the amount due.
  a. What credit will Mr. Nyman receive for the 40% payment?
  b. What balance will Mr. Nyman owe after receiving the credit for the payment?

	R & D Furniture Co 9 Walnut St. Pineville, U.S.A.	NO. 112 Date May 28
Sold To	L. D. Nyman 7 Main St. Airville, U.S.A.	Terms 25/20/10 3/10, 1/20, n/30 EOM

Quantity		Amount
1	Dining Room Set	$1,308.80
6	Arm chairs	948.00
	Prepaid Shipping Charges	218.20
	Total Invoice	$2,475.00

Step 1. Find the list price of the merchandise:

$2,475.00 Total invoice price
   218.20 Prepaid shipping
− 316.00 Credit for returned goods
$1,940.80 List price

Step 2. Find net price of merchandise:

$1,940.80 × .75 × .80 × .90 = $1,048.03 Net price

Step 3. Find the discount date:

Invoice date	May 28
E.O.M. date	May 31
Additional month	June 30 (invoice date after the 26th)
Discount days	+ 10
Discount date	July 10
Payment date	July 2

Step 4. Payment:

$1,048.03 × .40 = $419.21

Step 5. Calculate credit for payment:

$$\frac{\$419.21}{.97} = \$432.18 \text{ Credit } (\textbf{Ans. } a)$$

Step 6. Calculate balance due:

Net price	$1,048.03
Less credit	− 432.18
Add shipping	+ 218.20
Balance due	$ 834.05 (**Ans.** *b*)

Practice exercises

Answer

1. An invoice dated January 14 in the amount of $1,215.75 included trade discount terms of 40/15/5 and cash discounts of 2/10, n/30. What amount would be paid on January 20? $577.25

2. Find the amount to be paid on an invoice for $1,075.00 if trade discounts of 20/12½/5, as well as cash discounts of 3/10, n/30, were allowed by the seller. The invoice was dated April 24 and paid in full on May 4.   _____

3. James A. Walters sent an invoice to Alice W. Ray for $3,820, plus prepaid shipping charges of $308.85. The invoice was dated April 27, with trade discounts of 30/15/2½ and cash discounts of 3/10, 1/20, n/30 EOM.
    a. On what date must the invoice be paid to take the 3% discount?
    b. Find the total amount that would be paid on the above date.   June 10
   $2,458.45

4. An invoice for $1,102, plus prepaid shipping charges of $296.85, was dated March 29, with cash discount terms of 5/10, n/30 EOM and trade discounts of 25/15/10.

  a. On what date would the 5% cash discount apply?
  b. What amount would be paid on this date?

5. An invoice dated September 10 for $725.50 was received from the Elean Manufacture Company. Terms included trade discounts of 20/10/2, as well as cash discounts of 2/10, n/30. The buyer decided to pay one half of the amount due on September 19 and the balance on October 1.
  a. What amount of credit would be given for the payment? $261.18
  b. What is the balance due on October 17? $250.73

6. Helen Mack received an invoice dated April 15 for $1,126.50 from a supplier. Terms of the sale included trade discounts of 25/10/5 and cash discounts of 3/10, 1/20, n/30. Ms. Mack paid 40% of the amount due on April 24 and the balance on May 14.
  a. What amount of credit would the seller give Ms. Mack for the payment?
  b. What amount would be due on May 14?

7. The M. O. Pepper Company received an invoice dated February 14 for $980.75, including prepaid freight charges of $83.40. The shipment was received on February 26 and damaged merchandise worth $164.80 was returned for credit. Trade discounts of 15/10/2, as well as cash discounts of 5/10, 2/20, n/30 ROG, were allowed.
  a. On what date must payment be made to take the 5% cash discount?   March 8
  b. What amount will the M. O. Pepper Company pay on this date? $605.13

8. The total invoice price, including prepaid shipping charges of $76.80, was $873.50. The merchandise was received on August 16. The buyer returned defective merchandise worth $86. Terms of the sale included trade discounts of 30/10/2 and cash discounts of 5/10, 2/20, n/30 ROG.
  a. What is the latest date on which 2% cash discount can be taken?
  b. What amount will the buyer pay on August 26?

9. An invoice dated June 10 for merchandise amounted to $798.65. Prepaid freight charges of $89.20 were also due but not included in the invoice price. Discount terms included trade discounts of 20/10/3 and cash discounts of 3/10, 1/20, n/30 EOM. What amount is due on July 9? $630.24

10. An invoice for $1,512.75 was dated May 28. Prepaid shipping charges of $163 were also due. Terms of the sale included trade discounts of 25/15/5 and cash discounts of 5/10, 2/20, n/30 EOM. What amount is due on July 9?

11. W. C. Gardner received an invoice dated July 27 for $1,063.50, which included $97.80 for prepaid shipping charges. Terms of the sale included cash discounts of 5/20, 2/30, n/30 EOM, as well as trade discounts of 15/5/2½. What net amount will be due on September 20? $820.09

12. The Morris Manufacturing Company received an invoice from one of its suppliers dated May 10 for $1,495.50, which included $156 for prepaid shipping charges. Terms of the sale included trade discounts of 25/10/2½, as well as cash discounts of 5/10, 1/20, n/30 ROG. When the goods were received on May 24, $318.50 worth of damaged goods were returned to the seller for credit.
    a. What is the latest date on which payment may be made to take the 5% cash discount?   _____
    b. What amount is due on this date?   _____

Review problems

		Answer
1.	A clothing store ordered 40 dozen hats at a price of $92.50 per dozen, less trade discounts of 25/20/5. What net price will the clothing store pay for the order?	$2,109.00
2.	Find the net price of an invoice for $245.50 if trade discounts of 20/10/2½ are allowed by the seller.	_____
3.	The Hall Knitting Mills purchased 40 spools of wool thread, each of which contained 50 meters of thread at a cost of $1.15 per meter. Terms of the sale included trade discounts of 30/10/5. What net amount would be due on the invoice?	$1,376.55
4.	A clothing store received an invoice from one of its suppliers for 20 dozen of women's vests priced at $8.65 each. Terms of the sale included trade discounts of 15/10/2½. What net amount will the store pay the supplier?	_____
5.	K & J Auto Supply Company had 5 invoices all subject to trade discounts of 20/10/5.	
	a. What net price equivalent could be applied to all of the invoices?	.684
	b. What net price will be due on each of the following invoices subject to 20/10/5?	

Invoice 1	List price	$1,026.00	$701.78
Invoice 2	List price	384.00	$262.66
Invoice 3	List price	612.80	$419.16
Invoice 4	List price	426.50	$291.73
Invoice 5	List price	976.25	$667.76

6. W. C. Jones had 4 invoices to be paid, all of which were subject to trade discounts of 30/15/5.
   a. Find the net price equivalent that could be applied to all of the invoices. (Round to 4 places.) _____
   b. What net amount is due on each of the following invoices?

Invoice 1	List price	$1,226.80	_____
Invoice 2	List price	982.60	_____
Invoice 3	List price	467.25	_____
Invoice 4	List price	1,027.00	_____

7. The Laura Shop received an invoice dated June 23 for 3 dozen cotton dresses at a price of $14.75 per dress. Terms of the sale included cash discounts of 4/10, 2/20, n/30.

     a. On what date must payment be made to take advantage of the 4% cash discount?   **July 3**
     b. What amount will be due on this date?   **$509.76**

8. The Roger Meat Packing Company received an invoice dated May 26 for 3,000 metal cans at $.15 per can. Terms of the sale were cash discounts of 2/10, 1/20, n/30.
    a. On what date must payment be made to take the 2% cash discount?   _____
    b. What amount would be due on or before the above date?   _____

9. The Harris Furniture Store received an invoice for merchandise it ordered from Southern Distributors. The total invoice, which was dated January 14, amounted to $1,785.60, including prepaid freight charges of $216.20. The merchandise was received on January 25, with cash discount terms of 5/10, 2/20, n/30 ROG.
    a. On what date must payment be made to take the 5% cash discount?   **February 4**
    b. What net amount will Harris Furniture pay on this date?   **$1,707.13**

10. An invoice dated May 6 for $926.50 included prepaid shipping charges of $62.90. The merchandise was received on May 21. The terms of the sale included cash discounts of 3/15, 2/10, n/30 ROG.
    a. What is the latest date payment can be made to take advantage of the 3% cash discount?   _____
    b. What net amount will be paid on this date?   _____

11. The Rensaw Sportswear Company received an invoice for $1,027.50, which included prepaid shipping charges of $90.25 for tennis and swimwear. The invoice was dated March 20, with cash discount terms of 5/15, 2/20, n/30 EOM. Damaged goods worth $116.80 were returned for credit.
    a. To take the 5% cash discount, by what date must payment be made?   **April 15**
    b. What amount will be paid?   **$869.68**

12. The Ross Jewelry Store received an invoice dated May 23 for $2,785.00, including prepaid delivery cost of $147.80. The jewelry store returned 2 rings that were damaged in shipment and worth a total of $682. The terms of the sale included cash discounts of 7/10, 3/20, n/30 EOM.
    a. On what date must the invoice be paid to take the 7% cash discount?   _____
    b. What net amount will be paid on this date?   _____

13. J. R. Paulson decided to pay 35% of an invoice dated July 12 for $1,208.60, with cash discount terms of 5/15, 3/20, n/60 EOM. Payment was made on August 13.

a. What credit will the seller give Mr. Paulson for the partial payment? $445.27
b. What balance is still due on the invoice? $763.33

14. Sally Walker received an invoice dated May 7 for supplies purchased for $2,895. Terms of the sale were cash discounts of 5/10, 3/20, n/60 EOM. Ms. Walker planned to pay 40% of the invoice price on June 8. What credit will she receive for the payment? _____

15. An invoice dated August 16 had cash discount terms of 2/10, 1/20, n/60 ROG and showed a total of $1,609.20. The merchandise was received on August 29. The buyer made a payment of $325 on September 2 and another payment of $210 on September 15. What balance would be due on September 15? $1,065.45

16. W. S. Fuller received an invoice dated September 20 for supplies he ordered for $916.20, with cash discount terms of 3/15, 1/30, n/60. Mr. Fuller planned to make a payment of $250 to take advantage of the 3% discount and a payment of $300 for the 1% discount.
a. On what dates will Mr. Fuller make the payments? _____
b. What balance will Fuller owe after receiving credit for the payments? _____

17. Terms of sale included trade discounts of 30/6/2½ and cash discounts of 5/10, 2/20, n/30. Find the amount needed to pay the net amount due on an invoice dated February 15 for $768.65 if payment is made on February 24. $468.47

18. The list price of an invoice was $785, with trade discounts of 25/6/2½, as well as cash discount terms of 5/10, n/20. The invoice was dated February 13 and the full amount due was paid on February 23. What amount was paid? _____

19. J. I. Haines received an invoice from the McCoy Manufacturing Company for $1,096.75, which included prepaid shipping charges of $171.80 and dated September 28. Terms of the sale included trade discounts of 20/10/5, as well as cash discounts of 3/10, 1/20, n/30 EOM. Damaged merchandise worth $216 was returned for credit.
a. On what date must the invoice be paid to take advantage of the 3% cash discount? November 10
b. What amount would be paid on or before this date? $642.17

20. C & J Manufacturing Company sells refrigerators for $365 each, with trade discount terms of 25/5/2½ and cash discounts of 5/10, 3/20, n/30 EOM. The Acme Appliance Store ordered 6 of the refrigerators and received an invoice dated November 29 for $2,400, which included $210 prepaid shipping charges. Acme found

one of the refrigerators had been damaged and returned it for credit.
- a. On what date must the net invoice be paid to take the 5% cash discount? _____
- b. What amount will be paid on or before this date? _____

21. W & J Manufacturing Company sells a product for $675, with trade discounts of 30/15/5. The Evans Supply Company sells the same product for $725, with trade discount terms of 25/20/10. The Harrison Appliance Store plans to buy 7 such products. Which company offers the better buy?   W & J Manufacturing Company

22. An invoice dated March 10 for $1,003.50 included terms of sale of trade discounts 15/10/2½ and cash discounts of 3/10, 1/20, n/30 ROG. Additional shipping charges of $62.80 were also due on the invoice. When the merchandise was received on March 24, the buyer found $206 worth of merchandise was damaged in shipment and returned it for credit.
- a. To take advantage of the 3% cash discount, the invoice must be paid on or before what date? _____
- b. What amount will be paid on this date to pay the invoice in full? _____

23. K & M Manufacturing Company received an invoice dated August 12 from one of its suppliers for $926.50, subject to trade discounts of 20/10/5, as well as cash discounts of 2/10, 1/20, n/30 ROG. Additional shipping charges of $101 were due on the invoice. The supplies were received on September 3 when K & M found that $47 worth of merchandise was defective and returned it for credit.
- a. On what date will payment be made to take advantage of the 2% discount?   September 13
- b. What amount will K & M pay on this date? $690.55

24. Trade discounts of 30/6/2, as well as cash discounts of 5/10, 2/20, n/30, were available to the buyer who had received an invoice dated February 5 for $1,626.35, including shipping charges of $176.20. The buyer decided to pay $325 on February 9 and $260 on February 24.
- a. What credit will the buyer receive for each payment? _____
- b. What balance is due on the invoice on March 3? _____

25. On an invoice dated March 12, terms of the sale included trade discounts of 25/10/5 and cash discounts of 3/10, 1/20, n/60. The invoice price was $1,196.40, including prepaid freight charges for $136.40. The buyer paid $215 on March 21 and $405 on April 1.
- a. What credit will the buyer receive for each payment? $221.65 and $409.09
- b. What balance is still due on the invoice? $185.39

26. A home appliance store intends to buy 5 electric stoves for a sale it is planning. The store contacted two suppliers, one of which was the Billford Company, which offered trade discounts of 25/15/2. The other supplier, Cross Company, offered trade discounts of 25/10/5. Both suppliers quoted a list price of $515 per stove. Which supplier offered the lower net price? _____

27. C. R. Harris received an invoice dated March 19 for $2,096. Terms of the sale included cash discounts of 5/15, 2/20, n/30. Additional freight charges of $186.50 were shown on the invoice. Mr. Harris made a payment of $300 on March 28 and another payment on April 5 of $400.
   a. What amount of credit will the seller give Mr. Harris for each payment? $315.79 and $408.16
   b. What balance remains due on the invoice after credit has been given? $1,558.55

28. The terms of a sale included trade discounts of 30/20/5. The total invoice price was $445. What amount of discount would the buyer receive? _____

4 TRADE AND CASH DISCOUNT / 111

STUDY UNIT 5

Simple interest— bank discount

CALCULATION OF INTEREST
    Interest days and year
    Due date
    Maturity value
    Interest tables

BANK DISCOUNT PROCEDURE
    Proceeds of bank loans
    Proceeds of noninterest notes
    Proceeds of interest notes

COMPOUND INTEREST
    Compound interest table

A charge for borrowing money has been an accepted business practice since the days of the Roman Empire. Today this charge, known as interest, has become an important source of income for banks and other financial institutions. Under certain circumstances it may be advantageous to borrow money and pay the necessary interest to expand a business, to meet cash-flow problems, to take advantage of discounts, and for a variety of other reasons. It has also become an accepted business practice to extend credit to customers by accepting their interest-bearing note in payment for goods or services.

Transactions involving the borrowing and lending of money requires the borrower to sign a legal negotiable instrument known as a promissory note. (See Figures 5-1 and 5-2.) Thus, the emphasis in this unit is on the procedures involved and on the calculation of simple interest, bank discount, and the proceeds of both noninterest and interest bearing notes.

DEFINITIONS

Principal. The principal is the amount of money that is borrowed. It may be stated in a problem as "face value," "amount borrowed," or "debt." It is always the base for the calculation of interest.

Rate. The rate is the annual percent of the principal that is applied to calculate the amount of interest to be charged for the use of the borrowed money.

Time. Time is the number of days, months, or years the borrower will use the money. The length of time the borrowed money is used determines the amount of interest to be paid.

Maturity value. Maturity value is the amount the borrower will repay at the maturity date of the note. Maturity value is calculated by:

Principal + Interest = Maturity value

Simple interest. Interest is the amount of money the borrower pays for the use of borrowed funds.

Maturity date. Maturity date is when the borrowed money must be repaid to the lender.

RULES OF INTEREST

The basic formula to calculate interest is:

Principal × Rate × Time = Interest

The amount of interest paid for the use of borrowed money depends on:

1. The *principal*, which is stated on the note or in a problem as "amount borrowed," "face value," or "amount due," but is always identified by the dollar sign ($).
2. The *rate*, which can be identified by the percent sign (%).
3. The *time*, which is the length of the period the borrower has use of the money, and may be expressed as years, months, or days.

The Principal and Rate factors in the interest formula requires no calculation. They may be substituted in the interest formula just as they are stated in a problem. The Time factor, however, may require a calculation because time is always expressed in terms of a year or a fraction of a year.

Rule 1: TO DETERMINE THE TIME FOR WHICH INTEREST IS TO BE PAID:

a. *Time stated as years:* Substitute the number of years stated on the note or in the problem in the interest formula.

b. *Time expressed as months:* Substitute in the interest formula this fraction:

$$\frac{\text{Number of months}}{12}$$

c. *Time expressed as days:* Substitute in the interest formula this fraction:

$$\frac{\text{Interest days}}{\text{Days in interest year}}$$

Rule 2: CALCULATION OF INTEREST DAYS:

Exact days = Use the number of days stated in the problem.
 or
 Count the exact days between the effective date of the note and the due date.

30 days to a month = If the term of the note states that time is based on the 30-day month, consider 30 days to each month included in the term of the note.
 or
 If the term of the note is stated in months, consider 30 days to each month included in the term of the note.

Example 1 Find the *exact* interest days on a note dated April 15 due on July 10.
Step 1.

Days in April	=	30
Effective date	=	– 15 days
Days remaining in April	=	15
Days in May	=	31
Days in June	=	30
Days in July	=	10
Total interest days		86

Example 2 Find the interest days on a note that was dated January 12 and due in 4 months, based on 30 days to a month.
Step 1.

$$4 \text{ months} \times 30 \text{ days} = 120 \text{ interest days}$$

Rule 3: CALCULATION OF THE INTEREST YEAR:
  a. If *ordinary* interest is charged, use *360 days* to the interest year.
  b. If *exact* interest is charged, use *365 days* to the interest year.

Example 1 Find the interest days and interest year on a note dated February 14 due on June 25 with ordinary interest.
Step 1. Calculate interest days (exact days):

Days in February	=	28
Effective date	=	– 14 days
Days remaining in February	=	14
Days in March	=	31
Days in April	=	30
Days in May	=	31
Days in June	=	25
Total interest days		131

Step 2. Calculate interest year:

Ordinary interest = 360 days

$$\text{Time} = \frac{131 \text{ interest days}}{360 \text{ interest year}}$$

Example 2 Find the interest days and interest year on a note dated March 13 due in 85 days with exact interest.
Step 1.

$$\text{Interest days} = 85 \text{ days}$$

Step 2.

$$\text{Interest year} = 365 \text{ days}$$

Step 3.

$$\text{Time} = \frac{85 \text{ interest days}}{365 \text{ interest year}}$$

> Rule 4: TO DETERMINE A DUE DATE OF A NOTE:
> a. Add the exact number of days stated in the terms of the note to the effective date.
> b. Add the number of months stated in the note to the effective month of the note. The day stated in the month remains the same.

Example 1   Find the due date of a note dated April 12 that is due in 90 days.
Step 1.

Days in April	= 30
Effective date	= −12 days
Days remaining in April	= 18
Days in May	= 31
Days in June	= 30
Required days in July	= 11 (due date)
Total days on note	90

Example 2   Find the due date of a note dated September 4 due in 3 months.
Step 1.

Effective date of note	= September 4	*or*	9/4
Add terms of note	= 3 months		+ 3
Due date of note	= December 4	*or*	12/4

Note: The due day remains the same as the effective day.

Example 3   Find the due date of a note dated January 30 due in 1 month.
Step 1.

Effective date of note	= January 30	*or*	1/30
Add term of note	= 1		+ 1
Due date of note	= February 30	*or*	2/30
	or		*or*
	February 28		2/28

Note: Due date is the last day of the due month.

Example 4   Find the due date of a note dated March 31 due in 3 months.
Step 1.

Effective date of note	= March 31	*or*	3/31
Add term of note	= + 3		+ 3
Due date of note	= June 31 *or* June 30		6/31 *or* 6/30

Note: Due date is the last day of the due month.

Practice exercises

                                                                                                                                                  Answer

1. Find the exact days for the following notes:
    a. Note dated March 10 due on May 17.   **68 days**
    b. Effective date of note was October 4, due date was February 10.   _____
    c. Note dated September 27 due on November 14.   **48 days**
    d. The effective date of a note was August 15, the due date December 15.   _____
    e. Note dated May 25, due date August 8.   **75 days**

   f. Note that was dated January 20 and due on April 10.
   g. Effective date of note, June 1 due on August 25.   **85 days**
   h. Note dated October 14, due on January 15.

2. Find the number of interest days based on a 30-day month.
   a. Note dated January 10 due on April 5.   **85 days**
   b. Effective date of note, March 29, due in 4 months.
   c. Note was dated March 17 due on August 10.   **143 days**
   d. Note dated May 31 due in 6 months.
   e. A note with an effective date of June 10 due in 8 months.   **240 days**
   f. Note was dated July 12 due November 15.
   g. Effective date of note was August 31 due in 3 months.   **90 days**
   h. Note dated September 18 due on November 2.

3. Find the due date of the following notes.
   a. Effective date of note was May 10 due in 90 days.   **August 8**
   b. Note dated February 10 due in 120 days.
   c. A note dated June 26 due in 5 months.   **November 26**
   d. Effective date of note, March 15, due in 75 days.
   e. Note dated October 26 due in 100 days.   **February 3**
   f. Effective date of note was January 31 due in 3 months.
   g. Note was dated November 6 due in 75 days.   **January 20**
   h. A note that was dated December 20 was due in 60 days.

Rule 5: CALCULATION OF SIMPLE INTEREST:
Substitute data stated on the note in the interest formula:

Principal × Rate × Time = Interest
$P \times R \times T = I$

Rule 6: CALCULATION OF MATURITY VALUE:

Add: Interest + Principal = Maturity value
$I + P = Mat.V.$

  Step 1. Calculate the interest days and interest year that apply to the data stated on the note.
  Step 2. Substitute the principal, rate, and time in the interest formula.
  Step 3. Complete the arithmetic required by the interest formula.
  Step 4. Add interest calculated in step 3 to the principal of the note to find maturity value.

Example 1 Find the ordinary interest on a note with a face value of $600, which was dated April 4 due on June 3, with interest at 9%.

Step 1. Calculate interest days and interest year:

Interest days
April	30
Effective date	−4 days
Days remaining	26
Days in May	31
Days in June	3
Total interest days	60

Interest year = 360 days ordinary interest

Step 2. Substitute data in interest formula:

Principal × Rate × Time = Interest

$\$600 \times .09 \times \dfrac{60}{360}$ = Interest

Step 3. Complete the arithmetic of the interest formula:

Decimal solution: $\$600 \times .09 \times \dfrac{60}{360} = \$9.00$ Ordinary interest

Fraction solution: $\dfrac{\$600}{1} \times \dfrac{09}{100} \times \dfrac{60}{360} = \$9.00$

Example 2 Find the maturity value of a note with a face value of $596 that is dated January 29 and due on March 14. Exact interest of 8½% is charged.

Step 1. Calculate interest days and interest year:

Interest days
January	=	31
Effective date	=	−29 days
Remaining days	=	2
Days in February	=	28
Days in March	=	14
Total interest days	=	44

Interest year
Exact interest = 365 days

Step 2. Substitute the principal, rate, and time in the interest formula:

Principal × Rate × Time = Interest

$\$596 \times .085 \times \dfrac{44}{365}$ = Interest

Step 3. Complete the arithmetic of the interest formula:

Decimal solution: $\$596 \times .085 \times \dfrac{44}{365} = \$6.11$ Exact interest

Fraction solution: $\dfrac{\$596}{1} \times \dfrac{085}{1,000} \times \dfrac{44}{365} = \$6.11$

Step 4. Add:

Interest + Principal = Maturity value
$6.11 + $596.00 = $602.11

Example 3 Find the maturity value of the following note.

Figure 5-1

```
                                          Date  March 25
    75 days      after date  I   promise to pay
TO THE ORDER OF      Helen W. Keller
Nine Hundred Fifteen and 00/100 ---------------- DOLLARS
value received with interest at    9½% ordinary
at    1st National Bank
DUE   June 8
                              James R. Keyes
```

Step 1. Calculate interest days and interest year:

> Interest days = 75 days stated on note
> Interest year = 360 ordinary interest

Step 2. Substitute the principal, rate, and time in the interest formula:

$$\text{Principal} \times \text{Rate} \times \frac{\text{Interest days}}{\text{Interest year}} = \text{Interest}$$

$$\$915.00 \times .095 \times \frac{75}{360} = \text{Interest}$$

Step 3. Complete arithmetic of the interest formula:

$$\$915.00 \times .095 \times \frac{75}{360} = \$18.11$$

Step 4. Add:

> Interest + Principal = Maturity value
> $18.11 + $915.00 $933.11

Practice exercises

		Answer
1.	Find the ordinary interest on a note with a face value of $350 that is dated April 3 due on July 5 with interest at 8½%.	$7.68
2.	Find the interest to be paid on a note with a face value of $875 that is dated March 31 due in 3 months with ordinary interest of 11%.	_____
3.	If Ms. Brown borrows $950 on June 10 with ordinary interest at 8%, what amount must be repaid on September 15?	$970.47 or $970.48
4.	Find the maturity value of a note for $665 with ordinary interest of 9% if the note was dated February 10 and due on June 20.	_____
5.	Find the maturity value of a note for $6,500 if exact interest of 7½% is charged for 120 days.	$6,660.29 or $6,660.27

6. The face value of a note is $1,350. Find the maturity value of the note if exact interest of 9.5% is charged for 80 days. _____

7. What interest would be charged on a note with a face value of $370 if the note is dated March 11 with ordinary interest of 7.25% and due on June 12? $6.93

8. Find the amount of interest the borrower will pay at the maturity date on a note for $950 with ordinary interest of 8½% that was dated July 10 and due on September 16. _____

9. A note with a face value of $5,860 was due in 90 days with exact interest of 8.25%. The note was dated April 4.
   a. What was the due date of the note? July 3
   b. What amount would the borrower repay on the due date? $5,979.21 or $5,979.22

10. The face value of a note was $750. The note was dated December 7 and due in 180 days with exact interest of 7.3% payable.
    a. What was the due date of the note? _____
    b. What was the maturity value of the note? _____

11. Mr. O. T. Shaw obtained a construction loan from his bank for $5,750. The note was dated July 16 due in 5 months with ordinary interest of 10¼%.
    a. What was the due date of the note? December 16
    b. How much will Mr. Shaw repay on the due date? $5,995.57 or $5,995.59

12. What is the maturity value of a note for $9,825 dated August 20 due on December 7 with exact interest of 11½%? _____

13. Alice Soul borrowed $11,000 on a note dated March 4 due in 180 days and agreed to pay 12¼% ordinary interest. How much interest did she pay on the due date of the note? $673.75

14. Exact interest of 9½% was charged on a note with a face value of $1,550 that was dated November 14 due in 5 months. Interest was calculated on exact days. What was the maturity value of the note? _____

15. Betty Burrows borrowed $935 on a note dated January 23 due on April 23 with ordinary interest of 10¼%. What is the maturity value of the note? $958.96

16. What amount of exact interest would be charged on a note for $985 that is dated February 15 and due on March 29 with exact interest of 9%? _____

17. A note dated April 12, due on June 17, based on a 30-day month, had a face value of $550 with ordinary interest of 8½%. Find the maturity value of the note. $558.44

18. Find the maturity value of a note with a face value of $1,575. The ordinary interest rate was 9%. The note was dated March 12 and due on July 25. _____

INTEREST TABLES

The rules for calculating simple interest and maturity value that were reviewed in the prior section apply to the procedures used primarily by business persons. However, many banks and other lending institutions use tables to find the exact number of days and the amount of ordinary interest. The use of Table 5-1 to find the exact days between the effective and due dates of a note, and Table 5-2 to calculate ordinary interest, will be reviewed in this section. It should be noted that a variety of interest tables are in use. The two tables we will review are intended only to illustrate this method of calculating *ordinary interest for exact interest days.*

Table 5-1: EXACT INTEREST BETWEEN EFFECTIVE AND DUE DATES OF A NOTE.

To use Table 5-1:

1. Locate the effective *day* of the note in Column 1.
2. Move to the right on the effective day line to the effective *month* column and note the number of days on the *table.*
3. Locate the *due day* of the note in Column 1.
4. Move to the right on the due day line to the due *month* and note the number of days from the *table.*
5. Number of days for the *due date* minus number of days for the *effective date* equals exact number of days. Or:

$$\text{Due date days} - \text{Effective date days} = \text{Exact days}$$

Table 5-1
Exact number of days between two dates

Day of Month	Jan.	Feb.	Mar.	Apr.	May	June	July	Aug.	Sept.	Oct.	Nov.	Dec.
1	1	32	60	91	121	152	182	213	244	274	305	335
2	2	33	61	92	122	153	183	214	245	275	306	336
3	3	34	62	93	123	154	184	215	246	276	307	337
4	4	35	63	94	124	155	185	216	247	277	308	338
5	5	36	64	95	125	156	186	217	248	278	309	339
6	6	37	65	96	126	157	187	218	249	279	310	340
7	7	38	66	97	127	158	188	219	250	280	311	341
8	8	39	67	98	128	159	189	220	251	281	312	342
9	9	40	68	99	129	160	190	221	252	282	313	343
10	10	41	69	100	130	161	191	222	253	283	314	344
11	11	42	70	101	131	162	192	223	254	284	315	345
12	12	43	71	102	132	163	193	224	255	285	316	346
13	13	44	72	103	133	164	194	225	256	286	317	347
14	14	45	73	104	134	165	195	226	257	287	318	348
15	15	46	74	105	135	166	196	227	258	288	319	349
16	16	47	75	106	136	167	197	228	259	289	320	350
17	17	48	76	107	137	168	198	229	260	290	321	351
18	18	49	77	108	138	169	199	230	261	291	322	352
19	19	50	78	109	139	170	200	231	262	292	323	353
20	20	51	79	110	140	171	201	232	263	293	324	354
21	21	52	80	111	141	172	202	233	264	294	325	355
22	22	53	81	112	142	173	203	234	265	295	326	356
23	23	54	82	113	143	174	204	235	266	296	327	357
24	24	55	83	114	144	175	205	236	267	297	328	358
25	25	56	84	115	145	176	206	237	268	298	329	359
26	26	57	85	116	146	177	207	238	269	299	330	360
27	27	58	86	117	147	178	208	239	270	300	331	361
28	28	59	87	118	148	179	209	240	271	301	332	362
29	29		88	119	149	180	210	241	272	302	333	363
30	30		89	120	150	181	211	242	273	303	334	364
31	31		90		151		212	243		304		365

5 SIMPLE INTEREST—BANK DISCOUNT / 123

Example 1 Find the exact days on a note which was dated March 18 and due on August 10.

Step 1. Locate the effective day in Column 1:

Effective day = Line 18

Step 2. Follow line 18 to the right to the effective month and note the number of days on the table:

Effective month = March = 77 days

Step 3. Locate the due day in Column 1:

Due day = Line 10

Step 4. Follow Line 10 to the right to the due month and note the number of days on the table:

Due month = August = 222 days

Step 5.

Due date, August 10 = 222 days
Effective date, March 18 = − 77 days
Exact number of interest days = 145 days

Example 2 Note is dated May 25, due on October 4. Find the exact number of days on which interest will be charged.

Step 1. Locate the effective day in Column 1:

Effective day = Line 25

Step 2. Follow Line 25 to the right to the effective month and note the number of days on the table:

Effective month = May = 145 days

Step 3. Locate the due day in Column 1:

Due day = Line 4

Step 4. Follow Line 4 to the right to the due month and note the number of days on the table:

Due month = October = 277 days

Step 5.

Due date, October 4 = 277 days
Effective date, May 25 = −145 days
Exact number of interest days = 132 days

Table 5-2: ORDINARY INTEREST ON $1.00 OF PRINCIPAL.

To use Table 5-2:

1. Divide total interest days into days listed on Table 5-2.
2. Follow the day line to the right to the required percent column and note the amount of interest per $1.00. Add total interest for $1.00.
3. Multiply total interest for $1.00 by the face value of the note.

Example 1 Find the ordinary interest at 8½% that R. J. Jones will pay on a note for $765 that was dated July 12 and due in 135 days.

Table 5-2
Ordinary interest for $1.00

Days	7%	7½%	8%	8½%	9%	9½%	10%	10½%	11%	11½%	12%
1	.00019	.00021	.00022	.00025	.00026	.00028	.00029	.00031	.00032	.00033	.00033
2	.00039	.00042	.00044	.00047	.00050	.00053	.00058	.00058	.00061	.00064	.00067
3	.00058	.00063	.00067	.00071	.00075	.00079	.00083	.00088	.00092	.00096	.00100
4	.00078	.00083	.00089	.00094	.00100	.00106	.00111	.00117	.00122	.00128	.00133
5	.00097	.00104	.00111	.00118	.00125	.00132	.00139	.00146	.00153	.00160	.00167
6	.00117	.00125	.00133	.00142	.00150	.00158	.00167	.00175	.00183	.00192	.00200
7	.00136	.00146	.00156	.00165	.00175	.00185	.00194	.00204	.00214	.00224	.00233
8	.00156	.00167	.00178	.00189	.00200	.00211	.00222	.00233	.02444	.00256	.00267
9	.00175	.00188	.00200	.00213	.00225	.00238	.00250	.00263	.00275	.00289	.00300
10	.00194	.00208	.00222	.00236	.00250	.00264	.00278	.00292	.00306	.00319	.00333
11	.00214	.00229	.00244	.00260	.00275	.00290	.00306	.00321	.00336	.00336	.00367
12	.00233	.00250	.00267	.00283	.00300	.00317	.00333	.00350	.00367	.00383	.00400
13	.00253	.00271	.00289	.00307	.00325	.00343	.00361	.00379	.00397	.00415	.00433
14	.00272	.00292	.00311	.00331	.00350	.00369	.00389	.00408	.00428	.00447	.00467
15	.00291	.00313	.00333	.00354	.00375	.00396	.00417	.00438	.00458	.00479	.00500
16	.00311	.00333	.00356	.00378	.00400	.00422	.00444	.00467	.00489	.00511	.00533
17	.00331	.00354	.00378	.00401	.00425	.00449	.00472	.00496	.00519	.00543	.00567
18	.00350	.00375	.00400	.00425	.00450	.00475	.00500	.00525	.00550	.00575	.00600
19	.00369	.00396	.00422	.00449	.00475	.00501	.00528	.00554	.00581	.00607	.00633
20	.00389	.00417	.00444	.00472	.00500	.00528	.00556	.00583	.00611	.00639	.00667
21	.00408	.00438	.00467	.00496	.00525	.00554	.00583	.00613	.00642	.00671	.00700
22	.00428	.00458	.00489	.00519	.00550	.00581	.00611	.00642	.00672	.00703	.00733
23	.00447	.00479	.00511	.00543	.00575	.00607	.00639	.00671	.00703	.00735	.00767
24	.00467	.00500	.00533	.00567	.00600	.00633	.00667	.00700	.00733	.00767	.00800
25	.00486	.00521	.00556	.00590	.00625	.00660	.00694	.00729	.00764	.00800	.00833
26	.00506	.00542	.00578	.00614	.00650	.00686	.00722	.00758	.00794	.00831	.00867
27	.00525	.00563	.00600	.00638	.00675	.00713	.00750	.00788	.00825	.00863	.00900
28	.00544	.00583	.00622	.00661	.00700	.00739	.00778	.00817	.00856	.00894	.00933
29	.00563	.00604	.00644	.00684	.00725	.00765	.00806	.00846	.00886	.00926	.00967
30	.00583	.00625	.00667	.00708	.00750	.00792	.00833	.00875	.00917	.00958	.01000
40	.00778	.00833	.00889	.00944	.01000	.01056	.01111	.01167	.01222	.01667	.01333
50	.00972	.01042	.01111	.01181	.01250	.01319	.01389	.01458	.01528	.02083	.01667
60	.01167	.01250	.01333	.01417	.01500	.01583	.01667	.01750	.01833	.01917	.00240
90	.01750	.01875	.02000	.02125	.02250	.02375	.02500	.02625	.02750	.02875	.03000
100	.01944	.02083	.02222	.02361	.02500	.02639	.02778	.02917	.03056	.03194	.03333

Step 1. Divide total interest days into days listed on Table 5-2:

135 days = 100 days; 30 days; 5 days

Step 2. Follow each day line to the required percent column:

100 days at 8½% per $1.00 = $.02361
30 days at 8½% per $1.00 = .00708
5 days at 8½% per $1.00 = .00118
135 days at 8½% per $1.00 = $.03187

Step 3. Multiply total interest for $1.00 by face value:

$.03187 × $765 = $24.38 Ordinary interest

Example 2 Find the maturity value of a note dated February 16 due on September 20. Face value of the note was $1,500 with ordinary interest of 9½%.

Step 1. Determine the exact interest days from Table 5-1:

a. Effective day = Line 16
b. Effective month = February = 47 days
c. Due day = Line 20
d. Due month = September = 263 days
e. Due date September = 263 days
   Effective date February = − 47 days
   Exact interest days = 216 days

Step 2. Calculate ordinary interest from Table 5-2:

a. Total interest days = 216 days
Divide as:

100 days; 100 days; 10 days; 6 days

b. Follow day line to 9½% column and add interest:

100 days at 9½% per $1.00 = $.02639
100 days at 9½% per $1.00 = .02639
 10 days at 9½% per $1.00 = .00264
  6 days at 9½% per $1.00 = .00158
216 days at 9½% per $1.00 = $.05700

Step 3. Multiply total interest for $1.00 by face value:

$.05700 × $1,500 = $85.50 Ordinary interest

Step 4. Add:

Face value + Interest = Maturity value
$1,500.00 + $85.50 = $1,585.50

Practice exercises

Answer

Use Table 5-1 and Table 5-2 to solve the following problems.

1. P. C. Phillips borrowed $1,175 from his bank on a note dated April 24 due on November 10 at ordinary interest of 10%. How much interest will be due on November 10? $65.28

2. Find the interest due on a note for $575 which was dated January 18 due in 38 days with ordinary interest of 8%.   _____

3. Find the maturity value of a note which was dated April 16 due November 22 with a face value of $910 with ordinary interest of 11%. $971.18

4. Ms. Jane Wiggins borrowed $615 from the bank on a note dated June 16 due on August 28 at ordinary interest of 11½%. What amount will she repay on the due date?   _____

5. Find the maturity value of a note dated September 2 due in 23 days with ordinary interest at 12%. Face value of the note was $9,800. $9,875.17

6. Find the maturity value of a note with a face value of $6200 dated June 5 due in 37 days with ordinary interest of 11½%.   _____

7. W. R. Gifford signed a note for $906.50 dated March 30 due on October 15 with ordinary interest of 7½%. What amount of interest will be paid on the due date of the note? $37.58

8. Find the amount of interest that would be due on a note for $465 dated August 31 due in 77 days with ordinary interest of 9½%.   _____

9. T. C. Hester signed a note for $1,158 dated May 12 due on December 20 with ordinary interest at 8%. Find the maturity value of the note.

$1,215.12
or
$1,215.11

10. Find the maturity value of a note with a face value of $1,075 with ordinary interest of 8½%. The note was dated March 19 due on November 28.

BANK DISCOUNT PROCEDURES

Bank discount refers to a procedure of "selling" commercial papers, such as notes, drafts, trade acceptances, to a bank prior to their maturity or due date. For a variety of reasons, a businessperson may find he is in need of additional cash and will convert commercial papers he owns to cash by "discounting" them at his bank. Familiarity with the procedure of discounting commercial papers is necessary to make the decision as to when and how to convert negotiable papers to cash. The procedures and problems in this section will review the three major types of transactions that involve bank discount.

1. Direct loans from a bank.
2. Discounting a noninterest-bearing note by the holder.
3. Discounting an interest bearing note by the holder.

DEFINITIONS

Face value. The amount stated on the note. It is the same as Principal.

Maturity value. The value of the note on the due date.

Noninterest-bearing notes. A negotiable note that does not include an interest charge. On a direct bank note, interest may be deducted in advance of due date.

Maturity date. The date on which the face value or maturity value must be repaid.

Discount date. The date on which the holder of a note "sells" the note to a bank.

Term of discount. Also called discount days, the term of discount is always the *exact number of days* from the date of the discount to the due date of the note.

Discount rate. The annual percent charged for discounting the note prior to the due date. It is the percent that is applied to the maturity value of the note.

Discount. The amount charged by the bank for "buying" a note prior to its due date.

Proceeds. The amount the holder of the note receives after discount has been deducted from the maturity value of the note.

RULES OF DISCOUNT

Direct bank loans

Although most banks prefer to charge simple interest on bank loans, they do (on occasion) discount a direct bank loan. Discounting a direct bank loan simply means that interest on the loan is calculated at the *effective date* and is deducted from the face value of the note. The borrower receives the proceeds and repays the face value of the note.

> **Rule 1: TO CALCULATE PROCEEDS OF A DISCOUNTED BANK LOAN:**
>
> a. Face value × Discount rate × $\frac{\text{Discount days}}{360}$ = Discount
>
> b. Face value − Discount = Proceeds

Step 1. Calculate the exact days from date of the note to the due date. The 360-day year is always used.

Step 2. Substitute data stated on the note in the discount formula.

Step 3. Complete the arithmetic of the discount formula.

Step 4. Deduct the amount of discount from the face value of the note.

Example 1   E. H. Martin borrowed $835 from his bank on May 12 and due on July 11. The bank discounted the note on May 12 at a rate of 7%. What proceeds did the borrower receive?

Step 1. Calculate the exact days from date of the note to due date:

May	=	31 days
Effective date	=	−12 days
Days remaining	=	19
Days in June	=	30
Days in July	=	11
Total discount days	=	60

Discount year is always 360 days

Step 2. Substitute data in discount formula:

Face value × Discount rate × $\frac{\text{Discount days}}{360}$ = Discount

$835   ×   .07   × $\frac{60}{360}$ = Discount

Step 3. Complete the arithmetic of the discount formula:

$835 × .07 × $\frac{60}{360}$ = $9.74

Step 4. Deduct discount from face value of note = Proceeds:

$835 − $9.74 = $825.26

Note: Mr. Martin will receive $825.26 from the bank and repay $835 on July 11.

Discounting a noninterest-bearing note

If a noninterest-bearing note had been accepted from a customer in payment of a debt or merchandise, the note may be converted to cash by "selling" it to a bank any time prior to the due date of the note. The bank will "discount" the note and give the note-holder the proceeds. The maker of the note will repay the face value of the note to the bank. When a bank deducts interest in advance, it is also called discounting a noninterest-bearing note.

> **Rule 2: TO CALCULATE PROCEEDS OF A NONINTERESTING-BEARING NOTE:**
>
> a. Face value × Discount rate × $\frac{\text{Discount days}}{360}$ = Discount
>
> b. Face value − Discount = Proceeds

Step 1. Calculate discount days: exact days from date of discount to due date.

Step 2. Substitute data in discount formula:

$$\text{Face value} \times \text{Discount rate} \times \frac{\text{Discount days}}{360} = \text{Discount}$$

Step 3. Subtract discount from face value = proceeds.

Example 1   Ms. R. Keith accepted a noninterest-bearing note from a customer in payment of an invoice for $650. The note was dated March 26, due in 65 days. On April 10, Ms. Keith discounted the note at her bank at a discount rate of 6½%. What proceeds did Ms. Keith receive from the bank?

Step 1. Calculate discount days:

a. Due date:
March	=	31 days
Effective date	=	−26 days
Remaining days	=	5
April days		30
May days	=	30
Total days	=	65

Due date = May 30

b. Discount days: April 10 to May 30

Table 1:
May 30	=	150 days
April 10	=	−100 days
Discount days	=	50

or Exact days:
April days	=	30
Discount date	=	−10 days
Remaining days	=	20
May days	=	30
Total discount days	=	50

Step 2. Substitute data in discount formula:

$$\text{Face value} \times \text{Discount rate} \times \frac{\text{Discount days}}{360} = \text{Discount}$$

$$\$650 \times .065 \times \frac{50}{360} = \text{Discount}$$

Step 3. Complete arithmetic of the discount formula:

$$\$650 \times .065 \times \frac{50}{360} = \$5.87 \text{ Discount}$$

Step 4. Subtract discount from face value = proceeds:

$$\$650.00 - \$5.87 = \$644.13 \text{ Proceeds}$$

Note: Ms. Keith received $644.13 from the bank. The customer will repay the bank $650.

Example 2   Mr. R. Bailey accepted a noninterest-bearing note dated October 15 which was due on January 10 in payment of an invoice from a customer in the amount of $1,025. Mr. Bailey's bank accepted the note for discount on October 15 at a discount rate of 8%. What proceeds did Mr. Bailey receive?

Step 1. Calculate discount days:

Discount month: October	= 31
Discount effective date	= −15
October days	= 16
November days	= 30
December days	= 31
January days	= 10
Total discount days	= 87 days
Discount year	= 360 days

Step 2. Substitute data in the discount formula:

$$\text{Face value} \times \text{Discount rate} \times \frac{\text{Discount days}}{\text{Discount year}} = \text{Discount}$$

$$\$1{,}025 \times .08 \times \frac{87}{360} = \text{Discount}$$

Step 3. Complete the arithmetic of the discount formula:

$$\$1{,}025 \times .08 \times \frac{87}{360} = \$19.82$$

Step 4. Subtract discount from face value = proceeds:

$$\$1{,}025 - \$19.82 = \$1{,}005.18 \text{ Proceeds}$$

Note: Mr. Bailey will receive $1,005.18 from the bank. The maker of the note will repay the bank $1,025.

DISCOUNTING AN INTEREST-BEARING NOTE

It is an accepted business practice to extend credit to selected customers by accepting an interest-bearing note in payment for goods sold. Such commercial papers may be discounted at a bank in much the same manner as the noninterest-bearing note.

The procedure to discount an interest-bearing note combines the rules for calculating simple interest and the rules of discounting.

Rule 1: TO CALCULATE ORDINARY OR EXACT INTEREST, WHICHEVER APPLIES TO THE DATA STATED ON THE NOTE, BY USE OF THE INTEREST FORMULA:

$$\text{Principal} \times \text{Rate} \times \frac{\text{Interest days}}{\text{Interest year}} = \text{Interest}$$

Rule 2: CALCULATE MATURITY VALUE:

Principal + Interest = Maturity value

Rule 3: CALCULATE BANK DISCOUNT:

$$\text{Maturity value} \times \text{Discount rate} \times \frac{\text{Discount days}}{360} = \text{Discount}$$

Rule 4: CALCULATE PROCEEDS:

Maturity value − Discount = Proceeds

Example 1 A note dated March 25 due on July 23 had a face value of $1,950. Ordinary interest of 7½% was charged. Find the proceeds of the note if the holder of the note discounted it on April 26 at a rate of 6%.

Step 1. Calculate the simple interest due on the note:

$$\text{Principal} \times \text{Rate} \times \frac{\text{Interest days}}{\text{Interest year}} = \text{Interest}$$

$$\$1,950 \times .075 \times \frac{120}{360} = \$48.75$$

Step 2. Calculate maturity value:

$$\text{Principal} + \text{Interest} = \text{Maturity value}$$
$$\$1,950 + \$48.75 \quad \$1,998.75$$

Step 3. Calculate bank discount:

$$\text{Maturity value} \times \text{Discount rate} \times \frac{\text{Discount days}}{360} = \text{Discount}$$

$$\$1,998.75 \times .06 \times \frac{88}{360} = \$29.31 \text{ Discount}$$

Discount days = Exact days between April 26 to July 23

Step 4. Calculate proceeds:

$$\text{Maturity value} - \text{Discount} = \text{Proceeds}$$
$$\$1,998.75 - \$29.31 = \$1,969.44$$

Example 2 The following note was discounted on September 26 by William Bailey, who had accepted this interest-bearing note from Marie Kelley in payment of an invoice for merchandise Ms. Kelley had purchased. What proceeds did Mr. Bailey receive from his bank? Discount rate was 8%.

Figure 5-2

$1,250.00	June 26, 19—

145 days after date _I_ promise to pay
TO THE ORDER OF William Bailey
One Thousand Two Hundred Fifty 00/100 - - - - - - - - - - - - - dollars
at Erie Bank
   Campton, N.Y.
value received with ordinary interest at 9%
DUE November 18, 19—   *Marie C. Kelley*

Step 1. Calculate ordinary interest:

$$\text{Principal} \times \text{Rate} \times \frac{\text{Interest days}}{\text{Interest year}} = \text{Interest}$$

$$\$1,250 \times .09 \times \frac{145}{360} = \$45.31$$

Step 2. Calculate maturity value:

$$\text{Principal} + \text{Interest} = \text{Maturity value}$$
$$\$1,250 + \$45.31 = \$1,295.31$$

Step 3. Calculate bank discount:

Discount days	= September 26 to November 18
September days	= 30
Discount date	= −26
Remaining days	= 4
October days	= 31
November days	= 18
Total discount days	= 53

Maturity value × Discount rate × $\dfrac{\text{Discount days}}{360}$ = Discount

$1,295.31 × .08 × $\dfrac{53}{360}$ = $15.26

Step 4. Calculate proceeds:

Maturity value − Discount = Proceeds
$1,295.31 − $15.26 = $1,280.05

Note: Mr. Bailey received $1,280.05 from the bank. Ms. Kelley will pay the bank $1,295.31.

Practice exercises

Answer

1. A note with a face value of $3,575 was dated April 11 due on September 10 for exact days with exact interest of 8½%. The note was discounted on July 21 at a discount rate of 7%.
   a. Find the amount of interest. $126.53
   b. Find the amount of discount the bank will charge. $36.72
   c. Find the proceeds of the note. $3,664.81

2. A note with a face value of $545 was dated March 31 due in 3 months. Ordinary interest of 7.5% was charged for the exact days. The note was discounted on May 2 at a discount rate of 8%. Find:
   a. The interest earned on the note. _____
   b. The discount charged by the bank. _____
   c. The proceeds of the note. _____

3. Find the proceeds of a note with a face value of $437 if ordinary interest is charged at the rate of 8%. The note is dated April 26 due in 80 days. The note is discounted on May 5 at a discount rate of 6%. $439.51

4. The bank discounted a note on May 12 for R. C. Willis dated May 12 due on November 13 for $895 at a discount rate of 7%. What proceeds did Mr. Willis receive? _____

5. Find the proceeds of a noninterest-bearing note with a face value of $650 dated August 15 due in 90 days which the holder discounted on September 20. The bank charged a discount rate of 7¼%. $642.93

6. A noninterest-bearing note with a face value of $650 was dated August 15 due in 75 days. The holder of the note discounted the note on September 20 at a discount rate of 6½%. What proceeds did the note holder receive? _____

7. Ms. E. Elwell borrowed $1,750 from her bank on June 22 due in 90 days. The bank discounted the note on June 22 at a discount rate of 7%.
    a. What proceeds did Ms. Elwell receive? $1,719.37
    b. What amount will Ms. Elwell repay the bank? $1,750.00

8. A note having a face value of $1,520 with ordinary interest at 9% was dated June 9 due on October 9. The holder of the note discounted it on August 20 at a discount rate of 6½%. Time was based on 30 days to a month. Find:
    a. The amount of interest. _____
    b. The discount. _____
    c. The proceeds the holder of the note would receive. _____

9. A note for $475 was dated February 19 due in 4 months including exact interest at 8¼% based on exact days. The note was discounted on March 26 at a discount rate of 5½%. Find:
    a. Due date of the note.   June 19
    b. The interest. $12.88
    c. The discount. $6.34
    d. The proceeds. $481.54

10. *a.* What is the due date of a note dated July 31 due in 2 months? _____
    b. If the above note was discounted on August 14, find the discount days. _____

11. W. O. Young took a noninterest-bearing note with a face value of $375 due in 90 days to his bank for discounting. The bank discounted the note on May 15 at a discount rate of 9%. The note was dated March 30. What proceeds were received? $370.88

12. Mr. M. A. Moore discounted a noninterest-bearing note for $200 at his bank. The note was dated December 7 due on April 7. The bank discounted the note on March 7 at a rate of 7%. What discount did the bank charge Mr. Moore and what proceeds did he receive? _____

13. John Gibbons signed a note at his bank for $1,150. The note was dated June 15 due in 70 days. The bank discounted the note on June 15 at a discount rate of 8¼%. What proceeds did Mr. Gibbons receive? $1,131.56

14. A note for $1,250 was dated March 25 and due on July 23 with exact time. Ordinary interest of 9% was charged and the note was discounted on April 26 at a discount rate of 7½%. Find the proceeds the holder of the note will receive. _____

15. Find the proceeds of a note with a face value of $1,000 if ordinary interest is charged at a rate of 10%. The note was dated May 5 and due in 75 days. The note was discounted on June 20 at a rate of 7%. $1,015.07

16. A note for $7,200 dated May 10 due on September 10 with ordinary interest of 8½% was discounted on July 14 at a discount rate of 6%. Interest time was based on exact days. Find:
    a. The amount of interest. _____
    b. The discount. _____
    c. The proceeds the holder of the note will receive. _____

17. If a note dated April 10 due in 5 months for exact time had a face value of $650 with ordinary interest at 8½% is discounted on May 23 at a discount rate of 7%, find:
    a. The due date of the note.   September 10
    b. The interest. $23.48
    c. The discount. $14.41
    d. The proceeds the holder of the note will receive. $659.07

18. Edna Evans borrowed $850 from her bank on a note dated April 16 due on August 16. The bank discounted the note at a rate of 8%. What proceeds did Edna Evans receive? _____

19. On May 20 the bank discounted a note Ms. M. A. Martin signed for a loan of $975. The note was due on August 12 and the bank's discount rate was 6¼%.
    a. What amount of discount did the bank charge? $14.22
    b. What proceeds did Ms. Martin receive? $960.78

20. A note with a face value of $375 was dated March 9 due in 90 days with exact interest of 7½% and was discounted on April 4 at a discount rate of 6%. Find:
    a. The due date of the note. _____
    b. The interest earned on the note. _____
    c. The discount charged. _____
    d. The proceeds the noteholder would receive from the bank. _____

COMPOUND INTEREST

Compound interest is calculated on the sum of the principal, plus all prior interest earned. Thus, the principal increases at the end of each interest period. The interest period is the number of times interest will be calculated in a year. For example, interest compounded annually is 1 interest period, interest compounded semiannually is 2 interest periods, interest compounded quarterly would be 4 interest periods, and interest compounded monthly would be 12 interest periods. Compound interest may be calculated by (1) the formula method, or (2) the use of a compound interest table.

COMPOUND INTEREST FORMULAS

$$\text{Principal + Prior interest} \times \text{Annual interest rate} \times \frac{1}{\text{Compound interest periods}} = \text{Interest}$$

Principal + Interest = Accumulated principal
Accumulated principal − Original principal = Compound interest

Example 1   Find the amount of compound interest earned on a deposit of $800 with 8% interest compounded semiannually for 2 years.

Step 1. Determine the compound interest periods:

Semiannual compound interest = 2 Interest periods

Step 2. Calculate interest for each interest period and add interest to the prior principal:

$$P \times R \times T$$

$\$800 \times .08 \times \frac{1}{2} = \$32.00$ Semiannual interest
Interest + 32
$\$832.00 \times .08 \times \frac{1}{2} = \$33.28$ Semiannual interest
Interest + 33.28
$\$865.28 \times .08 \times \frac{1}{2} = \$34.61$ Semiannual interest
Interest + 34.61
$\$899.89 \times .08 \times \frac{1}{2} = \$36.00$ Semiannual interest
Interest + 36.00
$\$935.89$ Accumulated principal after 2 years

Step 3. Calculate compound interest:

Accumulated principal − Original principal = Compound interest
$935.89 − $800.00 = $135.89 Compound interest

Example 2   Find the interest on $900 at 8% interest compounded quarterly for 1 year.

Step 1. Determine compound interest periods:

Quarterly compound interest = 4 periods/year

Step 2. Calculate interest for each interest period and add interest to the prior principal:

Principal × Rate × Time = Interest

$\$900.00 \times .08 \times \frac{1}{4} = \$18.00$ Quarterly interest
Interest + 18.00
$\$918.00 \times .08 \times \frac{1}{4} = \$18.36$ Quarterly interest
Interest + 18.36
$\$936.36 \times .08 \times \frac{1}{4} = \$18.73$ Quarterly interest
Interest + 18.73
$\$955.09 \times .08 \times \frac{1}{4} = \$19.10$ Quarterly interest
Interest + 19.10
$\$974.19$ Accumulated principal after 1 year

Step 3. Calculate compound interest:

Accumulated principal − Original principal = Compound interest
$974.19 − $900.00 = $74.19 Compound interest

Table 5-3
Compound Interest Per $1.00

Period	½%	1%	1½%	2%	3%	4%
1	1.005	1.01	1.015	1.02	1.03	1.04
2	1.01003	1.02010	1.03023	1.04040	1.06090	1.0816
3	1.01508	1.03030	1.04568	1.06121	1.09273	1.12486
4	1.02015	1.04060	1.06136	1.08243	1.12551	1.16986
5	1.02525	1.05101	1.07728	1.10408	1.15927	1.21665
6	1.03038	1.06152	1.09344	1.12616	1.19405	1.26532
8	1.04071	1.08286	1.12649	1.17166	1.26677	1.36857
10	1.05114	1.10462	1.16054	1.21899	1.34392	1.48024
12	1.06168	1.12683	1.19562	1.26824	1.42576	1.60103
14	1.07232	1.14947	1.23176	1.31948	1.51260	1.73168
16	1.08307	1.17258	1.26899	1.37279	1.60471	1.87298
20	1.10490	1.22019	1.34686	1.48595	1.80611	2.19112
24	1.12716	1.26973	1.42950	1.60844	2.03279	2.56330
28	1.14987	1.32129	1.51722	1.74102	2.28792	2.99870
32	1.17304	1.37494	1.61032	1.88454	2.57508	3.50805
36	1.19668	1.43077	1.70914	2.03989	2.89827	4.10392

COMPOUND INTEREST TABLE

The use of the compound interest table is a convenient method of calculating compound interest and accumulated principal for long periods of time.

Example 1   Find the value of $700 invested at 6% interest compounded semiannually for 10 years.

Step 1. Determine the interest periods:

10 years × 2 interest periods per year = 20 interest periods

Step 2. Determine interest rate per compound interest period:

$$\frac{\text{Annual interest rate}}{\text{Yearly compound interest periods}} = \frac{.06}{2} = .03$$

Thus, 3% interest rate for each semiannual period.

Step 3.   *a.* Locate total interest periods in the left-hand column of table = Line 20.
   b. Follow Line 20 to the right to the rate column for 3%.
   c. Factor for 20 periods at 3% = 1.80611.

Step 4. Multiply the interest factor by the principal:

$700.00 × 1.80611 = $1,264.28 Accumulated principal

Step 5.

Accumulated principal − Original principal = Compound interest:

$1,264.28 − $700.00 = $564.28

Example 2   Bob Gray deposited $1,200 in a savings bank that pays 4% interest compounded quarterly.
   a. What will be the balance in his account at the end of 7 years?
   b. How much interest will be earned on the deposit?

Step 1. Determine the interest periods:

7 years × 4 quarterly interest periods = 28

Step 2. Determine interest rate per compound interest period:

$$\frac{\text{Annual interest rate}}{\text{Compound interest periods}} = \frac{.04}{4} = .01$$

Thus, 1% interest rate for each quarterly interest period.

Step 3.

Total interest periods = Line 28
Compound interest rate = .01
Interest factor = 1.32129

Step 4. Multiply the interest factor by the principal:

$1,200 × 1.32129 = $1,585.55 Accumulated balance
$1,585.55 − $1,200.00 = $385.55 Interest

Practice exercises

Answer

1. Find the balance of a savings account for $500 that earns 6% interest compounded semiannually at the end of 2 years. $562.75

2. What amount of compound interest would an investment of $1,500 that earned 8% interest compounded quarterly earn at the end of 6 years? _____

3. Calculate the compound interest and the accumulated balance on an investment of $1,000 at 6% interest compounded quarterly at the end of 5 years. Int. = $346.86
Bal. = $1,346.86

4. Find the balance of a savings account with a balance of $800 with 8% interest compounded quarterly for 4 years. _____

5. If an investment of $2,600 earns 6% interest compounded semiannually, what would the accumulated principal be at the end of 10 years? $4,695.89

6. Find:
    a. The compound interest.
    b. The accumulated principal on a bank account with a balance of $400 that earns 4% interest compounded quarterly at the end of 2 years. _____

7. $11,000 was invested at 8% interest compounded semi-annually.
    a. What will the accumulated principal be at the end of 8 years? $20,602.78
    b. What amount of interest was earned? $9,602.78

8. Phyllis Rayburn invested $1,300 in savings certificate which paid 6% compounded monthly.
    a. Find the accumulated principal at the end of 2 years. _____
    b. How much interest did the investment earn? _____

Review problems

		Answer
1.	Find the maturity value of a note with a face value of $435.60 if ordinary interest of 8% is charged for the exact days from September 27 to December 11.	$442.86
2.	What interest would be charged on a note with a face value of $1,345 dated May 10 due on September 15 if ordinary interest is charged and time is based on a 30-day month? The rate of interest is 9%.	_____
3.	If a note with a face value of $375 was dated March 9 due in 90 days with ordinary interest of 7% and was discounted on April 24 at a discount rate of 6%, find:	
	a. The amount of interest.	$6.56
	b. The amount of discount.	$2.80
	c. The proceeds the noteholder would receive.	$378.76
4.	A noninterest-bearing note with a face value of $650 dated August 15 due in 90 days was discounted on September 20 at a discount rate of 7.5%. Find:	
	a. The due date of the note.	_____
	b. The amount of discount.	_____
	c. The proceeds the borrower would receive.	_____
5.	Find the maturity value of a note with a face value of $860 with exact interest of 8% that was dated October 1 due on February 1 for the exact days.	$883.19
6.	A note with a face value of $325 dated October 10 due on November 24 is discounted by the bank on October 10. What proceeds were given to the borrower if the discount rate was 7.5%?	_____
7.	Find the maturity value of a note with a face value of $6,173.50 if exact interest of 8% is charged. The note is dated April 10 and due in 85 days.	$6,288.52
8.	Ms. M. Marshell borrowed $850 from the bank and signed a note dated September 12 due on January 10. The bank discounted the note at a rate of 9½%. What proceeds did Ms. Marshell receive?	_____
9.	A note with a face value of $450 was dated February 15 due in 4 months with time based on a 30-day month. Find the maturity value of the note if ordinary interest of 8¼% is charged.	$462.37 or $462.38
10.	On June 3rd Nora Morris took a note with a face value of $1,100 with ordinary interest at 7¼% to the bank for discount. The bank charged a discount rate of 6%. The note was dated March 26 and due on August 10.	

5 SIMPLE INTEREST—BANK DISCOUNT / 139

a. The interest on the note was how much?
  b. How much was the discount charged by the bank?
  c. Find the proceeds that were received.

11. A note with a face value of $550 was dated February 19 due in 4 months (time based on a 30-day month). Ordinary interest of 9% was charged. The note was discounted on February 28 at a rate of 7½%. Find:
    a. The due date of the note.   June 19
    b. The amount of interest. $16.50
    c. The amount of discount. $13.10
    d. The proceeds the noteholder will receive from the bank. $553.40

12. To finance the upcoming selling season, Mr. Allen borrowed $1,800 and agreed to pay it back in 145 days at 8% ordinary interest. What amount did Mr. Allen repay?

13. Joan Winters borrowed $850 from the bank and signed a 90-day note dated March 24. The bank charged a discount rate of 9½%. What proceeds did Ms. Winters receive? $829.81

14. A note with a face value of $450 was dated December 7 and due in 180 days. Exact interest of 8% was charged. The holder of the note discounted it at his bank on April 12 at a rate of 6%. Find:
    a. The due date of the note.
    b. The amount of interest.
    c. The amount of discount.
    d. The proceeds the noteholder would receive.

15. Ms. B. Wells accepted a note for $760 from one of her customers. The note was dated June 16 due in 90 days with ordinary interest of 7½%. On August 1, Ms. Wells discounted the note at the bank at a rate of 6%. What proceeds did she receive? $768.57

16. C. R. Simms needed $1,000 to pay an invoice for merchandise. He held a note from a customer for $1,000 with ordinary interest of 7% that was dated April 12 due in 70 days. On May 20, Mr. Simms decided to discount the note at his bank at a discount rate of 6%. What proceeds did Mr. Simms receive from the bank?

17. What proceeds would the borrower receive from a note he signed for $600 dated November 10 due in 120 days if the bank discounted the note on November 10 at a rate of 6.8%? $586.40

18. Find the proceeds of a note with a face value of $10,000 dated April 3 due in 4 months with exact interest at 9% if the note was discounted on July 5 at a discount rate of 7½%. Time of the note was based on exact days.

19. What amount would the borrower repay on a note for $500 that was dated April 12 due on June 17 with time

based on exact days if ordinary interest is charged at a rate of 8¼%? $507.56

20. Find the amount of compound interest that would be earned on a savings account with a balance of $1,150 if 5½% interest compounded semiannually is paid for a period of 2 years. (Use the compound interest formula.)   _____

21. What is the balance of a savings account at the end of 1 year if 6½% interest, compounded quarterly, is paid on a beginning balance of $750? (Use the compound interest formula.) $799.96

22. Find the amount of interest earned on an investment of $2,600 that paid 4% interest compounded quarterly at the end of 5 years. (Use the compound interest table.)   _____

23. What is the balance of J. W. Singer's savings account at the end of 3 years if 6% compound interest is paid quarterly on a beginning balance of $1,685. (Use compound interest table.) $2,014.62

24. Using the compound interest table, find the amount of interest that would be earned on an investment of $2,000 that paid 8% interest compounded semiannually at the end of 10 years. (Use compound interest Table 5-3.)   _____

25. J. F. Darwell invested $800 at 6% interest compounded quarterly. What is the total value of the investment at the end of 8 years? (Use the compound interest Table 5-3.) $1,288.26

STUDY UNIT **6**

Retail merchandising

RULES OF MARKUP
    Markup in dollars
    Selling price: Markup based on cost
    Cost: Markup based on selling price

MARKUP PERCENTS
    Rate of markup based on cost
    Rate of markup based on selling price

MARKDOWN
    Markdown percent of selling price
    Rate of markdown based on selling price

NET MARKUP-MARKDOWN
    Final selling price

PROFIT AND LOSS

Every merchant, wholesaler, or retailer is in business to make a profit by buying goods or services and reselling them for more than their cost. The amount of profit a merchant makes depends, in part, on the selling price that is established for the goods sold. The selling price must be sufficient to recover the cost of the merchandise, to pay for all the expenses of doing business, and to provide a reasonable profit. In this unit the amount or percent added to the cost of goods or services to determine selling price will be called "markup."

The rules of procedure and practice exercises in this unit concentrate on the retailer's calculation of:

1. Markup and markdown.
2. Net markup and net markdown.
3. Gross and net profit.

The term *markup* as used in this unit refers to all expenses of doing business plus a profit. The markup may be expressed as dollars and cents, as a percent of the cost, or as a percent of the selling price. Markdown also may be expressed as either dollars and cents or as a percent of the selling price that is to be reduced.

DEFINITIONS

Selling price. The amount a merchant charges his customers for his goods or services.

Cost. The amount a merchant pays for the goods and services she plans to resell.

Markup. The difference between the selling price and the cost.

Markdown. The percent or an amount that is deducted from the selling price period.

Gross profit. The difference between the selling price and the cost. This is also the markup on an item.

Net profit. The difference between gross profit and expenses.

RULES OF MARKUP

If any two of the quantities in the basic markup formula are known, the remaining quantity can be calculated by substituting the facts stated in the problem in one of the following formulas:

1. Cost + Markup = Selling price
2. Selling price − Cost = Markup
3. Selling price − Markup = Cost

> **Rule 1:** SUBSTITUTE *DOLLARS* STATED IN THE PROBLEM IN THE APPLICABLE FORMULA:

Example 1   The cost of an item was $24; the merchant planned a markup of $7. Find the selling price.
   Step 1. Substitute dollars in the formula:

$$\text{Cost} + \text{Markup} = \text{Selling price}$$
$$\$24 + \$7 = \$31$$

Example 2   The selling price of an item was $31, the cost was $24. Find the markup:
   Step 1. Substitute dollars in the formula:

$$\text{Selling price} - \text{Cost} = \text{Markup}$$
$$\$31 - \$24 = \$7$$

Example 3   The selling price of an item was $31, the markup was $7. Find the cost:
   Step 1. Substitute dollars in the formula:

$$\text{Selling price} - \text{Markup} = \text{Cost}$$
$$\$31 - \$7 = \$24$$

> **Rule 2:** SUBSTITUTE PERCENTS STATED IN THE PROBLEM IN THE APPROPRIATE FORMULA:

Step 1. Assign 100% to the base of the markup.
Step 2. Calculate the remaining quantity.

Example 1   Cost is 60% of the selling price. What percent of the selling price is the markup?
   Step 1. Assign 100% to the base of the markup.

   Assign 100% to the selling price because it is the basis of the markup.

   Step 2. Substitute percents stated in the problem in the formula:

$$\text{Selling price} - \text{Cost} = \text{Markup}$$
$$100\% - 60\% = 40\%$$

Example 2   Markup is 25% of the selling price. What percent of the selling price is the cost?
   Step 1. Assign 100% to selling price because it is the basis of the markup.
   Step 2. Substitute percents stated in the problem in the formula:

$$\text{Selling price} - \text{Markup} = \text{Cost}$$
$$100\% - 25\% = 75\%$$

Example 3 Markup is 20% of the cost. Find the percent selling price is of cost.
Step 1. Assign 100% to the cost because it is the basis of markup.
Step 2. Substitute percents stated in the problem in the formula:

$$\text{Cost} + \text{Markup} = \text{Selling price}$$
$$100\% + 20\% = 120\%$$

Rule 3: TO FIND THE *SELLING PRICE* WHEN THE PERCENT OF MARKUP IS BASED ON THE COST:

$$\text{Selling price} = \frac{\text{Cost}}{\text{Percent cost is of S.P.}}$$

Note: The use of a markup table may facilitate identifying the relationship of the facts stated in the problem and the required arithmetic.

Step 1. Draw the following Markup table:

	Cost	+ Markup	= Selling price
Dollars			
Percent			

Step 2. Assign 100% to the base of markup and enter the dollars and percents given in the problem in the appropriate box.

Step 3. Complete the arithmetic on the percent line.

Step 4. If the dollars and percent are in the same column, *divide* dollars by the percent to find the dollar value of 100%. Enter answer on table and complete the dollar line.

Step 5. If the dollars and 100% are entered in the same column, *multiply* the dollars by the *markup* percent and enter the amount in the markup block. Complete the arithmetic on the dollar line.

Example 1 An item cost $50. Markup was 20% of the selling price. Find (*a*) the selling price and (*b*) the amount of markup.

Step 1. Draw a markup table.
Step 2. Assign 100% to the base of markup.

	Cost	+ Markup	= Selling price
Dollars	$50.00		
Percent	80%	20%	100%

Step 3. Enter the dollars and percents in the markup table.
Note: 100% assigned to Selling price
       (base of markup)
       −20% percent of Markup
       80% percent of Cost

Step 4. Divide dollars and percent in the same column and enter answer on dollar line:

	Cost	+ Markup	= Selling price
Dollars	$50.00	+ $12.50	= $62.50
Percent	80%	+ 20%	= 100%

$$\frac{\$50.00}{.80} = \$62.50 = \text{Selling price}$$

Complete dollar line:

$62.50 − $50.00 = $12.50 Markup

Example 2 The cost of an item was $60. The markup was 15% of the cost. Find (*a*) the selling price and (*b*) the markup.

Step 1. Draw a markup table.

Step 2. Assign 100% to the base of markup and enter dollars and percent in the appropriate box:

	Cost	+ Markup	= Selling price
Dollars	$60.00		
Percent	100%	+ 15%	= 115%

Step 3. Multiply:

Cost × Markup percent = Markup
$60. ×   .15   = $9.00 (**Ans.** *b*)

Step 4. Complete the dollar line:

	Cost	+ Markup	= Selling price
Dollars	$60.00	+ $9.00	= $69.00 (**Ans.** *a*)
Percent	100%	+ 15%	= 115%

Rule 4: TO FIND *COST* WHEN THE PERCENT OF MARKUP IS BASED ON *SELLING PRICE*:

$$\text{Cost} = \frac{\text{Selling price}}{\text{Percent selling price is of cost}}$$

Step 1. Draw a markup table.

Step 2. Assign 100% to the base of markup, and enter dollars and cents stated in problem in the appropriate block on the table.

Step 3. Complete the arithmetic on the percent line.

Step 4. If the dollars and percent are in the same column, *divide* dollars by the percent to find the dollar value of 100%. Complete the dollar line.

Step 5. If the dollars and 100% are entered in the same column, *multiply* the dollars by the markup percent.

Example 1 The selling price of an item was $80. The markup was 16% of the cost. Find (*a*) the cost and (*b*) the markup.

Step 1. Draw a markup table.

Step 2. Assign 100% to the base of the markup and enter dollars and percent stated in problem in the appropriate blocks:

	Cost	+ Markup	= Selling price
Dollars			= $80.00
Percent	100%	+ 16%	= 116%

Step 3. Divide dollars by percent to find the dollar value of 100%. Complete the dollar line.

	Cost	+ Markup	= Selling price
Dollars	$68.97	+ $11.03	= $80.00
Percent	100%	+ 16%	= 116%

$$\frac{\$80.00}{1.16} = \$68.97 \quad (\textbf{Ans.}\ a)$$

Selling price − Cost = Markup
$80.00 − $68.97 = $11.03

Example 2 The selling price of an item was $75. Markup was 30% of the selling price. Find (a) the cost and (b) the markup.

Step 1. Draw a markup table.

Step 2. Assign 100% to the base of the markup and enter dollars and percent stated in the problem in the appropriate block:

	Cost	+ Markup	= Selling price
Dollars			= $75.00
Percent	70%	+ 30%	= 100%

Step 3. If 100% and dollars are in the same column, *multiply* the markup percent by the dollars stated in the problem and complete the dollar line:

	Cost	+ Markup	= Selling price
Dollars	$52.50	+ $22.50	= $75.00
Percent	70%	+ 30%	= 100%

$75 × .30 = $22.50 Markup (**Ans.** b)
Selling price − Markup = Cost
$75.00 − $22.50 = $22.50 (**Ans.** a)

Practice exercises

Answer

1. a. An item cost $145; markup was $40. Find the selling price. — $185
   b. If an item sold for $95.85 and markup was $22.50, what was the cost? — $73.35
   c. The cost of an item was $14.95; the selling price was $21.60. Find the markup. — $6.65
   d. Find the selling price if markup was $11 and the cost was $20. — $31
   e. Find the cost of an item if the selling price was $35.60 and the markup was $12.40. — $23.20
2. a. If the markup of an item is 20% of cost, what percent of cost is the selling price? — _____
   b. Markup was 12½% of the selling price. What percent of the selling price is cost? — _____

    c. If the cost of an item was 72% of the selling price, what percent of the selling price would be the markup?

    d. The selling price was 127% of cost. What percent of cost was the markup?

    e. If the selling price was 100% and the markup was 33⅓% of the selling price, what percent of the selling price was cost?

3. An article costing $218.50 is to be sold at a markup of 15½% of the selling price. Find :
    a. The selling price. $258.58
    b. The markup. $40.08

4. A manufacturer of leather goods priced pocketbooks to include a markup of $7.65, which was 24.6% of the cost. Find the selling price.

5. A grocer sold coffee that cost $1,000 at a markup of 30% of cost. What was the total selling price? $1,300

6. Find the cost of 96 robes if the retail price of one robe is $21.60 and the markup is 27% of the cost.

7. A buyer for a clothing store paid $119.50 per dozen for wool gloves. If the markup is 17.5% of the selling price, what is the selling price per pair of gloves? $12.07

8. Find the selling price of one pair of shoes if 40 pairs cost $780 and a markup of 15% was based on the selling price.

9. Find the cost of a tennis racket if the selling price is $25.85 and a markup of 18.5% was based on the cost. $21.81

10. The cost of woolen shirts was $16.50 each. Find the selling price if a markup of 38% based on cost is included in the selling price.

11. Find the amount of markup on a dress that cost $11.50 and the markup was 22.5% of the selling price. $3.34

12. Merchandise which sold for $1,620 included a markup of 12½% of the cost. Find the cost of the merchandise.

13. Ruth Wells paid $385 for an electric portable typewriter, which she planned to sell at a markup of 26% of cost. Find:
    a. The amount of the markup. $100.10
    b. The selling price. $485.10

14. The Mack Furniture Store purchased 2 dozen chairs at a total cost of $406.52. Find the selling price per chair if they were marked up 18½% of the selling price.

15. The selling price of a desk was $1,290. Find the cost if the markup was 35% of the selling price. $838.50

16. Clarke's Hardware Store purchased 50 gallons of white house paint, which they plan to resell for $12.50 per gallon. Find the cost of the 50 gallons if a markup of 31% based on the cost was charged.

17. J. & T. Sporting Goods Store purchased 12 pair of ice skates at a cost of $235.50. It planned a markup of 27½% based on the selling price. Find the selling price of 1 pair of skates. $27.07

18. Find the selling price of an item that cost $21.90 if a markup of 15% based on cost was charged.   _____

MARKUP PERCENT BASED ON COST OR SELLING PRICE

At times a merchant may have to change a desired selling price to meet competition or to reduce inventory of slow-selling merchandise. To make an appropriate change in the selling price, the merchant must know what percent of markup was included in the original selling price and whether it was based on cost of the item or its selling price.

> **Rule 1: TO FIND *RATE OF MARKUP* BASED ON *COST*:**
>
> $$\frac{\text{Markup}}{\text{Cost}} = \text{Rate of markup}$$

Step 1. Calculate the amount of markup:

$$\text{Selling price} - \text{Cost} = \text{Markup}$$

Step 2. Calculate rate of markup:

$$\frac{\text{Markup}}{\text{Cost}} = \text{Rate of markup}$$

Example 1   The selling price of an item was $84 and the cost was $70. Find the rate of markup based on the cost.

Step 1. Calculate the amount of markup:

$$\text{Selling price} - \text{Cost} = \text{Markup}$$
$$\$84 - \$70 = \$14$$

Step 2. Calculate rate of markup:

$$\frac{\text{Markup}}{\text{Cost}} = \text{Rate of markup}$$
$$\frac{\$14.00}{\$70.00} = .20 = 20\%$$

Example 2   Find the percent of markup on cost if the selling price of an item is $84.42 and the markup is $17.42.

Step 1. Calculate the amount of the cost:

$$\text{Selling price} - \text{Markup} = \text{Cost}$$
$$\$84.42 - \$17.42 = \$67.00$$

Step 2. Calculate rate of markup:

$$\frac{\text{Markup}}{\text{Cost}} = \text{Rate of markup}$$
$$\frac{\$17.42}{\$67.00} = .26 = 26\%$$

> **Rule 2: TO FIND RATE OF MARKUP BASED ON SELLING PRICE:**
> $$\frac{\text{Markup}}{\text{Selling price}} = \text{Rate of markup}$$

Step 1. Calculate amount of markup:

$$\text{Selling price} - \text{Cost} = \text{Markup}$$
or
$$\text{Cost} + \text{Markup} = \text{Selling price}$$

Step 2. Calculate rate of markup:

$$\frac{\text{Markup}}{\text{Selling price}} = \text{Rate of markup}$$

Example 1   The selling price of an item was $90, the cost was $72. Find the rate of markup based on selling price.

Step 1. Calculate amount of markup:

$$\text{Selling price} - \text{Cost} = \text{Markup}$$
$$\$90 - \$72 = \$18$$

Step 2. Calculate rate of markup:

$$\frac{\text{Markup}}{\text{Selling price}} = \text{Rate of markup}$$
$$\frac{\$18.00}{\$90.00} = .20 = 20\%$$

Example 2   S & C Department Store purchased wool sweaters at a cost of $37.83 and added a markup of $10.67. What was the rate of markup based on selling price?

Step 1. Calculate amount of markup:

Stated in problem: $10.67

Step 2. Calculate selling price:

$$\text{Cost} + \text{Markup} = \text{Selling price}$$
$$\$37.83 + \$10.67 = \$48.50$$
$$\frac{\text{Markup}}{\text{Selling price}} = \text{Rate of markup}$$
$$\frac{\$10.67}{\$48.50} = .22 = 22\%$$

Practice exercises

Answer

1. The markup on an item was $18.46. The cost was $56.80. What is the percent of markup based on cost?   **32.5%**

2. If markup is $23.26 and cost is $162.80, what is the percent of markup based on the selling price?   _____

3. A job lot of 35 sweaters cost $297.50. The retail price of 8 sweaters was $15.25 each, 15 sweaters sold for $12.35 each, and 12 sweaters were $10.50 each. What is the percent of markup based on selling price?   **31.33%**

4. A wholesale plumbing company priced water pumps to sell for $385. If the cost was $312.62, find the rate of markup based on the selling price.

5. An article which cost the retailer $16.98 was priced to sell for $22.96. What is the percent of markup based on the selling price? **26.05%**

6. Find the percent of markup based on cost if the markup is $7 and the selling price is $35.

7. What is the percent of markup on cost if the selling price is $79.67 and the markup is $17.67? **28.5%**

8. R. T. Wells paid $530.25 for a shipment of 50 pairs of shoes. Later, 15 pairs of the shoes were sold for $12.50 per pair, 20 pairs for $15 per pair, 12 pairs for $17.50 per pair, and 3 pairs for $20 per pair. Find the percent of markup based on total selling price.

9. An item that cost $483.60 is to be sold at a markup of 6.25% of the cost. Find:
   a. The selling price. **$513.83**
   b. The percent the selling price is of cost. **106.25%**

10. The total cost of the stock in a drugstore was $13,045.52. The sales were $21,212.22. What was the percent of markup based on the selling price?

MARKDOWN

For a variety of reasons the original selling price of merchandise may be reduced by either a stated amount of dollars and cents or by a stated percent of the current selling price. The amount of the reduction is called the *markdown*. The final selling price after the markdown, however, must be sufficient to cover the cost of the merchandise and business expenses to prevent a loss.

> **Rule 1:** WHEN *MARKDOWN* IS EXPRESSED IN DOLLARS AND CENTS, FIND THE REDUCED SELLING PRICE BY:
>
> Selling price − Markdown = Sale price

Step 1. Calculate the reduced selling price:

Selling price − Markdown = Sale price

Example 1   The selling price of an item was $32.50. It was decided to reduce the selling price by $7.50 during a clearance sale. Find the sales price.

Step 1. Calculate the reduced selling price:

Selling price − Markdown = Sale price
$32.50 − $7.50 = $25.00

> **Rule 2:** WHEN *MARKDOWN* IS STATED AS A PERCENT OF THE ORIGINAL SELLING PRICE:
>
> a. Selling price × Rate of markdown = Markdown
> b. Selling price − Markdown = Sales price

Step 1. Calculate amount of markdown.
Step 2. Deduct markdown from original selling price.

Example 1 The selling price of an item was $35. This price was reduced by 12%. Find (a) the markdown and (b) the reduced selling price.

Step 1. Calculate amount of markdown:

Selling price × Rate of markdown = Markdown
$35.00   ×   .12   = $4.20   (Ans. a)

Step 2. Deduct markdown from selling price:

Selling price − Markdown = Sales price
$35.00   − $4.20 $30.80   (Ans. b)

Example 2 A desk lamp was reduced to sell for $32 during an inventory sale. This price was 15% less than the original selling price. Find (a) the original selling price and (b) the amount of markdown.

Step 1.

Sale price +	Markdown =	Selling price
$32.00		
85% +	15% =	100%

$$\text{Original selling price} = \frac{\$32.00}{.85} = \$37.65 \text{ (Ans. } a\text{)}$$

Calculate markdown:

Selling price × Rate of markdown = Markdown
$37.65   ×   .15   = $5.65   (Ans. b)

Rule 3: TO FIND THE RATE OF MARKDOWN

$$\frac{\text{Markdown}}{\text{Original selling price}} = \text{Rate of markdown}$$

Step 1. Calculate amount of markdown.
Step 2. Calculate rate of markdown.

Example 1 An item sold for $12 but a markdown of $3 was made during a clearance sale. Find the rate of markdown.

Step 1. Calculate amount of markdown:

$3 = markdown stated in problem

Step 2. Calculate rate of markdown:

$$\frac{\text{Markdown}}{\text{Selling price}} = \frac{\$3.00}{\$12.00} = .25 = 25\%$$

Example 2 Woolen scarfs were sold for $14.75 each. At the end of the season, the merchant sold the scarfs for $11.50. What was the rate of markdown?

Step 1. Calculate amount of markdown:

Original selling price $14.75
Sale price   −11.50
Markdown $ 3.25

Step 2. Calculate rate of markdown:

$$\frac{\text{Markdown}}{\text{Selling price}} = \frac{\$3.25}{\$14.75} = .2203 = 22.03\%$$

Practice exercises

	Answer

1. The selling price of a color TV set was $875. The merchant decided to reduce the selling price to $700 during a sale. Find:
    a. The amount of the markdown. — $175
    b. The rate of markdown. — 20%

2. Wool shirts were priced to sell for $25. A decision was made to reduce this selling price by 18% during a sale. Find the sale price of a wool shirt. — _____

3. Suits were priced to sell for $175. During a clearance sale they were sold for $120.75. What was the rate of markdown? — 31%

4. The Home Appliance Store offered a refrigerator at a selling price of $670 less a markdown of 12½%. Find:
    a. The reduced sales price. — _____
    b. Amount of markdown. — _____

5. At the end of the summer season, the Home Garden Shop offered a 50-foot garden hose at a markdown price of $14.50. The regular selling price was $20.00. If the entire inventory of 16 hoses were sold at the reduced price, find:
    a. Total markdown. — $88.00
    b. Percent of markdown. — 27.5%

6. Find the reduced sales price of ladies dresses that were priced to sell for $39.95 and marked down 8½%. — _____

7. A hardware store priced wood saws to sell for $22.50. During an inventory sale the selling price was reduced to $17.75. Find:
    a. The amount of markdown. — $4.75
    b. Percent of markdown. — 21.11%

8. An item was originally priced to sell for $12.45 but finally sold for $10.25. What was the rate of markdown? — _____

9. During an inventory sale a set of golf clubs were sold for $165. This price was 22.5% less than the original selling price. Find:
    a. The original selling price. — $212.90
    b. Amount of the markdown. — $47.90

10. A merchant is planning to reduce spring coats from an original selling price of $75.00 to $62.50. What is the rate of markdown? — _____

11. The Haynes Nursery sold miniature crabapple trees for $11.95 each. At the end of the season, Haynes marked down the selling price to $8.40. Find the rate of markdown. — 29.71%

MARKUP AND MARKDOWN

After the selling price of an item has been determined by the markup and markdown procedures we have just reviewed, it may be desirable for a businessman to make further changes in the selling price. Because of seasonal sales, inventory clearances, competition, and so on, the original selling price may be marked up and marked down several times before the merchandise is sold. To determine whether the final selling price is adequate to at least cover operating expenses, the businessman may calculate the *net markup* and the *net markdown*.

> Rule 1: TO CALCULATE THE *FINAL SELLING PRICE:*
> a. Calculate the original selling price, if necessary, by the rules of markup.
> b. Apply all subsequent markups and markdowns in the order in which they were made to the latest selling price.

Step 1. Calculate original selling price, if necessary.
Step 2. Apply first markup or markdown to the original selling price.
Step 3. Apply additional markups and markdowns to the last selling price.

Example 1   An art dealer purchased a painting at a cost of $1,020 and planned to sell it at a markup of 25% based on its selling price. After one month the original selling price was marked down by 8% and later marked down again by 12%. This price was too low to cover expenses and the price was marked up by 6%. Finally the picture was sold. Find the final selling price.

Step 1. Calculate the original selling price:

Cost $1,020 + Markup = Selling price
     75%   + 25% =   100%   (Base of markup)

$$\frac{\$1,020}{.75} = \$1,360 \text{ Original selling price}$$

Step 2. Apply first markdown:

Original selling price × Rate of markdown = Markdown
$1,360 × .08 = $108.80 = Markdown
$1,360 − $108.80 = $1,251.20 Sale price

Step 3. Apply additional markdowns and markups:

$1,251.20 × .12 = $150.14 Markdown
$1,251.20 − $150.14 = $1,101.06 Sale price

$1,101.06 × .06 = $66.06 Markup
$1,101.06 + $66.06 = $1,167.12 Final selling price

Example 2   A dealer planned to sell garden tractors for $785.50 each. The original selling price was marked down 12⅛% during a clearance sale. After one month, the price was marked down another 6½%. What would the final selling price be for one tractor?

Step 1. Calculate original selling price:

Original selling price stated in the problem = $785.50

Step 2. Apply the first markdown:

Original selling price × Rate of markdown = Markdown
$785.50   ×   .12125   = $95.24 Markdown
$785.50   − $95.24   = $690.26 Sale price

Step 3. Apply additional markdowns:

$690.26 × .065 = $44.87 Markdown
$690.26 − $44.87 = $645.39 Final selling price

Rule 2: TO CALCULATE *NET MARKUP* AND *NET MARKDOWN:*
  a. Final selling price − Cost = *Net markup*
  b. Original selling price − Final selling price = *Net markdown*

Step 1. Calculate final selling price.
Step 2. Calculate net markup.
Step 3. Calculate net markdown.

Example 1   An automobile dealer bought a used car for $1,113.25. The selling price was to include a markup of 27% based on the selling price. The car did not sell at this price so the dealer marked the price down by 10%. Two weeks later the price was marked down another 15%. The dealer decided this price was too low to cover all operating expenses and marked the price up by 7%. Find (*a*) the final selling price, (*b*) the net markup, and (*c*) the net markdown.

Step 1. Calculate final selling price:

Cost $1,113.25 + Markup = Selling price
      73%   +   27% =   100%   (Base of markup)

$$\frac{\$1{,}113.25}{.73} = \$1{,}525 \text{ Original selling price}$$

Apply all markdowns and markups:

$1,525 × .10 = $152.50 Markdown
$1,525 − $152.50 = $1,372.50 Sale price

$1,372.50 × .15 = $205.88 Markdown
$1,372.50 − $205.88 = $1,166.62 Sale price

$1,166.62 × .07 = $81.66 = Markup
$1,166.62 + $81.66 = $1,248.28 = Final selling price

Step 2. Calculate net markup:

Final selling price −   Cost   = Net markup
  $1,248.28   − $1,113.25 = $135.03   (Ans. *b*)

Step 3. Calculate net markdown:

Original selling price − Final selling price = Net markdown
  $1,525.00   − $1,248.28   = $276.72   (Ans. *c*)

Practice exercises

Answer

1. Find the final selling price on an item that cost $412 and had a markup of 25% based on the selling price that was

originally charged. During an inventory sale the selling price was marked down 15%.   **$466.93**

2. A manufacturer of leather goods priced overnight bags to include a markup of $7.75, which was 24.6% of the cost. During a discount sale, the price was marked down by 12½%. Find the final selling price.   _____

3. The cost of a tennis racket was $21.80. A markup of 18.5% was based on cost. After the summer season, the merchant had a clearance sale and marked the original selling price down by 16%. What was the sale price of the racket?   **$21.70**

4. An article that cost $156.80 was to be sold at a markup of 30% based on the selling price. To meet a competitor's price, the merchant marked down the original selling price by 20%. Find the sale price of the article.   _____

5. If the cost of a chair was $204.75 and the markup was 33⅓% based on the selling price, find the final selling price if the owner of the store marked down the original selling price by 25%.   **$230.33**

6. A retail merchant purchased sweaters at a cost of $7.95 each, planning to sell the sweaters at a markup of 35% based on the selling price. At the end of the season, the merchant marked down the original selling price on 150 sweaters in stock by 17% of the original selling price. Find the total reduced selling price of the 150 sweaters.   _____

7. An item costing $118.20 included a markup of 20% based on its selling price. Later a markdown of 33⅓% was made on the original selling price. During a sale an additional markdown of $4 was made and finally the price was marked up by 27%. Find:
    a. Net markup.   **$1.82**
    b. Net markdown.   **$27.73**

8. The King Novelty and Gift Shop purchased a sculpture from a local artist for $600 and marked the cost up by 40%. After one month the original selling price was marked down 20%. Two weeks later another markdown of 8% was made. The owner felt that the price was now too low and marked it up by $7. Finally the sculpture sold at the latest selling price. Find the sale's:
    a. Net markup.   _____
    b. Net markdown.   _____

9. Wallets that cost $8.10 were marked up 29% based on the selling price. When the wallets were put on sale, the price was marked down by 10%. Find, when the inventory of 35 wallets were sold:
    a. The net markup.   **$75.95**
    b. The net markdown.   **$39.90**

10. The cost of an item was $240. The markup was 40% of its selling price. Later the selling price was reduced by 16⅔% and at a later date reduced again by 5%. Finally   _____

the item was sold. Find (*a*) the final selling price, (*b*) the net markup, and (*c*) the net markdown.

11. The Wilson Galleries purchased a painting for $340 and marked it up by 45% of the cost. Later, when the painting did not sell, the original selling price was marked down 15% and an additional markdown of 12% was made before it was sold. Find the sale's:
    a. Net markup. $28.76
    b. Net markdown. $124.24

12. An item was priced to sell at a markup of $107.75 which was 24.6% of the cost. The item was later put on sale with a markdown of $8\frac{1}{3}\%$ of the original selling price. The price was reduced further by $12\frac{1}{2}\%$. The manager thought the last selling price was too low and marked the price up by 20%. Find:
    a. The net markup.
    b. Net markdown.

13. A dealer purchased a used car for $1,750 and planned to sell it for $2,100. After 2 months the car was not sold and the price was marked down by 12%. During an inventory sale, the last selling price was marked down again by $7\frac{1}{2}\%$. After the sale, the last selling price was marked up 9%. Finally the car was sold. Find:
    a. Net markup. $113.25
    b. Net markdown. $236.75

14. Find the final selling price of an item that cost the merchant $356.75 and on which he made a markup of 22% based on selling price. Several weeks later another markup of 10% was made. During an inventory sale, the last selling price was marked down by $33\frac{1}{3}\%$.

PROFITS AND LOSSES

Markup was defined as the difference between the selling price and the cost of the merchandise sold. This difference must be sufficient to cover the cost of operating the business and a reasonable profit for the merchant. Thus Markup = Operating expenses + Profit. Periodically, the merchant will calculate his profit on a single item of merchandise, on the entire inventory of one or more items of merchandise, or on the entire business.

The calculation of profit consists of (1) the determination of gross profit, which will indicate if the selling price is sufficient to at least recover the cost of the merchandise sold, and (2) the determination of net profit, which will indicate how much profit the merchant has made after operating expenses are paid.

> **Rule 1: TO CALCULATE GROSS PROFIT:**
>
> Sales or Selling price – Cost = Gross profit

Example 1   The R. T. Thomas Gift Shop had total sales for the month of $18,946. The cost of the merchandise sold during the month was $14,426.

Step 1. Substitute data in the problem in the formula:

Sales   -   Cost   = Gross profit
$18,946 - $14,426 = $4,520 Gross profit

Example 2   Barnshaw Equipment Company sold a piece of heavy equipment for $24,500. The cost of the equipment was $19,435. Find the gross profit on the piece of equipment.

Selling price -   Cost   = Gross profit
$24,500   - $19,435 = $5,065

Rule 2: TO CALCULATE NET PROFIT OR NET LOSS:

Gross profit - Operating expenses = Net profit or Net loss
Sales - Cost - Operating expenses = Net profit or Net loss

Note: Operating expenses may include such expenses as salaries or wages, rent, heat and light, advertising, commissions, insurance, shipping cost.

If operating expenses exceed gross profit, the result will be a *net loss*.
Step 1. Calculate gross profit.
Step 2. Calculate operating expenses.
Step 3. Calculate net profit or net loss.

Example 1   The Hardwick Hardware Company had sales of $119,486.50 for the month. The cost of the merchandise sold amounted to $101,260. Expenses for the month included; rent, $2,500; salaries, $13,640; advertising, $850; and heat and light, $416.80. What net profit did Hardwick have at the end of the month?

Step 1. Calculate gross profit:

Sales   -   Cost   = Gross profit
$119,486.50 - $101,260 = $18,226.50

Step 2. Calculate total operating expenses:

Rent	$ 2,500.00
Salaries.............................	13,640.00
Advertising......................	850.00
Heat and light	416.80
Total	$17,406.80

Step 3. Calculate net profit:

Gross profit - Expenses   = Net profit
$18,226.50 - $17,406.80 = $819.70 = Net profit

Example 2   Bay City Furniture Store purchased a living room sofa for $980. The sofa sold for $1,220. Operating expenses charged to the sale of the sofa included: commission, $150; rent expense, $1/5$% of the selling price; heat and light, $1/2$% of the selling price. Find the net profit that was made on the sale.

Step 1. Calculate gross profit:

Selling price - Cost   = Gross profit
$1,220   - $980 = $240

Step 2. Calculate operating expenses:

Commission	$150.00
Rent expense (.002 × $1,220)	2.44
Heat and light (.005 × $1,220)	6.10
Total expenses	$158.54

Step 3. Calculate net profit:

Gross profit − Expenses = Net profit
$240.00 − $158.54 = $81.46

Example 3 The Bushwick Rug Company purchased a hand-woven India rug for $680. They added a markup of 20% based on the selling price. Operating expenses charged to the rug included: commission, $80; heat and light, $4.80, rent, $9.40; advertising, $90. Find: the net profit or loss that was made on the sale.

Step 1. Calculate gross profit:

Selling price −   Cost   = Gross profit
 $850.00   − $680.00 = $170.00
($680 ÷ .80)

Step 2. Calculate operating expenses:

Commission	$ 80.00
Heat and light	4.80
Rent	9.40
Advertising	90.00
Total	$184.20

Step 3. Calculate net profit or loss:

Gross profit − Expenses = Net profit or Net loss
 $170.00   − $184.20 = $14.20 = Net loss

Note: Operating expenses exceeded gross profit.

Practice exercises

Answer

1. An item cost $576 and was marked up 45% of its cost. Operating expenses related to the item included: commission, $137.50; installation cost, $64.00; storage, $41.80; and insurance cost, $27.50. Find:
   a. Gross profit. $259.20
   b. The net profit. $11.60 loss

2. An office equipment company purchased file cabinets at a cost of $210 each. The markup was 35% of the selling price. Expenses for each file cabinet included: storage, $26.50; advertising, $26.20; insurance, $37.80. What was the net profit or loss on the sale of 4 cabinets. _____

3. An item that sold for $620.30 cost the buyer $406.20. Expenses related to the sale of the item included: insurance, $36.00; storage, $32.20; commission, $60.00. Find the net profit or loss made on the sale. $85.90 profit

4. If an item that cost $64.00 was marked up 32% of its selling price and expenses related to the sale of the item included: delivery charges, $12.50; commissions, $9.40; storage, $17.50, what was the net profit or loss made on the sale?

5. The Jones Equipment Company bought a backhoe for $16,850. The company marked up the cost 33⅓% of its selling price. The backhoe did not sell, so the price was marked down 12%. Two weeks later the price was marked down again by 8%. Expenses related to the sale of the backhoe included: assembly, $410; commission, $1,026; advertising, $92; and shipping cost, $310. Did Jones make a profit or loss when the equipment was sold? How much?

    Yes
    $1,773.62
    profit

6. Find the gross and net profit on an item that cost $325 and was sold for $458.25. Advertising expenses were $50, repairs amounted to $35, and the salesman's commission was $21.

7. The James Automatic Equipment Company paid $2,102 for a tractor which it intended to sell at a markup of 33⅓% based on its selling price. The selling price was marked down $50 before the tractor was sold. Expenses related to the sale of the tractor included: repairs to the motor, $408; commission, $195; other expenses, $63.50. What were the gross and net profit the company made on the sale?

    $1,000.84
    or
    $1,001.00
    gross profit.
    $334.34
    or
    $334.50
    net profit

8. The Fisher Furniture Company bought dining room furniture from a supplier at a cost of $1,600. Fisher marked up the cost by 25% of the selling price. A customer agreed to buy the set if Fisher would mark down the selling price by 5%. Fisher agreed to the markdown. Expenses related to the sale were; advertising, $65; shipping cost, $45; commission, $70; and $60 in miscellaneous expenses. Find the net profit that was made on the sale.

Review problems

		Answer
1.	A grocer sold tea that cost him $1,000 at a markup of 30% of the cost. What was the total selling price of the tea?	$1,300
2.	Find the cost of a tennis racket if the selling price is $25.85 and the markup is $4.35.	_____
3.	A jewelry store priced a set of silverplated flatware to sell for $53.20. If the cost was $45, find the percent (rate) of markup based on cost.	18.22%
4.	The cost of an item was $38.46. The selling price was $56.80. What is the rate of markup based on the selling price?	_____
5.	The selling price of an item is $174. The markup is 20% of the cost. Find:	
	a. The cost of the item.	$145
	b. What the percent cost is of the selling price.	83.33%
6.	The S & W Clothing Store paid $117.18 per dozen for wool vests. If the markup is 27.5% of the selling price, what is the selling price of each vest?	_____
7.	A leather-goods manufacturer priced ladies purses to sell for $35 each, which was 122.4% of the cost. Find the amount of markup on each purse.	$6.41
8.	If the markup on an item was 18.75% of the cost, what percent of the cost is the selling price?	_____
9.	Find the selling price of 1 overcoat when 30 overcoats cost $2,164.50 and a markup of 22% based on selling price is charged.	$92.50
10.	Wool socks that cost $36 a dozen pairs are sold for $4.50 per pair. What was the rate of markup based on cost?	_____
11.	Jack's Western Shop bought a fancy saddle for $680. They added a markup of 32% based on the selling price. After 2 months and the saddle had not been sold, the price was marked down 16⅔%. Finally the saddle was sold. Find:	
	a. Net markup.	$153.30
	b. Net markdown.	$166.70
12.	The T & R Sporting Goods Store purchased 200 pairs of ice skates at a cost of $4,751.45. They priced 80 pairs to sell for $31.50 per pair, 50 pairs at $27.50 per pair, 30 pairs at $24.50 per pair and the remainder at $22.50 per pair. Find:	
	a. The amount of markup they will receive if all skates are sold at the expected selling price and	_____

  b. The rate of markup based on the expected selling price.

13. The Arnold Ford Company purchased a used car for $1,657.50. A markup of 35% of the selling price was added. After 2 weeks, the selling price was marked down 15%. Repair costs amounted to $185.60, advertising expenses were $22.80, and a commission of $200 was paid when the car was sold. Find:
  a. The net markup on the sale. $510.00
  b. The net markdown. $382.50
  c. The net profit or loss the dealer made on the sale. $101.60 profit

14. The MacDonald Boat Company purchased a power motor from a supplier at a cost of $402.25. MacDonald marked the cost up by 45% of the selling price. It spent $7.50 for advertising, $55.00 for commission, and $26.08 for overhead expense. Find the net profit MacDonald made on the sale.

15. The selling price of cotton shirts was $20.36. During a clearance sale, the selling price was marked down to $12.95. Find:
  a. The amount of markdown. $7.41
  b. The rate of markdown based on selling price.   36.39%

16. The Sharp Fur Company purchased a fur coat at a cost of $2,238.60 and marked it up 28% based on its selling price. The coat did not sell, so the selling price was marked down 12½%. An additional markdown of 8% was made during a sale. After the sale, the manager marked the selling price up 5%. Finally the coat was sold. Find:
  a. Net markup.
  b. Net markdown.

17. An item was priced to sell for $90. During an inventory sale, the price was marked down to $78.75. Find:
  a. The amount of the markdown. $11.25
  b. The rate of markdown based on the original selling price.   12½%

18. The Ellery Book Store purchased a rare book for $1,050. They added a markup of 22% based on the selling price. When the book did not sell, another markdown of 5% was made. Three weeks later an additional markdown of 8⅓% was made. The last selling price was too low, so the manager added a markup of 7½%. Finally the book was sold. Expenses related to the sale of the book included: advertising costs, $96.50; commission, $125; insurance, $42.60; shipping costs $31.85. Find:
  a. Net markup.
  b. Net markdown.
  c. The profit or loss made on the sale.

19. An item was priced to sell for $146.50. The markup was 27.5% of the cost. Find:

  a. The amount of markup. $31.60
  b. The cost of the item. $114.90

20. Sales during a month for the WJR Company amounted to $186,420. The cost of the goods sold was $114,645. Operating expenses for the month included: salaries, $12,946; heat and light, $1,326.35; rent, $1,800; insurance, $316.25; shipping charges, $216.20; advertising, $1,700. Find the net profit or loss for the month.

STUDY UNIT **7**

Consumer credit

RULES OF PROCEDURE
  Installment charges
  Amount financed
  Add-on interest
  Monthly interest rates
  Annual percentage rate
    APR tables
    APR formula
  Installment payments
    Simple add-on interest
    Amortized installment payments

OPEN-END CREDIT PLANS
  Amount due
  Minimum payment
  Finance charges

INTRODUCTION

With the increase in the use of various types of consumer credit plans and in federal regulation of information the consumer must have, it is important that you know something about the arithmetic involved in both extending and using credit. The extension of credit has become an important service that a business offers its customers and has become very competitive in the retail market. The consumer should know how much the use of credit costs and the interest rate charged so that comparisons can be made among the various sources of credit.

There is a wide variety of credit plans available to consumers for the purchase of goods or services as well as the borrowing of money. The material included in this unit should be regarded as illustrations of the calculations used in consumer credit plans rather than a complete study of consumer credit.

The formulas and their required arithmetic are those that are common to most installment plans, and includes the calculation of:

1. The cost of installment buying.
2. Methods of calculating interest.
3. Calculation of interest rates.
4. Determination of installment payments.
5. Amortized payments.
6. Open-end credit plans.

These six calculations will be discussed in the following pages.

RULES OF PROCEDURE

1. The cost of installment buying

Installment (or finance) charges include all charges made by the lender for the use of credit. Such charges may include one or all of the following: interest, loan fees, carrying charges, application fees, credit investigation fees, insurance, service fees.

> **Rule 1: TO CALCULATE INSTALLMENT CHARGES:**
>
>   Amount to be repaid
> +Any additional charge stated
> <u>−Cash price less down payment if one was required</u>
>   Installment charges

Step 1. Calculate the amount to be repaid:

      Number of payments × Amount of each payment

Step 2. Add any additional charges stated in the problem.
Step 3. Deduct:

      Cash price
    − Down payment (if one is required)

Example 1   An item was on sale for $235 cash or $35 down payment and the balance to be paid in 10 equal payments of $24. A credit fee of $15 and an application fee of $5 were also charged. Find the installment charges.

Step 1.   Calculate amount to be repaid:

Number of payments × Amount of payment
      10   × $24.00   = $240.00

Step 2. Add additional charges:

Credit fee	$15.00	
Application fee	<u>5.00</u>	+ 20.00
		$260.00

Step 3. Deduct cash price minus down payment:

      $235.00   − $35.00 = <u>−200.00</u>
      Installment charges $ 60.00

Amount financed

This is the amount of the unpaid balance that the consumer must borrow to complete the transaction. It is also the amount of credit the seller will extend to the consumer.

> **Rule 2: TO CALCULATE THE AMOUNT FINANCED:**
>
> Cash or Selling price − Down payment = Amount financed

Step 1. If down payment is a percent of the selling price, multiply the selling price by the required rate.
Step 2. Substitute data in the formula:

      Selling price − Down payment = Amount financed

Example 1 A. T. Ball purchased merchandise totaling $1,226.75 and agreed to pay 15% of the selling price as a down payment and the balance in 8 equal payments. What amount was financed?

Step 1. Calculate down payment:

Selling price × Rate = Down payment
$1,226.75 × .15 = $184.01

Step 2. Substitute data in formula:

Selling price − Down payment = Amount financed
$1,226.75 − $184.01 = $1,042.74

Example 2 An item of merchandise was on sale for $975 cash or $150 down payment and the balance in 15 equal payments. Find the amount the buyer would finance.

Step 1. Calculate down payment:

Down payment stated as $150

Step 2. Substitute data in formula:

Selling price − Down payment = Amount financed
$975.00 − $150.00 = $825.00

Practice exercises

Answer

1. Ellen Allwell bought a stereo priced to sell for $650. An installment plan was available that required a down payment of $150, a $20 service charge, a $15 credit fee, and 4 monthly payments of $125. What were the total installment charges? $35

2. An item of merchandise was offered on sale for $312.60 or on an installment plan that required 12½% of the sale price as a down payment and the balance in 6 monthly payments of $50 per payment. A credit investigation fee of $15 and a service fee of $3 were also charged. Find the total installment charge.   _____

3. C. B. Dillon purchased a motor bike on the installment plan that was priced to sell for $2,785. The installment plan required a down payment of 15% of the sale price as well as a credit fee of $10, insurance of $4, an application fee of $7.50, and the balance payable in 30 monthly payments of $110 each. Find:
   a. The amount he had to finance. $2,367.25
   b. The total installment charges. $954.25

4. Kim Kelly purchased a used car priced to sell for $2,350. Terms of the sale on the installment plan required 22% of the selling price as a down payment and the balance in 15 equal payments. What amount must Kim finance to purchase the car on the installment plan?   _____

5. A motorboat was advertised for sale at a cash price of $14,780. Installment plan terms were available, which

included a down payment of 35% of the cash price and monthly payments of $300 for 36 months. Find:
- a. The total installment charges. — $1,193.00
- b. The amount the buyer would have to finance to purchase the boat on the installment plan. — $9,607.00

6. Mrs. Allen purchased a rug shampooer on the installment plan that required a down payment of $25 and 20 weekly payments of $10 each. The cash price of the shampooer was advertised as $195.
   - a. What was the amount Mrs. Allen financed to purchase the shampooer on the installment plan? _____
   - b. What were the total installment charges? _____

7. A sporting goods store offered ski equipment for $275 cash or an installment plan that required $40 down payment and the balance in 20 payments of $13 each. Carrying charges of $8.50 plus insurance of $6 and a service charge of $3 were also charged. Find the total installment charges if the ski equipment is purchased on the installment plan. — $42.50

8. The R & S Finance Company charged a $10 service fee, a $15 application fee, and a $7.50 insurance charge on all loans in excess of $1,000. June Wilson decided to purchase an organ on the installment plan, which required 15% of the cash price as a down payment and to borrow the balance from R & S Finance Company. The finance company required 30 monthly payments of $52.50 each. The cash price of the organ was $1,435. Find the total installment charges. _____

9. J. C. Wallace purchased 15 storm windows for his house at a cash price of $27.50 each. The seller offered an installment plan that required 20% of the cash price as a down payment and the balance to be paid in 25 payments of $14 each. A service fee of $5 and a credit fee of $12.50 was also charged. Find:
   - a. The amount that would be financed if purchase was made on the installment plan. — $330.00
   - b. The total installment charges. — $37.50

10. Find the amount a buyer would have to finance on a purchase of merchandise that sold for $2,685.20 on an installment plan that required 27¾% as a down payment and the balance to be paid in equal payments over the next 12 months. _____

2. Methods of calculating interest

   a. When the interest rate is stated in the installment terms, interest is calculated by the simple interest formula. Interest is charged on the amount financed for the life of the loan or for the total installment periods.

   The amount to be repaid by the consumer is the sum of the amount financed plus the interest. This method of calculating interest is called *add-on* interest.

> **Rule 1:** *a.* **TO CALCULATE ADD-ON INTEREST:**
>
> Amount financed × Rate × Time = Interest
>
> *b.* **TO CALCULATE AMOUNT TO BE REPAID:**
>
> Amount financed + Interest = Amount repaid

Step 1. Calculate the amount financed:

Selling price − Down payment = Amount financed

Step 2. Calculate add-on interest:

Amount financed × Rate × Time = Interest

Step 3. Calculate amount to be repaid:

Amount financed + Interest = Repayment

Example 1 The cash price of a refrigerator-freezer was $875. Ms. J. Barton elected to buy the freezer on an installment plan that required a down payment of 15% of the cash price and the balance payable in 24 equal payments. Simple add-on interest of 7% was charged. Find:
  a. The total amount of interest she will pay.
  b. The total amount she will repay.

Step 1. Calculate the amount financed:

$875 × .15 = $131.25 Down payment

Selling price − Down payment = Amount financed
$875.00 − $131.25 = $743.75

Step 2. Calculate add-on interest:

Amount financed × Rate × Time = Interest

$743.75 × .07 × $\frac{24 \text{ months}}{12}$ = $104.13

Step 3. Calculate amount to be repaid:

Amount financed + Interest = Repayment
$743.75 + $104.13 = $847.88

b. When the interest rate is not stated in the installment terms, interest is calculated by Rule 2. It is assumed that if additional installment charges are part of the credit terms, they are included in the amount of the payment, and are considered as interest.

> **Rule 2:** **TO CALCULATE INTEREST WHEN NO INTEREST RATE IS STATED:**
> *a.* **Calculate the amount to be** *repaid:*
>
> Number of payments × Amount of payment = Repayment
>
> *b.* Repayment − Amount financed = Interest

Step 1. Calculate the amount to be repaid:

Number of payments × Amount of payment = Repayment

Step 2. Calculate amount financed:

Selling price − Down payment = Amount financed

Step 3. Calculate amount of interest:

Repayment − Amount financed = Interest

Example 1   F. C. Allen borrowed $1,450 and agreed to repay the loan in 26 weeks by a weekly payment of $60.29. Find:
  a. The amount to be repaid.
  b. The amount of interest that was paid.
Step 1. Calculate the amount to be repaid:

Number of payments × Amount of payment = Repayment
        26   × $60.29   = $1,567.54 (**Ans.** *a*)

Step 2. Calculate amount financed.

Stated in problem = $1,450

Step 3. Calculate interest:

Repayment − Amount financed = Interest
$1,567.54 − $1,450.00   = $117.54 (**Ans.** *b*)

Example 2   Tom Kramer purchased a garden tractor that was priced to sell for $625 on an installment plan. Terms of the sale included a down payment of 20% of the selling price and the balance to be paid in 10 monthly payments of $55.25 each. Find:
  a. The total amount that Mr. Kramer will repay.
  b. The amount of interest that was charged.
Step 1. Calculate the amount to be repaid:

Number of payments × Amount of payment = Repayment
        10   × $55.25   = $552.50 (**Ans.** *a*)

Step 2. Calculate the amount financed:

$625 × .20 = $125.00 Down payment
$625 − $125 = $500.00 Amount financed

Step 3. Calculate amount of interest:

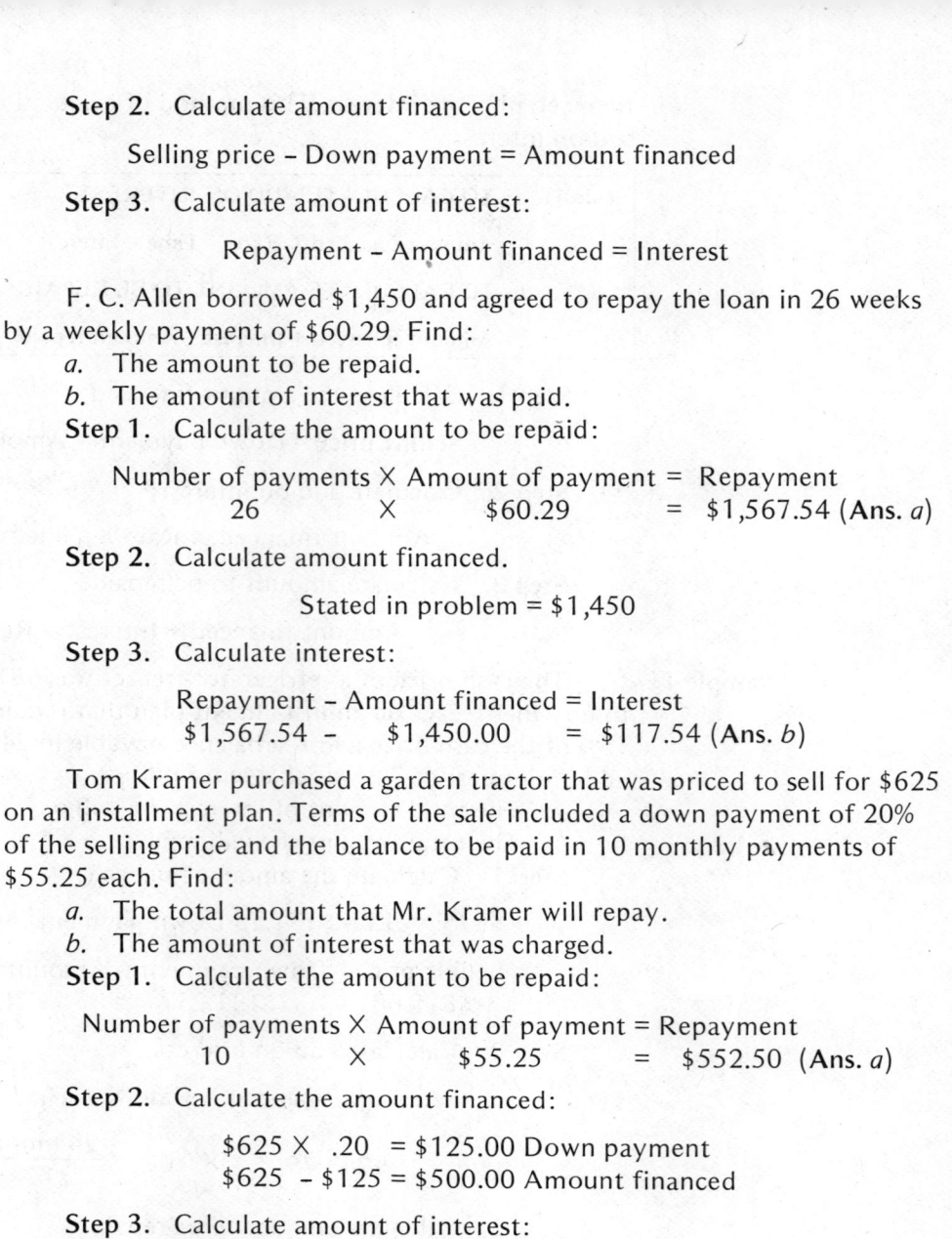

Repayment − Amount financed = Interest
$552.50   − $500.00   = $52.50 (**Ans.** *b*)

Practice exercises

                                                                    Answer

1. An order of merchandise totaled $1,226.75. Terms of the sale required 15% of the selling price as a down payment. The balance was to be paid in 12 monthly payments of $97.50. What was the amount of interest paid? $127.26
2. A washing machine was priced to sell for $205. The installment plan required no down payment and $3 weekly installments for 77 weeks. If the installment plan is elected:
  a. How much was the amount repaid?   _____
  b. What is the amount of interest paid?   _____

3. A washer-dryer was advertised to sell for $575, or 10% of the selling price down and the balance to be paid in 26 weekly payments with add-on interest of 8½%. What amount of interest would the buyer pay? $21.99

4. Find the total amount to be repaid on a loan for $700 payable in 2 years with simple add-on interest of 7¼%.   _____

5. D. W. Haynes borrowed $650 to pay his outstanding bills. He made arrangements to repay the loan in 24 equal monthly payments of $31.25. He also had to pay a credit fee of $5. Find:
    a. The amount of interest he paid. $100.00
    b. Total installment charges. $105.00

6. Ms. C. A. Bradley purchased a used car that was priced to sell for $2,715. She decided to purchase the car on an installment plan that required a 20% down payment and the balance in 24 monthly payments of $110.50. Find:
    a. The amount of interest that was charged.
    b. The total amount she would repay.   _____

7. A living room set was on sale at a price of $1,950 or on an installment plan that required 15% of the sale price as a down payment and 52 weekly payments of $33.60. If the living room set was purchased on the installment plan:
    a. What amount of interest would the buyer pay? $89.70
    b. What amount would be repaid? $1,747.20

8. What amount of interest would be paid on a loan of $1,126.80 that required simple add-on interest of 11¼% for 30 months?   _____

9. Ms. T. Harris had an opportunity to buy the inventory of a bankrupt company for a total of $4,268. She borrowed the money from a bank and agreed to repay the loan in 28 months with simple add-on interest of 10½%. Find:
    a. The amount of interest to be paid. $1,045.66
    b. The total amount to be repaid. $5,313.66

10. Mrs. John Irvine purchased wall-to-wall carpeting for her office that was priced to sell for $11.25 per square yard. She needed 114 square yards to cover the floor space. The carpeting was purchased on an installment plan that required 18% of the sale price as a down payment and the balance payable in 15 months at $76.95 per month.
    a. What amount would be repaid?
    b. What amount of interest would be paid?   _____

3. Calculation of interest rates

The Truth in Lending Law requires all creditors extending consumer credit—including, banks, credit unions, retail stores, gasoline companies, and so on—to notify the consumer of the actual annual interest rate they charge for the use of credit. The law further states that all installment charges must be included in the calculation of the interest rate, even though such charges as credit fees, insurance charges, service fees, and the like, are not listed separately or, in some cases, are paid in cash.

Methods of calculating the annual percentage rate (APR) include:

a. Use of monthly interest rates.
b. Annual percentage rate tables.
c. Annual percentage rate formula.

a. Monthly interest rates

If consumer credit is extended on an open-end or revolving credit account, as do many retail stores, bank credit cards, and credit unions, a monthly interest rate is stated based on the limit of credit used. For example, a monthly interest rate of 1½% may be charged on an unpaid balance up to $500 and 1% per month charged on unpaid balances over $500.

> **Rule 1: TO CALCULATE THE ANNUAL INTEREST RATE:**
> a. Monthly interest rate × 12 = Annual interest rate
> b. Unpaid balance × Monthly rate = Monthly interest

Step 1. Calculate annual interest rate.
Step 2. Calculate monthly interest.

Example 1 George Smith received his monthly gasoline bill, which stated a monthly interest rate of 1½% payable on the unpaid balance of less than $500. Mr. Smith's bill was for $104.95.

a. What was the annual rate of interest charged?
b. What amount of interest would he pay?

Step 1. Calculate annual interest rate:

Monthly rate × 12 = Annual interest rate
.015 × 12 = .18 or 18%   (**Ans.** *a*)

Step 2. Calculate monthly interest:

Monthly rate × Unpaid balance = Monthly interest
.015 × $104.95 = $1.57   (**Ans.** *b*)

b. Annual percentage rate (APR) per table

Regulation Z of the Truth in Lending Law requires all businesses that extend consumer credit by loans or installment accounts that are to be repaid in equal installment payments, to calculate the actual annual percentage rate by use of APR tables. These tables are available from Federal Reserve banks and show the installment charges for $100 borrowed or financed for various periods of time at a variety of interest rates. A portion of a Federal Reserve APR Table is shown on Table 7-1 for use in completing example problems and practice exercises.

> **Rule 2: TO CALCULATE THE APR FROM A TABLE:**
> a. $\dfrac{\text{Total installment charges}}{\text{Amount financed}} \times 100$ = Installment charges per $100
> b. On the number of payment line, locate the installment charges nearest to those calculated in Step *a*.
> c. Refer to top of column to find the APR that applies.

Table 7-1
Annual percentage rate table for monthly payment plans (see instructions for use of tables)

Number of Payments	18.00%	18.25%	18.50%	18.75%	19.00%	19.25%	19.50%	19.75%	20.00%	20.25%	20.50%	20.75%	21.00%	21.25%	21.50%	21.75%
1	1.50	1.52	1.54	1.56	1.58	1.60	1.62	1.65	1.67	1.69	1.71	1.73	1.75	1.77	1.79	1.81
2	2.26	2.29	2.32	2.35	2.38	2.41	2.44	2.48	2.51	2.54	2.57	2.60	2.63	2.66	2.70	2.73
3	3.01	3.06	3.10	3.14	3.18	3.23	3.27	3.31	3.35	3.39	3.44	3.48	3.52	3.56	3.60	3.65
4	3.78	3.83	3.88	3.94	3.99	4.04	4.10	4.15	4.20	4.25	4.31	4.36	4.41	4.47	4.52	4.57
5	4.54	4.61	4.67	4.74	4.80	4.86	4.93	4.99	5.06	5.12	5.18	5.25	5.31	5.37	5.44	5.50
6	5.32	5.39	5.46	5.54	5.61	5.69	5.76	5.84	5.91	5.99	6.06	6.14	6.21	6.29	6.36	6.44
7	6.09	6.18	6.26	6.35	6.43	6.52	6.60	6.69	6.78	6.86	6.95	7.04	7.12	7.21	7.29	7.38
8	6.87	6.96	7.06	7.16	7.26	7.35	7.45	7.55	7.64	7.74	7.84	7.94	8.03	8.13	8.23	8.33
9	7.65	7.76	7.87	7.97	8.08	8.19	8.30	8.41	8.52	8.63	8.84	8.84	8.95	9.06	9.17	9.28
10	8.43	8.55	8.67	8.79	8.91	9.03	9.15	9.27	9.39	9.51	9.63	9.75	9.88	10.00	10.12	10.24
11	9.22	9.35	9.49	9.62	9.75	9.88	10.01	10.14	10.28	10.41	10.54	10.67	10.80	10.94	11.07	11.20
12	10.02	10.16	10.30	10.44	10.59	10.73	10.87	11.02	11.16	11.31	11.45	11.59	11.74	11.88	12.02	12.17
13	10.81	10.97	11.12	11.28	11.43	11.59	11.74	11.90	12.05	12.21	12.36	12.52	12.67	12.83	12.99	13.14
14	11.61	11.78	11.95	12.11	12.28	12.45	12.61	12.78	12.95	13.11	13.28	13.45	13.62	13.79	13.95	14.12
15	12.42	12.59	12.77	12.95	13.13	13.31	13.49	13.67	13.85	14.03	14.21	14.39	14.57	14.75	14.93	15.11
16	13.22	13.41	13.60	13.80	13.99	14.18	14.37	14.56	14.75	14.94	15.13	15.33	15.52	15.71	15.90	16.10
17	14.04	14.24	14.44	14.64	14.85	15.05	15.25	15.46	15.66	15.86	16.07	16.27	16.48	16.68	16.89	17.09
18	14.85	15.07	15.28	15.49	15.71	15.93	16.14	16.36	16.57	16.79	17.01	17.22	17.44	17.66	17.88	18.09
19	15.67	15.90	16.12	16.35	16.58	16.81	17.03	17.26	17.49	17.72	17.95	18.18	18.41	18.64	18.87	19.10
20	16.49	16.73	16.97	17.21	17.45	17.69	17.93	18.17	18.41	18.66	18.90	19.14	19.38	19.63	19.87	20.11
21	17.32	17.57	17.82	18.07	18.33	18.58	18.83	19.09	19.34	19.60	19.85	20.11	20.36	20.62	20.87	21.13
22	18.15	18.41	18.68	18.94	19.21	19.47	19.74	20.01	20.27	20.54	20.81	21.08	21.34	21.61	21.88	22.15
23	18.98	19.26	19.54	19.81	20.09	20.37	20.65	20.93	21.21	21.49	21.77	22.05	22.33	22.61	22.90	23.18
24	19.82	20.11	20.40	20.69	20.98	21.27	21.56	21.86	22.15	22.44	22.74	23.03	23.33	23.62	23.92	24.21
25	20.66	20.96	21.27	21.57	21.87	22.18	22.48	22.79	23.10	23.40	23.71	24.02	24.32	24.63	24.94	25.25
26	21.50	21.82	22.14	22.45	22.77	23.09	23.41	23.73	24.04	24.36	24.68	25.01	25.33	25.65	25.97	26.29
27	22.35	22.68	23.01	23.34	23.67	24.00	24.33	24.67	25.00	25.33	25.67	26.00	26.34	26.67	27.01	27.34
28	23.20	23.55	23.89	24.23	24.58	24.92	25.27	25.61	25.96	26.30	26.65	27.00	27.35	27.70	28.05	28.40
29	24.06	24.41	24.77	25.13	25.49	25.84	26.20	26.56	26.92	27.28	27.64	28.00	28.37	28.73	29.09	29.46
30	24.92	25.29	25.66	26.03	26.40	26.77	27.14	27.52	27.89	28.26	28.64	29.01	29.39	29.77	30.14	30.52

Step 1. Calculate amount financed.
Step 2. Calculate installment charges.
Step 3. Calculate $100 installment charges:

$$\frac{\text{Total installment charges}}{\text{Amount financed}} \times 100 = \text{Installment charges per }\$100$$

Step 4. Locate nearest installment charges on Table 7-1.
Step 5. Locate APR at top of column on Table 7-1.

Example 1 The Bellow Company advertised a sale price of pianos as $1,240. Installment terms included $100 down payment and 10 payments of $125 each. Find the annual percentage rate (APR) by use of Table 7-1.

Step 1. Calculate the amount financed:

Selling price − Down payment = Amount financed
$1,240 − $100 = $1,140

Step 2. Calculate the installment charges:

Repayments − Amount financed = Installment charges
$1,250 ($125 × 10) − $1,140 = $110

Step 3. Calculate $100 installment charges:

$$\frac{\text{Installment charges}}{\text{Amount financed}} \times 100 = \text{Installment charges per }\$100$$

$$\frac{\$110}{\$1,140} \times 100 = \$9.65$$

7 CONSUMER CREDIT / 177

Step 4. Locate installment charges on Table 7-1.

Line 10 = $9.63 nearest to 9.65

Step 5. Locate APR rate at top of column:

9.63 = 20.5% Annual percentage rate

Example 2 L. C. Monty purchased an acre of undeveloped land for $3,085. A down payment of 25% of the selling price was borrowed from the bank and the balance to be paid in 24 months. Simple add-on interest of 11¼% was charged, as was a service charge of $7.50, a credit fee of $5 and an insurance charge of $9.50. Find the APR by use of Table 7-1.

Step 1. Calculate the amount financed:

Selling price − Down payment = Amount financed
$3,085.00 − $771.25 = $2,313.75

Step 2. Calculate installment charges:

$$\$2,313.75 \times .1125 \times \frac{24}{12} = \$520.59 \text{ Interest}$$

Additional Charges:

Service charge	$ 7.50
Credit fee	5.00
Insurance charge	9.50
	22.00

Total installment charges: $542.59

Step 3. Calculate $100 installment charges:

$$100 \times \frac{\text{Total installment charges}}{\text{Amount financed}} = \frac{\$542.59}{\$2,313.75} = 23.45$$

Step 4. Locate installment charges on Table 7-1:

Line 24 = 23.33 − 23.62
23.45 is nearer 23.33

Step 5. Locate APR at top of column:

23.33 = 21% the Annual percentage rate

c. **Annual percentage rate (APR) formula**

Annual percentage rate tables may not be available to consumers. However, the approximate APR may be calculated by the use of the APR formula, which will enable the consumer to compare the cost of credit among the various sources of credit. The lower the APR the less costly the use of credit. Note that add-on interest rates may be used to calculate the installment charges but cannot be used as the annual percentage rate that is charged. All fees and additional credit charges must be included in calculating the APR, even though some may be paid in cash.

> **Rule 3: TO CALCULATE THE APR BY FORMULA:**
>
> $$\frac{2 \times \text{Number of payments in 1 year*} \times \text{Interest}}{\text{Selling price or amount financed} \times (\text{Number of required payments} + 1)} = \text{APR}$$
>
> *Use: 52 if weekly payments are required,
> 12 if monthly payments are required,
> 4 if quarterly payments are required,
> 1 if annual payments are required.

Step 1. Calculate the amount financed:

Selling price − Down payment = Amount financed

Step 2. Calculate interest, include any additional credit charges.

Step 3. Substitute data in the APR formula.

Example 1   A. R. Downs purchased a boat for $3,875 and agreed to pay $400 down and the balance in 24 equal monthly payments of $175. Find the annual percentage rate that was charged.

Step 1. Calculate the amount financed:

Selling price − Down payment = Amount financed
$3,875   − $400   = $3,475

Step 2. Calculate interest:

Number of payments × Amount of payment = Repayments
          24   × $175   = $4,200
          Less amount financed   −3,475
          Total interest $ 725

Step 3. Substitute data in APR formula:

$$\frac{2 \times \text{Number of payments in 1 year} \times \text{Interest}}{\text{Selling price or Amount financed} \times (\text{Required payments} + 1)} = \text{APR}$$

$$\frac{2 \times 12 \times \$725}{\$3,475 \times (24 + 1)} = .2003 = 20.03\% \text{ APR}$$

Example 2   Jean Martin purchased bedroom curtains and bedspreads that were priced to sell for $206.75 on an installment plan. Terms of the plan included 12% down and the balance in 50 equal weekly payments. Simple add-on interest of 9½% plus $3.50 carrying charges were also charged.

Step 1. Calculate amount financed:

Selling price − Down payment = Amount financed
$206.75   − $24.81   = $181.94

Step 2. Calculate interest:

$\$181.94 \times .095 \times \frac{50}{52}$ = $16.62
Carrying charges   3.50
Total installment charges = $20.12

7 CONSUMER CREDIT / 179

Step 3. Substitute data in APR formula:

$$\frac{2 \times \text{Number of payments in 1 year} \times \text{Interest}}{\text{Amount financed} \times (\text{Required payments} + 1)} = \text{APR}$$

$$\frac{2 \times 52 \times 20.12}{\$181.94 \times (50 + 1)} = 22.55\% \text{ APR}$$

Practice exercises

	Answer

Use the APR formula unless the problem states to use Table 7-1.

1. A portable organ was advertised to sell for $750 or on an installment plan that required a down payment of 12½% with the balance payable over 18 months at $42.61 per month. The organ was purchased on the installment plan. What was the APR? (See Table 7-1.)   **20.25%**

2. Find the APR paid on a loan for $500 to be repaid in 12 months at $46.17 per month. There were no installment charges except the interest. (See Table 7-1.)   _____

3. Marion Keller received a monthly bill from the S & C Department Store that showed a prior balance of $312.50. Interest on this balance was 1¼% per month.
   a. What annual rate of interest was charged?   **15%**
   b. What amount of interest would she pay on the prior balance for the month?   **$3.91**

4. Fred Zeeley had a revolving charge account at the F & T Auto Supply Company. He received a monthly bill that showed a prior balance of $820.65. Interest for this balance was calculated at 2% per month.
   a. What annual rate interest was he paying?   _____
   b. What amount of interest would he pay on the current bill?   _____

5. R. C. Cullen purchased a lathe for the plant at a cost of $26,945. Credit terms included a 20% down payment and 36 monthly payments of $861.50. No other installment charges were payable. To compare the cost of the credit to other plans available, Ms. Cullen calculated the annual percentage rate by use of the APR formula. What APR would this plan require?   **28.46%**

6. Mr. James wanted to purchase a bedroom set. Store 1 offered a set at a selling price of $1,285 cash or an installment plan that required 15% down and $62.75 per month for 20 months and an insurance charge of $9.85 as well as carrying charges of $7.50. Store 2 offered a set for $1,095 cash or an installment plan that required a 10% down payment and $64.25 per month for 18 months. A credit fee of $8 and carrying charges of $10.50 were also payable. To compare the cost of credit offered by the two stores, Mr. James calculated

the annual percentage rate for both plans. Using the APR formula, find the APR charged by each store.

7. Anne Norris had a charge account with the Ace Sporting Goods Store. She received the monthly bill which showed a prior balance of $185.65. The store charged 1½% interest for balance under $500.
   a. What annual percent rate did the store charge? **18%**
   b. What amount of interest would be charged on the current bill? **$2.78**

8. The Dayton Book Supply Company sent the Kelly Book Store a monthly bill with an unpaid balance of $785.20. Monthly interest was charged at the rate of 1½% for unpaid balances of $500 or less and 2% for unpaid balances over $500.
   a. What annual percentage rate would Kelly Book Store pay on the current bill?
   b. What amount of interest would they pay?

9. An item of merchandise that was priced to sell for $495 was purchased on an installment plan that required a down payment of 8% and the balance payable in 20 equal monthly payments. Simple add-on interest of 12% was charged. No other charges were payable. Find the annual percentage rate that was charged, by use of Table 7-1. **21.75%**

10. Using the APR Table 7-1, find the annual percentage rate on a purchase of $945.95 on an installment plan that required 17½% down payment and the balance payable in 15 equal monthly payments. Simple add-on interest of 10.5% was charged. No other installment charges were payable.

11. R. P. Thomas purchased a set of electric tools and workbench for $312 on an installment plan. Credit terms included a down payment of 14% of the selling price and $5.00 per week for 60 weeks. No additional installment costs were payable. Using the APR formula, what APR would be paid? **20.13%**

12. Lois Grange purchased supplies for $816.50 on an installment plan that required no down payment. The amount due was payable over 16 months with simple add-on interest of 9.75%. Insurance charges of $14.75 and a credit fee of $9.20 were charged. Using Table 7-1, find the annual percentage rate that was charged.

4. **Installment payments**

When an installment payment plan is offered the customers of a business, it is necessary to determine the amount of the installment payment. Many businesses include the interest as well as additional installment charges, such as carrying charges, service fees, and insurance, in calculating the monthly or weekly installment payment. In some transactions the consumer may be required to pay certain fees in cash at the time of purchase.

You can assume in the following example problems and practice exercises that all installment charges are included in calculating the installment payments.

We will concentrate our review on the calculation of (*a*) installment payments when simple add-on interest is part of the installment terms, and (*b*) the calculation of amortized installment payments and the amortized schedule.

Rule 1: TO CALCULATE INSTALLMENT PAYMENTS WHEN SIMPLE ADD-ON INTEREST IS CHARGED:

$$\frac{\text{Amount financed} + \text{Total installment charges}}{\text{Number of required payments}} = \text{Installment payment}$$

Step 1. Calculate amount financed:

Selling price − Down payment = Amount financed

Step 2. Calculate interest + other installment charges.

Step 3. Substitute data in the installment payment formula.

Example 1   W. C. Bellows offered a dining room set priced to sell for $2,150 on an installment plan that required 15% down and the balance in 18 equal monthly payments. Add-on simple interest of 7% was charged as well as a $5.00 credit fee, $7.50 for insurance, and a $10.00 application fee. Find the monthly installment payment the buyer will pay.

Step 1. Calculate the amount financed:

Selling price − Down payment = Amount financed
$2,150.00 − $322.50 (.15 × $2,150) = $1,827.50

Step 2. Calculate interest and other installment charges:

$$\$1{,}827.50 \times .07 \times \frac{18}{12} = \$191.89$$

Credit fee	=	5.00
Insurance	=	7.50
Application fee	=	10.00

Total installment charges = $214.39

Step 3. Substitute data in the installment payment formula:

$$\frac{\text{Amount financed} + \text{Installment charges}}{\text{Number of required payments}} = \text{Installment payment}$$

$$\frac{\$1{,}827.50 + \$214.39}{18} = \$113.44 \text{ Monthly installment payment}$$

Example 2   Mrs. James Walls purchased merchandise that was priced to sell for $303.50 on the installment plan. Terms of the plan required a down payment of 10% of the selling price and the balance payable in 52 weekly payments. Simple add-on interest of 10¼% was charged, as was a carrying charge of $8.50 and insurance of $11.75. What weekly installment payment would she make?

Step 1. Calculate the amount financed:

Selling price − Down payment = Amount financed
$303.50 − $30.35 (303.50 × .10) = $273.15

Step 2. Calculate interest and other installment charges:

$$\$273.15 \times .1025 \times \frac{52}{52} = \$28.00$$

Carrying charges = 8.50
Insurance = 11.75
Total installment charges $48.25

Step 3. Substitute data in installment payment formula:

$$\frac{\text{Amount financed} + \text{Installment charges}}{\text{Number of required payments}} = \text{Installment payments}$$

$$\frac{\$273.15 + \$48.25}{52} = \$6.18 \text{ Weekly installment payment}$$

Amortized installment payments

When installment payments include interest calculated on simple add-on interest, the consumer is paying interest on the total amount financed for the life of the installment plan, even though they do not have use of the money for the full credit period. Amortized installment plans provide for the application of a portion of each payment to interest on only the unpaid balance of the debt, and the remainder of the payment is applied to the reduction of the debt. Each payment reduces the amount of interest as well as the amount of the unpaid debt. Such payment plans use *annual* rates of interest rather than simple add-on interest rates.

Rule 2:   TO CALCULATE AMORTIZED INSTALLMENT PAYMENTS:
   a. Calculate the amount financed.
   b. Convert "time" to the number of months involved in the life of the debt.
   c. Convert the annual rate of interest to a monthly rate.
   d. Select factor from amortized table.
   e. Amount financed × Table factor = Monthly payment.

Step 1. Calculate amount financed:

Selling price − Down payment = Amount financed

Step 2. Convert "time" to months:

Step 3. Convert annual rate of interest to monthly rate:

$$\frac{\text{Rate of interest}}{.12} = \text{Monthly interest rate}$$

Step 4. Locate *factor* on the number of payment line in the column for the monthly interest rate.

Step 5.

Amount financed × Table factor = Monthly payment

Example 1   C. J. Webb purchased a dining room set for $1,600. Terms of the sale required a down payment of $400 and the balance to be paid in 2 years with an annual rate of 8% interest. Find the monthly payments Mr. Webb will pay.

Table 7–2
Amortization table

Month	1/2%	3/5%	7/12%	2/3%	3/4%	4/5%	5/6%	1%	1 1/3%	1 1/2%
1	1.00500	1.00600	1.00583	1.00666	1.00750	1.00800	1.00834	1.01000	1.01333	1.01500
2	.50375	.50450	.50438	.50501	.50563	.50601	.50626	.50751	.51002	.51128
3	.33667	.33734	.33723	.33779	.33835	.33868	.33891	.34002	.34226	.34338
4	.25313	.25376	.25366	.25418	.25471	.25502	.25523	.25628	.25839	.25945
5	.20301	.20361	.20351	.20402	.20452	.20483	.20503	.20604	.20807	.20909
6	.16959	.17018	.17009	.17058	.17107	.17136	.17156	.17255	.17453	.17553
7	.14573	.14631	.14621	.14669	.14718	.14747	.14766	.14863	.15058	.15156
8	.12783	.12840	.12830	.12878	.12926	.12954	.12973	.13069	.13262	.13358
9	.11391	.11447	.11438	.11485	.11532	.11560	.11579	.11674	.11865	.11961
10	.10277	.10333	.10324	.10370	.10417	.10445	.10464	.10558	.10748	.10843
11	.09366	.09421	.09412	.09459	.09505	.09533	.09552	.09645	.09834	.09929
12	.08607	.08662	.08653	.08699	.08745	.08773	.08792	.08885	.09073	.09168
13	.07964	.08019	.08010	.08056	.08102	.08130	.08149	.08242	.08429	.08524
14	.07414	.07469	.07459	.07505	.07551	.07579	.07597	.07690	.07878	.07972
15	.06936	.06991	.06982	.07028	.07074	.07101	.07120	.07212	.07400	.07494
16	.06519	.06574	.06564	.06610	.06656	.06684	.06702	.06795	.06982	.07077
17	.06151	.06205	.06196	.06242	.06287	.06315	.06333	.06426	.06613	.06708
18	.05823	.05878	.05869	.05914	.05960	.05987	.06001	.06098	.06286	.06381
19	.05530	.05585	.05576	.05621	.05667	.05694	.05713	.05805	.05993	.06088
20	.05267	.05321	.05312	.05357	.05403	.05431	.05449	.05542	.05729	.05825
21	.05028	.05083	.05073	.05119	.05165	.05192	.05211	.05303	.05491	.05587
22	.04811	.04866	.04857	.04902	.04948	.04975	.04994	.05086	.05275	.05370
23	.04614	.04668	.04659	.04704	.04750	.04777	.04796	.04889	.05077	.05173
24	.04432	.04486	.04477	.04523	.04569	.04596	.04615	.04707	.04896	.04992
25	.04265	.04320	.04310	.04356	.04402	.04429	.04448	.04541	.04730	.04826
26	.04111	.04166	.04156	.04202	.04248	.04275	.04294	.04387	.04577	.04673
27	.03969	.04023	.04014	.04059	.04105	.04133	.04151	.04245	.04435	.04532
28	.03836	.03891	.03881	.03927	.03973	.04001	.04019	.04113	.04303	.04400
29	.03713	.03767	.03758	.03804	.03850	.03877	.03896	.03990	.04181	.04278
30	.03598	.03652	.03643	.03689	.03735	.03763	.03781	.03875	.04066	.04164
31	.03490	.03545	.03536	.03581	.03627	.03655	.03674	.03768	.03959	.04057
32	.03390	.03444	.03435	.03481	.03527	.03555	.03573	.03667	.03859	.03958
33	.03295	.03349	.03340	.03386	.03432	.03460	.03479	.03573	.03766	.03864
34	.03206	.03260	.03251	.03297	.03343	.03371	.03390	.03484	.03677	.03776
35	.03122	.03176	.03167	.03213	.03259	.03287	.03306	.03400	.03594	.03693
36	.03042	.03097	.03088	.03134	.03180	.03208	.03227	.03321	.03516	.03615

Step 1. Calculate the amount financed:

Selling price − Down payment = Amount financed
$1,600 − $400 = $1,200

Step 2. Convert years to months:

2 years = 2 × 12 = 24 months

Step 3. Convert annual rate of interest to a monthly rate:

$$\frac{.08}{.12} = \frac{2}{3} \% \text{ per month}$$

Step 4. Locate factor on table:

Line 24, column $\frac{2}{3}$% = .04523

Step 5.

Amount financed × factor = Monthly payment
$1,200 × .04523 = $54.28

Amortized installment schedules

Banks, savings and loan companies, and finance companies will provide the consumer with a schedule of amortized payments, which indicates the reduction of the debt and the amount of interest that is applied each payment period.

> **Rule 3: CALCULATIONS OF AN AMORTIZATION SCHEDULE:**
> a. Calculate monthly payments as outlined in Rule 2.
> b. Calculate the interest on the unpaid balance for each payment period.
> c. Deduct interest from monthly payment and deduct the remainder from the unpaid balance.

Step 1. Calculate the monthly amortized payment (see Rule 2).
Step 2.

Unpaid balance × Monthly interest rate = Monthly interest

Step 3.

Monthly payment − Monthly interest = Monthly reduction in debt

Step 4.

Unpaid balance − Reduction in debt = Current unpaid balance

Step 5. Calculate interest on the current unpaid balance for each payment. Continue this procedure until debt is paid.

Example 1 The Thomas Manufacturing Company borrowed $3,600 from the local bank and agreed to repay the loan in 6 monthly payments at the annual rate of 9%. Develop an amortization schedule for the first 4 payments.

Step 1. Calculate the monthly amortized payment:

$$\text{Amount financed} = \$3{,}600$$
$$\text{Time} = 6 \text{ Monthly payments}$$
$$\text{Monthly interest rate} = \frac{.09}{.12} = \frac{3}{4}\%$$

Line 6 on table: Column $\frac{3}{4}\%$ = .17107 Factor

$3,600 × .17107 = $615.85 Monthly payment

Step 2.

Unpaid balance × Monthly interest rate = Monthly interest

$$\$3{,}600 \times \frac{3}{4}\% \ (.0075) = \$27.00$$

Step 3.

Monthly payment − Monthly interest = Reduction in debt
  $615.85   − $27.00   = $588.85

Step 4.

Unpaid balance − Reduction in debt = Current unpaid balance
  $3,600   − $588.85   = $3,011.15

Step 5. Follow Steps 2, 3, and 4 for each of the payments. The current unpaid balance is used to calculate monthly interest.

A completed amortization schedule for the first 4 payments would be:

Amortization schedule

Payment number	Unpaid balance	Amount of payment		Interest ¾%		Reduction of debt
1	$3,600.00 - 588.85	$615.85	-	$27.00	=	$588.85
2	$3,011.15 - 593.27	$615.85	-	$22.58*	=	$593.27
3	$2,417.88 - 597.72	$615.85	-	$18.13†	=	$597.72
4	$1,820.16 - 602.20	$615.85	-	$13.65‡	=	$602.20

$1,217.96 Unpaid balance after the 4th payment

* 2d payment interest: $3,011.15 X .0075 = $22.58
† 3d payment interest: $2,417.88 X .0075 = $18.13
‡ 4th payment interest: $1,820.16 X .0075 = $13.65

Practice exercises

Answer

1. Calculate the monthly payments for loans that included simple add-on interest:
   a. Loan for $1,800; simple interest of 8% for 2 years. — $87.00
   b. Loan for $1,200; simple interest at 9% for 18 months. — $75.67

2. Ms. R. Brown purchased a new swimming pool for $6,300. Installment terms included $1,500 down payment and the balance in 3 years at an annual rate of 10% interest. What is the amortized monthly payment? (Use Table 7-2.) — _____

3. Carol Brown purchased a used car for $2,500. Terms of the sale required a down payment of $500 and the balance to be paid over a 3-year period with 7% annual interest. Find the amortized monthly payment. (Use Table 7-2.) — $61.76

4. Sally Bean bought a snowmobile for $2,400. She made a down payment of $800 and agreed to pay the balance over 2½ years at 9% simple add-on interest. Find the monthly payment she will pay. — _____

5. The advertised price of an item was $425, or, if purchased on the installment plan, a 15% down payment and 15 monthly payments with add-on interest of 9½%. What monthly payment would the buyer pay on the installment plan? — $26.94

6. Ms. A. C. Thomas purchased merchandise totaling $1,226.75. She agreed to pay 12½% of the purchase price as a down payment and the balance in 1½ years at an annual interest rate of 9%. Using Table 7-2 find the monthly payment. — _____

7. R. W. Smalley borrowed $1,500 at 12% annual interest for 10 months. What amount is the unpaid balance of the debt after the 5th payment? — $768.68

8. Prepare an amortization schedule for the first 4 payments on a loan for $500 with annual interest of 12% payable in 10 monthly payments. What is the unpaid balance at the end of the 4th payment? _____

9. A refrigerator-freezer was advertised to sell for $825 on an installment plan that required an 8% down payment and the balance payable over 2½ years at an annual interest rate of 16%. Find the monthly payments using Table 7–2. $30.86

10. An item of merchandise was offered for sale at a price of $950. An installment plan was available which required no down payment. Add-on simple interest of 11% was charged, with 40 weekly payments for the balance due. Find the amount of the weekly payments. _____

11. A used car was purchased for $2,050 on an installment plan that required 14% of the selling price as a down payment and the balance in 24 equal payments. Add-on simple 11¼% interest was charged, as was a credit fee of $9, insurance of $14.50, and carrying charges of $6.50. What will be the monthly payments? $91.24

12. Joan Carter purchased a fur coat on an installment plan that required a down payment of 20% of the selling price and the balance in 60 weekly payments. The selling price of the coat was $1,975. Add-on simple interest of 12% was charged, as well as $16.20 for insurance and carrying charges of $11.50. Find the weekly payments she will pay. _____

13. Terry Whitefield purchased a motorcycle on an installment plan that required a down payment of 20% of the selling price, which was $2,175. Annual interest of 16% was charged and the balance due was amortized over 2½ years. What were the monthly payments? $70.75

14. Prepare a schedule of amortized payments on a loan of $1,500 with 12% annual interest that is to be repaid over 1½ years. What is the amount still due after the 4th payment? _____

OPEN-END CREDIT PLANS

Retail stores, bank credit cards, and gasoline credit cards are examples of open-end credit plans. Such plans are also known as "revolving credit accounts."

Open-end credit plans usually offer the consumer a choice of payment plans. If the consumer pays the full amount due upon receipt of the bill, no finance charge or minimum payment is applicable. If, however, payment is any amount less than the full payment, a monthly finance charge and a minimum payment is usually required by the creditor. Our review will include the calculations the creditor makes to determine the balance due on open-end credit accounts.

The finance charge may be stated as a monthly rate, such as 1½% of the unpaid balances of less than $500 and 1% on unpaid balances in excess of $500, or as a flat amount regardless of the balance of the account. The amount of minimum payment also differs among creditors of open-end credit accounts. The minimum payment is usually stated as a rate of the unpaid balance or an amount such as $15, $10, and so on, whichever is higher.

In the example problems and practice exercises, we will use the method frequently applied by creditors of deducting any payment from the beginning balance to determine the balance to which the finance charge is to be applied.

> **Rule 1: TO CALCULATE THE AMOUNT DUE:**
> a. When the full amount due is paid.
> b. No finance charge or minimum payment is applicable.

Example 1 Mrs. James Bolin had a charge account with the Fashion Dress Shop. The shop charged 1½% finance charges and a minimum payment charge of $10 if the unpaid balance was less than $500. Mrs. Bolin purchased a dress for $82.90 during the current month. There was no beginning balance. Find the balance due on her account.

Step 1.

Beginning balance	$00.00
Finance charge	0.00
Minimum payment	10.00
Purchase	82.90

Step 2.

Balance due is $82.90
Minimum payment is $10.00

> **Rule 2: TO CALCULATE THE MINIMUM PAYMENT:**
> a. Beginning balance × Minimum rate = Percent minimum payment
> b. Compare percent minimum payment to dollar minimum payment. The greater amount is payable.

Step 1. Calculate the minimum percent payment:

Beginning balance × Minimum rate = Percent minimum payment

Step 2. Compare percent minimum payment and the dollar minimum. Whichever amount is greater is payable.

Example 1 Richard Dawson received a bill from the T & W Gasoline Company that required a minimum payment of 25% or $10, whichever is greater. The bill showed a beginning balance of $62.80. No payments or additional purchases were made during the credit period. What minimum payment will Mr. Dawson be required to make?

Step 1. Calculate the percent minimum payment:

Beginning balance × Rate = Percent minimum payment
$62.80 × .25 = $15.70

Step 2. Compare percent minimum payment to dollar minimum:

Percent minimum payment = $15.70
Dollar minimum payment = $10.00

Step 3. Percent minimum payment $15.70 is greater and due for payment.

Example 2   Mrs. Ann Cullen had a revolving credit account with the J & C Department Store. Her account had a beginning balance of $32.50. The store required a minimum payment of 10% or $10, whichever is greater. What minimum payment would Mrs. Cullen pay?

Step 1. Calculate the percent minimum payment:

Beginning balance × Rate = Percent minimum payment
$32.50   × .10 = $3.25

Step 2. Compare percent minimum payment with dollar minimum:

Percent minimum payment = $ 3.25
Dollar minimum payment = $10.00

Dollar minimum payment of $10 is payable.

Rule 3: TO CALCULATE THE FINANCE CHARGE:

Beginning balance − Payments × Rate = Finance charge

Step 1. Calculate the unpaid balance:

Beginning balance − Payments = Unpaid balance

Step 2. Calculate the applicable finance charge:

Unpaid balance × Applicable rate = Finance charge

Example 1   R. C. Fellows received the monthly bill from the Merit Credit Card Company. The beginning balance of his account was $186.70. The company required a finance charge of 1½% on unpaid balances of less than $500. Mr. Fellows had made a payment of $75. What finance charge would the company make?

Step 1. Calculate the unpaid balance:

Beginning balance − Payment = Unpaid balance
$186.70   − $75.00 = $111.70

Step 2. Calculate the finance charge:

Unpaid balance × Rate = Finance charge
$111.70   × .015 = $1.68

$1.68 would be charged on current bill.

Rule 4: TO CALCULATE TOTAL AMOUNT DUE:

Beginning balance
− Payment (minimum or actual payment)
+ Finance charge
+ Additional purchases
Current account balance

Step 1. Calculate the applicable minimum payment.
Step 2. Calculate the finance charge.
Step 3. Add all purchases made in the current credit period.
Step 4. Complete arithmetic in the amount due formula.

Example 1   Marion Oman had an open-end credit account with the Swanson Credit Card Company. The beginning balance of her account was $516.20. A minimum payment of $25 or 15% of the balance was required. A finance charge

7 CONSUMER CREDIT / 189

of 1½% on unpaid balances of less than $500 and 1% on balances in excess of $500. During the credit period, Ms. Oman purchased merchandise for $11.90, $31.50, and $19.45. Find the balance of her account at the end of the current period.

Step 1. Calculate the applicable minimum payment:

Beginning balance × Rate = Percent minimum payment
$516.20 × .15 = $77.43

Dollar Minimum payment = $25.00
Percent minimum payment of $77.43 is payable.

Step 2. Calculate finance charge:

Unpaid balance × Rate = Finance charge
$516.20 − 77.43 × .015 = $438.77
$438.77 × .015 = $6.58

Step 3. Add all purchases:

$11.90 + $31.50 + $19.45 = $62.85

Step 4. Complete the arithmetic of the amount due formula:

Beginning balance	$516.20
− Minimum payment	− 77.43
Unpaid balance	$438.77
Finance charge $438.77 × .015	= + 6.58
Purchases	+ 62.85
Account balance	$508.20

Practice exercises

Answer

1. Richard Lee's bill at Hermann's at the beginning of December was $275. During the month he purchased $105 additional merchandise and paid the required minimum of 10% or $10, whichever was greater. A finance charge of 2% on unpaid balances of less than $500 was charged. What was the balance of his account at the end of December? $357.45

2. Ms. Jean Cann had a revolving charge account at the Fowler Shop. The beginning balance of the account was $75. During the month she purchased $125 worth of merchandise and paid the required minimum payment of $10 or 15%, whichever was greater. A finance charge of 1½% of unpaid balances of less than $500 was charged. What was the amount due on the bill received at the end of the month?   _____

3. Jan Crane had an open-end credit account at Lacy's Department Store. The store required a minimum payment of $15 or 15% of unpaid balances of less than $500. Finance charges included 2¼% on unpaid balances of less

than $500. The beginning balance of the account was $410. No additional purchases were made during the credit period and the account was paid in full at the end of the credit period. What amount was paid? $410

4. Mary Smith had an open-end charge account at the S & C Department Store. Her account showed a beginning balance of $90. A finance charge of 2% was charged on unpaid balances of less than $500. A minimum payment of 15% of the unpaid balance was payable. She made a payment of $39 during the month and purchased additional merchandise for $65.95. What was the amount of her bill at the end of the month?   _____

5. J. T. Walker received the monthly bill for $216.80 from the Shell and Shell Company on September 1. On September 12 the minimum payment, which was 20% of the beginning balance, was paid. A finance charge of 2% was charged on the unpaid balance. Additional purchases included: $52.50, $12.95, and $27.90. What was the balance of the account on October 1? $270.26

6. J. T. Flanders received a bill for $101.60 from the Newton Gasoline Company. The company required a 1½% finance charge on unpaid balances of less than $500 and a minimum payment of $15 or 15%, whichever is greater. The required minimum was paid and additional purchases totaling $56.40 were made.
   a. What was the amount of the payment?   _____
   b. What was the balance of the account at the beginning of the following month?   _____

7. Mrs. James Hampton received a bill from a local department store that had a beginning balance of $619. The store required a finance charge of 1½% on unpaid balances of less than $500 and 1% on unpaid balances in excess of $500. A payment of $85.50 had been made. What was the amount of finance charge the store would make? $5.34

8. The A & W Sporting Goods Store sent its monthly bill to the Seymour Gym with a beginning balance of $416. A & W required a minimum payment of 22% of the unpaid balance and a monthly finance charge of 1½% on balances less than $500. The gym had purchased merchandise for $30 and paid $175 on account. What was the balance of the bill they received?   _____

9. The MacDowell Department Store was calculating the monthly bill for a customer. The beginning balance was $311.80. The customer had made a payment of $65 and had purchased additional merchandise for $119.40. The store charged a finance charge of 1½% on unpaid balances of less than $500 and 1% on balances in excess of $500. The required minimum payment was $15 or 15% of the unpaid balance. What was the amount of the bill they sent the customer? $369.90

10. Ms. H. W. Webb had an open-end credit account with the local garage. On August 1 the balance in the account was $709.80. Charges for the month included $95.20 and $114.60. Ms. Webb had paid the required minimum of 20% of the unpaid balance. The garage also made a finance charge of 1½% on unpaid balances of less than $500 and 1% on unpaid balances in excess of $500.
    a. What minimum payment was paid? _____
    b. What was the balance of the bill received on August 31? _____

Review problems

		Answer
1.	An item was on sale at a cash price of $400 or on an installment plan that required 6 monthly payments of $80 each. A credit fee of $5, insurance of $2.50, and an application fee of $7.50 was charged. Find the total installment charges.	$95.00
2.	An item was on sale for $565 cash or $50 down payment and the balance to be paid in 15 equal monthly payments of $38.50. A credit fee of $5, insurance premium of $6.50 and an application fee of $2.50 were also charged. Find the total installment charges.	_____
3.	A combination washer-dryer was on sale for $610. Installment arrangements included a 20% down payment and 10 monthly payments of $54.75 each. Find:	
	a. The amount that was financed.	$488.00
	b. The amount of interest that was paid.	$59.50
4.	The cash price of a stove was $280. The seller required 10% down and 18 equal monthly payments to purchase the stove on the installment plan. Add-on interest of 10% was charged. Find:	
	a. The installment charges.	_____
	b. Monthly payment.	_____
5.	Find the monthly payments for each of the following loans:	
	a. Loan for $1,500; add-on interest of 7%; term of the loan was 2½ years.	$58.75
	b. Loan for $900; add-on interest of 3%; term of the loan, 9 months.	$102.25
6.	Sue Allen borrowed $1,450 and agreed to repay the loan in 26 weeks by a payment of $60.29 each week. What was the amount of interest paid?	_____
7.	Mr. J. Burk arranged to pay 30 equal payments to repay a loan of $1,200 of $41.75 each week. Calculate the annual percentage rate he paid, (using the APR formula).	14.68%
8.	The Gray Home Furniture Store advertised carpeting for $8.75 per square yard. A customer purchased 63 square yards of the carpeting and agreed to pay 12% of the selling price as a down payment and the balance in 12 monthly installments of $50. Using the APR formula, find the APR that was charged?	_____
9.	Find the monthly payment Kay Holland will pay on the purchase of a boat that sold for $12,800 on an installment plan that required a down payment of 15% of the

7 CONSUMER CREDIT / 193

selling price, an annual interest rate of 10%, and was due in 3 years. (Use Table 7-2.) $351.10

10. Find the monthly payment on a loan for $2,500 to be repaid in 36 months with add-on interest of 11.5%.   _____

11. What amount is still due after the third payment on a loan in the amount of $980 with an annual interest rate of 9%? Monthly payments were to be made over a period of 1½ years. (Prepare an amortization schedule.) $825.67

12. The W & S Department Store sent Mr. Edwards a bill on July 1 that had a beginning balance of $325.50. The store required a minimum payment of $15 or 15%, whichever was greater, as well as a finance charge of 1¼% of the unpaid balance. Mr. Edwards paid the minimum payment but made no additional purchases during the month. What was the balance of his account on August 1?   _____

13. Mrs. John Haddon received a bill from the Gaylord Department Store that showed a beginning balance of $119.45. The store required a minimum payment of $10 or 10% of the beginning balance, whichever was the greater. There was also a monthly finance charge of 1¼% on unpaid balances of less than $500. Find the balance of Mrs. Haddon's account at the end of the credit period if she paid the minimum payment and made additional purchases of $19.95, $37.50, and $26.85. $193.14

14. An item sold for $1,300 on an installment plan that required 12½% of the selling price as a down payment, with the balance to be paid in 12 monthly payments of $129.50 each. The seller also charged a $15 credit investigation fee, a $5 insurance premium, and an application fee of $7.50. Find the total installment charges.   _____

15. Ms. I. Shelling purchased merchandise for a total of $1,237.75. She agreed to pay a down payment of $500 and the balance in 15 months with simple add-on interest at a rate of 9¼%. Find:
   a. The amount of interest paid. $85.30
   b. Amount of the monthly payment. $54.87

16. J. T. Stewart borrowed $7,850 to pay off the mortgage on his store. Agreement was made to repay the loan in monthly payments over the next 3 years at an annual rate of interest of 8%. Find:
   a. The monthly payment that will be made.   _____
   b. The amount still due after the 4th payment.   _____
    (Use an amortization schedule.)

17. M & J Manufacturing Company purchased merchandise for $4,846. Terms of the sale included a down payment of $1,000 and the balance to be paid in 2½ years at an annual interest rate of 9%. Find the amount of the monthly payment. (Use Table 7-2.) $143.65

18. What is the APR on a loan for $375 that was to be

repaid in 10 monthly payments of $43? (Use the APR formula.)

19. L. O. Pelly borrowed $2,500 that was to be repaid in 2½ years with annual interest of 6%. Using Table 7-2, find:
    a. The monthly payment. — $89.95
    b. The amount of interest that was paid. — $198.50

20. Ms. Stewart purchased a stereo that was on sale for $675. The installment plan terms required a 10% down payment and the balance to be paid in 10 months. The annual interest rate was 10%. Find the monthly payment that would be paid on the installment arrangements. (Use Table 7-2.)

21. The Keller Company offered an installment plan that required a 15% down payment and the balance to be paid in 20 monthly payments. Simple add-on interest of 9½% was charged, as was a credit fee of $7.50 and an insurance charge of $11.75. Find the annual percentage rate on a purchase of $1,075. (Use the APR formula.) — 20.5%

22. A used car was on sale for $4,067. An installment plan, which required a down payment of 17% of the sale price and the balance to be paid in 24 monthly payments of $172.50 each, was available. Tim Wells decided to purchase the car on the installment plan. Additional installment charges totaling $74.42 were also payable. What was the annual percentage rate according to the APR Table 7-1?

23. Find the annual interest rate on the following:
    a. A loan for $275 with a monthly interest rate of 2¼%. — 27%
    b. A loan payable in 30 months, with a monthly interest rate of 1¾% per month. — 21%

24. Mrs. Jean Ray received a bill from the Avon Shop for $114.25. A monthly interest charge of 1.2% was charged.
    a. What was the annual interest rate she was charged?
    b. How much interest would she pay on the bill for 1 month?

25. The Knox Sporting Goods Store was preparing the monthly bill for a customer. The account had a beginning balance of $742.50. A minimum payment of 15% or $25, whichever was the greater, was required, as was a finance charge of 2% on unpaid balances of less than $500 and 1½% on balances over $500. The customer had paid the required minimum payment and had purchased $111.20 additional merchandise. What was the balance of the current bill? — $751.79

STUDY UNIT **8**

Payroll computations

    HOURLY WAGES

    GROSS PAY

    OVERTIME PAYMENTS

    INCENTIVE PAYMENT PLANS
        Piecework plans
        Hourly rate and bonus
        Hourly rate and premium payments
        Differential piecework rates

    SALARIES

    COMMISSION PAYMENT PLANS
        Straight commission
        Commission—drawing—travel expense
        Commission and salary
        Sliding scale commission

    COMMISSION MERCHANT PAYMENT PLANS
        Sales commission merchants
        Purchase commission merchants

In order to comply with state and federal regulations, and with cost accounting system requirements or negotiated labor contract conditions, employers are required to keep detailed records of employees earnings. Employees are concerned with their gross and net incomes, to comply with state and federal income tax requirements.

Whether payroll records are computed and recorded by a computer, as in large companies, or by an accountant, as is often done in small companies, you should be familiar with the arithmetic involved in computing both gross and net payrolls.

In this unit, the concentration will be on the arithmetic calculations used to compute only gross income, as required by wage and salary plans, including hourly wages, incentive wage plans, salaries and commission plans. The calculation of net income will be covered in Unit 9, Taxes. Because of the wide variety of payroll plans that are used by businesses, the wage and salary plans used in the Rules of Procedure and the Example Problems should be regarded as illustrations of existing plans rather than a complete study of payroll computations.

HOURLY WAGES

RULES OF PROCEDURE   The Fair Labor Standard Act of the federal government requires a minimum hourly rate be paid for a standard work week of 40 hours or for a standard work day of 8 hours for companies engaged in interstate commerce. Many states have established minimum hourly rates and standard hours for companies engaged in intrastate commerce. A company may set its own minimum hourly rates and standard hours within the limits set by government agencies. You can assume that the hourly rates and hours used here in the Rules of Procedure and Example Problems comply with the limitations of federal, state, and company laws regarding hourly rates and standard hours.

> **Rule 1: TO CALCULATE GROSS PAY:**
>
> Hourly pay rate × Standard hours worked = Gross pay

Step 1. Calculate the standard hours worked.

Step 2. Calculate gross pay by completing the arithmetic of the gross pay formula.

Example 1 Find the gross pay of Henry Green, who worked 39½ standard hours in one week. His hourly rate of pay was $4.15.

Step 1. Calculate the standard hours worked:

Standard hours stated as 39½ hours

Step 2. Calculate gross pay by use of formula:

Hourly pay rate × Standard hours worked = Gross pay
$4.15 × 39.5 = $163.93

Example 2 From the time card of Helen Graham, calculate her gross weekly pay.

TIME CARD

name __Helen Graham__   job __#41__
hourly rate __$5.26__

DAY	IN	OUT	IN	OUT	TOTAL HOURS
Monday	8:00	12:00	12:30	4:30	8
Tuesday	8:00	12:00	12:30	3:30	7
Wednesday	8:00	12:00	12:30	4:30	8
Thursday	8:00	12:00	12:30	5:30	9
Friday	9:00	12:00	12:30	4:30	7
Total hours					

Step 1. Calculate standard hours:

Monday 8
Tuesday 7
Wednesday 8
Thursday 9
Friday 7
Total   39 Standard hours

Step 2. Calculate gross pay:

Standard hours × Hourly rate = Gross pay
39 × $5.26 $205.14

OVERTIME PAY

Federal and most state labor regulations require that overtime pay be given for all hours worked in excess of the standard weekly or daily hours at a rate that is 1½ times the regular rate of pay.

STRAIGHT OVERTIME PAY

> Rule 2: TO CALCULATE GROSS PAY, INCLUDING OVERTIME PAYMENTS:
> a. Regular hourly rate × Standard hours = Regular pay
> b. Overtime hours × (Regular hourly rate × 1.5) = Overtime pay
> c. Regular pay + Overtime pay = Gross pay

Step 1. Calculate standard and overtime hours.
Step 2. Calculate regular pay.
Step 3. Calculate overtime pay.
Step 4. Calculate gross pay:

Regular pay + Overtime pay

Example 1   The Edwards Manufacturing Company paid overtime at a rate of time and a half for all hours worked in excess of a standard work week of 40 hours. Find the total gross pay for A. T. Jackson, who worked 46½ hours in one week and was paid a regular rate of $5.90 per hour.

Step 1. Calculate standard hours and overtime hours:

```
Total hours worked =   46.5
Standard hours     = -40.0
Overtime hours          6.5
```

Step 2. Calculate regular wages:

Standard hours × Regular pay rate = Gross regular pay
    40   × $5.90   = $236.00

Step 3. Calculate overtime payments:

Regular pay rate × 1.5 = Overtime pay rate
    $5.90   × 1.5 = $8.85

Overtime hours × Overtime pay rate = Overtime payment
    6.5   × $8.85   = $57.53

Step 4. Calculate total gross pay:

Gross regular pay + Overtime payment = Gross pay
   $236.00   + $57.53   = $293.53

Example 2   The A.B.C. Company paid time and a half for all hours worked in excess of a standard work day of 8 hours. Find the gross pay of Joy Franklin, who worked 9 hours on Monday, 8 on Tuesday, 6½ on Wednesday, 10 on Thursday, and 8½ on Friday. Franklin's hourly regular pay rate was $6.05 per hour.

Step 1. Calculate standard and overtime hours:

	Total hours	Standard hours	Overtime hours
Monday	9	8	1
Tuesday	8	8	0
Wednesday	6½	6½	0
Thursday	10	8	2
Friday	8½	8	½
	42	38½	3½

Step 2. Calculate regular wages:

$$\text{Standard hours} \times \text{Regular pay rate} = \text{Gross regular pay}$$
$$38.5 \times \$6.05 = \$232.93$$

Step 3. Calculate overtime payment:

$$\text{Regular pay rate} \times 1.5 = \text{Overtime pay rate}$$
$$\$6.05 \times 1.5 = \$9.075$$
$$\text{Overtime hours} \times \text{Overtime pay rate} = \text{Overtime payment}$$
$$3.5 \times \$9.075 = \$31.76$$

Step 4.

$$\text{Regular pay} + \text{Overtime payment} = \text{Total gross pay}$$
$$\$232.93 + \$31.76 = \$264.69$$

EXCESS OVERTIME PAYMENTS

To comply with the requirements of some cost accounting systems or to take advantage of a lower workman's compensation insurance premium, many employers will maintain their payroll records to show payments for only the half-time when overtime payments are due. The total wages paid to the employee remains the same regardless of how overtime is calculated.

Rule 3: **TO CALCULATE GROSS PAY WHEN EXCESS OVERTIME IS RECORDED:**

a. Calculate regular pay:

Total hours worked $\times$ Regular pay rate = Total regular pay

b. Calculate excess overtime payment:

Overtime hours $\times$ (Regular pay rate $\times$ .5) = Excess overtime pay

---

Step 1. Calculate standard and overtime hours.
Step 2. Calculate total regular pay by use of formula.
Step 3. Calculate excess overtime pay by use of the formula.
Step 4. Calculate total gross pay:

Total regular pay + Excess overtime pay

Example 1   The Edwards Manufacturing Company paid their employees time and a half for all hours worked in excess of a standard work day of 8 hours. A. T. Jackson was paid an hourly rate of $6. Hours worked during one week included 9 hours on Monday, 10 hours on Tuesday, 11 hours on Wednesday, 6 hours on Thursday, and 10½ hours on Friday. Find (a) the excess overtime, (b) the total wages for the week.

Step 1. Calculate standard and overtime hours:

	Total hours	Standard hours	Overtime hours
Monday	9	8	1
Tuesday	10	8	2
Wednesday	11	8	3
Thursday	6	6	0
Friday	10½	8	2½
Total	46½	38	8½

Step 2. Calculate total regular pay:

Total hours worked × Regular rate of pay = Regular pay
46.5   × $6.00   = $279.00

Step 3. Calculate excess overtime payment:

Overtime hours × (Regular rate × .5) = Excess overtime pay
8.5   ×   ($6.00 × .5)   = $25.50

Step 4. Calculate total gross pay:

Total regular pay + Excess overtime pay = Total gross pay
$279.00   + $25.50   = $304.50

Practice exercises

Answer

1. Edna Oman was paid $5.20 per hour for a standard work week of 40 hours. Overtime was paid for all hours worked in excess of the standard week at a rate of time and a half. Find her total gross pay for a week in which she worked a total of 48 hours. $270.40

2. Employees of a bakery are paid $6.15 an hour for a standard work day of 8 hours and time and a half for all hours worked in excess of the standard day. Find the weekly gross pay for K. Hubbs, who worked 9 hours on Monday, 8 on Tuesday, 6½ on Wednesday, 10 on Thursday, and 10.75 on Friday.   _____

3. Jerry Brown was paid $4.50 per hour and time and a half for all hours worked in excess of a standard 8-hour work day. In one week he worked 11 hours on Monday, 9 on Tuesday, 6 on Wednesday, 9 on Thursday, and 10½ on Friday. Find:
    a. His total pay for the week. $221.63
    b. His overtime pay. $50.63

4. Find the gross weekly pay for an employee who earned $6.80 per hour for a standard work week of 40 hours and time and a half for all hours worked in excess of 40 hours. The time card indicated that a total of 52 hours were worked in the week. Find:
    a. The total pay for the week.   _____
    b. The amount of overtime pay.   _____

5. Dorothy Brown was paid $7.30 per hour and time and a half for all hours worked in excess of 40 hours per week. She worked 12 hours on Monday, 6½ on Tuesday, 9 on Wednesday, 8 on Thursday, and 10½ on Friday.
    a. What amount of excess overtime did she receive? $21.90
    b. What was her total pay for the week? $357.70

6. R. T. Thomas was paid $6.42 per hour and time and a half for all hours worked in excess of a standard work week of 40 hours. Find his gross weekly pay for a week in which he worked 9½ hours on Monday, 8 on Tuesday, 6½ on Wednesday, 10 on Thursday, and 6 on Friday.   _____

7. An employee who worked 49 hours in one week was paid $8.10 per hour, with time and a half for all hours worked in excess of a standard work week of 40 hours. Find:
   a. The amount of excess overtime that was paid. $36.45
   b. Total pay for the week. $433.35

8. Ms. C. Kelley was paid $7.05 per hour and time and a half for all hours worked in excess of a standard work day of 8 hours. What was her total gross pay for a week in which she worked 8 hours on Monday, 10½ on Tuesday, 11 on Wednesday, 6 on Thursday, and 7½ on Friday?   _____

9. Find the gross weekly pay for Elane Towers, who was paid $8.85 an hour, with time and a half for all hours worked in excess of a standard work day of 8 hours. She worked 7½ hours Monday, 9 on Tuesday, 10 on Wednesday, 4½ on Thursday, and 9¼ on Friday. $375.02

10. The Loomis Company paid its production workers $5.90 per hour and time and a half for all hours worked in excess of a standard work week of 40 hours. Find the gross weekly pay for the following employees:
    a. O. C. Morris, who worked 38¼ hours.   _____
    b. B. R. Poppin, who worked 51¼ hours.   _____
    c. M. T. Russell, who worked 39.75 hours.   _____

11. Complete the following time card and calculate:
    a. The amount of excess overtime paid. $11.70
    b. The total gross pay received by the employee. $243.10

TIME CARD

name ___Jean Harris___   job ___#21___

rate ___$5.20___   standard day ___8 hr___

Day	In	Out	In	Out	Total
Monday	8:00	11:00	12:00	5:00	
Tuesday	8:00	12:00	1:00	5:00	
Wednesday	8:00	12:00	12:30	6:00	
Thursday	8:00	12:00	12:00	6:00	
Friday	8:00	12:00	12:30	5:30	
Total					

12. The Standard Tool Company paid their production employees time and a half for all hours worked in excess of a standard work week of 37½ hours. Calculate:
    a. The regular overtime pay.   _____
    b. The total gross pay of an employee who worked 46½ hours in a week at a pay rate of $6.60 per hour.   _____

INCENTIVE PAYMENT PLANS

Many types of incentive plans have been developed to encourage employees to increase their production of acceptable work units. The following plans represent those plans that are used frequently by manufacturing companies.

PIECEWORK PLANS **Straight piecework rates**

This method is one of the oldest incentive pay plans. It has been replaced with a variety of modifications of the basic piecework rate but is used in many businesses producing small units of work.

> **Rule 1: TO CALCULATE GROSS WAGES:**
>
> Number of units produced × Rate per work unit = Gross wages

Step 1. Calculate the number of units produced.
Step 2. Calculate gross wages by substituting data in gross wage formula.

Example 1 Jack Ommar completed 36 units of work in one week and was paid $2.50 per unit. What was his gross pay for the week?

Step 1. Calculate the number of units produced:

Production stated was 36 units

Step 2. Calculate gross wages:

Number of units produced × Rate per work unit = Gross wages
36 × $2.50 = $90.00

Piecework rate with minimum wage

To comply with federal or state regulations regarding minimum wages, this plan guarantees the employee a minimum wage based on an hourly rate for a standard work period or a stated rate per unit produced, whichever is greater.

> **Rule 2: TO CALCULATE GROSS WAGES:**
>
> a. Standard hours × Hourly rate = Guaranteed wage
> b. Number of units produced × Rate per work unit = Gross wage
> c. Employee receives the greater wage.

Step 1. Calculate guaranteed wage by substituting data in the guaranteed wage formula.
Step 2. Calculate number of units produced.
Step 3. Calculate gross wage by substituting data in gross wage formula.
Step 4. Compare guaranteed wage to gross wage of the employee, whichever is greater.

Example 1 The Bailey Manufacturing Company paid $1.50 for each unit of work that passed inspection or paid $4.10 per hour for a standard work week of 40 hours, whichever is greater. Find the weekly gross pay for the following employees who had worked a 40 hour week:

8 PAYROLL COMPUTATIONS / 205

a. Eleanor Walker produced 140 units.

Step 1. Calculate guaranteed wage:

Standard hours × Hourly rate = Guaranteed wage
40 × $4.10 = $164.00

Step 2. Calculate number of units produced:

Production = 140 units

Step 3. Calculate gross wage:

Number of units produced × Rate per work unit = Gross wage
140 × $1.50 = $210.00

Step 4. Compare wages:

Guaranteed wage = $164
Gross wage = $210

Step 5. Eleanor Walker would be paid $210.

b. William T. Hadden produced 15 units on Monday, 16 on Tuesday, 20 on Wednesday, 21 on Thursday, and 18 on Friday.

Step 1. Calculate guaranteed wage:

Standard hours × Hourly rate = Guaranteed wage
40 × $4.10 = $164.00

Step 2. Calculate number of units produced:

15 + 16 + 20 + 21 + 18 = 90 units

Step 3. Calculate Gross Wage:

Number of units produced × Rate per work unit = Gross wage
90 × $1.50 $135.00

Step 4. Compare wages:

Guaranteed wage = $164
Gross wage = $135

Step 5. Mr. Hadden would receive the guaranteed wage of $164.

WAGE AND BONUS PLANS

Hourly rate + bonus

Under this plan of incentment, the employee is paid a bonus rate per unit if he or she exceeds a standard rate of production.

> **Rule 3: TO CALCULATE GROSS WAGES:**
>
> *a.* Minimum hourly rate × Standard hours = Standard wages
> *b.* Bonus rate per unit × Bonus production = Bonus wages
> *c.* Standard wages + Bonus wages = Gross wages

Step 1. Calculate standard wages by substituting data in standard wage formula.

Step 2. Calculate bonus production and substitute data in bonus wage formula.

Step 3. Calculate total gross wages:

Standard wages + Bonus wages = Total gross wage

Example 1 The New Products Company paid production workers $7.25 per hour for a standard production of 100 units completed in a standard 8-hour day. A bonus of 40 cents per unit was paid for production in excess of the standard production. Find the daily gross wage for Betty Hansen, who produced 123 units in an 8-hour day.

  Step 1. Calculate standard wage:

  Minimum hourly rate × Standard hours = Standard wage
  $7.25   ×   8   = $58.00

  Step 2. Calculate bonus production and bonus wage:

  Actual production   =   123 units
  Standard production   =   −100 units
  Bonus production   =   23 units

  Bonus rate per unit × Bonus production = Bonus wage
  $.40   ×   23 units   = $9.20

  Step 3. Calculate total gross wage:

  Standard wage + Bonus wage = Total gross wage
  $58.00   + $9.20   = $67.20

Example 2 Mary Martin was paid $5.45 per hour for a standard work week of 40 hours, plus a bonus of $.45 per unit for all production in excess of the standard production of 250 units. Find her gross pay for a week in which she produced 45 units on Monday, 39 on Tuesday, 43 on Wednesday, 52 on Thursday, and 48 on Friday.

  Step 1. Calculate standard wage:

  Minimum hourly rate × Standard hours = Standard wage
  $5.45   ×   40   = $218.00

  Step 2. Calculate bonus production and bonus wage:

  Actual production:
  45 + 39 + 43 + 52 + 48 = 227 units
  Standard production   = 250 units

Actual production did not exceed standard production. No bonus wage is paid.

  Step 3. Calculate total gross wage:

  Standard wage   = $218.00
  Bonus wage   =   00.00
  Total gross wage = $218.00

Hourly rate + premium pay

Under this plan, if production is below or equal to a standard-unit production, the employee is paid the standard hourly pay. A premium rate per hour is paid if production exceeds the standard production.

Rule 4: TO CALCULATE TOTAL GROSS PAY:

  a. Hourly rate × Standard hours = Standard pay

  b. $\dfrac{\text{Units produced in excess of standard}}{\text{Standard units}} \times$ Standard pay = Premium pay

  c. Standard pay + Premium pay = Total gross pay

Step 1. Calculate standard pay by substituting data in standard pay formula.
Step 2. Calculate premium pay by substituting data in premium pay formula.
Step 3.

$$\text{Standard pay} + \text{Premium pay} = \text{Total gross pay}$$

Example 1   The New Market Basket Company paid its production employees $5.125 per hour for a standard week of 40 hours. The company also paid a premium for production in excess of the standard unit production of 500 units. Find the gross wages of James Morris, who produced 543 units in the standard 40-hour week.

Step 1. Calculate standard pay:

$$\text{Hourly rate} \times \text{Standard hours} = \text{Standard pay}$$
$$\$5.125 \quad \times \quad 40 \quad = \quad \$205.00$$

Step 2. Calculate premium pay:

$$\frac{\text{Units produced in excess of standard}}{\text{Standard units}} \times \text{Standard pay} = \text{Premium pay}$$

$$\frac{543 - 500}{500} \times \$205.00 = \$17.63 \text{ Premium pay}$$

Step 3.

$$\text{Standard pay} + \text{Premium pay} = \text{Total gross pay}$$
$$\$205.00 \quad + \quad \$17.63 \quad = \quad \$222.63$$

Example 2   Janet Less was paid $6.035 per hour for a standard work week of 40 hours with a standard production of 475 units. Her production of the 40-hour week included 118 units on Monday, 102 on Tuesday, 91 on Wednesday, 85 on Thursday, and 64 on Friday. Find her total gross pay for the week.

Step 1. Calculate standard pay:

$$\text{Hourly rate} \times \text{Standard hours} = \text{Standard pay}$$
$$\$6.035 \quad \times \quad 40 \quad = \quad \$241.40$$

Step 2. Calculate premium pay:

Actual production = 118 + 102 + 91 + 85 + 64 + = 460
Standard production =   = 475

Actual production did not exceed the standard production. No premium pay is due.

Step 3. Calculate total gross pay:

$$\text{Standard pay} + \text{Premium pay} = \text{Total gross pay}$$
$$\$241.40 \quad + \quad 00.00 \quad = \quad \$241.40$$

Differential piecework rate

This plan provides for a higher unit rate on all produced units as the production of an employee increases.

> Rule 5: **TO CALCULATE GROSS PAY:**
>
> a. Calculate total production.
> b. Total production × Applicable unit rate = Total gross pay

Step 1. Calculate total unit production.
Step 2. Select applicable unit rate from the differential pay scale:

Total production × Applicable unit rate = Total gross pay

Example 1   The Burbank Manufacturing Company paid its production employees on the following differential piecework scale:

Total production	Rate per each unit
0–9	.90
10–50	1.50
51–100	1.70
101–150	1.95
151–200	2.05

a. Find the gross wages of the following employees:

1. Alice Creeley, who produced 126 units.
2. Vickey Duncan, who produced 104 units.
3. Frank Nixon, who produced 167 units.
4. George Pepper, who produced 42 units.

b. What was the total gross wages paid?

Step 1. Calculate total production:

Total production is given in problem

Step 2. Select applicable unit rate and calculate gross pay (**Ans.** *a*):

a. Creeley: 126 × $1.95 = $245.70
b. Duncan: 104 × $1.95 = $202.80
c. Nixon: 167 × $2.05 = $342.35
d. Pepper: 42 × $1.50 = $ 63.00

Step 3. Calculate total gross pay, which is $853.85 (**Ans.** *b*).

Example 2   The Kelsey Dress Manufacturing Company pays its sewing machine operators a daily differential piecework rate of:

$.40 for 30 to 80 completed units
$.60 for 81 to 100 completed units
$.80 for 101 to 130 completed units

Mary Greene produced lots of 20, 15, 25, and 16 on Monday; lots of 20, 35, and 27 on Tuesday; and lots of 30, 40, 25, and 8 on Wednesday. She did not work on Thursday or Friday.

a. Find her daily gross pay.
b. What amount did she receive for the week?

Step 1. Calculate total unit production:

Monday: 20 + 15 + 25 + 16 = 76 units
Tuesday: 20 + 35 + 27   = 82 units
Wednesday: 30 + 40 + 25 + 8 = 103 units

Step 2. Select applicable unit rate and calculate gross pay (**Ans.** *a*):

$$\begin{aligned}\text{Monday:} \quad & 76 \text{ units} \times \$.40 = \$30.40\\ \text{Tuesday:} \quad & 82 \text{ units} \times \$.60 = \$49.20\\ \text{Wednesday:} \quad & 103 \text{ units} \times \$.80 = \$82.40\end{aligned}$$

Step 3. Calculate total gross pay (**Ans.** *b*):

$$\$30.40 + \$49.20 + \$82.40 = \$162.00$$

Practice exercises

Answer

1. The Farwell Company paid its employees on a piecework rate that required a payment of $0.455 per unit for all units that passed inspection or a guaranteed weekly wage of $4.50 per hour for a standard work week of 40 hours. Find the weekly gross wages for the following employees:
    a. P. Peters, who produced 450 units. $204.75
    b. B. Broomley, who produced 503 units. $228.87
    c. S. Evans, who produced 390 units. $180.00 (min.)
    d. T. Thomas, who produced 520 units. $236.60

2. The production employees of the Jenson Company were paid a guaranteed hourly wage of $4 for a standard work week of 40 hours. A piecework rate of $0.60 per unit was also available to the employees. Find the gross wages of:
    a. Larry Lowell, who produced 236 units.   _____
    b. Nora Fallon, who produced 316 units.   _____

3. The Reynolds Company paid its production employees $5.05 per hour for a standard work week of 40 hours. A premium for production in excess of the standard 235 units is also paid. Find the gross wages for:
    a. T. Kristy, who produced 264 units. $226.93
    b. P. Kercher, who produced 233 units. $202.00
                                                                    (no premium)

4. The production employees of the R & R Manufacturing Company were paid $5.625 per hour for a standard work day of 8 hours. Standard production for the day was 110 units, with a premium wage for all units produced in excess of the standard. Calculate the daily gross wage for:
    a. Alice Palmer, who produced 92 units.   _____
    b. Joyce Goldey, who produced 136 units.   _____

5. Find the daily and weekly gross pay of the following employees, who were paid on a differential piecework rate of:

    $ 9 for 1 to 4 units completed
    $10 for 5 to 10 units completed
    $12 for 11 to 15 units completed

    On Monday H. Jones completed 2, 3, and 4 units. On Tuesday it was 3, 4, and 5 units, and on Wednesday, 2, 4, and 5 units.   Mon. $90
                                                                    Tues. $144

    a. Find the daily gross pay.   Wed. $132
    b. What was the gross pay for the 3 days worked? $366

6. Find the daily gross pay of Joann Peoples, who produced these units: 16, 9, 4, and 5. Refer to the differential scale in Example 1.   _____

7. S & H Manufacturing Company paid its plant employees on a piecework rate of $.515 per unit. R. T. Smith completed 305 units and C. B. Collie completed 210 units. Who earned the higher wages for the week?   R. T. Smith

8. May and Edna Watson were employed as assemblers of flip-flops for the Reliable Semiconductor Company, which paid a straight piecework rate of 21¢ per flip-flop. Find their individual gross wage for a week in which May assembled 1,182 units and Edna assembled 1,300.   _____

9. The production workers of the R. A. C. Assembly Plant were paid $4.20 per hour for a standard work week of 40 hours. Standard production for the week was 120 units. A premium was paid for all units produced in excess of the standard. Find the weekly gross wage of Bill Haas who produced 153 units in the standard work week. $214.20

10. The Dalton Company paid all production employees $5.15 per hour for a minimum production of 185 units that are completed in a standard work week of 40 hours. A bonus of $0.80 per unit is paid for production in excess of minimum production. How much did Helen Mack receive for her production of 218 units completed in the standard work week?   _____

11. Wilson & Wilcox Manufacturing Company established a minimum production of 40 work units to be completed in a standard work day of 8 hours. The minimum hourly rate was $4.65. A bonus of $0.22 per unit for all production in excess of the standard was also paid. What gross wage did Abby Kelly earn in an 8-hour day in which 61 units were completed? $41.82

12. The Claypoole Company paid 25¢ for each gasket treated with a special compound. Standard production was 700 gaskets for a standard work week of 40 hours. A bonus piecework rate of 19¢ each for all gaskets produced in excess of standard was also paid. All employees were guaranteed a weekly wage of $175 for the standard work week. Find the weekly wage for the following employees, all of whom worked the standard work week:
    a. Fred White, who produced 583 gaskets.   _____
    b. Polly Oliver, who produced 803 gaskets.   _____

SALARIES

    Salaries are generally paid for services rendered or performance of assigned duties regardless of time spent. Salaries may be paid weekly, bi-weekly, semimonthly, or monthly.

1. Weekly salary means 52 payments per year.
2. Bi-weekly salary means 26 payments per year.
3. Semimonthly salary means 24 payments per year.
4. Monthly salary means 12 payments per year.

Rule 1: TO CONVERT ONE TYPE OF PAY PERIOD TO ANOTHER PERIOD:

a. Calculate salary for 1 year.

b. $\dfrac{\text{Yearly salary}}{\text{Desired pay period}} = \text{Required salary}$

Step 1. Calculate salary for 1 year:

Salary × Pay periods in 1 year = Yearly salary

Step 2. $\dfrac{\text{Yearly salary}}{\text{Desired pay period}} = \text{Required salary}$

Example 1 A. R. Allen received a weekly salary of $165. What salary would be received if the pay period was changed to (a) a bi-weekly pay period, (b) a semimonthly pay period, and (c) a monthly pay period?

Step 1. Calculate salary for 1 year:

Salary × Pay periods in 1 year = Yearly salary
$165 ×   52   = $8,580

Step 2. $\dfrac{\text{Yearly salary}}{\text{Desired pay period}} = \text{Required salary}$

$\dfrac{\$8,580}{26 \text{ (bi-weekly)}} = \$330$ Bi-weekly Pay (a)

Step 1. Calculate salary for 1 year:

Salary × Pay periods in 1 year = Yearly salary
$165 ×   52   = $8,580

Step 2. $\dfrac{\text{Yearly salary}}{\text{Desired pay period}} = \text{Required salary}$

$\dfrac{\$8,580}{24} = \$357.50$ Semimonthly salary (b)

Step 1. $\dfrac{\text{Yearly salary}}{\text{Desired pay period}} = \text{Required salary}$

Step 2. $\dfrac{\$8,580}{12} = \$715$ Monthly salary (c)

Example 2 Mary Morrison earned a bi-weekly salary of $525. What salary would she receive if the pay period was changed to weekly?

Step 1. Calculate salary for 1 year:

Salary × Pay periods in 1 year = Yearly salary
$525 ×   26   = $13,650

Step 2. $\dfrac{\text{Yearly salary}}{\text{Desired pay period}} = \text{Required salary}$

$\dfrac{\$13,650}{52} = \$262.50$ Weekly salary

Example 3   Mrs. J. C. Rather was paid $915 per month. Find her salary if the pay period was changed to (*a*) a weekly pay period, (*b*) a bi-weekly pay period, and (*c*) a semimonthly pay period.

Step 1.   Calculate salary for 1 year:

$$\text{Salary} \times \text{Pay periods in 1 year} = \text{Yearly salary}$$
$$\$915 \times 12 = \$10,980$$

Step 2.   (Ans. *a*):

$$\frac{\text{Yearly salary}}{\text{Desired pay period}} = \text{Required salary}$$

$$\frac{\$10,980}{52} = \$211.15 \text{ Weekly salary}$$

Step 2.   (Ans. *b*):

$$\frac{\text{Yearly salary}}{\text{Desired pay period}} = \text{Required salary}$$

$$\frac{\$10,980}{26} = \$422.31 \text{ Bi-weekly salary}$$

Step 2.   (Ans. *c*):

$$\frac{\text{Yearly salary}}{\text{Desired pay period}} = \text{Required salary}$$

$$\frac{\$10,980}{24} = \$457.50 \text{ Semimonthly salary}$$

Practice exercises

		Answer
1.	Joan Kelly was offered a job with a weekly salary of $265. She also had an opportunity for a job that paid $535 bi-weekly. Which job provides the greater monthly salary?	Bi-weekly salary
2.	Find the annual salary of James Crow, who earns $627.50 semimonthly.	————
3.	What is the weekly salary of Marie Wilson, who earns a salary of $412.65 bi-weekly?	$206.33
4.	The Raymond Insurance Agency had a semimonthly payroll of $18,427.50. What was its annual salary expense?	————
5.	Joan Jones was hired at a weekly salary of $147.50. She was promoted to a position with a bi-weekly salary of $352.69. How much was her monthly increase?	$124.99
6.	If the annual salary expense of the R & T Company was $116,438, what was the amount of its semimonthly salary expense?	————
7.	Wilma Wright was offered a position that paid $712 per bi-weekly pay period. In her present position she earns $1,485 per month. What increase or decrease per month will she receive if she accepts the new position?	$57.67 increase
8.	Jane Barber earns $1,085 per month. What weekly salary does she earn?	

9. J. T. Stevens has a semimonthly payroll of $36,840.60. If no salary increases are given, what would the payroll be if it changed to a bi-weekly pay period? $34,006.71
10. Peter Paul earns a monthly salary of $1,119.00. Find his salary if the pay period was changed to:
   a. A weekly period.   _____
   b. A bi-weekly period.   _____
   c. A semimonthly period.   _____

COMMISSION PAYMENT PLANS

A variety of commission payment plans have been developed to meet the needs of numerous businesses and industries who market their product by salespeople. Most plans are a variation of the straight commission payment plan.

Straight commission payments

> **Rule 1: TO CALCULATE COMMISSION PAYMENT:**
>
> Net sales × Commission rate = Commission payment

Step 1. Calculate net sales:

Total sales − Returned goods = Net sales

Step 2. Calculate commission payment:

Net sales × Commission rate = Commission payment

Example 1   Ms. C. Wells earns a commission of 12½% of net sales. In the month of August, Ms. Wells sold a total of $12,865. During the month, $426.50 worth of goods were returned by the customers. What commission did Ms. Wells receive for the month?

Step 1. Calculate net sales:

Total sales − Returned goods =   Net sales
$12,865   − $426.50   = $12,438.50

Step 2. Calculate commission payment:

Net sales   × Commission rate = Commission payment
$12,438.50 ×   .125   = $1,554.81

Commission payments including drawing account and travel expenses

To provide salespeople with a regular income, many employers permit them to periodically withdraw a stated amount to be charged against future commissions. It is customary to reimburse salespeople for travel expenses incurred in the course of selling the company's products.

> **Rule 2: TO CALCULATE NET COMMISSION:**
> a. Calculate commission payment.
> b. Calculate amount of drawings.
> c. Calculate travel expenses.
> d. Add commission payments and travel expenses, then deduct drawings, which equals net commission payment.

Step 1. Calculate commission payment:

Net sales × Commission rate = Commission payment

Step 2. Calculate drawings:

Amount of drawings × Number of periods = Drawings

Step 3. Calculate travel expenses: Add all expenses reported by the salesperson.

Step 4.

    Total commission
+ Travel expenses
− Total drawings
    Net commission payment

Example 1 R. A. Lenox earned a commission of 15% of monthly net sales. He had a drawing account of $250 per week. Find his total income for a month in which he sold $46,840 worth of merchandise, $1,645 worth of goods were returned, and he had withdrawn 4 weeks of his allowable drawings. Travel expenses amounted to $185.

Step 1. Calculate commission payment:

    Net sales   × Commission rate = Commission payment
($46,840 − $1,645) ×   .15   = $6,779.25

Step 2. Calculate drawings:

Amount of drawings × Number of periods = Total drawings
    $250   ×   4 weeks   = $1,000

Step 3. Calculate travel expenses:

Total travel expenses = $185

Step 4. Calculate net commission:

Commission payment	$6,779.25
Add travel expenses	+ 185.00
Deduct drawings	−1,000.00
Net commission payment	$5,964.25

Commission and salary payments

One of the more common variations of the straight commission payment plans is to guarantee the salesperson a stated salary plus a commission on net sales completed in a stated time.

> **Rule 3:** TO CALCULATE TOTAL INCOME INCLUDING COMMISSION AND SALARY:
> a. Calculate net commission payment.
> b. Convert salary payment to the same pay period used to calculate commissions.
> c. Commission + Salary = Total income

Step 1. Calculate net commission payment by substituting data in net commission formula.

Step 2. Convert salary (if necessary) to the same pay period used to calculate commissions by substituting data in salary formula.
Step 3.

Net commission payment + Converted salary = Total income

Example 1 An employee received a semimonthly salary of $325 plus a commission of 8¼% on net sales. Find the total monthly income for a month in which $11,827 worth of goods were sold and $912 were returned for credit.

Step 1. Calculate net commission payment:

Total sales − Returned goods = Net sales
$11,827 − $912 = $10,915
Net sales × Commission rate = Net commission payment
$10,915 × .0825 = $900.49

Step 2. Convert salary to monthly payment:

$$\frac{\$325 \times 24}{12} = \$650 \text{ Monthly salary}$$

Step 3. Calculate total income:

Commission payments + Salary = Total income
$900.49 + $650.00 = $1,550.49

Sliding scale commission payments

This commission plan provides different commission rates for different volume of sales completed by the salesperson.

> **Rule 4:** TO CALCULATE TOTAL COMMISSION PAYMENTS:
>
> Applicable sales volume × Commission rate = Commission payment

Step 1. To calculate total commission:

a. Total sales − First sales volume × Rate = 1st commission

b. Remaining sales − Subsequent sales vol. × Commission rate = Subsequent commission

Step 2. Add all commissions calculated in Step 1 *a* and *b*.

Example 1 Fred Freedman was paid 2% commission on the first $5,000 of monthly sales, 4% on the next $10,000 of sales, and 5% on all sales in excess of $15,000. Find his total commission for a month in which he sold $22,000 worth of merchandise.

Step 1.

Total sales − 1st sales volume × Rate = 1st commission

Total sales = $22,000
1st volume sale = − 5,000 × .02 = $100.00
Remaining sales = $17,000
2d volume sale = −10,000 × .04 = $400.00
Remaining sales = 7,000 × .05 = $350.00

Step 2. Add all commissions calculated in Step 1.

$100 + $400 + $350 = $850

Example Problem

To apply Rules 2, 3, and 4.

Dora Green earned a weekly salary of $235. She also earned a commission on net sales of 4% on the first $7,000 of sales, 5½% on the next $12,000, and 7% on all sales in excess of $19,000. Travel expenses, for which she was reimbursed, amounted to $216.40. Find the total income she received at the end of a month in which she sold $24,820 worth of merchandise. Returned sales amounted to $3,405.

Step 1. Calculate monthly salary:

$$\frac{\$235 \times 52}{12} = \$1,018.33$$

Step 2. Calculate monthly commission:

```
Total sales        = $24,820
Returned sales     = - 3,405
Net sales            $21,415                   Commissions
1st sales volume   -  7,000 × .04  =           $   280.00
Remaining sales      $14,415
2d sales volume    -12,000 × .055 =            $   660.00
Remaining sales      $ 2,415 × .07 =           $   169.05
Total monthly commissions                       $1,109.05
```

Step 3. Total monthly income:

Total monthly salary	$1,018.33
Total monthly commissions	1,109.05
Total travel expenses	216.40
Total monthly income	$2,343.78

COMMISSION MERCHANT PAYMENT PLANS

Sales commission merchants

When a producer or manufacturer sells his products through a commission merchant, he receives a statement and remittance from the commission merchant for the net amount of the sale completed by the commission merchant.

Rule 5: TO CALCULATE NET SALE:
a. Calculate total of merchandise sold.
b. Deduct all selling expenses.
c. Deduct commission charge.
d. Send total invoice and remittance to the producer or manufacturer.

Step 1. Calculate total merchandise sold:

Quantity sold × Unit price = Invoice price

Step 2. Commission charge:

Total invoice price × Rate = Commission

Step 3. Calculate net sale:

```
  Total invoice price
- Commission
- Expenses incurred in completing sale
  Net sale price
```

Note: Commission sales merchant sends invoice and remittance for the net sale to the producer or manufacturer. The merchant has collected the invoice price from the buyer.

Example 1

```
                    SALES ACCOUNT

                    N. T. REYNOLDS
                    commission merchant

Sold for:
  P. P. Eden
  Orlando, Florida              Date   May 15, 19—

  27   Crates of grapefruit   @ $12.40     $  334.80
  32   Crates of Oranges      @ $15.10        483.20
  20   Crates of Lemons       @ $ 8.45        169.00
  15   Crates of Celery       @ $11.25        168.75

       Total sale                         $1,155.75

       Charges:
         Commission (.09 X $1,155.75)    -  104.02
         Freight                         -  106.50
         Storage                         -   94.20

       Total Remittance                  $  851.03
```

Note: N. T. Reynolds will remit $851.03 to P. P. Eden for merchandise sold.

Purchase commission merchants

When a commission merchant purchases merchandise for a producer or manufacturer, he will pay for merchandise purchased and bill his customer for the total cost of the transaction, including his commission.

> **Rule 7: TO CALCULATE INVOICE SENT TO THE BUYER:**
> a. Calculate total invoice price of merchandise purchased.
> b. Add all expenses incurred.
> c. Add commission charged.
> d. Send total invoice to the buyer.

Example 1

```
                  PURCHASE ACCOUNT

                  THE KELLOGG COMPANY
                  Commission Merchants

Purchased for:
  The Rayco Company
  Oxford, Ohio                  Date   May 2, 19—

   35   C of paper            @ $26.80    $   938.00
   20   lbs. of #46 paste     @   .385          7.70
   60   C of Sealing Tape     @  1.97         118.20
  210   lbs. of #4 twine      @   .475         99.75

        Total purchase price              $1,163.65

        Additional charges:
          Commission (.11 X $1,163.65)   +  128.00
          Insurance                      +   57.85
          Freight                        +  146.20

        Total invoice cost                $1,495.70
```

218 /

Note: The Kellogg Company paid a total of $1,163.65 for merchandise purchased and will collect $1,495.70 from the Rayco Company.

Practice exercises

Answer

1. Paul Ames was paid a straight commission of 11.75%. Find his commission for a month in which he sold $32,458.75 worth of merchandise. $3,813.90

2. A salesperson was paid a commission of 11.5% of weekly sales. Find the total commission for a week in which $188 was sold on Monday, $316 on Tuesday, $284 on Wednesday, $308 on Thursday, $325 on Friday, and $507 on Saturday.   ———

3. A salesperson for a hardware supply company was reimbursed for travel expenses and received a commission of 11% on the first $45,000 of sales, 13½% on the next $20,000 of sales, and 16% on all sales in excess of $65,000. If travel expenses for the year were $8,212.00 and sales were $80,062, find the total amount received at the end of the year. $18,271.92

4. During a four-week period, Jane Stark sold the following merchandise:

    25 units at $35.75 each
    15 units at $59.50 each
    12 units at $125.00 each   ———

    Returned merchandise amounted to $250. She had a weekly drawing account of $250, which she had drawn each week. Commission was 16¼% of net sales. At the end of the four-week period, did Stark receive any commission? What was the status of her earnings?   ———

5. Ms. B. R. Brown earned a monthly salary of $900. She also earned a commission of 7¼% on total sales. Find her gross earnings for a week in which she sold $1,135 worth of merchandise. $289.98

6. Paula Smith was paid a commission of 4½% on the first $20,000 of sales, 8% on the next $30,000, and 6½% on all sales in excess of $50,000. Find her annual gross income for a year in which she sold a total of $144,500 worth of merchandise and received a bi-weekly salary of $512.   ———

7. Tony Rogers, a salesman for the Apex Company, received a commission of 9% on the first $50,000 of sales, 11% on the next $25,000, and 13% on all sales in excess of $75,000. Total sales amounted to $103,973 and $5,315 were returned. What was his total commission? $10,325.54

8. J. C. Whitley's gross income as a salesman was based on commission of 6½% on the first $20,000 of sales, 7% on the next $30,000, and 8% of all sales over $50,000. He also received a semimonthly salary of $410. Find the

annual income he received for a year in which he sold a total of $112,000 in merchandise.

9. R. A. Little, commission merchant, sold merchandise for the Acme Products Company in the total amount of $11,846. Shipping expenses of $216.40, storage charges of $186.40, and a commission of 8½% were incurred in completing the transaction. What amount will the commission merchant send the Acme Products Company? $10,436.29

10. R. A. Newhart Co. sold the following produce for the Farmer's Cooperative, Inc.:

    46 crates of asparagus   @ $52.50 per crate
    300 pounds of green beans   @ $ .46 per pound
    62 crates of lettuce   @ $37.50 per crate
    26 crates of strawberries   @ $26.80 per crate

Expenses necessary to complete the transaction included freight charges of $267.50, cold storage charges of $187.80, and a commission of 8¼%. What amount was remitted to the Farmer's Cooperative Inc.?

11. A commission merchant purchased material for R. J. Steward Company at a total invoice cost of $9,645. Expenses incurred in completing the transaction involved special handling charges of $137.85, storage charges of $179.60, and a commission of 11½%. What was the amount of the bill sent to the Steward Company by the commission merchant? $11,071.63

12. T. C. Elliott purchased the following material for the Baker Manufacturing Company:

    129 yards of blue denim   @ $2.375 per yard
    60 spools of 30 thread   @ $3.96 per spool
    40 sewing machine belts   @ $7.40 each
    280 yards of yellow cotton   @ $2.06 per yard

Additional expenses incurred in completing the transaction included: shipping costs of $226.85, insurance of $56.90, delivery costs of $119.40, and a commission of 14½%. What was the amount of the bill sent to the Baker Manufacturing Company?

13. The Shell-Rite Company paid their sales personnel 4½% commission on total sales completed. Find the annual income of Peg Hays for a year in which total sales amounted to $45,426 and her salary was $505 semimonthly. $14,164.17

14. Ms. T. White is paid a straight commission of 9½% of total sales. She has a drawing account of $195 per week and is reimbursed for traveling expenses. Find her total gross income for a month in which she sold a total of $26,847 worth of merchandise. Traveling expenses were $318.40 and she had withdrawn four weeks of the allowable drawings.

METHODS OF PAYROLL PAYMENTS

Most employers, large and small, pay their employees by check. The increase in the use of checks in paying employees is due in part to the requirements of Internal Revenue Service, federal and state regulations, and union agreements. Cancelled checks provide a verifiable record, should such be required. Furthermore, the increase in computer services to small companies provide payroll checks for a very modest fee. However, it is still the practice of some companies to pay part-time or temporary employees by cash.

Check payment method

A check payable to the individual employee for the net amount due is issued each pay period. Although a wide variety of checks is in use, the employee is provided with a record of gross earnings as well as all deductions made from the gross earnings.

Cash payment method

The cash payment method may be used to pay part-time, temporary, or one or two full-time employees. The following procedure is applicable when cash payments are made:

Step 1. Complete a money distribution sheet similar to the following example:

Employee	Total net pay	$50	$20	$10	$5	$1	.50	.25	.10	.05	.01
Marie Hutton	$164.80	1	4	2	2	4	1	1		1	
Helen Black	$196.47	1	4	4	5	1		1	2		2
Bob Wilson	$153.18	1	2	4	4	3			1	1	3
Total	$514.45	3	10	10	11	8	1	2	3	2	5

Step 2. Use the figures from Step 1 in the following manner:

Proof of money distribution
$50 X 3 = $150.00
$20 X 10 = 200.00
$10 X 10 = 100.00
$5 X 11 = 55.00
$1 X 8 = 8.00
$.50 X 1 = .50
$.25 X 2 = .50
$.10 X 3 = .30
$.05 X 2 = .10
$.01 X 5 = .05
Total $514.45

Step 3. Prepare a copy of the proof sheet for use by the bank teller in the payroll check for the total net payroll.

Step 4. Using the money distribution sheet, prepare an individual envelope for each employee.

Review problems

		Answer
1.	Henry Baar was paid $4.26 per hour. What was his weekly pay for a week in which he worked 7½ hours on Monday, 9 on Tuesday, 6 on Wednesday, 10 on Thursday, and 6 on Friday?	$164.01
2.	Ann Copley was paid $5.15 per hour with time and a half for all hours worked in excess of 8 hours per day. She worked 10 hours on Monday, 8 on Tuesday, 6 on Wednesday, 11 on Thursday, and 9 on Friday. What was her total gross pay for the week?	_____
3.	Carol Wolf was paid $4.80 per hour with time and a half for all hours worked in excess of 8 hours per day. She worked 9½ hours on Monday, 10 on Tuesday, 6 on Wednesday, 8 on Thursday, and 11 on Friday. Find:	
	a. The amount of *excess* overtime she was paid.	$15.60
	b. Her total pay for the week.	$229.20
4.	The W & W Manufacturing Company paid its production employees time and a half for all hours worked in excess of 40 hours per week. It also recorded *excess* overtime. Find:	
	a. The amount of excess overtime paid an employee who earned $6.10 per hour and had worked 7 hours on Monday, 10 on Tuesday, 9½ on Wednesday, 10.75 on Thursday, and 11 on Friday.	_____
	b. What was the total pay for the week?	_____
5.	The Graymore Company paid its employees on a straight piecework rate. Laura Smalley was paid $1.15 and Marie Thomas $.955 for each unit completed. What was the gross pay of each employee if Laura completed 164 units and Marie completed 187 units?	Laura: $188.60 Marie: $178.59
6.	The J. S. Marten Company paid its employees $0.165 for each work unit that passed inspection or a minimum wage of $4.95 per hour for a standard work week of 40 hours. Bill Adler completed 1,200 units and Sarah Willis 1,328 units, all of which passed inspection. Find the weekly pay of each employee.	_____ _____
7.	The Jenkins Manufacturing Company paid its plant employees a minimum hourly rate of $5 per hour for a minimum production of 35 units per day of 8 hours. A bonus of 55¢ per unit for all production in excess of the standard was also paid. Find the gross earnings of:	
	a. W. Ellis, who produced 54 units in the 8-hour day.	Ellis: $50.45
	b. P. Young, who produced 31 units.	Young: $40.00

8. The Holly Manufacturing paid its production employees an hourly rate of $4.06 for a standard production of 375 units completed in a 40-hour work week and a premium for all work units produced in excess of the standard. Find the weekly gross pay of an employee who produced 412 units in the standard work week. _____

9. The Baylor Clothing Manufacturing Company paid plant employees on a differential pay scale of:

1–300 units	$.40 per unit
301–400 units	$.50 per unit
401–500 units	$.65 per unit
501 and over	$.75 per unit

Find the weekly pay for:
   a. John Mooney, who produced 297 units.
   b. Doris Newman, who produced 512 units.
   c. Janet Peterson, who produced 438 units.

Mooney: $118.80
Newman: $384.00
Peterson: $284.70

10. Find the daily pay of the following employees who were paid on a differential pay scale of:

1–15 units	$8.25 per unit
16–25 units	$8.75 per unit
26–35 units	$9.30 per unit
36 and over	$9.80 per unit

   a. Steve George, who produced 18 units.
   b. Mary St. John, who produced 27 units.
   c. Ann Synder, who produced 39 units.

11. Edwin Arnold was paid a monthly salary of $1,109. What will he earn if the pay period is changed to a weekly period?

$255.92 per week

12. T. C. White is paid a straight commission of 17.5% on total sales. What was her annual income on total sales of $137,850? _____

13. A salesperson received a bi-weekly salary of $215 and a 6½% commission on total sales. Find the monthly income if total sales for the month amounted to $9,827.

$1,104.59

14. Paula Wills was reimbursed for her travel expenses and received a commission of 7½% on the first $12,000 of total sales, 9% on the next $16,000 of sales, and 11% on all sales in excess of $28,000. Her travel expenses were $206 and she withdrew $600 of the allowable drawings. What amount was received at the end of the month if total sales were $32,500? _____

15. R. Boxter received a commission of 4½% on the first $5,000 of sales, 5½% on the next $12,000, and 7% on all sales over $17,000. Find the monthly income if total sales amounted to $23,750.

$1,357.50

16. Hilton & Son were commission merchants in Chicago. They sold the following merchandise for Halstead and Company:

>   275 crates of blueberries at $6.80 per crate
>   310 crates of strawberries at $10.40 per crate
>   1,240 10-pound bags of potatoes at $2.35 per bag

  Freight charges were $108.60, storage charges were $137.50. Hilton and Son charged 5½% commission. What amount did Halstead and Company receive from the sale?   _____

17. The Hermann Realty Company was a commission agent for Ms. H. Williams. The company sold an office building for Ms. Williams for $118,945. Expenses incurred in completing the transaction totaled $915.50, plus a commission of 9.125%. What amount did Ms. Williams receive from the sale?   **$107,175.77**

18. Heller and Wagner, commission merchants, purchased the following merchandise for Parkes and Tull:

    >   625 pounds of coffee at $9.45 per pound
    >   540 pounds of tea at $.52 per pound

    Expenses incurred in completing the transaction included: storage charges of $81.60, insurance charges of $48.90, and a commission of 7½%. What amount did the commission merchants charge the Parkes and Tull Company?   _____

19. A commission merchant purchased 3,400 bushels of rye grass seed at a cost of $2.04 per bushel for the Hagan Feed and Grain Company. Freight charges were $461.80 and the commission was 7¼%. What was the amount of the bill sent the Hagan Feed and Grain Company by the commission merchant?   **$7,900.66**

20. Morris & Smith Company paid their salespeople 4½% commission of the first $5,000 of sales, 6% on the next $10,000, and 7½% on all sales over $15,000, as well as a bi-weekly salary of $395. Each salesperson had a drawing account of $150 per week and were reimbursed for all travel expenses. Helen Gray sold $22,700 worth of merchandise during the month of June. She withdrew three weeks of drawings and travel expenses were $308.70. Find the total amount that she received at the end of the month.   _____

21. Stanley Bridges earned $4.95 per hour and time and a half for all hours worked in excess of 8 hours per day. What gross pay would Bridges receive for a week in which he worked 9 hours on Monday, 10½ on Tuesday, 6 on Wednesday, 11 on Thursday, and 9 on Friday?   **$243.79**

22. The Harris Company paid its plant employees a minimum hourly wage of $5.80 per hour for a minimum production of 60 work units completed in 8 hours. A premium was paid for daily production in excess of the standard. Find the daily gross earnings of:
    a. Joy Farr, who produced 56 units.   _____
    b. Stacy Whelan, who produced 71 units in an 8-hour day.   _____

23. The employees of the Abbott Dress Company were guaranteed a weekly wage of $152.50 plus a bonus of $.165 for each unit produced in excess of 122 units completed in a 40-hour week. What gross pay would:
    a. Paul Saylor receive for his production of 146 units? $156.46
    b. Henry Kennedy for his production of 118 units? $152.50
24. Joan McKay earned a straight commission of 12½% on net sales. Find her commission for a week in which she sold $2,409.50 worth of merchandise, $42.95 of which was returned. _____

STUDY UNIT **9**

Taxes

FEDERAL TAXES
  FICA
  Federal income withholding taxes
  Net income

LOCAL TAXES
  Sales tax
  Property taxes
    Tax Rate
    Property Taxes
    Assessed Value

The major source of revenue of local, state, and federal governments comes from taxes that are levied on employers, employees, consumers, and property owners. In this unit, we will review the mathematics involved in the computation of two federal taxes (FICA and income withholding tax) and two local or state taxes (property and sales).

FEDERAL TAXES

Federal Insurance Contribution Act (FICA)

In Unit 8, the arithmetic of calculating gross income earned by an employee was reviewed. In this unit, the arithmetic involved in calculating net income received by the employee will be included. One of the deductions made from gross income is the FICA, or social security tax.

The Federal Insurance Contribution Act requires an employer to deduct a stated percent of the gross earnings of each employee up to a maximum taxable base for each pay period. The deductible percent and taxable base has changed many times since the FICA became law. The deductible rate and the taxable base for the year 1981 and the rates for 1982 through 1985 include:

1981 6.65% on earnings up to and including $29,700
1982 6.7%
1985 7.05%
1986 7.15%

Note: The taxable wage base may increase automatically according to increases in average wage levels.

Several methods of making the required deductions are available. Both the tax table method and the percent method are acceptable by the federal government. The 1981 percent method and wage base have been used in the following examples and problems.

> Rule 1: TO CALCULATE TAXABLE GROSS EARNINGS:
> a. Current Gross earnings = Taxable gross earnings
>
> or
>
> b. Maximum wage base − Earnings to date = Taxable gross earnings

Step 1. If earnings to date are less than $29,700, the current earnings are taxable.
Step 2.

Maximum wage base − Earnings to date = Taxable gross earnings

Example 1 Keith Ginger's earnings to date were $18,950. Gross earnings for the current pay period were $964.50. What are his taxable gross earnings for the current period?
Step 1.

Earnings to date = $18,950.00
Current earnings =   964.50
                            $19,914.50

Total earnings are less than $29,700.
Taxable earnings for current pay period = $964.50

Example 2 Linda Darby's earnings to date were $28,700. Earnings for the current pay period were $1,265. What are the taxable earnings for the current pay period?
Steps 1 and 2.

Maximum wage base	$29,700
Earnings to date	−28,700
Taxable earnings current period	$ 1,000

> Rule 2: TO CALCULATE FICA TAX:
>
> Tax Rate × Current taxable earnings = FICA tax

Step 1. Determine taxable earnings for current pay period (see Rule 1).
Step 2. Calculate FICA tax:

Tax rate × Current taxable earnings = FICA tax

Example 1 B. A. Thomas earns $216.50 per week. Earnings to date amount to $2,598. What amount will be deducted from the current pay for FICA taxes?
Step 1. Determine taxable earnings for current pay period:

Earnings to date	$2,598.00
Current earnings	216.50
Total	$2,814.50

Total earnings to date is less than $29,700. Current taxable earnings = $216.50

Step 2. Calculate FICA tax:

.0665 × $216.50 = $14.40 FICA tax

230 /

Example 2 C. J. Jackson's gross earnings to date were $28,950. What amount of FICA tax will be deducted from the current pay of $985?

Step 1.

$$\begin{aligned}\text{Maximum wage base} &= \$29{,}700 \\ \text{Earnings to date} &= -28{,}950 \\ \text{Taxable earnings---current pay} &= \$750\end{aligned}$$

Step 2. Calculate FICA tax:

$$.0665 \times \$750 = \$49.88 \text{ FICA tax}$$

Federal income withholding tax

Another deduction usually made from an employees gross earnings is for federal income tax. Employers usually deduct a portion of the employee's income tax from each pay, and at the end of the tax year supply the employee with a record of the total tax that has been withheld from his or her earnings. The amount of the deduction is determined by:

1. Gross earnings for the pay period.
2. Length of the pay period.
3. The marital status of the employee.
4. The number of exemptions claimed by the employee.

Several methods are available to employers to compute the amount of federal withholding tax that should be deducted from the employee's pay. The calculation of state income withholding tax, where required, is similar to the federal income withholding tax except for the difference in the applicable percents and wage brackets.

TAX TABLE METHOD Tables showing the amount of deduction to be made for various wage brackets for weekly, biweekly, semimonthly, and monthly pay periods are available from the Internal Revenue Service.

PERCENT METHOD By the use of the schedule of allowances and Tables 9-1, 9-2, 9-3, and 9-4, an employer may compute the withholding tax for all employees with very acceptable accuracy. It is this method that has been used in completing the calculations in the following examples and problems.

Rule 1: TO CALCULATE INCOME WITHHOLDING TAX PERCENT METHOD:*
  a. Calculate allowance for exemptions claimed by the employee.
  b. Calculate taxable wage.
  c. Calculate withholding tax for the applicable pay period and marital status of the employee.

*Circular E: Employer's Tax Guide, Internal Revenue Service

Step 1. Calculate total allowance for exemptions:

Number of exemptions × Allowance for one exemption = Total allowance

Step 2. Calculate taxable wage:

Gross wage − Total allowance = Taxable wage

Step 3. Refer to appropriate table for employees marital status and pay period and:

a. Select wage bracket that includes the employees taxable wage.

  b. Select tax from table for the lower wage bracket.
  c. Calculate tax on remaining taxable wage:

$$\text{Taxable wage} - \text{Lower bracket} \times \text{Percent}$$

  d. Lower bracket tax + Remaining tax = Total withholding tax

Example 1 Marie Worth is single, claims 1 exemption and earns $175 per week. What withholding tax will be deducted from the gross earnings?

 Step 1. Calculate total allowance for exemptions:

$$1 \times \$14.40 = \$14.40 \text{ (see Schedule)}$$

 Step 2. Calculate taxable wage:

Total gross earnings	=	$175.00
Allowance	=	− 14.40
Taxable wage	=	$160.60

 Step 3. Calculate withholding tax:

  a. Locate wage bracket on Table 9-1a:

$$\text{Wage bracket that includes taxable wage} = \$143 - \$182$$

  b. Tax on lower bracket:

$$\$143 \text{ tax} = \$18.94$$

  c. $\$160.60 - \$143 \times .22 = \$3.87$

  d. $\$18.94 + \$3.87 = \$22.81$ Withholding tax

Example 2 James Grove is married, claims 4 exemptions, and earns $365 bi-weekly. What amount of withholding tax will be deducted from his pay?

 Step 1. Exemptions claimed equals 4 (see Schedule).

$$4 \times \$28.80 = \$115.20$$

 Step 2. Calculate taxable wage:

Total wage	=	$365.00
Allowance	=	−115.20
Taxable wage	=	$249.80

 Step 3. Calculate withholding tax:

  a. Select wage bracket that includes taxable wage. Locate wage bracket on Table 9-2b:

$$\text{Wage bracket} = \$210 - \$445$$

  b. Tax on lower bracket of $210 = $13.35

  c. $\$249.80 - \$210.00 \times .18 = \$7.16$

  d. $\$13.35 + \$7.16 = \$20.51$ Withholding tax

Example 3 Marie Wilcox is married and claims 3 exemptions. Find the amount of withholding tax that will be deducted from her monthly salary of $880.

 Step 1. Calculate total allowance (see Schedule):

$$3 \times \$62.50 = \$187.50$$

Step 2. Calculate taxable wage:

$$\begin{array}{ll}\text{Total wages} & \$880.00 \\ \text{Allowance} & \underline{187.50} \\ \text{Taxable wage} & \$692.50\end{array}$$

Step 3.
a. Select wage bracket that includes taxable wage. Locate wage bracket on Table 9–4b:

Wage bracket = $454 – $965

b.   Tax on lower bracket $454 = $28.65

c. $692.50 – $454.00 × .18 = $42.93

d. $28.65 + $42.93 = $71.58 Withholding tax

Schedule of Allowance for One Exemption	
Payroll period	One allowance
Weekly	$ 14.40
Biweekly	28.80
Semimonthly	31.30
Monthly	62.50
Quarterly	187.50
Semiannual	375.00
Annual	750.00
Daily	2.10

Rule 2: TO CALCULATE NET INCOME:

Gross pay – FICA tax – Withholding tax = Net income

Step 1. Calculate FICA tax:

Gross pay × Rate = FICA tax

Subject to maximum of $29,700 earnings to date.
Step 2. Calculate income withholding tax: Refer to Rule 1.
Step 3. Gross wage – FICA – Withholding tax = Net income

Example 1   Paula Peterson is married, has claimed 4 exemptions, is paid a semimonthly salary of $509. Her gross earnings to date are $10,180. What is the amount of her net income?

Step 1. Calculate taxable earnings:

$$\begin{array}{ll}\text{Earnings to date} = & \$10,180.00 \\ \text{Current earnings} = + & \underline{509.00} \\ \text{Total earnings} & \$10,689.00\end{array}$$

Total earnings are less than maximum of $29,700. Current earnings of $509 is the taxable earnings. Calculate FICA tax:

$509 × .0665 = $33.85

Step 2. Calculate income withholding tax:
a. Calculate total allowance (see Schedule):

4 × $31.30 = $125.20

Table 9-1 Weekly payroll period

(a) SINGLE person—including head of household:

If the amount of wage is:	The amount of income tax to be withheld shall be:
Not over $33 . . .0	

Over—	But not over—		of excess over—
$33	—$ 76	16%	—$33
$76	—$143	$6.88 plus 18%	—$76
$143	—$182	$18.94 plus 22%	—$143
$182	—$220	$27.52 plus 24%	—$182
$220	—$297	$36.64 plus 28%	—$220
$297	—$355	$58.20 plus 32%	—$297
$355	. . . .	$76.76 plus 36%	—$355

(b) MARRIED person—

If the amount of wages is:	The amount of income tax to be withheld shall be:
Not over $61 . . .0	

Over—	But not over—		of excess over—
$61	—$105	15%	—$61
$105	—$223	$6.60 plus 18%	—$105
$223	—$278	$27.84 plus 22%	—$223
$278	—$355	$39.94 plus 25%	—$278
$355	—$432	$59.19 plus 28%	—$355
$432	—$509	$80.75 plus 32%	—$432
$509	. . . .	$105.39 plus 36%	—$509

Table 9-2 Biweekly payroll period

(a) SINGLE person—including head of household:

If the amount of wage is:	The amount of income tax to be withheld shall be:
Not over $65 . . .0	

Over—	But not over—		of excess over—
$65	—$152	16%	—$65
$152	—$287	$13.92 plus 18%	—$152
$287	—$363	$38.22 plus 22%	—$287
$363	—$440	$54.94 plus 24%	—$363
$440	—$594	$73.42 plus 28%	—$440
$594	—$710	$116.54 plus 32%	—$594
$710	. . . .	$153.66 plus 36%	—$710

(b) MARRIED person—

If the amount of wages is:	The amount of income tax to be withheld shall be:
Not over $121 . . .0	

Over—	But not over—		of excess over—
$121	—$210	15%	—$121
$210	—$445	$13.35 plus 18%	—$210
$445	—$556	$55.65 plus 22%	—$445
$556	—$710	$80.07 plus 25%	—$556
$710	—$863	$118.57 plus 28%	—$710
$863	—$1,017	$161.41 plus 32%	—$863
$1,017	. . . .	$210.69 plus 36%	—$1,017

Table 9-3 Semimonthly payroll period

(a) SINGLE PERSON—including head of household:

If the amount of wages is:	The amount of income tax to be withheld shall be:
Not over $71 . . .0	

Over—	But not over—		of excess over—
$71	—$165	16%	—$71
$165	—$310	$15.04 plus 18%	—$165
$310	—$394	$41.14 plus 22%	—$310
$394	—$477	$59.62 plus 24%	—$394
$477	—$644	$79.54 plus 28%	—$477
$644	—$769	$126.30 plus 32%	—$644
$769	. . . .	$166.30 plus 36%	—$769

(b) MARRIED person—

If the amount of wages is:	The amount of income tax to be withheld shall be:
Not over $131 . . .0	

Over—	But not over—		of excess over—
$131	—$227	15%	—$131
$227	—$482	$14.40 plus 18%	—$227
$482	—$602	$60.30 plus 22%	—$482
$602	—$769	$86.70 plus 25%	—$602
$769	—$935	$128.45 plus 28%	—$769
$935	—$1,102	$174.93 plus 32%	—$935
$1,102	. . . .	$228.37 plus 36%	—$1,102

Table 9-4 Monthly payroll period

(a) SINGLE person—including head of household:

If the amount of wages is:	The amount of income tax to be withheld shall be:
Not over $142 . . .0	

Over—	But not over—		of excess over—
$142	—$329	16%	—$142
$329	—$621	$29.92 plus 18%	—$329
$621	—$788	$82.48 plus 22%	—$621
$788	—$954	$119.22 plus 24%	—$788
$954	—$1,288	$159.06 plus 28%	—$954
$1,288	—$1,538	$252.58 plus 32%	—$1,288
$1,538	. . . .	$332.58 plus 36%	—$1,538

(b) MARRIED person—

If the amount of wages is:	The amount of income tax to be withheld shall be:
Not over $263 . . .0	

Over—	But not over—		of excess over—
$263	—$454	15%	—$263
$454	—$965	$28.65 plus 18%	—$454
$965	—$1,204	$120.63 plus 22%	—$965
$1,204	—$1,538	$173.21 plus 25%	—$1,204
$1,538	—$1,871	$256.71 plus 28%	—$1,538
$1,871	—$2,204	$349.95 plus 32%	—$1,871
$2,204	. . . .	$456.51 plus 36%	—$2,204

Source: *Circular E (Supplement)*, Publication 15 (May 1977).

b. Calculate taxable wage:

$$\begin{aligned}\text{Total wage} &= \$509.00 \\ \text{Allowance} &= -125.20 \\ \text{Taxable wage} &= \$383.80\end{aligned}$$

Wage bracket (Table 9-3b) = $227 - $482
Tax on lower bracket, $227 = $14.40

c. Tax on remaining wages:

$$\$383.80 - \$227.00 \times .18 = \$28.22$$

Total tax: $14.40 + $28.22 = $42.62

Step 3. Calculate net income:

Gross income − FICA tax − Withholding tax = Net income
$509.00 − $33.85 − $42.62 = $432.53

Practice exercises

		Answer

1. Find the FICA tax that would be made on the gross earnings of the following employees:
   a. R. P. Cookford earned a gross monthly salary of $1,500. Gross earnings to date were $15,000. — $99.75
   b. A. J. Zero earned a biweekly salary of $1,012. His gross earnings to date were $24,038. — $67.30
   c. T. C. Haines had gross earnings to date of $24,964. His weekly salary for this pay period was $418.06. — $27.80
   d. E. J. Mack earned a semimonthly salary of $1,065. Gross earnings to date were $24,300. — $70.82

2. Calculate the withholding tax that will be deducted from the gross income of an employee who earns $2,675 per month, is single, and claims 2 exemptions. — _____

3. Ms. S. E. Hogan earns a weekly salary of $365. She is married and claims 5 exemptions. Find the amount of withholding tax that would be deducted from her weekly pay. — $43.69

4. Mrs. L. O. O'Keefe, who is married and claims 2 exemptions, earns $425 biweekly. What amount of withholding tax will be deducted from her pay each pay period? — _____

5. The semimonthly pay of an employee was $685. The employee was married and claimed 6 exemptions. What was the amount of his withholding tax? — $63.64

6. Ms. B. W. Allen is paid a biweekly salary of $650. Her gross earnings to date were $20,945. Ms. Allen is married and claims 4 exemptions.
   a. What is the amount of FICA tax that will be deducted from her pay? — _____

  b. Calculate the withholding tax that will be deducted from her pay. _____

  c. What is the amount of her net income each pay period? _____

7. John S. Barlow is paid a monthly salary of $2,100. His gross earnings to date are $29,200. Mr. Barlow is married and claims 5 exemptions.
   - *a.* Calculate the amount of the FICA tax he will pay this pay period. $33.25
   - *b.* What amount of withholding tax will be deducted from his current pay? $326.57
   - *c.* What is the amount of his net pay? $1,740.18

8. Find the net pay of Barbara Shippley who was paid a weekly salary of $185. Her gross earnings to date were $8,880. Barbara was single and claimed 2 exemptions. _____

9. Roberta I. Walters was paid a semimonthly salary of $675. Her gross earnings to date were $6,075. Ms. Walters is single and claims 3 exemptions. What net pay will be received the next pay period? $521.42

10. A. G. Gray is married, has claimed 4 exemptions, and is paid a salary of $1,050 biweekly. Total earnings to date are $21,940. What net pay will be received next pay day? _____

11. Larry O'Neal earns $2,846 per month, is married, and claims 3 exemptions. His earnings to date are $28,412. What net pay will he receive on his next pay day? $2,140.22

12. Find the withholding tax on the following employee's next pay day.
    - *a.* Rita Mellon, married, 6 exemptions, semimonthly pay of $1,345. _____
    - *b.* Carol Jones, single, 2 exemptions, is paid biweekly and earns $809.50 per pay period. _____

13. Calculate the FICA tax that will be deducted from the pay checks of the following employees.
    - *a.* Ruth C. Norris, who is paid $2,628.50 per month. Her earnings to date are $20,126.40. $174.80
    - *b.* Charles Kelly's earnings to date are $29,900 and he earns $1,100 per week.   No tax
    - *c.* Nellie Fellows earns $1,095 semimonthly. Her earnings to date are $24,590. $72.82

14. Calculate the net income of Jay Ryan, who is single, is paid $2,210 monthly, and claims 3 exemptions. His earnings to date are $23,072. _____

LOCAL TAXES

SALES TAX The tax levied on the sale of retail goods is a fixed percent of the retail selling price that is generally set by state or local governments. Tax tables are available for merchants that show the tax for fractional parts of $1 or for a variety of retail prices. The percent method of calculating sales tax is also acceptable by government agencies.

> **Rule 1: TO CALCULATE SALES TAX:**
> a. Tax table method:
>
> $$\text{Retail price dollars} \times \text{Tax rate} = \text{Sales tax}$$
>
> + Refer to table for tax on the fractional part of $1 = Sales tax
>
> b. Percent method:
>
> $$\text{Retail price} \times \text{Sales tax rate} = \text{Sales tax}$$

Step 1. Calculate total retail price if more than one item is subject to the sales tax.
Step 2. Add all applicable tax rates.
Step 3. Substitute data in sales tax formula.

Example 1   A. J. Rose purchased merchandise for $169.47, which was subject to a 5% sales tax. What amount of sales tax was due? (Use 5% tax table.)

Step 1.
$$\text{Total retail price} = \$169.47$$

Step 2.
$$\text{Applicable tax rate} = 5\%$$

Step 3. Sales tax formula:

$$\text{Retail price dollars} \times \text{Tax rate} = \text{Sales tax}$$
$$\$169 \times .05 = \$8.45$$

Tax from table on $0.47 = .02
Total sales tax $8.47

Table 9-5
Sales tax tables

4% Tax table
1. Multiply the number of dollars in the retail price by 4%.
2. Tax on fractional parts of $1.00 include:
$.00 - $.12 = $.00
.13 - .37 = .01
.38 - .62 = .02
.63 - .87 = .03
.88 - .99 = .04

5% Tax table
1. Multiply the number of dollars in the retail price by 5%.
2. Tax on fractional parts of $1.00 include:
$.00 - $.10 = $.00
.11 - .27 = .01
.28 - .47 = .02
.48 - .68 = .03
.69 - .89 = .04
.90 - .99 = .05

6% Tax table
1. Multiply the number of dollars in the retail price by 6%.
2. Tax on fractional parts of $1.00 include:
$.00 - $.10 = $.00
.11 - .24 = .01
.25 - .41 = .02
.42 - .58 = .03
.59 - .74 = .04
.75 - .91 = .05
.92 - .99 = .06

7% Tax table
1. Multiply the number of dollars in the retail price by 7%.
2. Tax on fractional parts of $1.00 include:
$.00 - $.07 = $.00
.08 - .20 = .01
.21 - .33 = .02
.34 - .47 = .03
.48 - .62 = .04
.63 - .76 = .05
.77 - .91 = .06
.92 - .99 = .07

Example 2 R. T. Evans purchased 6 bed sheets for $77.52, 12 pillowcases for $59.43, 4 pillows for $60.00, and 4 bedspreads for $120.00. A sales tax of 5½% was also charged. What amount of tax is payable using the percent method?

Step 1. Total retail sale price:

$77.52 + $59.43 + $60.00 + $120.00 = $316.95

Step 2.

Applicable sales tax rate = .055

Step 3. Sales tax formula:

Retail price × Sales tax rate = Sales tax
$316.95   ×   .055   = $17.43

Rule 2: TO CALCULATE SALES TAX:
When multiple sales taxes apply:
Total retail price × Total sales taxes = Sales tax

Step 1. Calculate total retail price.
Step 2. Add all applicable sales tax rates.
Step 3. Substitute data in sales tax formula.

Example 1 Mrs. Gibbs purchased 2 small rugs for $61.80, 2 pairs of draperies for $206.20, 1 chair cover for $111.50, and 12 window shades for $167.30. The merchandise was subject to a city sales tax of 4%, a county sales tax of 2½%, and a state sales tax of 1½%. What was the total sales tax charged on the sale?

Step 1. Calculate total retail price:

$61.80 + $206.20 + $111.50 + $167.30 = $546.80

Step 2. Add all applicable sales taxes:

.04 + .025 + .015 = .080

Step 3. Substitute data in sales tax formula:

Retail price × Sales tax rates = Sales tax
$546.80   ×   .08   = $43.74

Rule 3: TO CALCULATE TOTAL RETAIL PRICE:
Retail price + Sales tax = Total price

Step 1. Calculate total sales tax:

Retail price × Sales tax rate = Sales tax

Step 2.

Retail price + Sales tax = Total retail price

Example 1 Mrs. E. A. Smith purchased a washer-dryer at a retail price of $567.85. A sales tax of 4½% was charged. What was the total retail price?

Step 1. Calculate total sales tax:

$567.85 × .045 = $25.55

Step 2.

Retail price + Sales tax = Total retail price
$567.85   + $25.55   = $593.40

Example 2 L. O. Jenkins purchased a lawn tractor for $903.50, a hauling cart for $164.80, and a seed spreader for $22.60. A city sales tax of 5½% and a state sales tax of 2% were charged. What was the total price Mr. Jenkins paid for the merchandise?

Step 1. Calculate total sales tax:

Retail price = $903.50 + $164.80 + $22.60 = $1,090.90
Total sales taxes = .055 + .02 = .075

Total retail price × Total sales tax rate = Sales tax
$1,090.90 × .075 = $81.82

Step 2. Calculate total price:

Total retail price + Total sales tax = Total price
$1,090.90 + $81.82 = $1,172.72

Rule 4: TO CALCULATE FINAL RETAIL PRICE:
When *discount* and additional charges are included in the transaction :
a. Apply allowable discount rate to total retail price.
b. Apply sales tax to net retail price.
c. Add additional charges.

Step 1. Calculate total retail price.
Step 2. Calculate allowable discount:

Total retail price × Discount rate = Discount

Step 3. Calculate net retail price:

Total retail price − Discount = Net retail price

Step 4. Calculate sales tax:

Net retail price × Sales tax rate = Sales tax

Step 5. Calculate final retail price:

Net retail price + Sales tax + Additional charges = Final retail price

Example 1 Mr. F. C. Albright purchased a color television from a store where a 5% sales tax applied for a retail price of $675. The store allowed a 6% discount for cash terms and charged $26.90 to deliver the set to his home. Mr. Albright paid cash. What was the final selling price to Mr. Albright?

Step 1.

Total retail price = $675.00

Step 2. Calculate allowable discount:

$675.00 × .06 = $40.50 Discount

Step 3. Calculate net retail price:

$675.00 − $40.50 = $634.50

Step 4. Calculate sales tax:

$634.50 × .05 = $31.73 Sales tax

Step 5. Calculate final retail price:

$634.50 + $31.75 + $26.90 = $693.15

> **Rule 5: TO CALCULATE APPLICABLE SALES TAX:**
> The point of delivery or destination determines the applicable sales tax.

Step 1. Calculate applicable sales tax.

Apply only the sales tax required at the point of delivery or destination of merchandise purchased.

Step 2. Calculate final retail price as outlined in Rule 4.

Example 1 Ms. Y. Wiggins purchased a vanity chest for $82.50 and a stereo system for $233.85 from a retail merchant in Erie, Pennsylvania, where a 5% sales tax was required. A 4% discount for cash term was allowed by the merchant and which Ms. Wiggins decided to take. The merchandise was delivered to her home in Buffalo, New York, where a sales tax of 4½% was required. Additional charges included: insurance charges of $22.35 and shipping charges of $56.70. Find the final retail price of the merchandise to Ms. Wiggins.

Step 1. The sales tax required in Buffalo, New York, of 4½% will apply.

Step 2.

Total retail price = $82.50 + $233.85 = $316.35
Allowable discount = $316.35 × .04 = $12.66
Net retail price = $316.35 − $12.66 = $303.69
Applicable sales tax = $303.69 × .045 = $13.67
Final retail price = $303.69
  + 13.67
  + 22.35
  + 56.70
Final retail price = $396.41

> **Rule 6: TO CALCULATE RETAIL PRICE WHEN TOTAL PRICE AND SALES TAX RATE ARE KNOWN:**
>
> $$\frac{\text{Total price}}{100\% + \text{Sales tax rate}} = \text{Retail price}$$

Step 1. Assign 100% to the unknown retail price and add the sales tax rate.

Step 2. Substitute data in the retail price formula.

Example 1 Dorothy Nixon paid a total of $516.40 for a round-trip airfare ticket. A sales tax of 6½% was included in the total price. Find the total retail price of the ticket.

Step 1.

Retail price of ticket = 100%
Sales tax rate = 6½%

Step 2. Calculate retail price:

$$\frac{\text{Total price}}{100\% + 6\frac{1}{2}\%} = \frac{\$516.40}{1.065} = \$484.88 \text{ Retail price of ticket}$$

PROPERTY TAXES Tax on real property is the basis on which property owners share the cost of financing government institutions and such services as police, parks and highways, fire departments, and schools.

To equally distribute the cost of government services, each property owner pays taxes based on the assessed value of his property. This assessment is an arbitrary value, usually a percent of the market value, set by a representative of the local government.

A summary of the cost of government services is presented in an annual budget, which represents the total amount that must be raised by taxes to support all the services to the community. We will review the calculations necessary to determine the tax rate, the property owner's taxes, and the assessed value of real property.

Rule 1: TO CALCULATE A TAX RATE:

$$\frac{\text{Budget}}{\text{Assessed value}} = \text{Tax rate}$$

Note: A tax rate may be quoted per $1, $100, or $1,000 of assessed value. Multiply the tax rate calculated by the formula by 1, 100, or 1,000 to find the applicable rate.

Step 1. Calculate total budget and, if necessary, total assessed value.
Step 2. Substitute data in the tax rate formula.
Step 3.

$$\text{Tax rate} \times 100 = \text{Tax rate per } \$100 \text{ assessed value}$$
$$\text{Tax rate} \times 1,000 = \text{Tax rate per } \$1,000 \text{ of assessed value}$$

Example 1   The annual budget of a town was $219,916. The total assessed value of the property in the town was $5,432,972. What is the tax rate that would be applied to the assessed value of a property owner, if:

a. Tax rate is based on $1 of assessed value.
b. Tax rate is based on $100 of assessed value.
c. Tax rate is based on $1,000 of assessed value.

Step 1.
$$\text{Total budget} = \$219,916$$
$$\text{Total assessed value} = \$5,432,972$$

Step 2. Substitute in formula:

$$\frac{\text{Budget}}{\text{Assessed value}} = \text{Tax rate}$$

$$\frac{\$219,916}{\$5,432,972} = .0405 \text{ tax rate}$$

Step 3.
a. Tax rate per $1.00 = .0405 × 1 = $.0405
b. Tax rate per $100 = .0405 × 100 = $4.05
c. Tax rate per $1,000 = .0405 × 1,000 = $40.50

Example 2   If a tax rate that includes budgets for local, county, and state governments is required, add all the budgets and assessed values.

The budget of the state was $284,815, for the county, $160,419, and for the city $175,845. The total assessed value of taxable property was $36,847,000. Find the combined tax rate the property owner will pay per $100 of assessed value of property owned.

Step 1. Calculate total budget:

$$\begin{aligned}
\text{State budget} &\ \ \$284{,}815 \\
\text{County budget} &\ \ 160{,}419 \\
\text{City budget} &\ \ \underline{175{,}845} \\
\text{Total tax budget} &\ \ \$621{,}079
\end{aligned}$$

Step 2. Tax rate formula:

$$\frac{\text{Budget}}{\text{Assessed value}} = \frac{\$621{,}079}{\$36{,}847{,}000} = .016856 \text{ Tax rate}$$

Step 3. Tax rate per $100 of assessed value:

$$.016856 \times 100 = \$1.6856 \text{ Tax rate}$$

Rule 2: TO CALCULATE PROPERTY TAXES:

Assessed value × Tax rate = Property taxes

Step 1. Calculate tax rate, if necessary.
Step 2. Substitute data in property tax formula.

Example 1 The assessed value of Mr. Stanley's home is $6,200. The tax rate is $3.47 per $100 of assessed value. What amount of taxes does Mr. Stanley pay?

Step 1. Tax rate is $3.47 per $100 of assessed value.
Step 2.

$$\text{Assessed value} \times \text{Tax rate} = \text{Property taxes}$$

$$\frac{\$6{,}200}{100} \times \$3.47 = \$215.14$$

Example 2 If separate tax rates for several governments are given, add the tax rates before calculating taxes.

Ms. F. Allen's home was assessed for $27,000. The tax rate included a state tax rate of $1.42 per $100 of assessed value, a county tax rate of $1.23 per $100 of assessed value, and a city tax rate of $1.96. What total tax was payable?

Step 1. Calculate the tax rate:

$$\begin{aligned}
\text{State tax rate} &= \$1.42 \\
\text{County tax rate} &= 1.23 \\
\text{City tax rate} &= \underline{1.96} \\
\text{Total tax rate} &\ \ \$4.61
\end{aligned}$$

Step 2.

$$\text{Assessed value} \times \text{Tax rate} = \text{Property taxes}$$

$$\frac{\$27{,}000}{100} \times \$4.61 = \$1{,}244.70 \text{ Property taxes}$$

Rule 3: TO CALCULATE THE ASSESSED VALUE:

a. $\dfrac{\text{Total budgets}}{\text{Tax rate}} = \text{Total assessed value}$

or

b. $\dfrac{\text{Taxes paid}}{\text{Tax rate}} = \text{Property assessed value}$

Step 1. Calculate total budgets, if necessary.
Step 2. Calculate total tax rate, if necessary.
Step 3. Substitute data in assessed value formal or in the property assessed value formula.

Example 1 Find the total assessed value of property in a county with a total tax rate of $0.94 per $1.00 of assessed value. The county budget was $19,627,416.
Step 1. Total budget is $19,627,416.
Step 2. Total tax rate is $0.94 per $1 of assessed value.
Step 3.

$$\frac{\text{Total budget}}{\text{Tax rate}} = \text{Total assessed value}$$

$$\frac{\$19,627,416}{\$.94} = \$20,880,229 \text{ Total assessed value}$$

Example 2 Mr. Albert Fremont pays an annual tax of $516.20 on his apartment building. The tax rate if $0.047 per $1.00 of assessed value. Find the assessed value of the property.
Step 2.

$$\frac{\text{Taxes paid}}{\text{Tax rate}} = \frac{\$516.20}{.047} = \$10,982.98 \text{ Assessed value of property}$$

Practice exercises

		Answer
1. The sales tax in a certain city was 4½% of the retail price. Find the total retail price of:		
a. An item with a retail price of $55.12.		$57.60
b. An item with a retail price of $119.45.		$124.83

2. Mrs. E. C. Hope purchased a dining room set at a retail price of $1,248.50. The sales tax in the city was 3½%, in the county the tax was 2%, and in the state, 3%.
   a. What was the total sales tax charged on the dining room set? _____
   b. What was the total retail price Mrs. Hope paid? _____

3. Ray Walsh purchased a car for $6,075 in Belford, Delaware, where a 5½% sales tax was required and had it delivered to his home in Chester, Pennsylvania, where a 6% sales tax was required. Mr. Walsh was charged $56.00 for delivery costs and a charge of $21.40 for insurance. What was the total price of the car to Mr. Walsh? $6,516.90

4. The total price of two theater tickets including a 7½% sales tax was $37.60. What was the retail price of one ticket? _____

5. The total invoice price of a shipment of merchandise including a 6½% sales tax was $8,065.40.
   a. What was the price of the merchandise? $7,573.15
   b. What was the amount of the sales tax? $492.25

6. Ms. Daly's home was assessed for $3,100. If the tax rate is $0.0261 per $1.00 of assessed value, what property tax does Ms. Daly pay?

7. A property owned by Mr. Welker was assessed for $10,820. The city tax rate was $7.06 and the county rate was $4.36 per $100 of assessed value. How much did Mr. Welker pay in property taxes? $1,235.64

8. The assessed value of the taxable property in Woodstown is $552,785,960. The budget for the state was $502,533, for the county, $4,856,843, and $609,452 for the town of Woodstown. What is the tax rate per $100 of assessed value the property owners will pay?

9. Evelyn Baylor paid a total property tax of $618.25. The property tax rate was $0.045 per $1.00 of assessed value. What was the assessed value of her property? $13,738.89

10. The budget for the city of Bridgeport was $1,465,590, with a property tax rate of $0.0375 per $1.00 of assessed value. The county budget amounted to $906,420, with a property tax rate of $.014, and the state tax budget was $926,000, with a tax rate of $0.0165. What was the total assessed value of the property in the city of Bridgeport?

11. The budget for the town of Maplewood included $10,200 for police, $27,800 for parks, $119,650 for highways, and $19,620 for garbage collection. The total assessed value of taxable property was $1,326,840. Ms. Wright owns property with an assessed value of $9,025. Find:
    a. The tax rate per $1,000 of assessed value. $133.60
    b. The amount of property taxes Ms. Wright pays. $1,205.74

12. Find the property tax rate per $100 of assessed value in a city whose budget included: $1,096,400 for the police department, $1,123,505 for the fire department, $894,225 for highways, and $3,040,155 for schools. The assessed value of property in the city was $18,960,000. What was the property tax rate per $100 of assessed value?

13. Mrs. Harry Jones paid $915.20 in property taxes last year. The tax rate included a city property tax of $0.096 per $1.00 of assessed value, a county property tax of $0.042 and a state property tax of $0.022. What was the assessed value of her property? $5,720

Review problems

		Answer
1.	a. Eleanor Burger earned $915.20 semimonthly. Her earnings to date were $29,085. What amount of FICA tax will be deducted from her next pay?	$40.90
	b. Wallace Yoder's earnings to date were $24,694. Based on his monthly salary of $1,206, what amount will his employer deduct from his next pay?	$80.20
	c. Bertha Mackey earned $257.85 for the week. Earnings to date were $14,026. What amount will be deducted from her pay for FICA tax?	$17.15
2.	Find the withholding tax deducted from the gross pay of:	
	a. Henry Warner, married with 3 exemptions, who is paid $570 semimonthly.	_____
	b. Sally Walton, single with 1 exemption, who is paid $172.50 weekly.	_____
3.	Find the withholding tax the following employees will have deducted from their next pay:	
	a. Gloria Bradford, who is single, claims 2 exemptions, and earns $490 bi-weekly.	$71.60
	b. James Parry, who is married, claims 5 exemptions, and earns $2,150 per month.	$340.57
4.	What net pay will Roger Williams, who is married, receive from his gross salary of $500 paid bi-weekly. His earnings to date are $11,500. Mr. Williams claims 3 exemptions.	_____
5.	Mildred Green, who is single, earned a semimonthly salary of $592.80 and claims 2 exemptions. Her earnings to date are $17,916.20. What net pay will she receive on the next pay day?	$458.94
6.	What amount of sales tax would be paid on merchandise that was sold for $312.90 if the city sales tax was 3½%, the county sales tax was 2%, and the state sales tax was 1%?	_____
7.	W. T. Andrews purchased a suit of clothes for $135.75. A city sales tax of 4%, a county sales tax of 2½%, and a sales tax in the state was 1%. What was the total cost of the suit to Mr. Andrews?	$145.93
8.	The sales tax in a certain city was 4½%. Find the total price of:	
	a. An item that cost $405.75 at retail price.	_____
	b. An item that sold at retail for $86.35.	_____
9.	Ms. Joan Mack purchased office furniture for $1,465 from a retail store in Canton, Ohio, where a sales tax of 7½% was required, and had the set delivered to her office	

in Greenville, Pennsylvania, where the required sales tax was 6%. The store offered a 4% discount for cash payment, which Ms. Mack accepted. Additional shipping charges of $24.15 was also charged. What was the total cost of the office furniture to Ms. Mack? $1,514.93

10. Allen Black purchased a used car from a dealer in Camden, Illinois, where a 5% sales tax was required. The car was priced to sell for $2,020; however, the dealer offered Mr. Black an 8% discount for cash payment. Mr. Black decided to pay cash and had the car delivered to his home in Westville, Kentucky, where a 4½% sales tax was required. Transportation charges of $62.80, insurance charges of $31.80, and a transfer fee of $11.50 were also payable. Find the final retail price of the car to Mr. Black. _____

11. Ms. Clair Harrison purchased an organ for $1,056.50 from a retail store in Coatsville, Pennsylvania, where a sales tax of 6½% was required, and had it shipped to her home in Columbus, Ohio, where a sales tax of 4% was required. Shipping charges amounted to $64.50. What was the total retail price of the organ? $1,163.26

12. The total price of an item was $136.80 including a sales tax of 7½%. What was the retail price of the item? _____

13. The Jay Moore Lumber Company received an invoice showing a total of $1,146.80 for a shipment of supplies. The total invoice included a sales tax of 5½%. Find the total price of the supplies. $1,087.01

14. The assessed value of the taxable property in a municipality was $152,785,960. The state budget was $601,525, the county budget was $3,258,583, and the municipal budget was $422,358. Find the combined tax rate the property owners in the municipality will pay on $100 of assessed value of their property. _____

15. What is the tax rate per $1,000 of assessed value in the town of Casselton, which has an annual budget of $614,752 and the total assessed value of property in the town is $14 million? $43.91

16. The assessed value of property in Newtown is $3,684,700. The Newtown budget included $33,083 for highways, $106,920 for police, $37,892 for schools, and $92,835 for social services.
    a. What is the tax rate per $100 of assessed value rounded to the 4th decimal place? _____
    b. What property tax will property owner pay on property that is assessed for $12,875? _____

17. Ms. K. Newman owned a building that was assessed for $76,000. What should her property tax payment be if the city tax rate was $2.80 per $100 of assessed value, the county tax was $1.75 per $100 of assessed value, and the state tax rate was $1.46? $4,567.60

246 /

18. Mr. Ted Hughes's property was assessed for $19,250. The property tax rate was $2.12 per $100 of assessed value. What amount of property tax does Mr. Hughes pay?

19. If the total annual tax payment on a building lot was $408, what was the assessed value of the lot with a tax rate of $.025 per $1.00 of assessed value? $16,320

20. The total annual budget of the town of Hopewell included $134,890 for the police department, $142,060 for the fire department, $63,906 for parks and highways, and $1,084,500 for schools. The property tax rate in the town was $.0834 per $1.00 of assessed value. What was the total assessed value of all property in the town. (Round answer to dollars.)

21. Find the amount of withholding tax that would be deducted from Jane Wilson's next pay. She is married, claims 4 exemptions, and earns $765 biweekly. $103.52

22. What net pay will Betty Weaver receive on her next pay day if her earnings to date are $24,994? She is married, claims 5 exemptions, and earns a semimonthly salary of $1,846.

STUDY UNIT **10**

Accounting procedures

METHODS OF DEPRECIATION
  Straight line
  Book value
  Declining balance
  Sum-of-the-years' digits

DISTRIBUTION OF OVERHEAD EXPENSES

INVENTORY EVALUATION
  Fifo inventory evaluation
  Lifo inventory evaluation
  Average unit cost method

Our review of the use of mathematics in accounting procedures is limited to the calculations used for:

Methods of depreciation.
Distribution of overhead.
Methods of evaluating inventories.

This limited application should not be regarded as the only use to be made of mathematics in the field of accounting, but rather as illustrations of the application of mathematics to accounting functions. The necessary journal entries and records to record the results of these calculations are covered extensively in accounting courses.

METHODS OF DEPRECIATION

To satisfy the requirements of their accounting systems and the Internal Revenue Service for depreciation allowances, a business must periodically calculate and record the decrease in the value of assets used in the production and creation of goods and services. However, land is not subject to depreciation.

Depreciation may be defined as the loss in value that occurs from the passage of time or from the use and obsolescence of productive assets. Such assets as buildings, machinery, trucks and automobiles, and production equipment are depreciated at least once a year. Land owned by a company is not subject to depreciation.

To illustrate the mathematics of depreciation, we will review the calculations involved in straight-line, declining-balance, and sum-of-the-years' digit methods of calculating depreciation. A fiscal year of January 1 to December 31 is used as the depreciation period.

STRAIGHT-LINE DEPRECIATION

To calculate the loss in value of an asset, the businessman will often use the simplest method of calculating depreciation, which is known as the straight-life method and distributes depreciation evenly over the life of the asset regardless of the basis of its "life."

To calculate straight-line depreciation, it is necessary to know or ascertain:

1. The original cost of the asset, plus any additional acquisition costs.
2. The salvage or trade-in value of the asset when it is no longer useful to the owner.
3. The estimated life of the asset, which may be expressed as *time (years), production units, production hours,* or *miles.*
4. The date of purchase.
5. The book value of the asset at any time during its lifetime.
6. The fiscal year used in the accounting system.
7. The application of an additional percent allowance that is permitted by the Internal Revenue Service on the first year of certain types of assets.

Rule 1: TO CALCULATE ANNUAL DEPRECIATION:

$$\frac{\text{Cost} - \text{Salvage (Trade-in) value}}{\text{Estimated life}} = \text{Annual depreciation}$$

Note: Estimated life may be years, units, hours, or miles.

Step 1. When the required data is ascertained, substitute data in the annual depreciation formula.

Example 1 Find the annual depreciation on an asset that cost $18,125 and that had a trade-in value of $1,275 after an estimated life of 8 years. The fiscal year is January 1 to December 31.

Step 1. Ascertain data:

$$\text{Cost} = \$18,125$$
$$\text{Estimated life} = 8 \text{ years}$$
$$\text{Trade-in value} = \$1,275$$

$$\frac{\text{Cost} - \text{Trade-in}}{\text{Estimated years}} = \text{Depreciation per year}$$

$$\frac{\$18,125 - \$1,275}{8 \text{ years}} = \$2,106.25 \text{ Depreciation per year}$$

Example 2 *Production units as estimated life.* The Emerson Company bought a machine at a cost of $5,000. The estimated life was 250,000 production units. Salvage value was expected to be $500. Find the depreciation after 26,000 units had been produced.

Step 1. Ascertain the data and calculate depreciation per unit:

$$\text{Cost} = \$5,000$$
$$\text{Salvage value} = \$500$$
$$\text{Estimated life} = 250,000 \text{ units}$$

$$\frac{\text{Cost} - \text{Salvage value}}{\text{Estimated life}} = \text{Depreciation per unit}$$

$$\frac{\$5,000 - \$500}{250,000} = \$.018 \text{ Depreciation per unit}$$

Step 2. Calculate total depreciation:

Units produced × Unit depreciation = Total depreciation
26,000   ×   .018   = $468.00

Example 3 *Production hours as the estimated life.* The Dumphy's Cabinet Shop purchased a planer at a cost of $1,400. The estimate life was 10,400 production hours and the scrap value was estimated to be $200. What was the depreciation after 4,170 hours of operation?

Step 1. Ascertain data and calculate depreciation per hour:

$$\frac{\text{Cost} - \text{Salvage value}}{\text{Estimated hours}} = \text{Depreciation per hour}$$

Cost   = $1,400
Scrap value = $ 200
Estimated life = 10,400 hours

$$\frac{\$1,400 - \$200}{10,400 \text{ hours}} = \$.1154 \text{ Depreciation per hour}$$

Step 2. Calculate total depreciation:

Production hours × Depreciation per hour = Total depreciation
4,170 hours   × $.1154   = $481.22

Example 4 *Miles as the estimated life.* A truck that cost $8,775 had been driven 87,500 miles when it was traded in for a value of $1,175. The estimated life of the truck was 120,000 miles. What was the total depreciation at the time of the trade-in?

Step 1. Ascertain the data and calculate the depreciation per mile:

$$\frac{\text{Cost} - \text{Trade-in}}{\text{Estimated miles}} = \text{Depreciation per mile}$$

$$\frac{\$8,775 - \$1,175}{120,000} = \$.0633 \text{ Depreciation per mile}$$

Step 2. Calculate total depreciation:

Miles driven × Depreciation per mile = Total depreciation
87,500   × $.0633   = $5,538.75

Practice exercises

Answer

1. The cost of a factory machine was $56,820, the salvage value was $4,620, and the estimated life was 12 years. Find the annual depreciation based on the calendar year. $4,350

2. The Edward Dress Manufacturing Company purchased an electric sewing machine at a cost of $27,890. The estimated life of the machine was 15 years, after which they expected to receive a salvage value of $1,820. Find the depreciation for one year.

3. The Dudley Company purchased a machine at a cost of $5,300. The life of the machine was estimated to be 200,000 units. The trade-in value was $500. In the first year, 38,000 units were produced and 46,000 units in the second year. Find the depreciation for each year.

$912 1st year
$1,104 2d year

4. The Appleton Company purchased a sorting machine at a cost of $16,750. Scrap value was estimated to be $2,500 after a life of 190,000 production units. Find the depreciation after 26,380 units had been produced.

_____

5. The U-Haul-Me Company purchased a truck for $11,740 and estimated its life to be 110,000 miles. Trade-in value was expected to be $1,400. What is the depreciation after the truck had been driven 62,575 miles?

$5,882.05

6. The N. B. Smith Company purchased a new car that cost $10,136. The life of the car was estimated to be 95,000 miles, after which a trade-in of $3,724 was expected. What was the depreciation on the car after it had been driven 46,134 miles?

_____

7. The Kelley Construction Company purchased a fork lift truck at a cost of $12,700. Scrap value was estimated to be $1,500 and the estimated life at 14,000 hours. The first year of operation the fork lift was used 824 hours and the second year it was used 712 hours. What was the depreciation for the 1st and 2nd years?

$659.20 1st year
$569.60 2d year

8. A piece of machinery, which had an estimated life of 13,680 production hours, cost $19,865. Salvage value was estimated to be $4,133. What was the depreciation after the machine had been used for 1,800 hours?

_____

First-year depreciation

If the purchase or trade-in of an asset does not occur exactly at the beginning of a fiscal year, the first year's depreciation will be a pro-rata portion of a full year's depreciation. If the purchase date is the 15th or before of a month, that month is included in the depreciation period. If the purchase date is after the 16th of the month, the depreciation period starts at the beginning of the following month. For example:

1. An asset purchased on April 10:
Depreciation period is April 1 to December 31, or 9 months, which is $9/12$ of a year.
2. An asset purchased April 18:
Depreciation period is May 1 to December 31, or 8 months, which is $8/12$ of a year.

Rule 2: TO CALCULATE THE FIRST-YEAR DEPRECIATION:
a. Calculate annual depreciation.
b. Determine the number of months in the first-year depreciation period.
c. $\dfrac{\text{Months in 1st year depreciation period}}{12} \times$ Annual depreciation = 1st year depreciation

---

254 /

Step 1. Calculate annual depreciation:

$$\frac{\text{Cost} - \text{Salvage or Trade-in value}}{\text{Estimated life}} = \text{Annual depreciation}$$

Step 2. Count number of months in the 1st-year depreciation period.
Step 3.

$$\frac{\text{Months in 1st year Depreciation period}}{12} \times \text{Annual depreciation} = \text{1st year depreciation}$$

Example 1 Find the depreciation for the 1st year on an asset that was purchased on August 9 at a cost of $11,825. The salvage value was $1,085 and the estimated life was 6 years. The fiscal year was the same as the calendar year.

Step 1. Calculate annual depreciation:

$$\frac{\text{Cost} - \text{Salvage value}}{\text{Estimated life}} = \text{Annual depreciation}$$

$$\frac{\$11,825 - \$1,085}{6 \text{ years}} = \$1,790 \text{ Annual depreciation}$$

Step 2. Number of months in depreciation period:

Purchase date = August 9
Depreciation period = August 9 to December 31, or 5 months

Step 3.

$$\frac{\text{Months in depreciation period}}{12} \times \text{Annual depreciation} = \text{1st year depreciation}$$

$$\frac{5}{12} \times \$1,790 = \$745.83 \text{ 1st-year depreciation}$$

Example 2 Calculate the 1st year's depreciation on an asset that was purchased on September 28 at a cost of $9,125. The salvage value was estimated to be $975 and the estimated life was 8 years. Depreciation was based on a calendar year.

Step 1. Calculate annual depreciation:

$$\frac{\text{Cost} - \text{Salvage value}}{\text{Estimated life}} = \text{Annual depreciation}$$

$$\frac{\$9,125 - \$975}{8 \text{ years}} = \$1,018.75$$

Step 2. Number of months in depreciation period:

Date of purchase = September 28
Depreciation period = October 1 to December 31, or 3 months

Step 3.

$$\frac{\text{Months in depreciation period}}{12} \times \text{Annual depreciation} = \text{1st-year depreciation}$$

$$\frac{3}{12} \times \$1,018.75 = \$254.69 \text{ 1st-year depreciation}$$

ADDITIONAL COST AND ANNUAL DEPRECIATION

Any cost, such as installation cost, remodeling cost, or "set-up" cost, that is necessary to make the asset productive is added to the original cost to determine the base of calculating depreciation.

Rule 3: TO CALCULATE DEPRECIATION WHEN ADDITIONAL COSTS ARE INCURRED:
 a. Calculate total cost:

 b. $\dfrac{\text{Total cost} - \text{Salvage or Trade-in value}}{\text{Estimated life}} = \text{Annual depreciation}$

Step 1. Calculate total costs:

Original costs + All costs to make the asset productive = Total cost

Step 2. Substitute data in annual depreciation formula.

Example 1 A milling machine that cost $47,815 had a salvage value of $9,060. Additional installation costs amounted to $1,745. Estimated life of the machine was 20 years. Calculate the annual depreciation.

Step 1. Calculate total costs:

$$\$47{,}815 + \$1{,}745 = \$49{,}560 \text{ Total cost}$$

Step 2. Substitute data in depreciation formula:

$$\frac{\$49{,}560 - \$9{,}060}{20 \text{ years}} = \$2{,}025 \text{ Annual depreciation}$$

First-year depreciation allowance

Because certain types of assets depreciate more rapidly in the early years of their useful life, Internal Revenue Service regulations permit an additional depreciation to be taken during the first year the asset is used. Although Internal Revenue Service regulations change from time to time, the current regulation permits a stated percent of the original cost of an asset to be deducted only for the first year of use. The first-year allowance applies to assets with an estimated life of at least 6 years and is subject to a maximum of 20% of the original cost.

Rule 4: TO CALCULATE DEPRECIATION WHEN FIRST-YEAR ALLOWANCE IS ELECTED:
 a. Calculate the 1st-year allowance.
 b. Calculate annual depreciation.
 c. Calculate the depreciation for 1st year:

 Annual depreciation + Allowance = 1st-year allowance

Step 1. Calculate 1st-year allowance:

Original cost × .20 = 1st-year allowance

Step 2. Calculate annual depreciation:

$$\frac{\text{Original cost} - \text{Allowance} - \text{Scrap or Trade-in}}{\text{Estimated life}} = \text{Annual depreciation}$$

Step 3. Calculate 1st-year depreciation:

Annual depreciation + Allowance = 1st-year depreciation

Step 4. Calculate subsequent years depreciation:

2d-year depreciation = Annual depreciation
3d-year depreciation = Annual depreciation

Example 1 Find the 1st-year depreciation on a piece of equipment that cost $26,845, had a salvage value of $9,120, and an estimated life of 15 years. The owner elected to take the additional 20% depreciation allowance. The equipment was purchased January 3.

Step 1. Calculate the 1st-year allowance:

$$\text{Original cost} \times .20 = \text{1st-year allowance}$$
$$\$26,845 \times .20 = \$5,369$$

Step 2. Calculate annual depreciation:

$$\frac{\text{Original cost} - \text{Allowance} - \text{Scrap or Trade-in}}{\text{Estimated life}} = \text{Annual depreciation}$$

$$\frac{\$26,845 - \$5,369 - \$9,120}{15 \text{ years}} = \$823.73 \text{ Annual depreciation}$$

Step 3. Calculate the 1st-year depreciation:

Annual depreciation + 1st-year allowance = 1st-year depreciation
$823.73 + $5,369 = $6,192.73

Example 2 The James Manufacturing Company purchased a piece of equipment at a cost of $18,125. The estimated life was 20 years, after which a salvage value of $2,165 was expected. The first year, 20% allowance was taken. Find:
 a. The depreciation for the first year.
 b. Depreciation for the second year. Purchase date was January 1.

Step 1. Calculate the 1st-year allowance:

$$\text{Original cost} \times .20 = \text{1st-year allowance}$$
$$\$18,125 \times .20 = \$3,625$$

Step 2. Calculate annual depreciation:

$$\frac{\text{Original cost} - \text{Allowance} - \text{Scrap or Trade-in}}{\text{Estimated life}} = \text{Annual depreciation}$$

$$\frac{\$18,125 - \$3,625 - \$2,165}{20 \text{ years}} = \$616.75 \text{ annual depreciation}$$

Step 3. Calculate 1st-year depreciation:

Annual depreciation + Allowance = 1st-year depreciation
$616.75 + $3,625 = $4,241.75

Step 4. Calculate 2d-year depreciation:

Annual depreciation = $616.75 = 2d-year depreciation

BOOK VALUE Book value is the recorded value of an asset at a specific point in time during the life of the asset. At least once during a fiscal or accounting year, depreciation is recorded on the books of the company and current book value of the asset is calculated.

> **Rule 5: TO CALCULATE BOOK VALUE:**
>
> Original cost − Accumulated depreciation = Book value

Step 1. Calculate accumulated depreciation:

All prior depreciation and depreciation of the current period = accumulated depreciation

Step 2. Substitute all data in book value formula.

Example 1 A lathe was purchased on June 6, 19—, at a cost of $24,640. The salvage value was $1,000 and the estimated life of the lathe was 12 years. What is the book value on December 31, 3 years after the lathe was purchased? No depreciation had previously been calculated. The fiscal year ended on December 31.

Step 1. Calculate accumulated depreciation:

a. Calculate annual depreciation:

$$\frac{\$24{,}640 - \$1{,}000}{12 \text{ years}} = \$1{,}970 = \text{Annual depreciation}$$

b. Calculate 1st-year depreciation:

June 6 to December 31 = 7 months

$\frac{7}{12} \times \$1{,}970$ = $1,149.17 1st year

Annual depreciation $1,970.00 2d year
Annual depreciation $1,970.00 3d year
Accumulated
 depreciation $5,089.17

Step 2. Calculate book value.

Original cost − Accumulated depreciation = Book value
 $24,640   − $5,089.17   = $19,550.83

Depreciation schedule

A schedule of the depreciation provides a convenient method of determining book value of an asset at any point during the life of the asset. It is often necessary to adjust the final year of depreciation to make the book value equal the scrap or trade-in value.

Example The Green Company purchased a piece of equipment at cost of $19,500. The estimated life was 6 years, after which a trade-in of $8,900 was expected. The purchase was made on January 5 and the fiscal year was the calendar year.

Step. 1 Calculate the annual depreciation:

$$\frac{\text{Original cost} - \text{Trade-in}}{\text{Estimated life}} = \text{Annual depreciation}$$

$$\frac{\$19{,}500 - \$8{,}900}{6} = \$1{,}766.67$$

Step 2. Calculate a depreciation schedule:

Year	Annual depreciation	Accumulated depreciation	Book value
1	Original cost		$19,500.00
1	$1,766.67	$ 1,766.67	- 1,766.67
2	$1,766.67	$ 3,533.34	$17,733.33 - 1,766.67
3	$1,766.67	$ 5,300.01	$15,966.66 - 1,766.67
4	$1,766.67	$ 7,066.68	$14,199.99 - 1,766.67
5	$1,766.67	$ 8,833.35	$12,433.32 - 1,766.67
6	$1,766.67	$10,600.02	$10,666.65 - 1,766.67 $ 8,899.98
6	Adjustment		+ .02 $ 8,900.00

Practice exercises

Answer

1. A. R. Wells purchased an office building for $137,500. He spent $82,000 to remodel the building and $18,000 for a new heating system. The estimated life of the building was 30 years. It was estimated that the value of the building would be $40,000 in 30 years. What is the annual depreciation on the building? $6,583.33

2. If an asset cost $9,267 and had a salvage value of $1,050 with an estimated life of 12 years, what depreciation would be charged for the 1st year if the asset was purchased on May 20 and depreciation was based on the calendar year? _____

3. Find the depreciation for the 1st year on an asset that was purchased on August 11 at a cost of $20,750. The salvage value was $1,586 and the estimated life was 12 years. Depreciation is based on a calendar year. $665.42

4. Find the depreciation on a piece of equipment which was purchased on March 23 for the 1st and 2d years if the cost was $26,845. Salvage value was $9,115 and the estimated life was 15 years. The 20% first-year allowance was taken by the owner. _____

5. A milling machine cost $129,850. The salvage value was $9,200 and the estimated life was 1,850,000 units. Find the depreciation for the first year if the 20% allowance was taken and units produced were 106,080. $31,401.30

6. Factory equipment was purchased at a cost of $38,750. The estimated life was 42,500 hours. The 20% allowance was taken in the 1st year. Find the book value of the equipment at the end of the 2d year if it was used 2,200 hours the 1st year and 2,925 hours the 2d year. _____

10 ACCOUNTING PROCEDURES / 259

7. Four and a half years ago the Bangor Company purchased a piece of machinery at a cost of $26,400.60. The estimated life was 8 years, after which a scrap value of $2,000 was expected. What is the present book value of the machine? Depreciation was based on a calendar year. $12,675.24

8. What is the book value of a drill press after 4 years if the cost was $6,750 and the press had an estimated life of 10 years? The estimated scrap value was $415. Depreciation was based on a calendar year. _____

9. A new assembly unit with an expected production life of 1,250,000 units and an estimated scrap value of $7,500 was purchased at a cost of $48,900. Special construction cost were $500, and setup charges were $1,500. What was the book value at the end of the 2d year? Production for the 1st year was 330,000 units and in the 2d year, 285,000 units. $29,559.50

10. A factory machine was purchased at a cost of $22,750. The estimated life was 20,000 hours. Installation costs were $593.50 and setup costs amounted to $570.00. What is the book value of the machine at the end of the second year? The machine was used 2,300 hours the first year and 3,125 hours the second year. _____

11. A milling machine was purchased on May 5 at a cost of $31,800. The salvage value was expected to be $3,600 and the estimated life was 12 years. What was the depreciation for 1st and 2d years? Depreciation was based on a calendar year. $1,566.67 1st year $2,350.00 2d year

12. Brownley Service Company purchased a minicomputer for $89,000 on April 8. The estimated life of the computer was 5 years, after which a resale value of $20,000 was expected. What is the book value of the computer after the 1st year and after the 2d year? Depreciation is based on a calendar year. _____ _____

13. Find the depreciation on an asset that was purchased on August 28 for $17,420 for the 1st and 2d years. Salvage value was $1,820 and an estimated life of 12 years was expected. $433.33 1st year $1,300 2d year

14. Find the annual depreciation on a piece of equipment that cost $24,800 and had an additional installation cost of $3,750. The salvage value was $6,250 and the estimated life was 15 years. _____

DECLINING-BALANCE METHOD OF CALCULATING DEPRECIATION

Some assets decrease more in value during the first few years of their estimated life than in later years. To more accurately record this accelerated rate of depreciation, the *declining-balance method* of depreciation is used. This method requires that a fixed rate of depreciation be applied to the book value of the prior year.

> **Rule 6: TO CALCULATE DECLINING-BALANCE DEPRECIATION:**
> a. Calculate the depreciation rate.
> b. Calculate the 1st-year depreciation:
>
> Original cost × Depreciation rate = 1st-year depreciation
>
> c. Calculate subsequent annual depreciation:
>
> $$\begin{pmatrix}\text{Original} \\ \text{Cost}\end{pmatrix} - \begin{pmatrix}\text{Accumulated} \\ \text{depreciation}\end{pmatrix} \times \begin{pmatrix}\text{Depreciation} \\ \text{rate}\end{pmatrix} = \begin{pmatrix}\text{Annual} \\ \text{depreciation}\end{pmatrix}$$

Step 1. Calculate the depreciation rate:

The depreciation rate is twice the straight-line rate.
Write a fraction using 2 as the numerator and the estimated life as the denominator:

$$\text{Fraction} = \frac{2}{\text{Estimated life}} = \text{Depreciation rate}$$

Step 2. Calculate the 1st-year depreciation:

Original cost × Depreciation rate = 1st-year depreciation

Note: Do not deduct scrap or trade-in from the original cost.

Step 3. Calculate subsequent annual depreciation:

Original cost − Accumulated depreciation × Depreciation rate
= Annual depreciation

Example 1 The Reynolds Manufacturing Company purchased an electric press at a cost of $21,840. The estimated life is 16 years, after which a scrap value of $3,125 is expected. Find the 1st-year depreciation by the declining balance method.

Step 1. Calculate the depreciation rate:

$$\frac{2}{\text{Estimated life}} = \frac{2}{16} = .125 \text{ or } 12.5\%$$

Step 2. Calculate the 1st-year depreciation:

Original cost × Depreciation rate = 1st-year depreciation
$21,840   ×   .125   = $2,730

Example 2 A piece of equipment was purchased at a cost of $14,635. A trade-in value of $2,900 was expected after an estimated life of 8 years. What was the depreciation:
  a. For the 1st year?
  b. For 2d year?
  c. For the 3d year?

Step 1. Calculate the depreciation rate:

$$\frac{2}{\text{Estimated life}} = \frac{2}{8} = .25 \text{ or } 25\%$$

Step 2. Calculate the 1st-year depreciation:

Original cost × Depreciation rate = 1st-year depreciation
$14,635   ×   .25   = $3,658.75

Step 3. Calculate subsequent annual depreciation:

Original cost − Accumulated depreciation × Depreciation rate
= Annual depreciation

$14,635 − $3,658.75 × .25 = $2,744.06 Depreciation 2d year

−$3,658.75
$14,635 − $2,744.06 × .25 = $2,058.05 Depreciation 3d year

SUM-OF-THE-YEARS'-DIGITS METHOD OF CALCULATING DEPRECIATION

Another accelerated method of calculating depreciation is the sum-of-the-years'-digits method, which is based on a decreasing rate of depreciation applied to the original cost of an asset less the scrap or trade-in value.

Rule 8: TO CALCULATE DEPRECIATION BY SUM-OF-THE-YEARS'-DIGITS METHOD:

  a. Add all the years involved in the estimated life.
  b. Write a fraction:

$$\frac{\text{The depreciation year in reverse order}}{\text{Sum of all years in the estimated life}} = \text{Depreciation rate}$$

  c. Calculate annual depreciation:

Original cost − Scrap or Trade-in × Depreciation rate = Annual depreciation

  d. Calculate book value:

Original cost − Accumulated depreciation = Book value

Step 1. Add all the years in the estimated life of the asset in reverse order.

Example: To get 7 years estimated life, add:

7 + 6 + 5 + 4 + 3 + 2 + 1 = 28 Years

Step 2. Write a fraction:

$$\frac{\text{Year in estimated life}}{\text{Total years in estimated life}}$$

Example:

$$\text{1st-year depreciation} = \frac{7}{28}$$

$$\text{2d-year depreciation} = \frac{6}{28}$$

$$\text{3d-year depreciation} = \frac{5}{28}$$

Step 3. Calculate annual depreciation:

Original cost − Scrap or Trade-in × Depreciation rate = Annual depreciation

Step 4. Calculate book value:

Original cost − Accumulated depreciation = Book value

Example 1 The Evans Manufacturing Company purchased a capping machine at a

cost of $12,485. The estimated life was 8 years, after which a scrap value of $1,042 was expected. Find:
   a. The depreciation for the 1st year.
   b. Depreciation for the 2d and 3d years.
   c. What was the book value at the end of the third year?

   Step 1. Add all the years in the estimated life:

$$8 + 7 + 6 + 5 + 4 + 3 + 2 + 1 = 36 \text{ total}$$

   Step 2. Write a fraction for 1st year:

$$\text{1st year} = \frac{8}{36}$$

   Step 3. Calculate annual depreciation:

$$\text{1st year} = \$12{,}485 - \$1{,}042 \times \frac{8}{36} = \$2{,}542.89$$

$$\text{2nd year} = \$12{,}485 - \$1{,}042 \times \frac{7}{36} = \$2{,}225.03$$

$$\text{3rd year} = \$12{,}485 - \$1{,}042 \times \frac{6}{36} = \$1{,}907.17$$

   Step 4. Calculate book value:

$$\$12{,}485 - \$6{,}675.09^* = \$5{,}809.91$$

*Accumulated depreciation:

1st year	$2,542.89
2nd year	2,225.03
3rd year	1,907.17
Total	$6,675.09

If the estimated life of an asset is for extended period of time, the sum-of-the-years'-digits may be calculated more conveniently by use of the formula.

Rule 9: SUM-OF-THE-YEARS'-DIGITS FORMULA (where N = estimated life):

$$\frac{N \times (N+1)}{2} = \text{Sum-of-the-years'-digit denominator}$$

Example 1 The original cost of a piece of equipment was $8,000. The estimated life was 15 years, after which a trade-in of $750 was expected. What is the 1st year's depreciation?

   Step 1. Calculate the sum-of-the-years' digits'

$$\frac{15 \times 16}{2} = \text{Sum-of-the-years' digits}$$

$$\frac{240}{2} = 120$$

   Step 2. Calculate the 1st year's depreciation:

$$\$8{,}000 - \$750 \times \frac{15}{120} = \$906.25 \text{ 1st-year depreciation}$$

Practice exercises

		Answer
1.	A bulldozer was purchased at a cost of $38,035. After an estimated life of 20 years, a trade-in value of $10,500 was expected. Calculate the depreciation for the 1st and 2d years by the declining-balance method.	$3,803.50 1st year $3,423.15 2d year
2.	The Progress Newspaper purchased a new press, which was estimated to have a life of 16 years. The original cost was $28,875 and the expected scrap value was $2,000. Find the depreciation for the first 3 years that accumulated by the declining-balance method.	_____ _____ _____
3.	A piece of equipment cost $9,038, with a scrap value of $910. The estimated life was 9 years. Find the first year depreciation by the sum-of-the-years'-digits method of depreciation.	$1,625.60
4.	Jane Barlow purchased a wide-screen television for her restaurant at a cost of $1,575. The estimated life was 5 years, after which a trade-in value of $610 was expected. Find: a. The depreciation for year 1, year 2, and year 3 by the sum-of-the-years'-digits method of depreciation. b. What was the book value of the set after 3 years?	_____ _____ _____ _____
5.	The Gibbs Manufacturing Company purchased new equipment for their factory at a total cost of $42,120. Estimated life was 18 years, after which a scrap value of $8,000 was expected. Using the declining-balance method of depreciation, find: a. The depreciation for each of the first 3 years. b. What the book value is after 3 years of use.	$4,680 1st year $4,160.78 2d year $3,697 3d year $29,582.22
6.	The Mid-Hunter Farm Corporation purchased a piece of farm equipment that was expected to have an estimated life of 12 years. The machinery cost $11,935. Using the declining-balance method of depreciation, find: a. The depreciation for the first 3 years. b. The book value after 3 years.	_____ _____ _____ _____
7.	The Harrison Company purchased three 16 H-P garden tractors at a cost of $1,695 each. The estimated life of the tractors was ten years, with a trade-in value of $325 each. By the sum-of-the-years'-digits method of depreciation, find the accumulated depreciation after the second year of use.	$1,419.82 or $1,419.81
8.	Using the sum-of-the-years'-digits method, find the accumulated depreciation after 4 years of use on an asset that cost $16,930 with an estimated life of 12 years and with a trade-in value of $1,525.	_____
9.	Mrs. Robert Willis purchased office furniture at a total cost of $7,560. Estimated life was 6 years after which a trade-in of $1,030 was expected. Using the declining-balance method, find:	

a. The depreciation for the 1st and 2d years. $2,520
b. The accumulated depreciation after the 3d year of use.
1st year
$1,680
2d year
$5,320

10. If the cost of an asset was $23,018 with a scrap value of $1,100 and an estimated life of 18 years, find the accumulated depreciation after 4 years by sum-of-the-years'-digits method. _____

DISTRIBUTION OF OVERHEAD

The accounting procedure of many business organizations requires the allocation of expenses that cannot be identified with a specific department but which benefit all departments. Such expenses as rent, heat, light, depreciation on buildings, insurance cost, taxes, and maintenance expenses are the type of expenditures that cannot be assigned to any one department and are considered to be part of overhead expenses.

For each department to share an equitable portion of overhead expenses, such expenses are distributed on a base most common to all departments, such as square feet occupied by a department, net sales, direct labor costs, or the number of people employed in each department.

Rule 1: TO CALCULATE THE ALLOCATION OF OVERHEAD EXPENSES:

$$\frac{\text{Department's share of allocation base}}{\text{Total base}} \times \text{Total overhead} = \text{Department overhead}$$

Step 1. Calculate the total base of overhead allocation, if necessary.
Step 2. Substitute data in the department overhead formula.

Example 1 Overhead expense on a factory building was $8,045. Overhead expenses were allocated on the basis of square feet of floor space occupied by each department. Calculate the distribution of total overhead to each of the following departments: Department A occupied 6,400 square feet; Department B occupied 3,600 square feet; Department C, 10,000 square feet; and the Office, which occupied 2,500 square feet.

Step 1. Calculate the total base of overhead allocation:

Department A	6,400
Department B	3,600
Department C	10,000
Office	2,500
Total square feet	22,500

Step 2. Substitute data in department overhead formula:

$$\frac{\text{Department share}}{\text{Total base}} \times \text{Overhead expenses} = \text{Department overhead}$$

$$\text{Department A} = \frac{6,400}{22,500} \times \$8,045 = \$2,288.36$$

$$\text{Department B} = \frac{3,600}{22,500} \times \$8,045 = \$1,287.20$$

$$\text{Department C} = \frac{10{,}000}{22{,}500} \times \$8{,}045 = \$3{,}575.55$$

$$\text{Office} = \frac{2{,}500}{22{,}500} \times \$8{,}045 = \$\underline{\ \ 893.89}$$

Proof: Total overhead   = $8,045.00

Example 2   The A & T Service Company distributed total overhead expenses on the basis of the number of employees in each of the 4 divisions of the company. Calculate the distribution of $12,427 in overhead expenses based on 112 employees in the marketing division, 406 employees in the service division, 60 employees in the advertising division, and 212 employees in the office.

Step 1. Calculate the total base of overhead allocation:

$$112 + 406 + 60 + 212 = 790 \text{ total employees}$$

Step 2. Substitute data in department overhead formula:

$$\text{Marketing division} = \frac{112}{790} \times \$12{,}427 = \$\ \ 1{,}761.80$$

$$\text{Service division} = \frac{406}{790} \times \$12{,}427 = \$\ \ 6{,}386.53$$

$$\text{Advertising division} = \frac{60}{790} \times \$12{,}427 = \$\ \ \ \ 943.82$$

$$\text{Office division} = \frac{212}{790} \times \$12{,}427 = \$\ \underline{3{,}334.85}$$

Total overhead expenses   = $12,427.00

Proof: Total overhead expenses   = $12,427.00

INVENTORY EVALUATION

At least once every fiscal or accounting year, the businessman should know the value of merchandise or raw material that is in stock. Since merchandise or raw material is purchased at different times at difference prices, a procedure that will account for these differences must be used to determine the value of the inventory on hand on a specific date. We will review the mathematics used in the accounting procedures used to evaluate inventories by the Fifo, Lifo, and average methods.

Fifo inventory evaluation

The Fifo method of evaluating an inventory is based on the concept that the merchandise sold or used *first* is the merchandise that was *purchased first*. Thus, this method is referred to as First-in, first-out. The units of stock in the ending inventory are those units that were purchased most recently. The value of the ending inventory is therefore based on the most recent prices paid.

Rule 1: FIFO EVALUATION OF ENDING INVENTORIES:

  a. Calculate remaining units in ending inventory.

  b. Units on the most recent purchase × Unit price on the purchase

  c. Continue steps *a* and *b* until all units in the ending inventory are priced.

Step 1.

Units in the   Units on the most   Remaining units in
ending inventory − recent purchase   = the ending inventory

Step 2.

Units on the   Unit price of
most recent purchase × most recent purchase = Inventory cost

Step 3.

Remaining units   Units in next
in inventory   − most recent purchase = Remaining units

Units in next most recent purchase × Unit price = Inventory value

Step 4. Continue the procedure in step 3 until all units in the ending inventory are priced.

Example 1   From the following data, calculate the value of the ending inventory of stock item #402 by the Fifo method. The ending inventory includes 1,427 units on December 31, 19—. Purchases included:

       January 16   315 units   at $1.14 each
       March 10   410 units   at $1.56 each
       June 20   500 units   at $1.72 each
       September 15   320 units   at $1.64 each
       November 27   600 units   at $1.78 each

Step 1. 1,427 units in ending inventory.

Step 2.   − 600 units × $1.78 (November 27 purchase) = $1,068.00
           827 remaining units

Step 3.   − 320 units × $1.64 (September 15 purchase) =   524.80
           507 remaining units

Step 4.   − 500 units × $1.72 (June 20 purchase)   =   860.00
              7 final units × $1.56 (March 10 purchase) =   10.92

         Total value of ending inventory   = $2,463.72

Lifo inventory evaluation

The lifo method of inventory evaluation is based on the concept that the last merchandise or raw material purchased is the first used or sold. This method is referred to as Last-in, first-out. The ending inventory will consist of units and unit prices of the earliest purchases.

Rule 2: LIFO EVALUATION OF ENDING INVENTORY:

    a. **Calculate the remaining units in the ending inventory.**

    b. **Units on the earliest purchase × Unit price = Inventory value**

    c. **Repeat steps *a* and *b* until all units in the ending inventory are priced.**

Step 1.

Units in the ending inventory − Units in earliest purchase = Remaining units

Units in earliest purchase × Unit price = Inventory value

Step 2.

Units in remaining inventory − Units in next earliest purchase = Remaining units

Units in next earliest purchase × Unit price = Inventory value

Example 1 From the data in the Fifo example 1, calculate the value of the ending inventory by the Lifo method.

Step 1. 1,427 units in ending inventory
        − 315 × $1.14 (January 16 purchase)   = $ 359.10

Step 2. 1,112 remaining units
          410 × $1.56 (March 10 purchase)   =   639.60

Step 3.   702 remaining units
        − 500 × $1.72 (June 20 purchase)   =   860.00
           202 remaining units
        − 202 × $1.64 (September 15 purchase) =   331.28

Value of ending inventory   = $2,189.98

Average unit cost method of evaluating ending inventories

The average method of evaluating an inventory is based on the concept that when a variety of prices are paid for merchandise or raw material during a period of time, the average price paid for the total units purchased should be the basis of calculating the value of the ending inventory.

Rule 3: AVERAGE UNIT COST METHOD OF EVALUATING ENDING INVENTORIES:

a. $\dfrac{\text{Total cost of units purchased}}{\text{Total units purchased}}$ = Average unit cost

b. Average unit cost × Units in the ending inventory = Total inventory value

---

Step 1. Calculate total cost of all purchases:

Number of units × Unit price = Cost of purchase

Step 2. Add all units purchased.

Step 3. Calculate average unit cost:

$\dfrac{\text{Total cost of all purchases}}{\text{Total units purchased}}$ = Average unit cost

Step 4. Calculate value of ending inventory:

Units in the ending inventory × Average unit cost = Inventory value

Example 1

INVENTORY RECORD

Max. Quan. 2,000
Min. Quan. 300

Stock Item #309

Date	Order no.	Quan. in	Unit cost	Req. no.	Quan. out	Balance
February 2	122	400	$ .855			400
March 16	123	615	$ .94			1,015
March 20				16	300	715
June 24	124	520	$1.15			1,235
July 7				17	400	835
September 12	125	390	$1.135			1,225
November 23	126	520	$1.19			1,745

Based on the above information, what is the value of the ending inventory using the average unit cost method?

Step 1. Calculate total cost of all purchases:

$$\begin{aligned}
400 \text{ units @ } \$.855 &= \$\ 342.00 \\
615 \text{ units @ } \$.940 &= 578.10 \\
520 \text{ units @ } \$1.15 &= 598.00 \\
390 \text{ units @ } \$1.135 &= 442.65 \\
520 \text{ units @ } \$1.190 &= 618.80 \\
\overline{2,445} & \quad \overline{\$2,579.55}
\end{aligned}$$

Step 2. 2,445 units cost $2,579.55.

Step 3. Calculate average unit cost:

$$\frac{\$2,579.55}{2,445} = \$1.055 \text{ cost per unit}$$

Step 4. Calculate value of ending inventory:

1,745 units @ $1.055 = $1,840.98

Practice exercises

Answer

1. The P & T Department Store distributed overhead expenses on the basis of net sales. Total overhead expenses for the month amounted to $12,420. Calculate the distribution of overhead to the following departments:

    Department 1 net sales = $ 87,945
    Department 2 net sales = $106,415
    Department 3 net sales = $ 65,905

    $4,196.79
    Dept. 1
    $5,078.19
    Dept. 2
    $3,145.02
    Dept. 3

2. Monthly overhead expenses included: rent, $2,785; depreciation on buildings, $3,025; heat and light, $1,135; taxes, $2,250; insurance, $915; and maintenance expense, $7,065. Overhead was allocated on the basis of square

feet of floor space. Calculate the distribution of overhead to Department A, which occupied 6,300 square feet; Department B, which occupied 4,800 square feet; and Department C, 3,910 square feet.

3. Calculate the value of the ending inventory of stock item 18, which included 512 units, by the Fifo method. Purchased on October 20 were 146 units at a cost of $3.45 each; 218 units purchased on November 16 at a cost of $4.06 each; and 300 units purchased on December 12 at $4.36 each. $2,168.72

4. The Wells Company evaluates its ending inventory of suits by the Fifo method. Find the value of the ending inventory that included 56 suits on December 31. Purchases included:

    25 suits purchased on May 12 at $41.30 each.
    40 suits purchased on August 29 at $36.80 each.
    20 suits purchased on September 27 at $39.25.

5. Calculate the value of the ending inventory of Stock Item #116 which included 2,046 units by the Lifo method. Purchases included: 600 units purchased on April 10 at $.68 each; 564 units on June 24 at $.76 each; 915 units on September 9 at $.82 each; and 700 units on November 16 at $.815 each. $1,559.88

6. Find the value of an ending inventory which includes 20,140 tons of #31 steel by the Lifo method. Purchases included:

    9,026 tons purchased on March 21 at $86.50 per ton.
    10,800 tons purchased on May 16 at $94.80 per ton.
    15,420 tons purchased on August 20 at $106.20 per ton.
    11,465 tons purchased on October 1 at $104.10 per ton.
    7,020 tons purchased on December 4 at $107.40 per ton.

7. Total overhead expenses, which were allocated to all departments on the basis of square feet of floor space, amounted to $33,210. The total square feet occupied by the Diane Company was 206,340. The cutting department occupied 75,400 square feet; the sewing department, 82,360 square feet; the pressing department, 42,090; and the office, which occupied 6,490 square feet. Calculate the distribution of the overhead expenses. $12,135.48 (cutting) $13,255.67 (sewing) $6,774.30 (pressing) $1,044.55 (office)

8. The total heat and light expenses of the Johnson Shirt Company amounted to $11,485. Allocation of this overhead item was based on the number of employees in each department. Calculate the following department allocation of overhead: the purchasing department had 6 employees; sales, 18 employess; cutting, 22 employees; pressing, 7 employees; and general office, 10 employees.

9. The Aiken Manufacturing Company used the Fifo method to evaluate its inventory. What is the value of

the ending inventory that included 3,126 units of raw material? Purchases included:

 3,026 units at $.705 each, purchased February 2.
 4,110 units at $.76 each, purchased April 20.
 2,000 units at $.87 each, purchased May 10.
 1,050 units at $.895 each purchased October 12. $2,737.51

10. Calculate the value of the ending inventory which included 396 units by the Fifo method. Purchases included:

 May 10   125 units at $2.36 each.
 July 23   170 units at $2.16 each.
 October 10   205 units at $2.54 each.
 November 16   95 units at $2.675 each.

11. The ending inventory included 184 units of merchandise. Purchases included:

 75 units purchased on March 3   at $38.10 each.
 60 units purchased on May 10   at $39.20 each.
 82 units purchased on September 26   at $41.65 each.
 50 units purchased on October 13   at $40.22 each.

 Calculate the value of the ending inventory by:
  a. The Fifo method. $7,464.70
  b. The Lifo method. $7,250.35

12. W. J. Jones Company had an ending inventory that included 815 units of raw material. During the fiscal period, 2,016 units had been purchased for a total cost of $4,394.88. Using the average unit cost method, calculate the value of the ending inventory.

13. Using the average unit cost method, calculate the value of an ending inventory that included 619 units. Purchases included:

 236 units purchased at a cost of $2.065 each.
 316 units purchased at a cost of $1.985 each.
 185 units purchased at a cost of $2.160 each.
  95 units purchased for $2.584 each. $1,309.19

14. From the following data, calculate the value of an ending inventory that included 112 yards of woolen goods by:
  a. The Lifo method of evaluation.
  b. The Fifo method.
  c. Average unit cost method of evaluation.
 Purchases included:

55 yards purchased on February 10 at a cost of $4.105.
95 yards purchased on March 12 at a cost of $4.37.
80 yards purchased on April 14 at a cost of $4.125.
40 yards purchased at a cost of $4.70 on May 10.

Review problems

		Answer
1.	Find the depreciation allowed for the 1st and 2d years on a machine that cost $11,800. The salvage value was expected to be $1,600 after an estimated life of 12 years.	$850 1st year $1,700 2d year
2.	Find the accumulated depreciation allowed for the 1st and 2d years on a machine that cost $19,825. The estimated life was 16 years, after which a trade-in of $1,020 was expected.	
3.	A delivery truck was purchased at a cost of $12,875. Trade-in value was expected to be $4,825 after an estimated life of 96,000 miles. Find the depreciation after 23,485 miles.	$1,970.39
4.	The J. C. Jones Construction Company purchased a truck for $18,000 and expected to use the truck for 200,000 miles, after which a trade-in of $2,000 was expected. Find the depreciation after the truck had been driven 60,000 miles.	_____
5.	The Ryan Manufacturing Company purchased a piece of equipment for $18,975. Installation charges amounted to $1,050.50. The estimated life of the equipment was 35,000 production hours and a resale value of $3,750 was expected. What amount of depreciation would be charged after the equipment had been used for 3,120 hours?	$1,450.80
6.	A punch press was purchased at a cost of $25,600. The estimated life was 14,500 production hours, and a salvage value of $4,950 was expected. Find the depreciation for the 1st year in which the production hours were 2,600 and the 2d year after the press was used another 3,120 hours.	_____ _____
7.	Find the 1st and 2d years' depreciations on a machine that cost $14,860 that has an estimated life of 9 years. The salvage value is expected to be $3,100. The machine was purchased on April 13 and depreciation was based on a calendar year.	$980.00 1st year $1,306.67 2d year
8.	The Kahn Company purchased a sewing machine for $6,545. The estimated life of the machine was 8 years, and the salvage value was expected to be $940. Find the depreciation for the 1st year if the machine was purchased on May 12. What was the depreciation for the 2d year?	_____ _____
9.	The Elfred Company bought a building for $150,000. It spent $60,000 for remodeling and $20,000 for additional storage space. The estimated life of the building	

was 25 years and a resale value was estimated to be $80,000. What annual depreciation would be charged?   **$6,000**

10. A new packaging machine was purchased at a cost of $45,000. The estimated salvage value was $7,000 and the expected production life was 1,500,000 units. Setup costs amounted to $1,500. Find the total depreciation at the end of the 1st year based on production of 340,000 units.   _____

11. The Ryan Manufacturing Company purchased a piece of equipment for $18,975. Installation charges amounted to $1,050.50. The estimated life of the equipment was 35,000 hours and a resale value of $3,750 was expected. What was the amount of depreciation at the end of the 1st year during which the equipment was used 3,210 hours?   **$1,492.65**

12. A machine was purchased at a cost of $97,500. A resale value of $7,500 was expected after an estimated life of 6 million units. The owner elected to take the additional 20% depreciation allowance for the 1st year. Find the depreciation for the 1st and 2d years. The 1st year production was 215,000 units and 382,500 units were produced in the 2d year of operations.   _____ _____

13. The Neilson Construction Company purchased a piece of equipment for $20,870. The estimated life was 12 years and a salvage value of $2,710 was expected. After 6 years of use, what was the book value of the equipment?   **$11,790**

14. Find the book value of an asset at the end of 4 years of use when the original cost was $126,500 with a trade-in value of $7,600 and an estimated life of 12 years.   _____

15. The Bryant Manufacturing Company purchased new equipment at a cost of $12,675 that had an expected scrap value of $1,126 and an estimated life of 8 years. Calculate the 1st and 2d years' depreciation by the declining-balance method of depreciation.   **$3,168.75** 1st year   **$2,376.56** 2d year

16. Find the depreciation of each of the first 3 years of an asset that cost $18,700 with an estimated life of 16 years and a trade-in value of $4,200. Use the declining-balance method of calculating depreciation.   _____ _____ _____

17. An asset that was purchased for $8,017.50 had an estimated life of 6 years, after which a trade-in of $925 was expected. Using the sum-of-the-years'-digits method of depreciation, calculate the depreciation for year 1 and year 2.   **$2,026.43** 1st year   **$1,688.69** 2d year

18. The C & D Manufacturing Company purchased new office furniture at a cost of $4,000. A trade-in of $625 was expected after an estimated life of 10 years. What is the depreciation for each of the first 3 years using the sum-of-the-years'-digit method of depreciation?   _____ _____ _____

19. The Bracken Manufacturing Company allocated overhead expenses to all departments on the basis of square   Dept. A **$11,242.93**

feet of floor space occupied by each department. Total overhead expenses for the year amounted to $87,445. Department A occupied 3,600 square feet; Department B, 8,700 square feet; department C, 11,420 square feet; and General Office space occupied 4,280 square feet. Calculate the overhead allocation to each department.

Dept. B
$27,170.40
Dept. C
$35,665.06
Office
$13,366.59

20. The New Bedford Company distributed overhead expenses, which included heat and light amounting to $4,036, insurance cost of $1,012.50, maintenance expense of $8,076 on the basis of net sales. Calculate the distribution of total overhead to Department A with net sales of $26,046, Department B with net sales of $19,428, and Department C with net sales of $22,000.

_____
_____
_____

21. The ending inventory included 712 units of stock #106. What is the value of the ending inventory using the Fifo method of inventory evaluation? Purchases included:

 January 10 300 units at a cost of $1.065 each.
 April 28 270 units at a cost of $1.34 each.
 August 12 410 units at a cost of $1.56 each.
 October 19 156 units at a cost of $1.615 each.

$1,087.18

22. Find the value of an ending inventory that included 836 units and was evaluated by the Fifo method of evaluation. Purchases included:

 146 units purchased on May 10 for $2.06 each.
 305 units purchased on July 17 for $2.395 each.
 210 units purchased on September 26 for $2.41 each.
 390 units purchased on November 10 for $2.56 each.

_____

23. The G & M Hardware Store evaluated its inventory by the Lifo method of inventory evaluation. Calculate the value of the ending inventories of #4 house paint of 20 gallons and #32 paint brushes of 45 brushes. Purchases included:

10 gallons of house paint on May 2 @ $6.16 per gallon.
 6 gallons of house paint on July 6 @ $5.35 per gallon.
20 gallons of house paint on October 12 @ $6.06 per gallon.

$117.94
house
paint

25 paint brushes on April 28 @ $1.95 each.
30 paint brushes on August 21 @ $2.15 each.

$91.75
brushes

24. The Acme Bakery evaluated its ending inventory by the Lifo method. Find the value of the ending inventory, which included 2,012 pounds of sugar. Purchases included:

1,000 lbs. purchased on March 3 at $.125 per lb.
 600 lbs. purchased on May 16 at $.142 per lb.
1,400 lbs. purchased on August 27 at $.175 per lb.
2,200 lbs. purchased on November 10 at $.160 per lb.

_____

25. The Hollywood Arts and Craft Shop uses the average unit cost method to evaluate their ending inventory. Purchases during the fiscal period included:

110 units purchased on March 10 at $3.08 each.
64 units purchased on April 29 at $11.50 each.
208 units purchased on September 11 at $4.12 each.
96 units purchased on October 4 at $5.25 each.

What is the value of the ending inventory that included 212 units? $1,080.29

26. Using the average unit cost method of evaluating an ending inventory, what is the value of an ending inventory that included 1,016 units if a total of 2,018 units were purchased at a total cost of $9,797.39? _____

STUDY UNIT **11**

Stocks and bonds

STOCKS
    Price of a share of stock
    Stock quotations
    Commission
    Transfer tax
    Security and exchange fees
    Sale and purchase of stock
    Stock dividend
    Stock yields
    Price-earnings ratio

BONDS
    Quotations
    Interest
    Commission and fees
    Yield to maturity
    Purchase and sale of bonds

STOCKS

A corporation sells shares of its stock for the purpose of raising money for a variety of business reasons. Generally a corporation will offer several types of stock, such as common stock, preferred, participating preferred, cumulative preferred, and so on, each of which offers some preference in price, voting rights, or dividends. The individual investor purchases stock in anticipation of an increase in its value and for the dividend earnings he or she may receive. Each purchaser of corporate stock becomes part owner of the corporation and is entitled to participate in the election of members of the board of directors as well as any profit made by the corporation.

The purchase and sale of stocks are made through stockbrokers or agents who have access to local, regional, or, the most noted exchanges, the New York Stock Exchange and the American Stock Exchange.

The following explanations, examples, and practice problems are restricted to the mathematics involved in stock transactions of common and preferred stock. See Figure 11-1 for an example of a share of common stock.

Topics in this unit include: the price of a share of stock; the purchase and sale of stock; stock yields; stock dividends; purchase and sale of corporate bonds; bond yield and bond interest.

PRICE OF A SHARE

The dollar value of a share of stock varies with the demand and availability of the stock. One of the indicators of the current price of many stocks is in the stock quotations which are published daily in most major newspapers throughout the country. This summary of the transactions completed on the previous trading day is a guide to many investors and potential investors.

STOCK QUOTATIONS

Table 11-1 gives examples of stock quotations as they appear in a daily newspaper. Stock prices are quoted as a mixed number. The whole number represents the full dollar value, the fraction expresses the cents in the price of the stock. For example, a quotation of $12\frac{1}{8}$ means the price of the stock

Figure 11-1
An example of a share of common stock

Courtesy of Criner & Kercher Associates, Inc.

was $12.125 ($\frac{1}{8}$ = .125); a quotation of 14¼ means the price was $14.25 ($\frac{1}{4}$ = .25).

To illustrate reading the stock quotation, follow the IBM quotation on Table 11-1.

Column	1	High	80 means that the highest price of IBM stock for the current year was $80.
Column	2	Low	68½ means that the lowest price of IBM stock for the current year was $68.50 (current year = preceding 365 days).
Column	3	Name	IBM
Column	4	Dividend	means that the last annual dividend paid was $3.44 per share.
Column	5	P-E	is the price-earnings ratio. The 13 indicates that the selling price is 13 times the earnings per share.
Column	6	Sales	23,641 × 100 = 2,364,100 is the number of shares sold during the trading day.
Column	7	High	70⅝ means that the highest price of the stock during the trading day was $70.625.
Column	8	Low	68½ means that the lowest price of the stock during the trading day was $68.50.
Column	9	Closing	69¾ means that the selling price of the stock at the close of trading day was $69.75.

Column 10   Net change $-\frac{1}{8}$ or $.125 means that the closing price of the stock on the current trading day is $.125 less than the closing price on the previous day.

Rule 1: TO CALCULATE THE VALUE OF STOCK OWNED:

Number of shares × Quoted price = Stock value

Example 1 R. C. Appleton owned 406 shares of McDonald common stock. What is the value of the stock based on the closing price quoted on Table 11-1?

Step 1.

$$\text{Number of shares} \times \text{Quoted price} = \text{Stock value}$$
$$406 \times \$48.125 = \$19{,}538.75$$

Example 2 Find the difference in the value of 289 shares of Nabisco stock based on the high quoted price of the current year and the high quoted price of the trading day as reported on Table 11-1.

Step 1. Calculate value of stock based on the high quoted price of current year:

$$\text{Number of shares} \times \text{Quoted price} = \text{Stock value}$$
$$289 \times \$28 = \$8{,}092$$

Step 2. Calculate value of stock based on the high quoted price of trading day:

$$\text{Number of shares} \times \text{Quoted price} = \text{Stock value}$$
$$289 \times \$23.375 = \$6{,}755.38$$

Table 11-1
Stock quotations

①	②	③	④	⑤	⑥	⑦	⑧	⑨	⑩
High	Low	Company name	Dividend	P-E	Sales per 100 shares	High	Low	Close	Net change
80	68½	IBM	3.44	13	23,641	70⅝	68½	69¾	−⅛
66½	53⅛	Gen'l Motors	6.15	4	8,317	56⅜	54⅞	56⅛	+⅜
64⅜	57	AT&T	5.00	7	8,730	57⅞	57⅜	57⅛	+⅜
25	12	Con Edison	2.44	6	1,460	24¾	24⅛	24⅛	−⅜
48	39	Ford Motor	1.56	5	4,390	41⅞	40⅜	41⅞	+⅞
15⅝	7	East. Airlines	—	3	1,062	8⅛	7⅝	7¾	−⅛
64⅜	44⅛	CBS	2.60	7	2,288	51¼	50⅜	50⅞	+⅛
28	22	Nabisco	1.50	7	1,410	23⅜	22½	23⅛	+⅛
40⅛	28⅝	Chase Man. Bank	2.40	5	5,698	40⅛	37½	39⅝	+1
81	72	Chase Man. Bank	pf 6.75	—	36	76	76	76	—
60½	39⅛	McDonald	.56	11	2,745	46⅜	44⅝	48⅛	−1½
21⅞	16½	DuPonts	2.00	7	4,812	40½	38¾	39⅝	−⅜
58	36⅛	Delta Air	1.20	6	1,240	42¼	41⅜	41⅜	−¾

Step 3. Calculate the difference:

$$\begin{aligned}\text{Current year stock value} &= \$8{,}092.00\\ \text{Trading day stock value} &= -6{,}755.38\\ \text{Difference} &= \$1{,}336.62\end{aligned}$$

Practice exercises

		Answer
1.	A stockholder owned 312 shares of AT&T stock. What was the value of the stock at the close of trading as reported on Table 11-1?	$17,823
2.	What was the value of 64 shares of Delta Air stock at the "high" stock price of the trading day according to Table 11-1?	_____
3.	W. T. Baker owned 114 shares of Chase Manhattan common stock. What was the value of the stock at the high price of the trading day? (See Table 11-1.)	$4,574.25
4.	H. A. Anthony owned 209 shares of Con Edison stock. Find the total value of the stock at the closing price on the current trading day. (See Table 11-1.)	_____
5.	Find the difference in the value of 219 shares of General Motors stock valued at the high quoted price of the current year and the high quoted price of the trading day, from the data on Table 11-1.	$2,217.37
6.	Find the difference in the value of 612 shares of DuPont stock on the high quoted price of the current year and the high quoted price of the current trading day as reported on Table 11-1.	_____
7.	Ms. T. R. James owned 95 shares of CBS common stock.	
	a. Did the value of her stock increase or decrease from the prior trading day price?	Increased
	b. By what amount did the value of her stock change? (Refer to Table 11-1.)	$11.88
8.	Did the value of Ford Motor stock increase or decrease from the prior day price as quoted on Table 11-1? H. T. Clara owned 1,006 shares of the stock. What was the change in the value of the stock?	_____
9.	What was the value of a share of Delta Air stock on the prior day of trading according to the quoted prices on Table 11-1 net change?	$42.125
10.	The IBM stock decreased $1/8$ in value. What was the price of the stock at the close of trading on the prior day?	_____
11.	Y. J. Russell owned 1,238 shares of General Motors stock when the last dividend was declared and paid. What was the amount of dividend received? (Refer to Table 11-1.)	$7,613.70
12.	If you owned 2,405 shares of AT&T stock when the last dividend was declared and paid, how much dividend would you have received per the data on Table 11-1?	_____

COMMISSIONS

The commission charged by stockbrokers for completing a stock transaction is determined by negotiation between the stockbroker and his customer. The amount of the commission depends on the number of shares of stock and the selling price per share involved in the transaction. The rates of commission is also affected by round lot sales (100 and multiples of 100 shares) and by odd lot sales (less than 100 shares). A charge is made on odd lot sales, known as *odd lot differential,* which is outlined in Table 11-2.

Table 11-3 illustrates the minimum commission rate charged by many stockbrokers, but these are subject to change resulting from negotiation.

Table 11-2
Odd lot differential

Selling price per share below $54⅞ = $ .125
Selling price per share above $55   = $ .25
  Add the differential to the price per share of stock *purchased.*
  Subtract the differential from the price per share of stock sold.

Table 11-3

Amount of gross sales	Round lot commission per 100 shares	Odd lot commission rates
Sales under $100:	Negotiated rate:	Negotiated rate:
$ 100 to $ 399	2% + $ 2.50	2% + $ 1.00
$ 400 to $2,399	1% + 6.00	1% + 4.00
$2,400 — $4,999	½% + 18.00	½% + 15.00
$5,000 and over	¹⁄₁₀% + 38.00	¹⁄₁₀% + 35.00

Rule 2: TO CALCULATE COMMISSION ON THE SALE OF STOCK:

  a. Commission on round lot sales:

  Number of round lot shares × Price per share = Gross selling price

  Gross selling price × Commission rate = Round lot commission

  b. Commission on odd lot sales:

  Number of shares × (Price per share − Odd lot differential) = Gross selling price

  Gross selling price × Commission rate = Odd lot commission

  c. Total commission:

  Round lot commission + Odd lot commission = Total commission

---

Example 1 C. B. Collins sold 300 shares of common stock at $26⅜ per share. Find the amount of commission paid.

  Step 1. Calculate round lot gross selling price:

  300 shares × $26.375 = $7,912.50

  Step 2. Calculate round lot commission:

  ($7,912.50 × .001) + $38.00 = $45.91 Commission

  Note: See Table 11-3.

Example 2 C. W. Edwards sold 60 shares of common stock at a quoted price per share of $60⅛. What commission would be paid the broker?

Step 1. Calculate odd lot price per share:

Quoted price	$60.125
Odd lot differential	− .250
Odd lot price per share	$59.875

Step 2. Calculate odd lot gross selling price:

60 shares × $59.875 = $3,592.50

Step 3. Calculate odd lot commission:

($3,592.50 × .005) + $15.00 = $32.96 Commission

Note: See Table 11-3.

Example 3   F. T. Simmons sold 210 shares of stock through his broker at a selling price of $36½ per share. What was the broker's commission?

Step 1. Calculate commission on round lot sale:

200 shares × $36.50 = $7,300 Gross selling price

($7,300 × .001) + $38.00 = $45.30 Round lot commission

Note: See Table 11-3.

Step 2. Calculate commission on odd lot sale:

Odd lot quoted price	$36.50
Odd lot differential	− .125
Odd lot price per share	$36.375

10 × $36.375 = $363.75 Gross selling price

($363.75 × .02) + $1.00 = $8.28 Odd lot commission

Note: See Table 11-3.

Step 3. Calculate total commission:

Round lot commission	$45.30
Odd lot commission	+ 8.28
Total commission	$53.58

Rule 3: TO CALCULATE COMMISSION ON THE PURCHASE OF STOCK:

  a. Commission on round lot purchase:

Number of round lot shares × Price per share = Gross selling price

Gross selling price × Commission rate = Round lot commission

  b. Commission on odd lot purchases:

Quoted price × (Price per share + Odd lot differential) = Gross selling price

Gross selling price × Commission rate = Odd lot commission

  c. Total commission:

Round lot commission + Odd lot commission = Total commission

Example 1   Alice Brooks purchased 35 shares of common stock at a market price of $10⅛ per share. What commission would Ms. Brooks pay the broker?

Step 1. Calculate odd lot price per share:

Quoted price	$10.125
Odd lot differential	+ .125
Odd lot price per share	$10.250

Step 2. Calculate odd lot gross selling price:

$$35 \times \$10.25 = \$358.75 \text{ Gross selling price}$$

Step 3. Calculate odd lot commission:

$$(\$358.75 \times .02) + \$1.00 = \$8.18 \text{ Odd lot commission}$$

Note: See Table 11-3.

Example 2 Joan Killigan purchased 175 shares of common stock at a market price of $57⅜. What commission would she pay the broker?

Step 1. Calculate round lot commission:

$$100 \text{ shares} \times \$57.375 = \$5,737.50 \text{ Gross selling price}$$

$$(\$5,737.50 \times .001) + \$38 = \$43.74 \text{ Round lot commission}$$

Note: See Table 11-3.

Step 2. Calculate odd lot commission:

Quoted price	$57.375
Odd lot differential	.250
Odd lot price per share	$57.625

Step 3. Calculate odd lot commission:

$$75 \text{ shares} \times \$57.625 = \$4,321.88 \text{ Gross selling price}$$

$$(\$4,321.88 \times .005) + 15 = \$36.61 \text{ Odd lot commission}$$

Note: See Table 11-3.

Step 4. Calculate total commission:

Round lot commission	$43.74
Odd lot commission	+36.61
Total commission	$80.35

TRANSFER TAX A number of states require the *seller* of stock to pay a transfer tax on all sales. The tax rate will vary from state to state and will change periodically. The rates in Table 11-4 will illustrate the tax rates that are applied to all sales completed in New York State. These rates will be used in the following examples and practice problems where applicable.

Table 11-4

Price per share	Transfer tax rate
Under $5.00	$.0156
$ 5.00 to $ 9.88	.0313
$10.00 to $19.88	.0469
$20.00 and over	.0625

Rule 4: TO CALCULATE THE TRANSFER TAX:
Number of shares sold × Applicable tax rate = Transfer tax

Example 1   R. C. Jones sold 23 shares of common stock through his broker on the New York Stock Exchange at a price of $12½ per share. What amount of transfer tax would Mr. Jones pay?

Step 1.

Number of shares sold × Applicable tax rate = Transfer tax
23   × $.0469   = $1.08

Example 2   H. L. Willard sold 165 shares of common stock at a market price of $9.65 per share through his broker on the New York Stock Exchange. How much was the transfer tax on the sale?

Step 1. Calculate the transfer tax:

Number of shares sold × Applicable tax rate = Transfer tax
165   × $.0313   = $5.16

SECURITY AND EXCHANGE FEE

The seller of any stock is required to pay a Security and Exchange Commission fee of $.01 per $500 or fractional part of $500 of the total gross selling price.

> **Rule 5: TO CALCULATE THE SECURITY AND EXCHANGE FEE:**
>
> $$\frac{\text{Total selling price}}{500} = \text{Taxable units} \times \$.01 = \text{S\&E fee}$$

Example 1   A. B. Phillips sold 75 shares of common stock through his broker on the New York Stock Exchange at a market price of $21.30 per share. What amount of Security and Exchange fee will be charged?

Step 1. Calculate the total selling price:

Quoted price per share $21.300
Odd lot differential   − .125
Odd lot price per share $21.175

Number of odd lot shares × Price per share = Total selling price
75   × $21.175   = $1,588.13

Step 2. Calculate the Security and Exchange fee:

$$\frac{\text{Gross selling price}}{\$500} = \text{Taxable units} \times \$.01 = \text{Fee}$$

$$\frac{\$1,588.13}{\$500} = 3.18 = 4 \text{ units} \times \$.01 = \$.04 \text{ Fee}$$

SALE AND PURCHASE OF STOCK

The mathematics required to calculate the net proceeds the seller receives from a sale of stock differs from the total cost of purchase stock by the application of taxes and fees.

> **Rule 6: TO CALCULATE NET PROCEEDS FROM THE SALE OF STOCK:**
>
> Gross selling price
> − Total commission
> − Transfer taxes
> − Security & Exchange fee
> Net proceeds

Step 1. Calculate gross selling price for:
  a. Round lot sale.
  b. Odd lot sale, including differential

Step 2. Calculate total commission on:
  a. Round lot sale.
  b. Odd lot sale.
Step 3. Calculate the transfer tax.
Step 4. Calculate the net proceeds.

Example 1 R. E. Phelps sold 215 shares of Eastern Airlines stock through a broker on the New York Stock Exchange at the current "high" quoted price on Table 11-1. The stockbroker agreed to the commission rates on Table 11-3. Calculate the net proceeds from the sale.

Step 1. Calculate gross selling price:
  a. Round lots selling price:

Number of round lot shares × Price per share = Gross selling price
200 × 8.125 = $1,625.00

Gross selling price × Commission rate = Round lot commission
($1,625.00 × .01) + $6.00 = $22.25

  b. Odd lot selling price:

Quoted price	$8.125
Odd lot differential	− .125
Odd lot price	$8.00

Number of odd lot shares × Odd lot price = Gross selling price
15 × $8.00 = $120.00

Gross selling price × Commission rate = Odd lot commission
($120.00 × .02) + $1.00 = $3.40

Step 2. Calculate total commission:

Round lot commission + Odd lot commission = Total commission
$22.25 + $3.40 = $25.65

Step 3. Calculate transfer tax (Table 11-4):

Number of shares × Tax rate = Transfer tax
200 (round lot) × .0313 = $6.26
15 (odd lot) × .0313 = $ .47
Total transfer tax $6.73

Step 4. Calculate security & Exchange fee:

Round lot gross selling price = $1,625
Odd lot gross selling price = 120
Total gross selling price $1,745

$$\frac{\text{Gross selling price}}{500} = \text{Taxable units} \times .01 = \text{S\&E fee}$$

$$\frac{\$1,745}{500} = 3.49 = 4 \text{ units} \times .01 = \$.04 \text{ S\&E fee}$$

Step 5. Calculate net proceeds of the sale:

Gross selling price	$1,745.00
Total commission	− 25.65
Transfer tax	− 6.73
Security & Exchange fee	− 0.04
Net proceeds:	$1,712.58

> **Rule 7: TO CALCULATE TOTAL COST OF A PURCHASE OF STOCK:**
> Total gross selling price + Total commission = Total cost

Step 1. Calculate gross selling price:
  a. Round lot selling price.
  b. Odd lot selling price.

Step 2. Calculate total commission:
  a. Round lot shares.
  b. Odd lot shares.

Step 3. Calculate total commission:

Round lot commission + Odd lot commission = Total commission

Step 4. Calculate total cost:

Total selling price + Total commission = Total cost

Example 1 Ms. C. Russell purchased 195 shares of Ford Motors stock at the current low quoted price on Table 11-1. The commission rates on Table 11-3 applied to the purchase. The transaction was completed on the New York Stock Exchange. What was the total cost of the purchase to Ms. Russell?

Step 1. Calculate gross selling price:
  a.

Number of round lot shares × Quoted price = Gross selling price
            100   × $40.375   = $4,037.50

  b.

Quoted price $40.375
Add odd lot differential + .125
Odd lot price per share $40.500

Number of odd lot shares × Odd lot price = Gross selling price
            95   × $40.50   = $3,847.50

  c. Total gross selling price:

$4,037.50 + $3,847.50 = $7,885.00

Step 2. Calculate total commission:

Gross selling price × Commission rate = Round lot commission
    ($4,037.50   ×   .005) + $18 = $38.19

  b. Odd lot commission:

Gross selling price × Commission rate = Odd lot commission
    ($3,847.50   ×   .005) + $15 = $34.24

  c. Total commission:

$38.19 + $34.24 = $72.43

Step 3. Calculate total cost:

Total selling price + Total commission = Total cost
    $7,885.00   + $72.43   = $7,957.43

Practice exercises

		Answer
1.	Find the commission that would be paid on a sale of 400 shares of common stock with a quoted price of $7⅜. (See Table 11-3.)	$32.75
2.	W. T. Bower sold 300 shares of common stock at a quoted price of $20½. What commission was paid on the sale, using rates on Table 11-3?	_____
3.	Ms. L. O. Mooney sold 165 shares of common stock for $37⅛ per share. What amount of commission is payable on the sale according to the rates on Table 11-3?	$63.59
4.	What is the commission on a sale of 74 shares of common stock sold for $57⅛ per share? The rate of commission payable is on Table 11-3.	_____
5.	What amount of transfer tax would the seller pay on the sale of 136 shares of common stock that were sold for $4⅞ per share? Table 11-4.	$2.12
6.	James Gordon sold 65 shares of common stock for a quoted price of $27⅛. How much is the transfer tax to be paid on the sale? Use Table 11-4.	_____
7.	What Security & Exchange fee would be charged on a sale of 210 shares of common stock at a quoted price of $19⅜ per share? (See Rule 5.)	$.09
8.	B. R. Barton sold 916 shares of common stock for $20⅛ per share. What amount of Security and Exchange fee would he pay on the transaction?	_____
9.	Ms. T. Abbott sold 320 shares of common stock on the New York Stock Exchange at a price of $11⅞ per share. What proceeds did Ms. Abbott receive from the sale?	$3,740.91
10.	Find the proceeds of a sale of 155 shares of common stock that were sold on the New York Stock Exchange at a quoted price of $60⅜ per share.	_____
11.	What is the total cost of a purchase of 410 shares of Con Edison stock on the New York Stock Exchange at the quoted low price on Table 11-1?	$9,946
12.	Mr. C. Babson purchased 250 shares of McDonald stock on the New York Stock Exchange at the closing price of the stock on Table 11-1. What was the total cost of the purchase to Mr. Babson?	_____
13.	Ms. R. Dillon called her stockbroker and requested him (*a*) to sell 135 shares of AT&T common stock at the quoted low price on Table 11-1. Commission rates on Table 11-3 were agreed upon by Ms. Dillon and her broker, as well as to (*b*) purchase 165 shares of Chase Manhattan common stock at the closing price of the stock on Table 11-1. Commission rates on Table 11-3 apply to the purchase.	

  a. What is the net proceeds of the sale of the AT&T stock? $7,660.55

  b. What is the total cost of the purchase of Chase Manhattan stock? $6,611.98

14. Ms. T. P. Morrison requested her broker to sell 65 shares of DuPont common stock at the quoted high price on Table 11-1. She also requested the broker to purchase 225 shares of Eastern Airlines common stock at the low quoted price on Table 11-1. Commission rates on Table 11-3 apply.

  a. What proceeds were received from the sale of stock? _____

  b. What was the total cost of the purchase? _____

STOCK DIVIDENDS

Based on the amount of earnings, the board of directors of a corporation may decide to declare a dividend that is payable to all stockholders. If the corporation has issued both common and preferred stock, the preferred stock dividends are paid first and the remainder of the declared dividends are payable to the common stockholders.

The distribution of the declared dividends to the preferred and common stockholders is based on the rate of dividend and par value of preferred stock and the amount of dividends available to common stockholders and the number of outstanding shares.

Rule 1: TO CALCULATE DIVIDEND PER SHARE:

a. Preferred stock:

  Par value per share × Dividend rate = Dividend per share

b. Common stock:

$$\frac{\text{Total common stock dividends}}{\text{Outstanding common shares}} = \text{Dividend per share}$$

Step 1. Calculate preferred dividend per share.

Step 2. Calculate total preferred dividend:

 Dividend per share × Outstanding shares = Total preferred dividend

Step 3. Calculate total common stock dividend:

Total dividends declared − Total preferred dividend = Total common dividend

Step 4. Calculate dividend per share of common stock:

$$\frac{\text{Total common stock dividends}}{\text{Outstanding common shares}} = \text{Dividend per share}$$

Example 1   The board of directors of the ABC Corporation declared a total dividend of $205,000. There were 10,000 shares of 7%, $100 par value preferred stock, and 45,000 shares of common stock outstanding. What was the dividend per share for

 a. Preferred stock?

 b. Common stock?

Step 1. Calculate preferred dividend per share:

  Par value × Dividend rate = Dividend per share
   $100 × .07 = $7.00

Step 2. Calculate total preferred dividends:

Outstanding shares × Dividend per share = Total preferred dividend
10,000 × $7 = $70,000

Step 3. Calculate total common stock dividend:

Total dividends declared − Total preferred dividends = Total common stock dividends
$205,000 − $70,000 = $135,000

Step 4. Calculate dividend per share of common stock:

$$\frac{\text{Total common stock dividends}}{\text{Outstanding common stock}} = \text{Dividend per share common stock}$$

$$\frac{\$135,000}{45,000} = \$3 \text{ Dividend per share for common stock}$$

Rule 2: TO CALCULATE STOCKHOLDER'S DIVIDEND:

Number of shares owned × Dividend per share = Common stockholder's dividend

Number of shares owned × Par value × Dividend rate = Preferred stockholder's dividend

---

Example 1 E. B. Mull owns 55 shares of common stock on which a dividend of $4.04 per share was declared. What amount of dividend would Ms. Mull receive?

Step 1. Calculate stockholder's dividend:

Number of shares owned × Dividend per share = Stockholder's dividend
55 × $4.04 = $222.20

Example 2 What total dividend would Harry Reaper receive on 110 shares of 8½% par value $100 preferred stock?

Step 1. Calculate stockholder's dividend:

Number of shares owned × Par value × Dividend rate = Stockholder's dividend on preferred
110 × $100 × .085 = $935.00

Example 3 The board of directors of a corporation declared a total of $88,780 for dividends to be distributed to preferred and common stockholders. There were 1,100, 9% par value $100 shares of preferred stock outstanding and 11,600 shares of common stock. P. R. Patton owned 30 shares of preferred stock and 92 shares of common stock. What amount of dividend did he receive for (a) the preferred stock and (b) the common stock?

Step 1. Calculate stockholder's preferred stock dividend:

Number of shares owned × Par value × Dividend rate = Preferred dividend
30 × $100 × .09 = $270.00

Step 2. Calculate total preferred dividend:

Number of shares owned × Par value × Dividend rate = Preferred stock dividend
1,100 × $100 × .09 = $9,900

Step 3. Calculate common stock dividend per share:

Total dividend − Preferred dividend = Common stock dividend
$88,780 − $9,900 = $78,880

$$\frac{\text{Common stock dividend}}{\text{Outstanding shares}} = \text{Common stock dividend per share}$$

$$\frac{\$78,880}{11,600} = \$6.80 \text{ per share}$$

Step 4. Calculate common stockholder's dividend:

Number of shares owned × Dividend per share = Stockholder's dividend
92 × $6.80 = $625.60

STOCK YIELDS

Stock yields are percents that indicate the rate of return the stockholder could expect to receive on an investment in the stock. This information may be helpful to an investor or potential investor to compare the rate of return on a stock investment to the interest earned on bank savings, the interest rate on bonds, or other types of money investments.

> **Rule 1: TO CALCULATE STOCK YIELD:**
>
> $$\frac{\text{Annual dividend}}{\text{Stock price}} = \text{Stock yield}$$

Example 1

Find the stock yield on a share of common stock that was purchased for $132.00 per share and paid a quarterly dividend of $3.25.

Step 1. Calculate annual dividend:

$3.25 × 4 = $13.00 annual dividend

Step 2. Calculate stock yield (round to 4 decimals):

$$\frac{\text{Annual dividend}}{\text{Purchase price}} = \text{Stock yield}$$

$$\frac{\$13.00}{\$132.00} = .0985 = 9.85\%$$

Example 2

A. R. Thomas purchased 40 shares of 7%, $50 par value preferred stock for $57 per share. Find the stock yield per share.

Step 1. Calculate the annual dividend:

Par value × Dividend rate = Annual dividend
$50.00 × .07 = $3.50

Step 2. Calculate stock yield:

$$\frac{\text{Annual dividend}}{\text{Purchase price}} = \text{Stock yield}$$

$$\frac{\$3.50}{\$57.00} = .0614 = 6.14\%$$

PRICE-EARNINGS RATIO

The price-earnings ratio, which is part of the published stock quotations, is a comparison of the earnings per share of stock to the selling price. It is a measurement of the investor's willingness to invest in the corporation with confidence that the future of the corporation will be successful. The higher the ratio, the higher the investor's confidence. For example, a ratio of 5 means that the stock is selling for 5 times more than the earnings per share of the stock. A ratio of 14 means that the selling price is 14 times more than the earnings per share. The P-E of 14 indicates greater investor confidence than the P-E of 5.

> **Rule 1: TO CALCULATE THE PRICE-EARNINGS RATIO:**
>
> $$\frac{\text{Closing price per share}}{\text{Earnings per share}} = \text{Price-earnings ratio}$$

Example 1   The closing price of the R & T Manufacturing Company was $38.40 and the earnings per share was $3.20. Find the price-earnings ratio.
Step 1.   Calculate the P-E ratio:

$$\frac{\text{Closing price}}{\text{Earnings per share}} = \frac{\$38.40}{\$3.20} = 12 \text{ P-E ratio}$$

Example 2   The closing price of a share of common stock in the Gaylord Corporation was $60⅞. The earnings per share was $12.175. What is the P-E ratio?
Step 1.   Calculate the P-E ratio:

$$\frac{\text{Closing price}}{\text{Earnings per share}} = \frac{\$60.875}{\$12.175} = 5 \text{ P-E ratio}$$

Practice exercises

		Answer
1.	The board of directors of the Allen Concrete Company declared a total of $44,060 for dividends to be paid to both preferred and common stockholders. There were 2,000, 8% par value $100 preferred stock and 11,500 common stock outstanding.	
	a. Find the dividend per share that preferred stockholders will receive.	$8.00
	b. What per share dividend will the common stockholders receive?	$2.44
2.	Find the dividend per share paid to (a) preferred stockholders and (b) the common stockholders of a corporation that declared a total of $26,225 for dividends. The corporation had issued 3,000 shares of 7% par value $50 preferred stock and 8,500 shares of common stock.	_____ _____
3.	Ms. Brady was considering investing in common stock. One stock (a) paid an annual dividend of $7.24 and was selling for $76⅜ per share. Another stock (b) sold for 42⅞ and paid an annual dividend of $4.60. Find the stock yield on each of the stock Ms. Brady is considering. (Round answer to 4 decimals.)	9.48% 10.73%
4.	a. Find the stock yield on a share of stock that sold for $90⅝ and paid an annual dividend of $8.65.	_____
	b. What is the stock yield on a share of common stock that paid an annual dividend of $1.35 and sold for $18.50?	_____
5.	What is the price-earnings ratio of a share of stock that had a closing price of $24.60 and earnings per share were $4.10?	6 P-E
6.	The closing price of a share of common stock was $155.72 and earnings per share were $9.16. What is the P-E ratio?	_____

11 STOCKS AND BONDS / 293

7. A total of $67,500 was declared to be distributed among the preferred and common stockholders. There were 1,400 shares of 7½%, $50 par value preferred stock and 7,700 shares of common stock outstanding. Find the dividend received by a stockholder who owned:
   a. 62 shares of preferred stock. $232.50
   b. 110 shares of common stock. $888.80

8. The Magrum Corporation declared a total of $103,000 dividend to be distributed among the preferred and common stockholders. There were 2,400 shares of 8% par value $100 preferred stock and 8,200 shares of common stock outstanding.
   a. What dividend will a stockholder who owns 165 shares of preferred stock receive?   _____
   b. R. C. Billings owns 95 shares of common stock. What dividend will be received?   _____

9. You own 210 shares of common stock and 75 shares of preferred stock in the F & C Corporation. The corporation declared a dividend of $112,000 to be distributed among all stockholders. There was 1,650, 8½% par value of $100 preferred stock shares and 24,075 common stock shares outstanding. What total dividend would you receive from your investment? $1,492.20

10. The board of directors of the Ballard Import Corporation declared a total dividend of $67,500 to be distributed to all stockholders. There was 1,500, 9% par value $100 preferred stock shares and 17,300 common stock shares outstanding. Find the total dividend received by A. E. Brooks, who owned 105 shares of preferred stock and 350 shares of common stock.   _____

BONDS

A bond is a long-term interest-paying debt of a corporation and is reported on a balance sheet as a liability. Most bonds are issued with a face value of $1,000 or multiples of $1,000, with the interest rate and maturity date stated in the agreement.

Bonds are purchased and sold on a bond exchange through brokers much the same as stocks. The market value of a bond may differ from the face value because of premium and discount sales.

Discount selling price. When a bond is sold for less than its face value, it has been sold at a "discount." For example, if a $1,000 face value bond is quoted on the market as "98," it means the bond would be sold for $980 or at a "discount" of $20.

Premium selling price. When a bond is sold for more than its face value, it has been sold at a "premium." For example, if a bond with a face value of $1,000 is quoted on the market as "101," it means the bond would be sold for $1,010 or at a premium of $10. The market price of bonds will fluctuate from day to day but the face value remains the same during the life of the bond.

QUOTATIONS   The current market value of bonds is reported in the newspapers in most major cities. Table 11-5 is a sample of the bond market information that is included on the published bond quotation.

Table 11-5
Bond quotation*

	①	②	③	④	⑤	⑥	⑦	⑧	⑨
	Name	Int.	Mat. date	Curr. yield	Vol.	High	Low	Clos.	Net change
1.	ATT	2.6	86	3.8	5	68⅛	68⅛	68⅛	-⅛
2.	ATT	8.7	00	8.9	155	98¾	98½	98⅝	-⅛
3.	Anhr	9.2	05	9.1	5	100⅞	100⅞	100⅞	+⅛
4.	AppP	7.3	89	7.4	31	97½	97½	97½	—
5.	Arco	8.7	81	8.9	20	98	97½	97½	+⅛
6.	Arco	8.4	83	8.7	25	96¼	96¼	96¼	+⅝

*To read the bond quotation, follow Line 5:

Column 1 Name of the bond is Arco.
Column 2 The interest rate is 8.7% and is payable semiannually.
Column 3 Maturity date of the bond is 1981.
Column 4 The current yield or rate of return on the bond is 8.9%.
Column 5 20 bonds were traded during the trading day.
Column 6 The high price during the trading day was "98," which is 98% of $1,000 or $980.
Column 7 The low price during the trading day was "97½," which is 97.5% of $1,000 or $975.
Column 8 The closing price at the end of the trading day was also $975.
Column 9 The net change from the closing price of the prior day was $1.25 less than closing price (⅛% = .00125 × $1,000 or $1.25).

Source: "The Bond Book," "The Bond Book" is a copyrighted publication of Merrill Lynch Pierce Fenner & Smith Incorporated, and is reprinted here with its permission.

INTEREST

The rate of interest, the semiannual due dates, and the maturity date are part of the bond agreement.

Simple interest

The simple interest formula is used to calculate interest on all types of bonds. Interest days are based on a 30-day month and the interest year is always 360 days on corporate bonds.

Rule 1: TO CALCULATE BOND INTEREST:

$$\text{Face value} \times \text{Interest rate} \times \frac{\text{Interest days}}{360} = \text{Bond interest}$$

Step 1. Calculate interest days.
Step 2. Substitute data in the simple interest formula.

Example 1   R. C. Dawson owned four $1,000 bonds with 7½% interest due on April 1 and October 1. Interest was paid on April 1. What amount of interest will be paid on October 1?

Step 1. Calculate interest days:

April 1 to October 1 = 6 months
6 months × 30 days = 180 days

Step 2. Substitute data in the simple interest formula:

11 STOCKS AND BONDS / 295

$$\text{Face value} \times \text{Interest rate} \times \frac{\text{Interest days}}{360} = \text{Interest}$$

$$(4 \times \$1{,}000) \times .075 \times \frac{180}{360} = \$150.00$$

Accrued interest

When a bond is purchased or sold between interest dates, interest days are counted from the last interest payment date to *the day prior to settlement date*.

Settlement date. It is four working days after the purchase or sale date of the bond. It is day on which title to the bond changes and payment is due.

For example, if a bond is sold on April 2, the interest and settlement dates would be:

Tuesday   April 2   Sale date
Wednesday   April 3   day 1
Thursday   April 4   day 2
Friday   April 5   day 3   Interest date
Monday   April 6   day 4   Settlement date

Last interest payment was February 1.
Interest period was February 1 to April 5.
Interest days: 65 days.

Rule 2: TO CALCULATE ACCRUED INTEREST:

$$\text{Face value} \times \text{Interest rate} \times \frac{\text{Interest days}}{360} = \text{Interest}$$

Step 1. Calculate interest days:

Add 4 working days to date of sale to find settlement date.
Interest date is the day prior to settlement date.
Count days, using 30 days to a month, from date of last interest payment to interest date.

Step 2. Substitute data in simple interest formula.

Example 1   A bond with a face value of $1,000 with interest of 4½% payable on June 1 and December 1 was sold on Monday, October 12. What interest was due on the bond if last interest was paid June 1?

Step 1. Calculate interest days:

October 12   Monday
        13   Tuesday   day 1
        14   Wednesday   day 2
        15   Thursday   day 3   Interest day
        16   Friday   day 4   Settlement day

Interest days: June 1 to October 15 = 135 days.

Step 2. Substitute data in simple interest formula:

$$\$1{,}000 \times .045 \times \frac{135}{360} = \$16.88 \text{ Interest}$$

COMMISSION AND FEES   The broker's commission on a purchase and sale of bonds is a set fee that may range from $2.50 to $7.50 for each $1,000 face value involved in the transaction. A commission of $5 per $1,000 face value has been used in the examples and practice problems.

> **Rule 3: TO CALCULATE COMMISSION ON A BOND TRANSACTION:**
> $$\frac{\text{Total face value}}{\$1,000} \times \$5 = \text{Commission}$$

Example 1 S. A. Sullivan purchased six $5,000, 7½% interest bonds. What amount of commission would be paid the broker?

Step 1. Calculate total face value:

$$6 \times \$5,000 = \$30,000$$

Step 2. Calculate the commission:

$$\frac{\$30,000}{\$1,000} \times \$5 = \$150$$

A Security and Exchange Commission fee of 1 cent for each $500 or fractional part of the market price is payable by the seller.

> **Rule 4: TO CALCULATE SECURITY & EXCHANGE FEE:**
> $$\frac{\text{Total market price}}{\$500} = \text{Units} \times \$.01 = \text{S\&E fee}$$

Example 1 If you sold eight $1,000, 7½% interest bonds at a market price of $970 each, calculate the Security and Exchange fee you must pay.

Step 1. Calculate total market price:

$$8 \times \$970 = \$7,760 \text{ Total market price}$$

Step 2. Calculate the S & E fee:

$$\frac{\$7760}{500} = 15.52 = 16 \text{ units} \times \$.01 = \$.16 \text{ S \& E fee}$$

YIELDS

Current yield. It is a percent that indicates the interest rate earned on a bond for the year in which the bond was purchased. As the market price changes, the current yield will change, but it is a significant indicator to the investor.

> **Rule 5: TO CALCULATE CURRENT YIELD:**
> $$\frac{\text{Annual interest}}{\text{Current price + Commission}} = \text{Current yield}$$

Step 1. Calculate annual interest:

Face value × Interest rate = Annual interest

Step 2. Calculate commission:

Commission per share × Number of shares = Commission

Step 3. Substitute data in current yield formula.

Example 1 A bond with a face value of $1,000 and interest of 9% was offered at a market price of $970. Broker's commission was $5. What is the current yield of the bond? (Round percent to 4 decimals.)

Step 1. Calculate annual interest:

$$\$1{,}000 \times .09 = \$90.00 \text{ Annual interest}$$

Step 2. Calculate broker's commission:

$$1 \text{ bond} \times \$5 = \$5 \text{ Commission}$$

Step 3. Calculate current yield on the bond:

$$\frac{\$90}{\$970 + \$5} = \frac{\$90}{\$975} = .0923 = 9.23\%$$

Example 2 What is the current yield of a bond that was offered on the market for $5,010? The broker's commission was $15 per share and the face value of the 5½% interest bond was $5,000. What was the current yield of the bond?

Step 1. Calculate annual interest:

$$\$5{,}000 \times .055 = \$275.00$$

Step 2. Calculate broker's commission:

$$1 \text{ bond} \times \$15 = \$15 \text{ Commission}$$

Step 3. Calculate current yield of the bond:

$$\frac{\$275}{\$5{,}010 + \$15} = \frac{\$275}{\$5{,}025} = .0547 = 5.47\% \text{ Current yield}$$

YIELD TO MATURITY

A more significant measurement of the rate of return an investor could expect from an investment in bonds is the yield to maturity. Tables are available to calculate this yield; however, an approximate yield can be calculated by the use of the yield to maturity formula. The use of this formula is illustrated in the examples and applied in the practice problems.

Rule 6: TO CALCULATE YIELD TO MATURITY:

a. Premium purchases:

$$\frac{\text{Annual interest} - (\text{Amount of premium} \div \text{Years to maturity})}{(\text{Face value} + \text{Purchase price}) \div 2} = \text{Yield to maturity}$$

b. Discount purchases:

$$\frac{\text{Annual interest} + (\text{Amount of discount} \div \text{Years to maturity})}{(\text{Face value} + \text{Purchase price}) \div 2} = \text{Yield to maturity}$$

Example 1 A bond with a face value of $1,000 was purchased for $975. The bond paid 6% interest and matured in 10 years. What was the yield to maturity of the bond? (Round percent to 4 decimals.)

Step 1. Calculate annual interest:

$$\$1{,}000 \times .06 = \$60 \text{ Annual interest}$$

Step 2. Calculate the discount:

$$\text{Face value} - \text{Purchase price} = \text{Discount}$$
$$\$1{,}000 \quad - \quad \$975 \quad = \quad \$25$$

Step 3. Substitute data in yield to maturity formula:

$$\frac{\$60 + (\$25 \div 10)}{(\$1{,}000 + \$975) \div 2} = \frac{\$62.50}{\$987.50} = .0633 = 6.33\%$$

Example 2   A bond with a face value of $1,000 was purchased for $1,024, including the commission. The bond matured in 8 years and paid 8% interest. What was the yield to maturity on the bond?

Step 1.   Calculate the annual interest:

$$\$1,000 \times .08 = \$80.00$$

Step 2.   Calculate the premium:

$$\$1,024 - \$1,000 = \$24 \text{ premium}$$

Step 3.   Calculate the yield to maturity:

$$\frac{\$80 - (\$24 \div 8)}{(\$1,000 + \$1,024) \div 2} = \frac{\$77}{\$1,012} = .0761 - 7.61\%$$

PURCHASE AND SALE
Purchases

Rule 7: TO CALCULATE THE TOTAL COST OF A PURCHASE OF BONDS:

Total purchase price + Accrued interest + Commission = Total cost

Step 1.   Calculate total purchase price:

Number of bonds purchased × Market price = Total purchase price

Step 2.   Calculate accrued interest:

$$\text{Face value} \times \text{Interest rate} \times \frac{\text{Interest days}}{360} = \text{Accrued interest}$$

Interest days are based on a 30-day month from date of last interest payment to day prior to settlement date.

Step 3.   Calculate commission:

Number of bonds × Fee = Commission

Example 1   Ms. J. A. Mitchell purchased a $5,000 bond, with interest of 8½% payable on January 1 and July 1, on a Monday, September 10, at a quoted market price of $4,925. The broker's commission was $10.00 per bond.

  a. On what date will Ms. Mitchell settle with the broker?
  b. What is the total cost of the bond to Ms. Mitchell?

Step 1.   Calculate total purchase price:

1 bond × $4,925 = $4,925 Total price

Step 2.   Calculate accrued interest:

Settlement date = Monday, September 10 + 4 days =
  Friday, September 14   (**Ans.** *a*)
Interest date   = September 13
Interest days   = July 1 to September 13 = 73 days

$$\text{Face value} \times \text{Interest rate} \times \frac{\text{Interest days}}{360} = \text{Interest}$$

$$\$5,000 \times .085 \times \frac{73}{360} = \$86.18 \text{ Interest}$$

Step 3.   Calculate commission

1 bond × $10.00 = $10.00 Commission

Step 4. Calculate total cost:

Market price	$4,925.00
Accrued interest	+ 86.18
Commission	+ 10.00
Total cost	$5,021.18 (**Ans.** *b*)

Sale of bonds

> **Rule 8:** TO CALCULATE NET PROCEEDS FROM THE SALE OF BONDS:
> Total sale price + Accrued interest − Commission − S&E fee = Net proceeds

Step 1. Calculate total sales price:

Number of bonds sold × Quoted market price = Total sales price

Step 2. Calculate accrued interest:

$$\text{Face value} \times \text{Interest rate} \times \frac{\text{Interest days}}{360} = \text{Interest}$$

Interest days are based on a 30-day month from last interest date to day prior to settlement.

Step 3. Calculate commission:

Number of bonds × Fee = Commission

Step 4. Calculate Security & Exchange fee:

$$\frac{\text{Market price}}{500} = \text{Units} \times \$.01 = \text{Fee}$$

Step 5. Substitute data in the net proceeds formula.

Example 1 On Monday, November 20, Tony Johnson sold four $1,000 face value bonds with 9% interest payable on March 1 and September 1 for a market price of $985 each. Broker's commission was $5 per bond. The transaction was completed on the New York Bond Exchange. What were the proceeds received from the sale?

Step 1. Calculate total sales price:

Number of bonds sold × Market price = Total sales price
      4   × $985   = $3,940

Step 2. Calculate accrued interest:

Settlement date = Monday, November 20 + 4 days = November 24
Interest date   = November 23
Interest days   = September 1 to November 23 = 83 days

$$\text{Face value} \times \text{Interest rate} \times \frac{\text{Interest days}}{360} = \text{Interest}$$

$$(4 \times \$1,000) \times .09 \times \frac{83}{360} = \$83.00$$

Step 3. Calculate commission:

Number of bonds sold × Fee = Commission
       4   × $5 = $20

Step 4. Calculate Security & Exchange fee:

$$\frac{\text{Market price}}{\$500} = \text{Units} \times \$.01 = \text{Fee}$$

$$\frac{\$3,940}{\$500} = 7.88 = 8 \times \$.01 = \$.08$$

Step 5. Calculate net proceeds:

Total sales price		$3,940.00
Accrued interest	+	83.00
Commission	−	20.00
S & E fee	−	0.08
Net proceeds		$4,002.92

Practice exercises

Answer

1. On October 1, a bond was purchased that had a face value of $1,000. Interest of 9% was payable on April 1 and October 1. What is the amount of the accrued interest on the bond? $45.00

2. Marie James purchased four bonds with a face value of $1,000 each on August 1. The bonds paid 7½% interest payable on February 1 and August 1. What was the accrued interest on the bonds? _____

3. Find the accrued interest on a $5,000 bond that was purchased on Monday, May 16 if the bond paid 8½% on March 1 and September 1. $93.26

4. You purchased six $1,000 face value bonds on Monday, March 3. The bonds paid 6½% interest due on June 1 and December 1. What amount of accrued interest is payable on the bonds? _____

5. Morris U. Salder was considering purchasing a $5,000 bond with interest of 10½%, at a market price of $4,965. The broker's commission was $5 per $1,000 of face value. What was the current yield of the bond? 10.52%

6. Find the current yield on a bond with a face value of $2,000 that paid 9½% interest. The market price was $1,950 and a commission of $5 per $1,000 of face value was due the broker. _____

7. Calculate the yield to maturity on a 12-year bond with a face value of $1,000 with 8% interest that had a market value of $1,015. (Round rate to the 4th decimal.) 7.82%

8. Calculate the yield to maturity on a 10-year bond with a face value of $2,000 with 9½% interest that had a market value of $1,970. (Round rate to 4 decimal places.) _____

9. a. A. C. Burroughs purchased a 10-year $1,000 bond with interest of 12½% at a market price of $990. What is the yield to maturity on the bond? 12.66%

   b. Mr. Burroughs also purchased a bond with a face value of $1,000 maturing in 10 years with interest at 9% at a market price of $1,100. What was the yield to maturity on the bond? 7.62%

10. Find the total cost of a bond that was purchased at a market price of $980. The bond had a face value of $1,000 with interest of 11% payable on August 1 and February 1 was purchased on Monday, January 18. Broker's commission was $5 per bond. _____

11. F. E. Ellis purchased a $2,000 bond on Monday, September 25, at a market price $1,970. The bond paid 7½% interest due on June 1 and December 1. The broker's commission was $5 per $1,000 of face value. What was the total cost of the bond to Ms. Ellis? $2,029.17

12. On September 21, B. C. Jenkins sold 2 bonds with a face value of $4,000 each. The market price was $4,025 each. The bonds paid 9% interest payable on May 1 and November 1. The broker's commission was $5.00 per bond. The transaction was completed on the New York Bond Exchange. What proceeds did Ms. Jenkins receive from the sale of the bonds?   _____

Review problems

		Answer
1.	Refer to Table 11-1 and answer the following questions.	
	a. What was the closing price of the Ford Motor stock at the close of trading on the previous day?	$41.00
	b. If you owned 6 shares of Delta Air stock, what were they worth at the close of trading?	$248.25
2.	From the quotations reported on Table 11-1:	
	a. What would 230 shares of Con Edison stock be worth at the high quoted price of the day?	_____
	b. How much dividend did the owner of 390 shares of CBS stock receive when the dividend was paid?	_____
3.	S. O. Ryan sold 73 shares of AT&T stock at a market price of $56⅞ per share through a broker. What commission did the broker receive? (See Tables 11-2 and 11-3.)	$35.67
4.	An investor sold 92 shares of stock at a quoted market price of $4.125 per share through his broker. What commission was paid the broker?	_____
5.	L. N. Delly sold 167 shares of Eastern Airlines stock at a quoted price of $62⅝ through his broker on the New York Stock Exchange. What commission would be due the broker?	$80.16
6.	If 208 shares of CBS stock was sold at $50⅜ per share, what commission would the broker receive?	_____
7.	Ms. H. L. Roberts sold 246 shares of common stock at a quoted market price of $34¾ per share through her broker on the New York Stock Exchange. What net proceeds did Ms. Roberts receive from the sale?	$8,462.31
8.	Mr. Madden sold 175 shares of stock at a quoted market price of $61⅝ through his broker on the New York Stock Exchange. What net proceeds did Mr. Madden receive from the sale?	_____
9.	Lois Young purchased 105 shares of common stock at a quoted market price of $27½ through her broker on the New York Stock Exchange. What was the total cost of the stock to Ms. Young?	$2,923.64
10.	Find the total cost of the purchase of 126 shares of stock with a quoted market price of $58⅜. The broker's commission is the same as Table 3.	_____
11.	The board of directors of the RTC Corporation declared a dividend of $869,040 to be distributed among the pre-	

ferred and common stockholders. There were 48,000 6% preferred stock outstanding shares and 206,520 shares of common stock. What was the dividend per share for:
    a. The preferred stockholders, par value $100. $6.00
    b. The common stockholders? $2.81

12. A total dividend of $719,440 was declared. There were 18,000, 5% $100 par value preferred stock outstanding and 112,000 shares of common stock. What is the dividend per share for:
    a. The preferred stockholders?
    b. The common stockholders?

13. You owned 50 shares of preferred stock in the XYZ Corporation as well as 112 shares of common stock. The corporation declared a total of $66,500 in dividends to be distributed among 2,800, 6% $100 par value shares of preferred stock outstanding and 6,855 shares of outstanding common stock. What total dividend will you receive? $1,112.00

14. Find the total dividends received by a stockholder who owned 125 shares of preferred stock and 216 shares of common stock in the Bayburn Manufacturing Company. In dividends, $48,750 was declared to be distributed to preferred and common stockholders. There was 4,000 shares of 7% $100 par value preferred shares outstanding and 5,200 shares of common stock.

15. a. Find the current yield on a share of common stock if the total dividend of $7,600 was available to 1,948 outstanding shares. The market price of the stock was $29⅜ per share.   13.28%
    b. If the closing price of the stock in problem 15a was $27.30, what was the P-E ratio?   7

16. There was $29,287 dividends to be distributed to 10,650 common stockholders. The current market price was $12⅛.
    a. What is the current yield of the stock?
    b. If the closing price was $12.375, what was the P-E ratio?

17. On Monday, May 20, Ms. Walters purchased six $1,000 par value bonds which paid 7½% interest payable on February 1 and August 1 at a market price of $990 per share. The broker's commission was $5 per $1,000 of par value. What are the net proceeds Ms. Walters would receive from the sale? $6,111.25

18. Find the net proceeds the seller would receive from the sale of four bonds with a face value of $2,000 each and paid interest of 8% due on May 1 and November 1. The sale was made on Monday, September 8, at a market price of $1,980 each. The broker's commission was $5 per $1,000 of par value and the transaction was completed on the New York Stock Exchange.

19. You purchased a $5,000 par value bond that paid 9½% interest at a market price of $4,925. The bond matured in 8 years. The broker's commission was $5 per $1,000 of par value.
    a. What is the current yield on the bond? 9.6%
    b. What is the yield to maturity? 9.76%
20. Find: (a) the current yield and (b) the yield to maturity on a bond with a face value of $2,000 with interest of 10% that was purchased at a market price of $2,100. The bond matured in 10 years. Broker's commission was $5 per $1,000 par value.

STUDY UNIT **12**

Introduction to statistics

MEASUREMENTS OF CENTRAL TENDENCIES
    Mean
    Median
    Mode
    Weighted average

FREQUENCY DISTRIBUTION

SIMPLE DEVIATION

STANDARD DEVIATION

GRAPHS
    Line graphs
    Bar graphs
    Circle graphs

Every man and woman in business must make decisions regarding some aspect of the operations of the business, and each decision involves some degree of risk. A knowledge of basic statistics and the properties of statistical data may help reduce the risk in decision making.

The concentration in this study unit is on descriptive statistics, which involves the organization, summarization, and mathematics involved in converting collected data into information upon which business decisions can be made. The calculation of central tendencies in a series of data, including the *mean*, the *median*, the *mode*, the *weighted average*, as well as *frequency distributions* and *standard deviation*, are illustrated in examples and practice problems. The presentation of statistical data on *line*, *bar*, and *circle* graphs are discussed and illustrated. Inferential statistics involving interpretation, projections, and sampling data will be deferred to advanced courses in statistics.

MEASUREMENTS OF CENTRAL TENDENCIES

The most frequently used measurements of central tendencies are the *mean, median,* and the *mode.*

MEAN   The *mean* (arithmetic average) is a number that reflects the quantities or values in a series of data. It is an easily calculated and effective measurement of central tendency if the volume of data is relatively small and the series does not include extremely high or low quantities or value.

Rule 1: TO CALCULATE THE MEAN:
$$\frac{\text{Sum of the quantities or values in a series}}{\text{Number of items in the series}} = \text{Mean}$$

Example 1 The following production record of Department C shows the units completed each week during the first quarter of the year. What was the weekly mean production of the department?

692, 502, 718, 421, 596, 812, 593, 613,
767, 803, 412, 555, and 720

Step 1. Add all quantities involved in the series:

692 + 502 + 718 + 421 + 596 + 812 +
593 + 613 + 767 + 803 + 412 + 555 + 720 = 8,204

Step 2. Add the total quantities involved in the series:

Total items = 13

Step 3. Substitute data in the mean formula:

$$\frac{\text{Sum of all quantities in the series}}{\text{Number of data}} = \text{Mean}$$

$$\frac{8,204}{13} = 631 \text{ units: Weekly mean}$$

MEDIAN The *median* is the middle quantity or value in a series of data. It is another measurement of central tendency that is more accurate than the arithmetic mean when extremely high or low data are included in the series.

Rule 2: **TO CALCULATE THE MEDIAN VALUE OF QUANTITY OF A SERIES:**
  a. Arrange the data in descending or ascending order and count the number of items in the series.

  b. $\dfrac{\text{Number of items in the series} + 1}{2}$ = Median quantity or value

---

Step 1. Arrange items in descending or ascending order. Count the number of items in the series.

Step 2. Substitute data in the median formula.

If the series includes an even number of items, average the middle two quantities or values to determine the median.

If the series includes an odd number of items, the middle quantity or value will be the median.

Example 1 Find the median unit cost of the products produced in Department A of the Joy Manufacturing Company:

$19.06, $16.47, $18.23, $9.32, $10.29, $11.62, $13.18.

Step 1. Arrange items in descending order and count the number of items in the series:

1. $19.06
2. $18.23
3. $16.47
4. $13.18 . . . . Median value
5. $11.62
6. $10.29
7. $ 9.32

Number of items = 7

Step 2. Substitute data in median formula:

$$\frac{7+1}{2} = \text{4th item}$$

Example 2   Find the median number of boxes produced by the Hicks plant during a three-week period. Production included: 2,122; 2,026; 1,842; 1,026; 2,610; and 1,209 boxes.

Step 1. Arrange the items in descending order and count them:

1. 2,610
2. 2,122
3. 2,026
4. 1,842
5. 1,209
6. 1,026

$$\frac{2,026 + 1,842}{2} = 1,934 = \text{Median production}$$

Step 2. Substitute data in the median formula:

$$\frac{\text{Number of items in the series} + 1}{2} = \text{Median}$$

$$\frac{6+1}{2} = 3.5 \text{ item}$$

Note: The series includes an even number of items. Median is the average of the middle two quantities.

MODE   The third measurement of central tendency is the *mode* of a series of data. It is the value or quantity that is repeated most frequently in a set of data. This measurement is useful in identifying a characteristic of a product, such as size, color, number, and shape, that is purchased most frequently by consumers. Many marketing surveys include the mode in measuring the acceptance of a product by the public.

Rule 3: TO DETERMINE THE MODE OF A SERIES:
Prepare a tally sheet and record each item in the series. The *mode* will be the quantity or value repeated the most frequently.

Example 1   The General Food Company made a survey to determine what size package of breakfast food was purchased most frequently in a small grocery store. Sales records indicated the following sales: 4 oz. package, 6 oz. package, 16 oz. package, 8 oz. package, 6 oz. package, 12 oz. package, 16 oz. package, 8 oz. package, 8 oz. package, 4 oz. package, 8 oz. package, 16 oz. package, 8 oz. package, 16 oz. package, 8 oz. package, 12 oz. package, 6 oz. package, 8 oz. package, 12 oz. package, 8 oz. package, 8 oz. package, 4 oz. package, 8 oz. package. Find the *mode* of the survey.

Step 1. Prepare a tally sheet and count the most frequently repeated item:

4 oz. packages					3
6 oz. packages					3
8 oz. packages	ℳ ℳ	10
12 oz. packages					3
16 oz. packages						4

Step 2. Mode of the series is the 8 oz. package.

12 INTRODUCTION TO STATISTICS / 311

WEIGHTED AVERAGE   The weighted average method of measuring central tendency permits a more accurate mean when the individual items in a series are not of equal value.

> **Rule 4: TO CALCULATE THE WEIGHTED AVERAGE MEAN:**
> *a.* For each item in the series:
>
> Quantity of the item × Value of the item = Total value of item
>
> *b.* Then calculate:
>
> $$\frac{\text{Total value of all items}}{\text{Total quantities of all items}} = \text{Weighted average mean}$$

Step 1. Record quantities and values on a tally sheet.
Step 2. Multiply each quantity of the item by its value.
Step 3. Add all quantities and values.
Step 4. Substitute data in the weighted average mean formula.

Example 1   The Ace Sporting Goods Store made a survey to determine the average price of a pair of ice skates, with the following results:

Store 1 sold 32 pairs of skates for $19.95 each.
Store 2 sold 28 pairs of skates for $22.25 each.
Store 3 sold 31 pairs of skates for $28.75 each.
Store 4 sold 19 pairs of skates for $34.15.
Store 5 sold 37 pairs of skates for $20.95
Store 6 sold 40 pairs of skates for $18.75

What is the weighted average mean of the price of a pair of ice skates?
Steps 1 & 2. Record quantities and value on a tally sheet:

	Pairs sold		Price per share		Total value
Store 1	32	×	$19.95	=	$638.40
Store 2	28	×	22.25	=	623.00
Store 3	31	×	28.75	=	891.25
Store 4	19	×	34.15	=	648.85
Store 5	37	×	20.95	=	775.15
Store 6	40	×	18.75	=	750.00
	187				$4,326.65

Step 3. Substitute data in the weighted average mean formula:

Step 4. $\dfrac{\$4,326.65}{187} = \$23.14$ Weighted average

Practice exercises

Answer

1. The following sales were completed during a clearance sale:

   $12.96, $21.40, $18.95, $17.14, $9.26, $11.30, $9.95, $10.15, $26.90, $19.30, $17.35 and $8.10

   What was the mean of the sales completed? $15.23

2. What is the mean grade of the following test scores made on a business math test?

   92, 70, 64, 58, 86, 78, 94, 72, 68, 56, 62, 74, 80, 58, 66, and 96 _____

3. a. The monthly sales of the Albert Toy Manufacturing Company for last year were:

   $624, $806, $1,026, $512, $413, $309, $187, $319, $986, $1,942, $2,020 and $300.

   What is the median sale of the year? $568

   b. The following production record of Department C showed the following units completed during a two-week period:

   692, 502, 718, 421, 596, 812, 613, 803, 720, 555, and 412

   What was the median production for the two-week period? 613

4. a. The unit cost of manufacturing summer jackets included:

   $4.26, $8.10, $3.06, $9.13, $6.12, $4.30, $3.91, and $5.26

   What was the median unit cost? _____

   b. The ages of employees of the A & R Company who enrolled in a contributory retirement plan included:

   22, 43, 31, 23, 39, 27, 44, 39, 19, 26, 34, 22, and 36

   What was the median age of the employees who enrolled in the plan? _____

5. A survey of paint stores included the following selling prices charged for a 5 gallon can of driveway sealer:

   $7.99, $6.99, $9.10, $7.99, $8.20, $9.14, $7.99, $10.95, $7.99, $8.39 and $8.12

   What is the mode of the selling prices charged? $7.99

6. The temperatures recorded during a 12 hour period included the following. Find the mode.

   64 degrees, 68 degrees, 70 degrees, 74 degrees, 68 degrees, 66 degrees, 64 degrees, 68 degrees, 75 degrees, 70 degrees, 68 degrees, 64 degrees, and 60 degrees _____

7. The All-Good Manufacturing Company made a survey of the production in 5 of their plants during an 8-hour day and asked you to find the weighted average mean of their unit production. Results of the survey included the following data:

   Plant A produced 983 units at a unit cost of $2.125.
   Plant B produced 1,142 at a cost of $1.06 each.
   Plant C produced 1,055 units at a unit cost of $1.88.
   Plant D produced 963 units at a cost of $1.965 each.
   Plant E produced 1,215 units at a cost of $2.06 each. $1.806

8. Find the weighted average mean of the selling price per coat of spring coats sold in four specialty shops.

Store 1 sold 12 coats at $39.95.
Store 2 sold 16 coats at $44.95.
Store 3 sold 20 coats at $31.50.
Store 4 sold 9 coats at $57.90.

FREQUENCY DISTRIBUTION

When the number of items in a series of data is too large to conveniently use the weighted average method of calculating a mean, the data can be grouped into class intervals and the midpoint of the interval considered to be the mean of the class. This grouping is called a "frequency distribution" and permits the measurement of a large number of data resulting in an accurate weighted average mean. Many marketing surveys, studies to relocate a business, or studies to introduce new products are examples of the use of frequency distribution.

What follows is the procedure to prepare a frequency distribution table.

> **Rule 1: TO CALCULATE THE RANGE OF THE ITEMS IN A SERIES OF DATA:**
>
> Highest quantity or value in the series − Lowest quantity or value in the series = Range

Example   The highest quantity in a series was 220 units and the lowest quantity was 110 units. What is the range?

Step 1.

$$220 - 110 = 110 \text{ Distribution range}$$

> **Rule 2: TO CALCULATE CLASS INTERVALS:**
>
> $$\frac{\text{Range}}{\text{Number of classes desired}} = \text{Class interval}$$

Example   Distribution range = 110.

Step 1.

Desired number of classes = 10

$$\frac{110}{10} = 11 \text{ units per interval}$$

> **Rule 3: TO PREPARE A FREQUENCY DISTRIBUTION TABLE:**
> *a)* Establish class interval
> *b)* Calculate midpoint of class interval
> *c)* Class midpoint × Frequency = Total class value

Example   The personnel director of the B & M Insurance Agency was interested in the typing speed of the 125 typists employed by the agency in order to establish an acceptable typing speed for applicants. From the following information—in which *wpm* means words per minute—prepare a frequency distribution table:

52 wpm, 11 typists   67 wpm, 11 typists
44 wpm, 12 typists   77 wpm, 4 typists
62 wpm, 14 typists   90 wpm, 3 typists
56 wpm, 20 typists   60 wpm, 20 typists
48 wpm, 9 typists   65 wpm, 17 typists
92 wpm, 4 typists

Step 1. Calculate the range of the distribution:

$$\begin{aligned}\text{Highest wpm} &= 92\\ \text{Lowest wpm} &= -44\\ \text{Range} &= 48\end{aligned}$$

Step 2. Calculate the class interval for 7 classes:

$$\frac{\text{Range}}{\text{Number of classes}} = \frac{48}{7} = 6.86 = 7 \text{ wpm}$$

Step 3. Prepare a frequency distribution table:

	Class intervals	Class midpoint	X	Frequency	=	Total wpm
1.	86–92	89	X	7		623
2.	79–85	82	X	0		0
3.	72–78	75	X	4		300
4.	65–71	68	X	28		1,904
5.	58–64	61	X	34		2,074
6.	51–57	54	X	31		1,674
7.	44–50	47	X	21		987
Totals				125		7,562

Rule 4: TO CALCULATE THE WEIGHTED AVERAGE MEAN:

$$\frac{\text{Total value}}{\text{Total items}} = \text{Weighted average mean}$$

Step 1. From frequency distribution table in Step 3:

$$\frac{7,562}{125} = 60.5 \text{ wpm} = \text{weighted average mean}$$

SIMPLE DEVIATION

A simple deviation is the difference between an individual item in a series of data and the arithmetic mean of the series.

For example: if the mean of a series of data is 50, the deviation of an item of 40 would be −10 (50 − 40). If the mean of a series of data is 50 and the individual item is 60, the deviation would be +10.

STANDARD DEVIATION

The standard deviation is a statistical measurement that indicates the spread of the individual items in a series of data from the mean of the series. The deviation of an individual item is the difference between the mean of the series and the value or quantity of the individual item. For example:

$$\text{Value of an individual item} = 60$$
$$\text{Mean of the series} = -50$$
$$\text{Deviation} = +10$$

$$\text{Value of an individual item} = 40$$
$$\text{Mean of the series} = -50$$
$$\text{Deviation} = -10$$

Standard deviations are particularly helpful to the businessman in maintaining quality control in verifying test results, and in interpreting marketing survey results. A low standard deviation may indicate that the items in a series are clustered close to the mean of the data collected and represent a consistent quality or performance. A high standard deviation may indicate that extreme values or quantities are included in the series and may suggest that some inconsistency has developed in the data that were collected.

Table 12-1

	①	②	③	④	⑤	⑥	⑦
	Class interval	Midpoint of class	Frequency (f)	Total (f) × midpoint	Deviation (d)	Squared Deviation (d^2)	Total (f) × (d^2)
1.	56–64	60	3	180	+27	729	2,187
2.	47–55	51	4	204	+18	324	1,296
3.	38–46	42	7	294	+ 9	81	567
4.	29–37	33	11	363	0	0	0
5.	20–28	24	8	192	- 9	81	648
6.	10–19	14	5	70	-19	361	1,805
7.	1– 9	5	2	10	-28	784	1,568
	Total		40	1,313			8,071

$$\frac{1,313}{40} = 33 \text{ mean} \qquad\qquad \text{S.D.} \sqrt{\frac{8,071}{40}} = 202 = 14$$

Table 12-1 illustrates a frequency distribution and the calculation of a standard deviation. The steps of solution will explain the calculations that were made to complete the data included in the table.

Procedure   Step 1. Calculate the class interval (column 1).

$$\text{Highest quantity in series} = 64$$
$$\text{Lowest quantity in series} = -1$$
$$\text{Range} = 63$$

Class interval for 7 classes:

$$\frac{63}{7} = 9 \text{ units per class}$$

Step 2. Calculate midpoint of the class interval (Column 2):

$$\text{Odd number of items per class} = \frac{9+1}{2} = \text{5th item}$$

Line 1: Class interval = 56 – 64
56, 57, 58, 59, 60, 61, 62, 63, 64
↓
Midpoint

Continue this procedure for each class interval.

Step 3. Record frequencies from original data and add column 3:

3 + 4 + 7 + 11 + 8 + 5 + 2 = 40 Total frequencies

Table 12-2

Square root of	Square root of
4 = 2	196 = 14
9 = 3	225 = 15
16 = 4	256 = 16
25 = 5	289 = 17
36 = 6	324 = 18
49 = 7	361 = 19
64 = 8	400 = 20
81 = 9	441 = 21
100 = 10	484 = 22
121 = 11	529 = 23
144 = 12	576 = 24
169 = 13	625 = 25

Step 4. Calculate the total of Column 4:

Frequency X Midpoint = Class total
Line 1:   3   X   60   =   180

Continue this procedure for each class interval and total the column:

180 + 204 + 294 + 363 + 192 + 70 + 10 = 1,313

Step 5. Calculate the arithmetic mean of the series:

$$\frac{1,313}{40} = 33 \text{ Mean of the series}$$

Step 6. Calculate the individual deviations (Column 5):

	Midpoint of class interval	− Mean	= Deviation
Line 1:	60	− 33 =	+27
Line 2:	51	− 33 =	+18
Line 3:	42	− 33 =	+ 9
Line 4:	33	− 33 =	0
Line 5:	24	− 33 =	− 9
Line 6:	14	− 33 =	−19
Line 7:	5	− 33 =	−28

Step 7. Square the individual deviations (Column 6):

Deviation X Deviation = Squared deviation

Line 1: 27 X 27 = 729
Line 2: 18 X 18 = 324

Continue this procedure for each class interval.

Step 8. Calculate the total of Column 7:

	Frequency	X	Squared deviation	=	Total
Line 1:	3	X	729	=	2,187
Line 2:	4	X	324	=	1,296
Line 3:	7	X	81	=	567
Line 4:	11	X	0	=	0
Line 5:	8	X	81	=	648
Line 6:	5	X	361	=	1,805
Line 7:	2	X	784	=	1,568
Total					8,071

Step 9. Substitute data in the standard deviation formula:

$$\text{Standard deviation} = \frac{\text{Frequency} \times \text{Squared deviation}}{\text{Total frequencies}}$$

$$\text{Standard deviation} = \sqrt{\frac{8{,}071}{40}} = 202 = 14 \text{ S.D.}$$

GRAPHS

In addition to the mathematical properties we have just reviewed, a series of data can also provide meaningful comparisons and trends among the variables in the series. One easily understood method of communicating these additional properties is a visual presentation by use of graphs.

Although a graph may not show the precise accuracy as a tabulation of statistical data, it does permit a presentation of approximations that clearly indicate the direction and changes that have occurred in data over a period of time or when comparisons are made.

The construction and use of the line, bar, and circle graphs are discussed and illustrated in this section.

LINE GRAPHS

A line graph is constructed by using a horizontal and vertical axes. One variable in the series of data is identified on the horizontal axis and another variable on the vertical axis. The data in the series are plotted at the intersection of the axes and connected by a straight line.

The line graph is used primarily to present continuous data over a period of time. For example, the sales of a company for a period of one week, one month or a year may be presented on a line graph as illustrated in Figure 12-1.

Rule 1: TO CALCULATE THE SCALES ON THE LINE GRAPH AXES:
  a. The horizontal scale based on *time* must cover the same time period that was included in the development of the data.
  b. The vertical scale is calculated in the same manner as a class interval.

$$\frac{\text{Range}}{\text{Number of classes}} = \text{Approximate scale interval}$$

Example

Mr. T. P. Pringle prepared the following tabulation of the sales of the People's Sportswear Company for the year 19—. Prepare a line graph to present this data to the president of the company.

```
January sales  . . . . . . . . . . . . . . . . . . . . . $16,825
February sales . . . . . . . . . . . . . . . . . . . . .  20,295
March sales  . . . . . . . . . . . . . . . . . . . . . .  14,250
April sales  . . . . . . . . . . . . . . . . . . . . . .  22,750
May sales  . . . . . . . . . . . . . . . . . . . . . . .  19,650
June sales . . . . . . . . . . . . . . . . . . . . . . .  27,400
July sales . . . . . . . . . . . . . . . . . . . . . . .  20,120
August sales . . . . . . . . . . . . . . . . . . . . . .  18,412
September sales  . . . . . . . . . . . . . . . . . . . .  15,500
October sales  . . . . . . . . . . . . . . . . . . . . .  21,680
November sales . . . . . . . . . . . . . . . . . . . . .  29,250
December sales . . . . . . . . . . . . . . . . . . . . .  17,230
```

Step 1. *Horizontal scale:*

January through December

Vertical scale (use 5 classes):

$$\frac{\text{Range}}{\text{Number of classes}} = \text{Scale interval}$$

$$\begin{array}{r}\$29,250\\-14,250\\\hline 15,000\end{array}$$

$$\frac{\$15,000}{5} = \$3,000 \text{ Interval}$$

Step 2. Complete a line graph based on the tabulation.

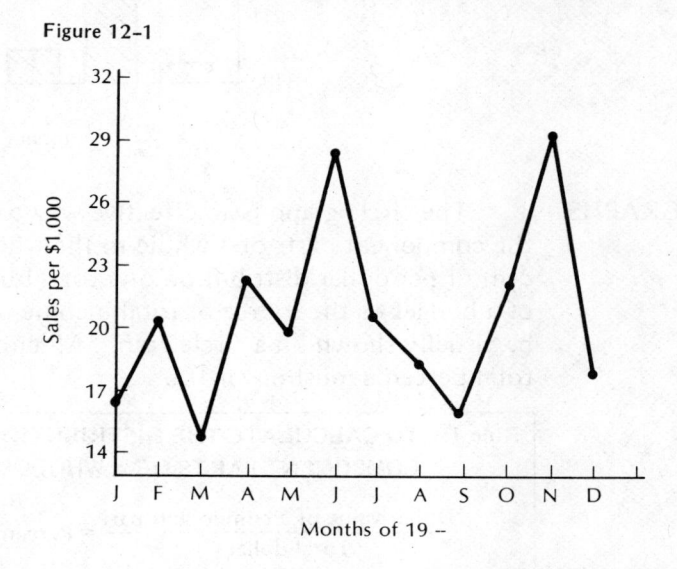

Figure 12-1

BAR GRAPHS

A bar graph is constructed on a horizontal and vertical axes similar to a line graph. The identification of the horizontal and vertical axes can be any of the variables included in the series of data. The graph may use vertical bars to indicate frequencies, time or value, or horizontal bars may be used. The bar graph is useful in presenting comparisons of size, value, or quantities among several variables in a series of data.

Example The Crawford Manufacturing Company produces five different products. The sales department made the following report of product sales for the last six months. Present the following data on a bar graph:

Product 1 .... $195,000
Product 2 .... $255,000
Product 3 .... $206,000
Product 4 .... $300,000
Product 5 .... $275,000

Step 1. Calculate the axes scale:

Horizontal scale: = Products 1 through 5

Vertical scale (use 5 classes):

$$\frac{\text{Range}}{\text{Number of classes}} = \$300,000 - 195,000 = \$105,000$$

$$\frac{105,000}{5} = \$21,000 \text{ Interval}$$

Step 2. Complete a bar graph

Figure 12-2

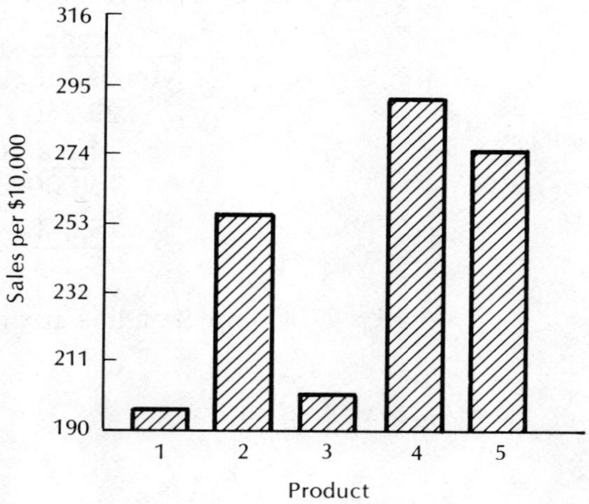

[Bar graph: Sales per $10,000 vs Product (1-5), y-axis values 190, 211, 232, 253, 274, 295, 316]

CIRCLE GRAPHS   The circle graph is an effective way to present the relationship between the component parts of a whole to the whole. For example, either the percent or per dollar distribution of a total budget among the individual items of a budget or the source of total income or the type of sales completed can be be visually shown on a circle graph. All circles are equal to 360 degrees. The total percents must equal 100%.

Rule 1: TO CALCULATE THE DISTRIBUTION OF A CIRCLE TO COMPONENT PARTS OF A WHOLE:

$$\frac{\text{Dollar value of a component part}}{\text{Total dollars}} = \text{Percent} \times 360 \text{ degrees} = \text{Component degrees}$$

Example   The accountant for the Marshall Company submitted the following analysis of expenses for the past six months:

Advertising expenses	$ 6,000
Administrative expenses	9,600
Selling expenses	36,000
Manufacturing costs	24,000
Salaries and wages	44,400
Total	$120,000

Present this data on a circle graph.

Step 1. Calculate the component parts degrees:

Advertising:

$$\frac{6,000}{120,000} = .05 \times 360 = 18 \text{ degrees}$$

Administrative expenses:

$$\frac{9,600}{120,000} = .08 \times 360 = 29 \text{ degrees}$$

Selling expenses:

$$\frac{36,000}{120,000} = .30 \times 360 = 108 \text{ degrees}$$

Manufacturing costs:

$$\frac{\$24,000}{\$120,000} = .20 \times 360 = 72 \text{ degrees}$$

Salaries and wages:

$$\frac{\$44,400}{\$120,000} = .37 \times 360 = 133 \text{ degrees}$$

Totals   100%   360 degrees

Figure 12-3

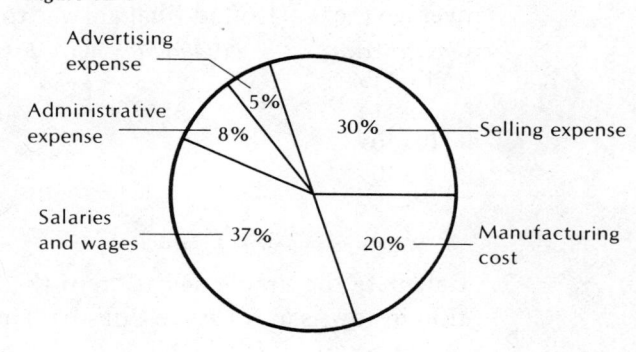

Practice exercises

                      Answer

1. The highest quantity in a series of data was 450 and the lowest quantity was 405. What class interval would be used on a frequency distribution for 5 classes?   9

2. A study of test results showed that the highest score recorded was 184 and the lowest score was 100. If 4 classes are desired, what class interval would be used?   _____

3. What is the mid-point (median) of the following class intervals?

   a.   1–11 =   6
   b.   22–26 =   24
   c.   32–41 =   36.5
   d.   15–28 =   21.5
   e.   14–20 =   17

4. From the following data determine: (*a*) the class interval   a. _____
   and (*b*) the midpoint (median) of the interval if 5 classes   b. _____
   are required.

   62, 89, 55, 67, 81, 69, 59, 87, 65, 54, 79, 73, 66, 71, 77, 84, 57, 75, 83

5. Complete a frequency distribution table and calculate a weighted average mean of the following data. (Round final answer to 2 decimal places.)

Class interval	Midpoint	Frequency	Total
560–570		2	
549–559		1	
538–548		2	
527–537		2	
516–526		2	
505–515		1	
494–504		3	
483–493		4	

Weighted average mean =　　　　　　　　　　　　　　519.71

6. From the following daily production records, complete a frequency distribution table and calculate the weighted average mean. (Round final answer to 2 decimal places.)

Class interval	Midpoint	Frequency	Total
115–119		6	
110–114		5	
105–109		11	
100–104		14	
95– 99		9	

Weighted average mean =

7. Calculate the simple deviation of the following population in towns in Birdseye County. The mean population of the county is 9,804.

			Simple deviation
a.	Maple Grove, population	11,012	+1,208
b.	Glen Cove, population	8,914	− 890
c.	Berlin, population	8,706	−1,098
d.	Swedesboro, population	12,312	+2,508
e.	Bridely, population	13,814	+4,010

8. Calculate the simple deviations of sales in the six sales districts of the T & W Company based on the following sales record:

District 1　Sales　$118,946
District 2　Sales　$123,019
District 3　Sales　$107,891
District 4　Sales　$126,784
District 5　Sales　$114,620
District 6　Sales　$130,000

　　Note: Calculate the arithmetic mean before completing the simple deviation.

9. Complete the following table and calculate the standard deviation of the data.

Class interval	Midpoint	Frequency	Total	Midpoint mean deviation	Squared deviation	Freq. × Dev.² Total
46–50		3				
41–45		2				
36–40		4				
31–35		7				
26–30		7				
21–25		6				
16–20		3				
11–15		4				
6–10		2				
0– 5		1				
		39				

Mean = 28

Standard deviation
11.32

10. Calculate the standard deviation from the following data.

Class interval	Midpoint	Frequency	Total	Midpoint mean deviation	Squared deviation	Freq. X Dev.² Total
91–99		3				
82–90		3				
73–81		4				
64–72		6				
55–63		8				
46–54		4				
37–45		7				
28–36		8				
19–27		9				
10–18		5				
0– 9		2				
		59				

11. To present the distribution of an annual budget by a circle graph, calculate the percent of the circle that would be assigned to each item of the budget.

Wages	$182,763	Wages 27%
Rent	74,459	Rent 11%
Advertising	115,073	Adv. 17%
Manufacturing cost	203,070	Mfg. cost 30%
Selling expense	101,535	Sell. exp. 15%
Total budget	$676,900	

12. What percent of the circle would be assigned to the sales of each product from the following record if the data was presented on a circle graph?

Men's suits sales	$71,437.50
Boys' jacket sales	34,290.00
Children's shoe sales	51,435.00
Ladies' coats & dresses	100,012.50
Ladies' accessories	28,575.00
Total sales	$285,750.00

APPENDIX

Use of the electric calculator

The following instructions apply to the use of a ten-key electric calculator. There is a wide variety of electric and hand calculators in use which include many features that permit a combination of arithmetic functions. The following instructions pertain only to the use of the *addition, subtraction, multiplication,* and *division function* keys on desk electric calculators that are used in most business offices. Refer to the manufacturer's instruction manual for use of additional function keys that may be available on your calculator.

There may be some differences between the operation of the electric desk calculator and the hand calculator in such operations as setting the decimal indicator, the total key, and in the addition and subtraction function keys. However, the following rules, examples, and practice exercises will assist in increasing your speed and accuracy in using either the desk or hand calculator and in solving applied problems. If you are not using a calculator, the material will provide additional practice to improve your accuracy in the basic functions of numbers.

| Step 1: SET THE DECIMAL INDICATOR |

The method of setting the decimal point will differ on each make of electric calculator. Refer to the manufacturer's instruction manual to set the decimal indicator on your calculator. The number of decimal places will be determined by the requirements of the problem.

Note: If the answer to a problem is to be given in dollars and cents, round the decimal to the 2d decimal place.

All answers to the examples and practice exercises and problems have been rounded to the 4th decimal place. To check your answers, set the decimal indicator at the 4th decimal setting.

> Step 2: CLEAR THE CALCULATOR

Before starting any calculation, depress the CLEAR or TOTAL key to remove all prior calculations that may be in the calculator. The CLEAR key on most calculators are the T, *, or CA keys.

> Step 3: ENTRY OF NUMBERS AND USE OF THE ARITHMETIC FUNCTION KEYS

ADDITION

The *addition* function is performed by use of the + key. Each digit in the number to be added is entered on the keyboard in the same order as you would read or write the number.

WHOLE NUMBERS

Clear the calculator and set Decimal Indicator at zero.

Example 1 Add 103 and 94.

Step 1 Enter the digits 1, 0, and 3 on the keyboard.
Step 2 Depress the + key.
Step 3 Enter the digits 9 and 4 on the keyboard.
Step 4 Depress the + key.
Step 5 Depress the TOTAL key.
The sum of 197 will appear on the tape or display window of the calculator.

Example 2 Add 123; 32; 1,234; and 6.

Step 1 Clear the calculator.
Step 2 Set the decimal indicator at zero.
Step 3 Enter 1, 2, and 3 on the keyboard. Depress the + key.
Enter 3 and 2 on the keyboard. Depress the + key.
Enter 1, 2, 3, and 4 on the keyboard and depress the + key.
Enter 6 on the keyboard and depress the + key.
Step 4 Depress the TOTAL key.
The sum of 1,395 will appear on the tape or display window of the calculator.

Practice exercises

		Answer
1.	18 + 92 + 24 + 86 + 43 + 81 + 39 =	383
2.	63 + 33 + 14 + 29 + 81 + 72 + 5 =	297
3.	415 + 713 + 505 + 135 + 346 + 627 =	2,741
4.	379 + 253 + 759 + 476 + 802 + 137 =	2,806
5.	4,569 + 103 + 8,629 + 7,420 + 1,956 =	22,677
6.	6,896 + 421 + 5,647 + 8,403 + 3,692 =	25,059
7.	3,467 + 143 + 11,369 + 7 + 8,739 =	23,725
8.	4,099 + 863 + 75,692 + 63,648 + 1,809 =	146,111
9.	2,194 + 486 + 87 + 10 + 7,209 + 3,250 =	13,236
10.	1,367 + 29,284 + 76 + 954 + 7,456 =	39,137
11.	1,906 + 47 + 3 + 246 + 926 + 2,047 =	5,175
12.	3,942 + 846 + 92 + 36 + 8 + 11,420 =	16,344

13.	306 + 4 + 1,964 + 726 + 8,432 + 505 =	11,937
14.	15 + 7,500 + 692 + 861 + 6,027 + 40 =	15,135
15.	11,826 + 1,924 + 429 + 4,112 + 691 + 3 =	18,985
16.	500 + 603 + 9,368 + 63 + 2 + 648 =	11,184
17.	4,621 + 6,426 + 4 + 307 + 768 + 5,974 =	18,100
18.	1,234 + 5,678 + 37 + 9 + 234 + 761 =	7,953
19.	52 + 8 + 2,098 + 7,521 + 16,847 =	26,526
20.	49,126 + 534 + 5,900 + 346 + 8,324 =	64,230

DECIMAL NUMBERS   Enter each digit in the numbers to be added including the decimal point. Set the decimal indicator at a number equal to the largest decimal in the numbers to be added.

Example 1   Add 26.4 + 196.425 + 1.006 + 62.0875.

Step 1   Set the decimal indicator at 4 decimal places.
Step 2   Clear the calculator.
Step 3   Remember to enter the decimal point.
Enter 2, 6, ., and 4 on the keyboard and depress the + key.
Enter 1, 9, 6, ., 4, 2, and 5 on the keyboard and depress the + key.
Enter 1, ., 0, 0, 6 on the keyboard and depress the + key.
Enter 6, 2, ., 0, 8, 7, and 5 on the keyboard and depress the + key.
Step 4   Depress the TOTAL key.
The sum of 285.9185 will appear on the tape or display window of the calculator.

Example 2   Add: .062 + .9 + .1435 + .005.

Step 1   Set the decimal indicator at 4 decimal places.
Step 2   Clear the calculator.
Step 3   Enter the decimal point ., 0, 6, and 2 on the keyboard and depress the + key.
Enter ., and 9 on the keyboard and depress the + key.
Enter ., 1, 4, 3, and 5 on the keyboard and depress the + key.
Enter ., 0, 0, and 5 on the keyboard and depress the + key.
Step 4   Depress the TOTAL key.
The sum of 1.1105 will appear on the tape or display window of the calculator.

Practice exercises

		Answer
1.	.6776 + .1234 + .06 + .375 =	1.236
2.	.7 + .1835 + .65 + .005 =	1.5385
3.	.875 + .5667 + .07 + .0003 =	1.5120
4.	112.45 + 50.62 + 4.20 + 32.80 =	200.07
5.	3,427.68 + 548.34 + 3.89 + 78.50 =	4,058.41
6.	11,450.00 + 43.20 + .85 + 548.90 =	12,042.95
7.	389.60 + 56.19 + 7.56 + 890.25 =	1,343.60
8.	3.21 + 420.78 + 4,523.09 + 44.67 =	4,991.75
9.	.003 + 41.1 + 7.8002 + .6 + 8.04 =	57.5432
10.	.125 + 16.68 + 2.0041 + 3.6097 =	22.4188
11.	303.35 + 23.56 + 78.74 + 119.56 =	525.21

12. 32.455 + 4.5735 + 102.00532 + .006 =   139.03982
13. 19.56 + 34.56 + 239.85 + 902.45 =   1,196.42
14. .012 + .87 + .4125 + .9062 =   2.2007
15. .87 + .0412 + .9 + .396 =   2.2072

SUBTRACTION

The *subtraction* function is completed by the use of the "–" key. Each digit in the numbers to be subtracted are entered on the keyboard as you would read or write the number. The amount to be reduced (minuend) should be entered first, followed by the number to be subtracted (subtrahend). The "difference" will be the result of the subtraction.

WHOLE NUMBERS

Example 1   Subtract 64 from 913.

Step 1   Set the decimal indicator at zero.
Step 2   Clear the calculator.
Step 3   Enter the digits 9, 1, and 3 on the keyboard and depress the + key. Enter the digits 6 and 4 on the keyboard and depress the "–" key.
Step 4   The answer 849 will appear on the tape or display window of the calculator.

Example 2   Subtract 132 from 96.

Note: When a larger number is subtracted from a smaller number, the difference will be a credit or minus amount.

Step 1   Set the decimal indicator at zero.
Step 2   Clear the calculator.
Step 3   Enter the digits 1, 3, and 2 on the keyboard and depress the + key. Enter the digits 9, and 6 on the keyboard and depress the – key.
Step 4   Depress the TOTAL key.
The answer 36 cr or –36 will appear on the tape or display window of the calculator.

Practice exercises

Complete the following exercises as rapidly as you can. If your answer does not agree with what is given, re-do the problem.

		Answer
1.	4,575 less 1,369 =	3,206
2.	327,546 – 785 =	326,761
3.	115,385 minus 4,271 =	111,114
4.	Subtract 12,305 from 4,506	–7,799
5.	575 less 32 =	543
6.	98,735 minus 56,047	42,688
7.	325,467 – 230,300 =	95,167
8.	Subtract 360 from 204	–156
9.	42,565 minus 5,678 =	36,887
10.	Subtract 4,503 from 7,912	3,409
11.	Subtract 964 from 438	–526

12.	1,042 less 891 =	**151**
13.	16,026 minus 12,743 =	**3,283**
14.	831 − 609 =	**222**
15.	Subtract 312 from 187	**−125**

DECIMAL NUMBERS   The subtraction of decimal numbers is completed in the same manner as it is in subtracting whole numbers. The decimal point must be entered as a digit. The calculator will align the decimal points according to the decimal setting. Set the decimal setting to agree with the larger decimal involved in the problem.

Example 1   Subtract .056 from .9348.

Step 1   Set the decimal indicator at 4 decimal places.
Step 2   Clear the calculator.
Step 3   Enter ., 9, 3, 4, and 8 on the keyboard and depress the + key.
Enter ., 0, 5, and 6 on the keyboard and depress the − key.
Step 4   Depress the TOTAL key.
The answer .8788 will appear on the tape or display window of the calculator.

Example 2   Subtract 12.375 from 92.6.

Step 1   Set the decimal indicator at 3 decimal places.
Step 2   Clear the calculator.
Step 3   Enter 9, 2, ., and 6 on the keyboard and depress the + key.
Enter 1, 2, ., 3, 7, 5 on the keyboard and depress the − key.
Step 4   Depress the TOTAL key.
The answer 80.225 will appear on the tape or display window of the calculator.

Practice exercises

		Answer
1.	.2091 − .0963 =	.1128
2.	.8456 less .473 =	.3726
3.	Subtract .28 from .3671	.0871
4.	.725 minus .004 =	.721
5.	45.375 less 15.0625 =	30.3125
6.	Subtract 34.045 from 98.2	64.155
7.	2,345.0875 − 1,872.325 =	472.7625
8.	3,452.0 less 2,873.075 =	578.925
9.	418.0875 − 206.02 =	212.0675
10.	$1,136.50 − $98.07 =	$1,038.43
11.	1.426 − .6285 =	.7975
12.	2,269.4 minus 913.25 =	1,356.15
13.	654.032 − 32.067 − 20.3 =	601.665
14.	45.09 − 1.0265 − 12.2 =	31.8635
15.	.9737 less .36 less .04 =	.5737

MULTIPLICATION

The *multiplication* function is performed by the use of the "X" ("times") key. Enter each digit in all numbers involved in the problem in the same order that you would read or write the number.

WHOLE NUMBERS

Example 1   Multiply 1,026 by 24.

Step 1 Set the decimal indicator at zero.
Step 2 Clear the calculator.
Step 3 Enter 1, 0, 2, and 6 on the keyboard and depress the "X" key.
Enter the 2 and 4 on the keyboard and depress the = key.
The answer 24,624 will appear on the tape or display window of the calculator.

Example 2   Multiply 426 times 12 times 4.

Step 1 Set the decimal indicator at zero.
Step 2 Clear the calculator.
Step 3 Enter 4, 2, and 6 on the keyboard and depress the X key.
Enter 1 and 2 on the keyboard and depress the X key.
Enter the 4 on the keyboard and depress the = key.
The answer 20,448 will appear on the tape or display window of the calculator.

Practice exercises

Complete the following exercises as rapidly as you can. If your answer does not agree with the given answer, re-do the problem.

		Answer
1.	4,567 X 48 =	219,216
2.	11,789 X 7 =	82,523
3.	89 X 62 =	5,518
4.	2,480 X 65 =	161,200
5.	732 X 6 X 13 =	57,096
6.	1,268 X 15 X 8 =	152,160
7.	908 X 42 =	38,136
8.	27 X 4 X 206 =	22,248
9.	92 X 56 X 187 =	963,424
10.	230 X 16 X 24 =	88,320
11.	2,796 X 517 =	1,445,532
12.	9,167 X 805 =	7,379,435
13.	3,600 X 185 X 6 =	3,996,000
14.	1,136 X 477 =	541,872
15.	2,760 X 132 X 9 =	3,278,880

DECIMAL NUMBERS

The multiplication of decimal numbers is completed by the same procedure used in the multiplication of whole numbers. The decimal point must be entered as a digit. The decimal indicator may be set at a desired decimal place or at a number equal to the decimal places in the multiplicand plus those in the multiplier. The decimal setting of 4 has been used in the following examples and practice exercises.

Example 1   Multiply 146.012 by 2.6.

Step 1 Set the decimal indicator at 4 decimal places.
Step 2 Clear the calculator.

Step 3   Enter 1, 4, 6, ., 0, 1, and 2 on the keyboard and depress the × key.
Enter 2, ., and 6 on the keyboard and depress the = key.
The answer 379.6312 will appear on the tape or the display window of the calculator.

Example 2   Multiply 16.5 × .06 × 135.

Step 1   Set the decimal indicator at 3 decimal places.
Step 2   Clear the calculator.
Step 3   Enter 1, 6, ., and 5 on the keyboard and depress the × key.
Enter ., 0, and 6 on the keyboard and depress the × key.
Enter 1, 3, and 5 on the keyboard and depress the = key.
The answer 133.65 will appear on the tape or display window of the calculator.

Practice exercises

		Answer
1.	$12.65 × .025 =	$.32
2.	46.054 × .125 =	5.7568
3.	$26.45 × .875 × 16 =	$370.30
4.	18.2 × .09 × 137 =	224.406
5.	$23.45 × 3.652 × 2.8 =	$239.79
6.	$205.67 × .0075 × 12.60	$19.44
7.	652.7 × .18 × 16.2 =	1,903.2732
8.	.123 × .06 =	.0074
9.	.6092 × .0725 =	.0442
10.	.42 × .0012 =	.0005
11.	.875 × .15 =	.1313
12.	.5674 × .328 =	.1861
13.	8.2 × 3.7 =	30.34
14.	36.4 × 6.9 =	251.16
15.	$32.83 × 1.08 =	$35.46

DIVISION

The *division* function is completed by the use of the ÷ key. Enter each digit in all the numbers involved in the division in the same order that you would read or write the number. Be sure to enter the number and any decimal point in the number that is to be divided (dividend) first.

The remainder that results from most division problems will be expressed as a decimal. The number of decimal places will be rounded to the decimal place set on the decimal indicator. It is important that the decimal indicator be set at the desired place before the division process is made. The remainders in the following examples and exercises are rounded to the 4th decimal place.

WHOLE NUMBERS
Example 1   Divide 1,075 by 25.

Step 1   Set the decimal indicator at 4 decimal places.

Step 2 Clear the calculator.
Step 3 Enter 1, 0, 7 and 5 on the keyboard and depress the ÷ key.
Enter 2 and 5 on the keyboard and depress the = key.
The answer 43 will appear on the tape or display window of the calculator.

Example 2 Divide 824 by 21.

Step 1 Set the decimal indicator at 4 decimal places.
Step 2 Clear the calculator.
Step 3 Enter 8, 2, and 4 on the keyboard and depress the ÷ key.
Enter 2 and 1 on the keyboard and depress the = key.
The answer 39.2381 will appear on the tape or display window of the calculator.

Practice exercises

Set the decimal indicator at 4 decimal places.

		Answer
1.	Divide 35,426 by 96	369.0208
2.	1,112 divided by 86 =	12.9302
3.	69,329 ÷ 1,267 =	54.7190
4.	142,583 ÷ 171 =	833.8187
5.	Divide 1,422 by 171	8.3158
6.	Divide 983 into 27,848	28.3296
7.	118 ÷ 11 =	10.7273
8.	256 ÷ 25 =	10.24
9.	40,065 ÷ 814 =	49.2199
10.	1,916 ÷ 121 =	15.8347
11.	1,400 divided into 64,498 =	46.07
12.	Divide 19,686 by 867	22.7059
13.	Divide 142,583 by 1,284	111.0460
14.	Divide 893 into 27,848	31.1848
15.	136,927 ÷ 562 =	243.6423

DECIMAL NUMBERS The division of decimal numbers is completed in the same manner as that used in dividing whole numbers. However, the decimal point in both the dividend and the divisor must be entered on the keyboard as a digit. The number of decimal places in the answer is determined by the setting of the decimal indicator. Such a decimal setting can be any number desired or required by a business. In the following examples and practice exercises, the decimal setting of 4 places has been used.

Example 1 Divide 1,280.40 by 10.82

Step 1 Set the decimal indicator at 4 decimal places.
Step 2 Clear the calculator.
Step 3 Enter 1, 2, 8, 0, ., 4, and 0 on the keyboard and depress the ÷ key.
Enter 1, 0, ., 8, and 2 on the keyboard and depress the = key.
The answer 118.3364 will appear on the tape or display window of the calculator.

Example 2 Divide .565 by .1276.

Step 1 Set the decimal indicator at 4 decimal places.

Step 2 Clear the calculator.
Step 3 Enter ., 5, 6, and 5 on the keyboard and depress the ÷ key.
Enter ., 1, 2, 7, and 6 on the keyboard and depress the = key.
The answer 4.4279 will appear on the tape or display window of the calculator.

Practice exercises

		Answer
1.	Divide 62.8 by 2.5	25.12
2.	669.2 ÷ 139.3 =	4.8040
3.	Divide .652 into 982.35	1,506.6718
4.	12.6 ÷ .003 =	4,200.0000
5.	Divide 425.381 by 43.27	9.8309
6.	62,024 ÷ 119.347 =	519.6947
7.	140.65 ÷ .086 =	1,635.4651
8.	Divide 1.75 into 946.1	540.6286
9.	6.21 ÷ .84 =	7.3929
10.	Divide 10.35 into 196.864	19.0207
11.	Divide 276.87 by 33.7	8.2157
12.	Divide 1,864.5 by .152	12,266.4474
13.	376.93 ÷ 17.04 =	22.1203
14.	66.912 ÷ 10.7 =	6.2535
15.	1,619.37 ÷ 202.4	8.0008

CONVERSION OF FRACTIONS TO DECIMALS

Many business measurements and amounts are expressed as common fractions or mixed numbers. Most calculators have no provision to calculate the arithmetic of fractions. However, the calculator can be used in solving problems involving fractions by converting the fraction to its decimal equivalent. To convert a fraction to its decimal equivalent, divide the numerator of the fraction by its denominator.

Example Convert the fraction ¾ to a decimal.

$$\begin{array}{r} .75 \\ 4\overline{)3.000} \\ \underline{2\ 8} \\ 20 \\ \underline{20} \\ 0 \end{array} = .75 \text{ Ans.}$$

Example Convert the fraction ⅓ to a decimal.

$$\begin{array}{r} .3333 \\ 3\overline{)1.0000} \\ \underline{9} \\ 10 \\ \underline{9} \\ 10 \\ \underline{9} \\ 10 \\ \underline{9} \\ 1 \end{array} = .3333 \text{ Ans.}$$

Practice exercises

The decimal indicator was set at the 4th decimal place in the following problems.

1. $\frac{3}{8}$ = .3750
2. $\frac{1}{6}$ = .1667
3. $\frac{5}{12}$ = .4167
4. $\frac{2}{3}$ = .6667
5. $\frac{3}{16}$ = .1875
6. $\frac{1}{2}$ = .5000
7. $\frac{4}{9}$ = .4444
8. $\frac{7}{8}$ = .8750
9. $\frac{3}{7}$ = .4286
10. $\frac{9}{14}$ = .6429
11. $\frac{23}{25}$ = .9200
12. $\frac{4}{5}$ = .8000
13. $\frac{4}{11}$ = .3636
14. $\frac{1}{12}$ = .0833
15. $\frac{7}{15}$ = .4667
16. $\frac{5}{6}$ = .8333
17. $\frac{5}{8}$ = .6250
18. $\frac{7}{16}$ = .4375
19. $\frac{21}{32}$ = .6563
20. $\frac{9}{16}$ = .5625

COMBINED CALCULATIONS

One advantage in using a calculator is that a combination of arithmetic functions can be completed in one operation.

Example   346 + 1,026 − 96 + 20 − 146 + 94 = ?

Step 1 Set the decimal indicator at zero.
Step 2 Clear the calculator.
Step 3 Enter 3, 4, and 6 on the keyboard and depress the + key.
Enter 1, 0, 2, and 6 on the keyboard and depress the + key.
Enter 9 and 6 on the keyboard and depress the − key.
Enter 2 and 0 on the keyboard and depress the + key.
Enter 1, 4, and 6 on the keyboard and depress the − key.
Enter 9 and 4 on the keyboard and depress the + key.
Step 4 Depress the TOTAL key.
The answer 1244 will appear on the tape or display window of the calculator.

Practice exercises

		Answer
1.	1,964 − 283 + 62 + 923 − 406 =	2,260
2.	563 + 358 + 81 − 192 − 426 =	384
3.	496 − 816 + 692 + 11 − 16 =	367

4. 12,942 + 1,940 − 10,487 − 167 =   4,228
5. 723 − 618 + 143 + 810 − 333 =   725
6. 92 + 86 + 62 − 48 − 52 − 73 =   67
7. 414 + 1,600 − 912 − 712 + 16 =   406
8. 1,636 − 1,442 − 800 + 912 + 4 =   310
9. 2,619 + 4,403 − 3,664 − 123 + 147 =   3,382
10. 296 − 406 − 518 − 6 + 847 =   213

The multiplication-division combination is useful in calculating some discounts and bank interest.

Example $\quad \dfrac{1{,}246 \times .06 \times 123}{360} = ?$

Step 1 Set the decimal indicator at 4 decimal places.
Step 2 Clear the calculator.
Step 3 Enter 1, 2, 4, and 6 on the keyboard and depress the × key.
Enter ., 0, and 6 on the keyboard and depress the × key.
Enter 1, 2, and 3 on the keyboard and depress the ÷ key.
Enter 3, 6, and 0 on the keyboard and depress the = key.
The answer 25.5430 will appear on the tape or display window of the calculator.

Practice exercises

		Answer
1.	$\dfrac{126 \times 11}{32}$	43.3125
2.	$\dfrac{\$1{,}050 \times .0875 \times 90}{365}$	$22.65
3.	$\dfrac{9{,}825 \times .573}{112} =$	50.2654
4.	$\dfrac{12 \times 3 \times 6 \times .5}{68.4} =$	1.5790
5.	$\dfrac{\$8.45 \times 36 \times 14}{144} =$	$29.58
6.	$\dfrac{\$5{,}025 \times .0925 \times 165}{360} =$	$213.04
7.	$\dfrac{18.95 \times 48}{12} =$	75.8
8.	$\dfrac{9{,}015 \times .875}{200} =$	39.4406
9.	$\dfrac{\$1{,}550 \times .115 \times 82}{365} =$	$40.05
10.	$\dfrac{29.75 \times 12 \times 4}{16} =$	89.25

Index

A

Accounting procedures, 249
Add-on interest, 173, 182
Addition
  decimal numbers, 6
  fractions, 18
  mixed numbers, 22
Additional charges, 95
Additional cost, 256
Allocation of overhead, 265
Amortization
  installment payments, 183
  schedule, 185-86
  tables, 184
Amount due, 102, 188-89
Amount financed, 170
Annual depreciation, 252, 254, 256
Annual percentage rate
  formula, 178
  table, 177
Assessed property value, 242
Average unit cost, 268

B

Bank discount, 127, 130
Bank statement, 29
Bar graph, 319
Base, 52
Biweekly salary, 212
Bonds
  interest, 295-96
  purchase, 299
  sale, 300
  quotation, 294-95
  yield, 298
Bonus and hourly pay rate, 206
Book value, 257-58

C

Cash and trade discount, 102
Cash discounts, 92
Cash payment method, 221
Check payment method, 221
Checking accounts, 27
Circle graphs, 321
Class intervals, 314
Commission
  payment plans, 214
  including drawing and travel, 214
  and salary, 215
  sliding scale, 216
  on stock, 283-84
  on bonds, 296
Commission merchant plans, 217

Common denominators, 18
Common fractions, 18
Compound interest, 132
Compound interest tables, 134
Consumer credit, 169
Conversion; see also Decimal numbers; Fractions; and Percent
  decimals to fractions, 41
  decimals to percents, 43
  fractions to decimals, 16
  percent to decimals, 40
  percent to fractions, 41
Conversion tables
  fraction to decimals, 17
  metric measurements, 74-75
Cost, 145
Cost of installment buying, 170
Credit: open end, 187

D

Decimal numbers
  addition, 7
  division, 15
  multiplication, 12
  rounding, 6
  subtraction, 9
Decimal point, 7, 15
Declining-balance depreciation, 260-61
Depreciation
  additional cost, 256
  declining balance, 260-61
  estimated life, 252
  first year, 254
  first year allowance, 256
  schedules, 258-59
  straight line method, 252
  sum-of-the-year's-digits method, 262
Differential piecework rate, 208
Direct bank loans, 127
Discount
  cash, 92
  discount dates, 93
  discount period, 92
  discount rate, 127
  interest-bearing notes, 130
  noninterest notes, 128
  trade, 83
Distribution of overhead, 265
Dividend: stock, 290-91
Division
  decimals, 15
  fractions, 22
  mixed numbers, 26

Division—Cont.
  whole numbers, 13
Drawing account, 214
Due dates, 118

E

End of month dating, 92
Equations, 67
Estimated life
  per hour, 253
  per mile, 253
  per units, 252
  years, 252
Exact interest, 130
Excess overtime, 202

F

Face value, 127
Federal income tax, 231
FICA, 229-30
Fifo inventory evaluation, 267
Final retail price, 239
Finance charge, 189
First year depreciation, 254
First year depreciation allowance, 256-57
Formulas, 59
Fractions
  addition, 18
  division, 22
  multiplication, 20
  subtraction, 20
Frequency distribution, 314

G

Graphs
  bar, 319
  circle, 321
  line, 318
Gross pay, 200-02, 205, 206-07, 209
Gross profit, 145, 159

H

Hourly pay rate, 199
Hourly pay rate and bonus, 206
Hourly pay rate and premium pay, 207

I

Incentive payment plans, 205
Installment charges, 170
Installment payments, 181-82
Interest, 115, 119
  add-on, 173
  bond, 295-96
  compound, 134
  days, 116

Interest—Cont.
  tables, 123, 125
  year, 117
Inventory methods
  average unit cost, 268–69
  Fifo, 266–67
  Lifo, 267–68

L

Lifo inventory, 267–68
Line graphs, 318
List price, 84, 102

M

Markdown, 145, 153
Markup, 145–46
  based on
    cost, 147
    selling price, 148
    percents, 146
  tables, 147
Maturity date, 118, 127
Maturity value, 115, 119, 127, 130
Mean, 309
Median, 310
Metric equivalent measurements, 75
Metric system, 73
Minimum payment, 188
Mixed numbers
  addition, 22
  division, 26
  multiplication, 24
  subtraction, 24
Mode, 311
Monthly interest rate, 183
Monthly payments, 183
Monthly salaries, 212
Multiplication
  decimal numbers, 12
  fractions, 20
  mixed numbers, 24
  whole numbers, 10

N

Net income, 233
Net loss, 160
Net markdown, 157
Net markup, 157
Net pay or wage, 233
Net price, 84, 102
  cash discount, 92
  trade discount, 84, 94–96
Net price equivalent, 84, 89
Net profit, 145, 160
Noninterest notes, 127

O

Open end credit, 187
Ordinary dating, 92
Ordinary interest, 117
Ordinary interest table, 125
Overhead distribution, 265
Overtime
  excess overtime, 202
  straight overtime, 201

P

Partial payments, 97, 102
Payment computations, 182–83
Payments
  installment payments, 181–83
  monthly payments, 183–84
Percent, 40, 43–44
  converted to a decimal, 40
  converted to a fraction, 41
  of markup based on cost, 151
  of markup based on selling price, 152
  method for income tax, 231
Piecework plans
  minimum wage payment, 205
  straight piecework payment, 205
Premium pay, 207
Price-earnings ratio, 293
Principal, 115
Proceeds
  interest bearing notes, 128, 130
  noninterest notes, 128
Profit and loss, 159
Proper fractions, 18
Property tax rate, 241
Property taxes, 242
Proof
  addition, 5
  division, 16
  multiplication, 11
  subtraction, 9
Purchase of
  bonds, 299
  stock, 284, 288
Purchase commission merchants, 218

Q

Quotations
  bonds, 294
  stock, 279

R

Range, 314–15, 318–19
Rate of
  decrease, 49
  increase, 49
  markdown, 154
  markup based on cost, 151
  markup based on selling price, 152
  percent, 47
Rates
  bank discount rate, 127
  cash discount rate, 92
  interest rate, 115, 175–76
  trade discount rate, 84
Receipt of goods (ROG), 93
Reconciliation of bank statement, 29
Remainders, 13, 14

Returned goods, 96
Review problems, 33, 55, 77, 107, 139, 163, 193, 223, 245, 303
ROG dating, 93
Rounding decimals, 6

S

Salaries
  biweekly, 212
  monthly, 212–13
  semimonthly, 212
  weekly, 212
Sale of
  bonds, 300
  stock, 283, 286
Sales commission
  merchant, 217
  sliding scale, 216
  straight, 214
Sales tax, 236–37, 240
  tables, 237
Security and exchange fees, 286, 297
Selling price, 145, 156
Single discount equivalent, 84, 89
Standard deviation, 315
Statistics, 307
Stocks
  commission, 283
  dividend, 290
  price, 279
  yield, 292
Straight line depreciation, 252
Straight overtime, 201
Straight piecework, 205
Subtraction
  decimals, 9
  fractions, 20
  mixed numbers, 24
  whole numbers, 8
Sum-of-the-years'-digits depreciation, 262

T

Tables
  annual percentage rate (APR), 177
  interest, 125, 136
  tax allowance exemptions, 233
  withholding tax, 234
Tax percent method, 231
Tax rates, 241
Tax table method, 231
Taxes
  FICA, 229
  property taxes, 240, 242
  sales tax, 236–37
  withholding tax, 234
Terms of
  discount, 92, 127
  an equation, 67
Time
  cash discount, 92–93
  interest, 115–16

340 /

Total amount due, 190
Trade and cash discounts, 102
Trade discount rates, 84
Trade discounts, 83–84
Transfer tax, 285

U–Y

Use of the electric calculator, 325

Wages
  hourly, 199
  hourly, and bonus, 206
  hourly, and premium pay, 207
Weekly salaries, 212
Weighted average mean, 315
Whole numbers
  addition, 3

Whole numbers—*Cont.*
  division, 13
  multiplication, 10
  subtraction, 8
Word problems, 33
Yield to maturity, bonds, 298

This book has been set in 11 point and 10 point theme leaded 2 points. Unit numbers are 48 point Optima and unit titles are 36 point Optima Medium. The size of the type page is 40 by 56 picas.